T0393993

The Political Economy of the Agri-Food System in Thailand

The mainstream agri-food system in Thailand has been shaped to aid capital accumulation by domestic and transnational hegemonic forces, and is currently sustained through hegemonic agri-food production–distribution, governance structures, and ideational order. However, sustainable agriculture and land reform movements have, to certain extents, managed to offer alternatives.

This book adopts a neo-Marxist and Gramscian approach to studying the political economy of the agricultural and food system in Thailand (1990–2014). The author argues that hegemonic forces have many measures to co-opt dissent into hegemonic structures, and that counter-hegemony should be seen as an ongoing process over a long period of time where predominantly counter-hegemonic forces, constrained by political-economic structural conditions, may at times retain some hegemonic elements. Contrary to what some academic studies suggest, the author argues that localist-inspired social movements in Thailand are not insular and anti-globalisation. Instead, they are selective in fostering collaborations and globalisation based on values such as sustainability, fairness, and partnership.

Providing new perspectives on polarised politics in Thailand, particularly how cross-class alliances can further or frustrate counter-hegemonic movements, the book points to the importance of analysing social movements in relation to established political authority. It will be of interest to academics in the field of Politics and International Relations, Sociology, Development Studies, and Asian Studies.

Prapimphan Chiengkul is a lecturer in the Department of International Relations, Faculty of Political Science, Thammasat University, Thailand. Her research interests are the political economy of development, international/global political economy, green politics, as well as transnational social movements and global governance.

Routledge Contemporary Southeast Asia Series

79 Political Institutions in East Timor
Semi-Presidentialism and Democratisation
Lydia M. Beuman

80 Religious Violence and Conciliation in Indonesia
Christians and Muslims in the Moluccas
Sumanto Al Qurtuby

81 Identity Politics and Elections in Malaysia and Indonesia
Ethnic Engineering in Borneo
Karolina Prasad

82 Rethinking Power Relations in Indonesia
Transforming the Margins
Edited by Michaela Haug, Martin Rössler and Anna-Teresa Grumblies

83 Indonesia and the Politics of Disaster
Power and Representation in Indonesia's Mud Volcano
Phillip Drake

84 Nation-Building and National Identity in Timor-Leste
Michael Leach

85 Visual Media in Indonesia
Video Vanguard
Edwin Jurriëns

86 Maritime Security and Indonesia
Cooperation, Interests and Strategies
Senia Febrica

87 The King and the Making of Modern Thailand
Antonio L. Rappa

88 Society in Contemporary Laos
Capitalism, Habitus and Belief
Boike Rehbein

89 Migrant Workers and ASEAN
A Two Level State and Regional Analysis
Anisa Santoso

90 The Political Economy of the Agri-Food System in Thailand
Hegemony, Counter-Hegemony, and Co-Optation of Oppositions
Prapimphan Chiengkul

91 Transforming Society
Strategies for Social Development from Singapore, Asia and Around the World
Edited by Ngoh Tiong Tan

The Political Economy of the Agri-Food System in Thailand

Hegemony, Counter-Hegemony, and Co-Optation of Oppositions

Prapimphan Chiengkul

LONDON AND NEW YORK

First published 2017
by Routledge
2 Park Square, Milton Park, Abingdon, Oxon OX14 4RN

and by Routledge
711 Third Avenue, New York, NY 10017

Routledge is an imprint of the Taylor & Francis Group, an informa business

British Library Cataloguing in Publication Data
A catalogue record for this book is available from the British Library

Library of Congress Cataloging in Publication Data
Names: Prapimphan Chiengkul, author.
Title: The political economy of the agri-food system in Thailand : hegemony, counter-hegemony, and co-optation of oppositions / Prapimphan Chiengkul.
Description: New York : Routledge, 2017. | Series: Routledge contemporary Southeast Asia series ; 90 | Includes bibliographical references and index.
Identifiers: LCCN 2016053009| ISBN 9781138288416 (hardback) | ISBN 9781315267920 (ebook)
Subjects: LCSH: Agriculture and politics–Thailand. | Agriculture–Economic aspects–Thailand. | Food industry and trade–Political aspects–Thailand. | Sustainable agriculture–Thailand. | Land reform–Thailand. | Economic development–Political aspects–Thailand. | Social movements–Political aspects–Thailand.
Classification: LCC HD9016.T552 P73 2017 | DDC 338.109593–dc23
LC record available at https://lccn.loc.gov/2016053009

ISBN: 978-1-138-28841-6 (hbk)
ISBN: 978-1-315-26792-0 (ebk)

Typeset in Times New Roman
by Wearset Ltd, Boldon, Tyne and Wear

Printed and bound in Great Britain by
TJ International Ltd, Padstow, Cornwall

Contents

Author's biography vii
Acknowledgements viii
List of abbreviations ix

1 An overview of *The Political Economy of the Agri-Food System in Thailand* 1

Introduction 1
Objectives, central research question and main arguments 2
Contributions to knowledge 4
Summary of the theoretical framework 4
Methodology and data collection 5
Chapter outline 7

2 Dynamics of the global capitalist agri-food system 10

Introduction 10
Part 1 Problems of the mainstream capitalist agri-food system 10
Part 2 A critique of neo-classical economics and neo-liberal ideologies 14
Part 3 Neo-Marxist critique of the capitalist agri-food system 17
Part 4 Hegemony and counter-hegemony in the agri-food system 20
Part 5 Insights from other theoretical perspectives 26
Part 6 Conclusion 28

3 Hegemony in the agri-food system in Thailand 36

Introduction 36
Part 1 Hegemonic agri-food production–distribution in Thailand 36
Part 2 Governance structures of the hegemonic agri-food system in Thailand 49

Part 3 Hegemonic ideational order of the agri-food system in Thailand 55
Conclusion 59

4 Counter-hegemony and co-optation of oppositions in the agri-food system in Thailand 70

Introduction 70
Part 1 Counter-hegemony in the agri-food system in Thailand 70
Part 2 Co-optation of oppositions in the agri-food system in Thailand 73
Conclusion 80

5 The sustainable agriculture movement in Thailand 86

Introduction 86
Part 1 Counter-hegemonic ideas and discourses 87
Part 2 Counter-hegemonic production–distribution practices 95
Part 3 Counter-hegemonic agri-food governance structures 109
Part 4 Grey areas and co-optation of oppositions 118
Conclusion 126

6 The land reform movement in Thailand 142

Introduction 142
Part 1 Counter-hegemonic ideas and discourses 143
Part 2 Counter-hegemonic governance of land 148
Part 3 Counter-hegemonic production–distribution practices 156
Part 4 Current obstacles and the possibility of co-optation of oppositions 160
Conclusion 164

7 Conclusion and reflections 174

Summary of important points 174
Reflections and future areas of research 175

Appendix: addresses of Sustainable Agriculture and Land Reform Groups 178
Bibliography 180
List of interviews and email correspondents 207
Index 210

Author's biography

Dr Prapimphan Chiengkul was awarded the degrees of Bachelor of Social Sciences in Economics from the National University of Singapore, Master of Arts (Research) in Political Economy from the University of Sydney, and Doctor of Philosophy in Politics and International Studies from the University of Warwick. She is now a lecturer in the Department of International Relations, Faculty of Political Science, Thammasat University.

Acknowledgements

This book has been adapted for publication from my Ph.D. thesis, which I completed at the Department of Politics and International Studies, University of Warwick, UK. It would not have been possible without the support of my family and I would like to give special thanks to my parents, grandmother, aunts, and Ben King, who helped me endure the demands of revising my manuscript at the same time as starting life as a lecturer. I would also like to thank my supervisor, Professor Jan Aart Scholte, who taught me a great deal while giving me intellectual freedom to explore, as well as other academics and friends I met during my time at the University of Warwick, whose friendships I treasure. Last, but certainly not least, I would like to thank all the interviewees who sacrificed their time for this research.

Abbreviations

AAN	Alternative Agriculture Network
ACIA	ASEAN Comprehensive Investment Agreement
ACMECS	Aeyawadee–Chaopraya–Mekong Economic Co-operation
ADB	Asian Development Bank
ALRO	Agricultural Land Reform Office
AoA	Agreement on Agriculture
ASEAN	Association of South East Asian Nations
BAAC	Bank for Agriculture and Agricultural Cooperatives
BioThai	Biodiversity and Community Rights Action Thailand
BOI	Board of Investment
CAE	Community of Agro-Ecology Foundation
CBD	Convention on Biological Diversity
CLTD	Community Land Title Deed
CP	Charoen Pokphand Group
CPB	Crown Property Bureau
CSA	Community Supported Agriculture
DAE	Department of Agricultural Extensions
FAO	Food and Agriculture Organization
FLO	Fairtrade Labeling Organisation International
FTA	Free Trade Agreement
GAP	Good Agricultural Practice
GDP	Gross Domestic Product
GM	genetically modified
GSP	Generalised System of Preferences
HYV	High Yielding Varieties
IAASTD	International Assessment of Agricultural Knowledge, Science and Technology for Development
ICARRD	International Conference on Agrarian Reform and Rural Development
IFAD	International Fund for Agricultural Development
IFOAM	International Federation of Organic Agriculture Movements
IMF	International Monetary Fund
IPE	International Political Economy

ISAC	Institute for a Sustainable Agriculture Community
LDD	Land Development Department
LRM	land reform movement
MOAC	Ministry of Agriculture and Co-operatives
MST	Movimento dos Trabalhadores Rurais Sem Terra [Landless Rural Workers Movement]
NACC	National Anti-Corruption Commission
NAFTA	North American Free Trade Agreement
NESDB	National Economic and Social Development Board
NGO	non-governmental organisation
OAE	Office of Agricultural Economics
OECD	Organisation for Economic Co-operation and Development
PAD	People's Alliance for Democracy
PDRC	People's Democratic Reform Committee
PFT	Peasants' Federation of Thailand
PRAI	Principles for Responsible Agricultural Investment
RFD	Royal Forestry Department
SAM	sustainable agriculture movement
SAO	Sub-district Administrative Organisation
SATHAI	Sustainable Agriculture Thailand Foundation
TDRI	Thailand Development Research Institute
TRF	Thailand Research Fund
TRIPS	Trade-Related Aspects of Intellectual Property Rights
TRT	Thai Rak Thai Party
UDD	United Front for Democracy Against Dictatorship
UN	United Nations
UNCTAD	United Nations Conference on Trade and Development
UNDP	United Nations Development Programme
UPOV	International Union for the Protection of New Varieties of Plants
WFP	World Food Programme
WTO	World Trade Organization

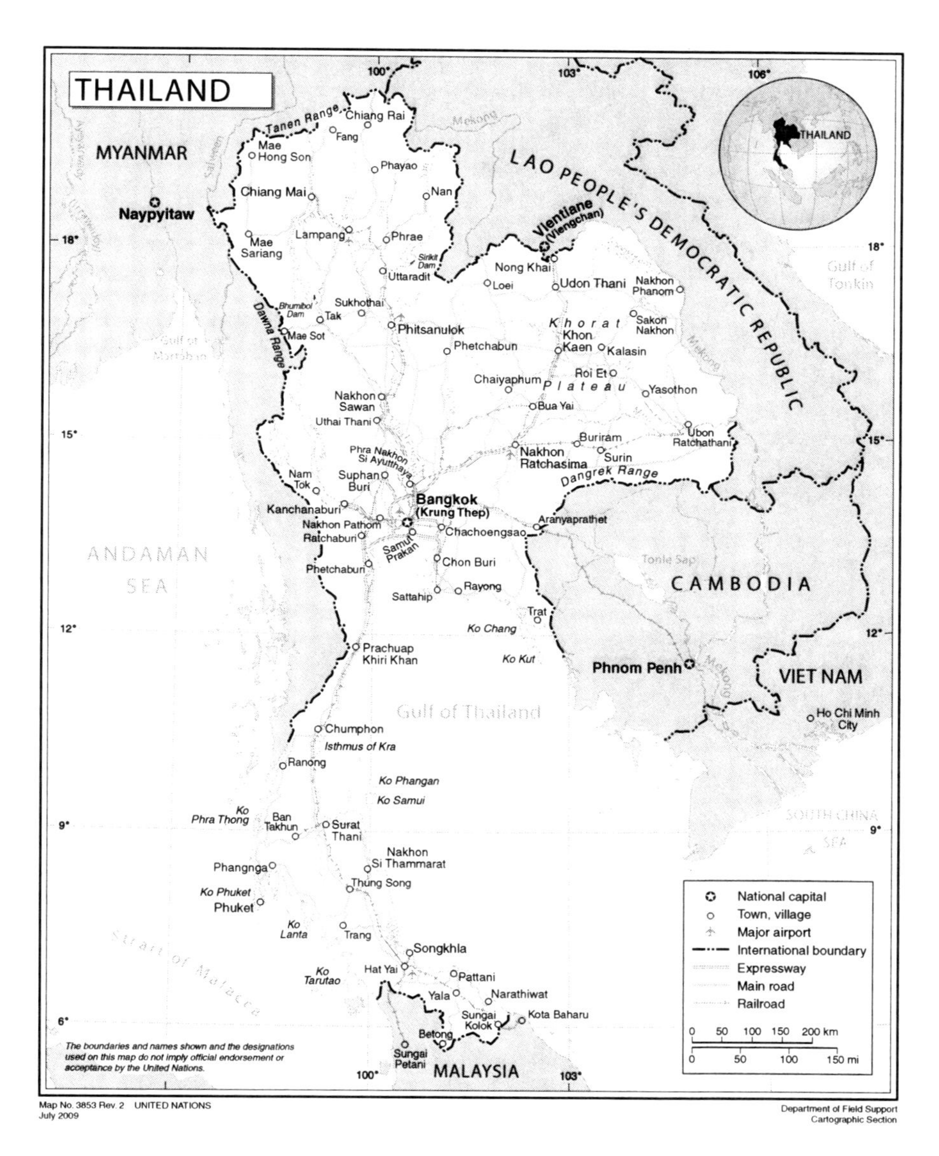

Figure 1 A map of Thailand. Thailand, Map No. 3853 Rev.2 (United Nations, July 2009).

Figure 2 Green Market in Surin.

Source: taken by the author on 22 December 2012.

1 An overview of *The Political Economy of the Agri-Food System in Thailand*

Introduction

Following the hikes in world food prices of 2007 and 2008, there have been renewed interests in agricultural investments as well as growing concerns over food security. Around 2.6 billion out of seven billion people on Earth, or around 37 per cent, rely on agriculture for their livelihood,[1] while 842 million people were unable to meet their dietary energy requirements between 2011 and 2013.[2] Of these 842 million, 827 million lived in developing regions.[3] Moreover, at least 70 per cent of the world's 1.4 billion poor people reside in rural areas.[4] These statistics suggest a large proportion of the world population's dependency on agriculture and rural economies, as well as their vulnerabilities to food insecurity.

Globally, mainstream discourses often use concerns over food security to call for increased investments in the agricultural sector to improve economic efficiency and productivity, such as to reduce labour in the agricultural sector through large-scale mechanised farming and with the help of biotechnology.[5] Global population growth and rising income levels in developing countries are also often cited in mainstream sources as main causes for global food security concerns.[6] Portraying food security as mainly a supply–demand issue, however, is only part of the story as statistics have shown that over the last two decades food supplies have grown faster than the population in developing countries, resulting in rising food availability per person.[7] Unfortunately, food supply availability does not necessarily translate into better food access and utilisation.[8] Moreover, mainstream focuses on high technologies of large corporations as solutions to global food security also neglect to address growing global concerns over the ecological unsustainability and political-economic inequality associated with how food is being produced. Specifically, some of these concerns include negative environmental and health consequences of industrial agriculture, financial speculations on agri-food commodities, the growth of agro-fuels production, as well as the economic and political power of large transnational agri-businesses.

Given the global importance of agriculture and food, this book's study of the political economy of the agri-food system in Thailand is very much relevant in the present-day context. In this book, an 'agri-food system' is defined as being comprised of the set of activities and relationships that interact to determine what and how much, by what method and for whom food is produced, processed, distributed and consumed.[9] The mainstream agri-food system is sometimes referred to in this book as the corporate or neo-liberal capitalist agri-food system to emphasise that, under this system, the main organising principle is the market[10] and that it is inseparable from the capitalist system.

Thailand is an interesting case study for many reasons. Thais are usually proud that their country is often referred to as 'the kitchen of the world' as it is a major exporter of agri-food products with some powerful transnational agri-businesses. On the other hand, the highly unequal political-economic power relations and ecological unsustainability in the Thai agri-food sector are serious causes to be concerned with. In Thailand, it is difficult to escape news reports, discussions and first-hand observations of problems facing small-scale farmers, as well as stark inequalities between rural and urban areas. Even though the agricultural sector accounted for only 11.46 per cent of Thailand's Gross Domestic Product (GDP) in 2009,[11] around 44.4 per cent of the total workforce was in the agricultural sector in 2010.[12] Hence, a large share of the population still depends on the agricultural sector (to varying extents) despite its small share in the country's GDP. Polarised politics in Thailand in recent years also bring to attention the complicated associations between Thai political-economic elites, agrarian development thoughts such as localism and sufficiency, as well as agrarian social movements.

As the following paragraphs elaborate, this book adopts a critical neo-Marxist and Gramsican international political economy theoretical approach to analyse the social, political-economic and ecological ills of the agri-food system in Thailand. Core to this system is an interplay between forces that try to sustain the status quo and forces that seek alternatives to the current agri-food system. Instead of identifying problems as isolated issues, the neo-Marxist and Gramscian approach in this book provides a frame to analyse problems of the agri-food system as having roots in interrelated ideational and material structures, and that transformation of the agri-food system requires extensive changes across local, regional, national, and global scales. In addition, by regarding the agri-food system in Thailand as part of the global agri-food system, it should become more salient as there are factors specific to Thailand as well as factors resulting from a globally interconnected agri-food system that have shaped the current agri-food system in Thailand. This supplements some Thai-centric literature which tends to focus on domestic factors. The following parts of this chapter discuss the objectives, central research questions, main arguments, contribution to knowledge, summary of the theoretical framework, methodology, and chapter outline of this book in greater detail.

Objectives, central research question and main arguments

This book has two main objectives: (1) to provide a critical political-economic study of the local-to-global interconnections and structural problems of the current agri-food system, using a case study of Thailand; and (2) to explore the possibilities that the current agri-food system can be transformed towards more socially and ecologically sustainable paths. With these two objectives in mind, the book asks the central research question: how have hegemonic and counter-hegemonic forces shaped the agri-food system in Thailand between 1990–2014? The Gramscian terms 'hegemonic' and 'counter-hegemonic' are discussed later in this chapter's summary of the theoretical framework. As the following paragraphs elaborate, this book has four main arguments.

First, this book argues that the mainstream agri-food system in Thailand has been shaped to aid capital accumulation by domestic and transnational hegemonic forces, and is sustained through the maintenance of hegemonic agri-food production –distribution, governance structures and ideational order. Important participants in the maintenance of the status quo often include transnational capital and global governance bodies, large domestic capital, and the Thai state. Hegemonic neoliberal ideas and practices in the agri-food system in Thailand have also been strengthened by some cultural-political ideologies and practices specific to Thai historical-social context, namely the 'Sakdina' (feudal/hierarchical) mentality and patron–client relations.

Second, this book argues that the sustainable agriculture movement's (SAM) and the land reform movement's (LRM) counter-hegemonic ideas, production–distribution practices, and governance structures have managed to influence the agri-food system in Thailand and offer alternatives to certain extents. Both the SAM and the LRM are influenced by local, national, as well as global factors. Hence, despite how they mostly operate within local and national boundaries, the SAM and the LRM can more appropriately be seen as part of global counter-hegemonic forces in the agri-food system. Despite some progress, there are still structural problems and limitations which prevent transformational changes of the mainstream agri-food system in Thailand.

Third, this book argues that hegemonic forces have many measures to co-opt dissent, alternative and reformist forces into hegemonic structures. To an extent, such measures have weakened alternative movements. The line between counter-hegemony and co-optation of oppositions is often unclear, but some examples of co-optation include attempts by large agri-businesses to enter organic niche markets and use similar terms as those in the SAM without wanting to radically transform the agri-food system, as well as some conservative forms of Thai localism and rural populist policies implemented by the Thai state.

Fourth, this book argues that counter-hegemony should be seen as a non-linear ongoing process over a long period of time, constrained by political-economic structural conditions, where forces that are predominantly counter-hegemonic may at times retain some hegemonic elements. Counter-hegemonic social movements do not necessarily have to resemble stereotypical images of politicised, structured, and leftist national movements, and one should not be too quick to pass judgments on counter-hegemonic ideas and practices which originated in different social contexts. The threat of co-optation suggests that counter-hegemonic forces should continually refine and develop clear ideas and practices to guard against co-optation. In addition, to implement structural reforms on wider scales and to bring about significant transformations of the mainstream agri-food system, counter-hegemonic movements should challenge not only local, but also national and global hegemonic governance structures.

Contributions to knowledge

This book makes many original empirical and conceptual contributions to knowledge. It brings new empirical information from Thailand into existing literature on the global corporate agri-food system and alternative agrarian movements. The following chapters will explore how there are historical, socio-cultural and political-economic conditions in Thailand which give rise to a unique form of hegemony and counter-hegemony in the agri-food system in Thailand. Empirical discussions of land grabs in Thailand in this book, for example, challenge stereotypical images of land grabs as large-scale acquisitions of land by suggesting how foreign land grabs can also occur through nominees.

This book also extends neo-Marxist and Gramscian theoretical perspectives in the study of the agri-food system, and suggests the importance of counter-hegemonic struggles at material and ideational levels which are locally as well as globally relevant. Viewing transformative change in the agri-food system as a process over a long period of time challenges agri-food studies from the Marxist tradition which tend to focus on crisis and change. Some authors have discussed hegemonic ideas and co-optations in the corporate agri-food system[13] but they have not explored the interconnections of ideas, production–distribution practices, and governance structures in the agri-food system to the same extent as this book.

Academic literature on Thai agrarian development and social movements tend to adopt Thai-centric approaches, so this book provides new perspectives by adopting a critical international political economy approach. It provides new perspectives on the practices and discourses of Thai localism and argues that contrary to what some studies suggest, Thai social movements which are partially inspired by localism are not insular and anti-globalisation, but are selective in fostering globalisation based on values such as sustainability, fairness and partnership. However, this does not mean that they are without problems. This book also provides new perspectives on polarised politics in Thailand by pointing out how polarised political discourses tend to reduce discussions on agrarian development to having only two opposing sides and divide social movements. Such simplistic portrayals distract people from structural social and ecological problems of capitalist agriculture, as well as the roles of political-economic elites from both sides of the political conflict in the maintenance of the status quo.

Summary of the theoretical framework

The decision to adopt a critical international political economy (IPE) framework in this book was derived from a critical inductive approach to research where starting points of theoretical generalisations are based on empirical observations, rather than treating theories and assumptions as facts or unambiguous truth.[14] The author had also observed that mainstream neo-classical economic analyses might be inadequate in addressing structural problems of the agri-food system, and that this inadequacy is likely to have political implications. Such observations have led the author to agree with foundational principles of critical IPE in the Coxian tradition, particularly the rejection of the belief that there is a value-free theory.[15] The term 'critical' in IPE in this context refers to a kind of analysis that sees existing social orders and their structural inequalities as products of history, and that the role of critical analysis is both to interpret and to help change existing social orders. In other words, to be critical means to have 'progressive commitment towards emancipation and the belief that the present social system can be transformed in order to address its injustices.'[16]

As Chapter 2 will elaborate, the combined neo-Marxist and Gramscian theoretical framework enables the book to analyse structural problems of the agri-food system in Thailand in ways that reflect the complexity of contemporary situations, taking into account the interconnections of ideational and material structures. Moreover, the framework helps the book to explore how the agri-food system might be directed in more socially equitable and ecologically sustainable directions. Chapter 2 will also discuss how poststructuralist and gendered perspectives also contributed some insights to the theoretical framework of the book. Specifically, poststructuralist studies point to the importance of ideas, values, knowledge and the power of consumers in the creation of alternative agri-food systems. The feminist/gendered perspectives enrich the neo-Marxist framework by pointing out the importance of non-commodified work and that both capitalism and patriarchy can be seen as sources of structural oppression.

There are two main parts to the neo-Marxist and Gramscian theoretical framework of the book. In the neo-Marxist part, agriculture and food are conceptualised as integral parts of global capital accumulation. Discussions of capitalism's exploitation of both nature and labour, as well as surplus appropriation through market relations, help the book to analyse structural problems of the hegemonic capitalist agri-food system. In the Gramscian part, concepts of 'hegemony' and 'counter-hegemony' are used to classify main types of forces which shape the agri-food system. Practices and ideas that sustain the mainstream capitalist agri-food system are seen as part of hegemony, whereas forces which try to change and transform such hegemonic ideas and practices are portrayed as counter-hegemonic forces. The book also uses a Gramscian concept of 'co-optation of oppositions' to understand hegemonic forces' attempts to integrate or subsume dissent so that it does not become a major threat to the status quo. As the following chapters will discuss, in reality, distinctions between hegemony, counter-hegemony, and co-optation of oppositions are not always clear-cut.

Methodology and data collection

The data collection period for this book was between 2011 and early 2014. This book draws on a wide range of English and Thai secondary sources that are related to the study of the global agri-food system and Thai agrarian social movements. Literature that has been surveyed comes from various disciplines across the social sciences including politics, sociology, and economics. Academic books, journal articles, dissertations, studies by various governmental and non-governmental institutions, as well as other secondary sources, were mostly obtained from universities in the UK and in Thailand. Primary documents used in the research include government publications and statistics made available online, such as by the Thai National Statistical Office and the Office of Agricultural Economics.

Substantial primary data was collected through semi-structured interviews, as well as materials from conferences and public forums, obtained in Thailand from October 2012 to February 2013. Semi-structured interviews as a method was preferred over quantitative surveys and structured interviews because they allowed for collections of more open-minded, comprehensive, and multi-dimensional information.[17] Predetermined structured questions and quantitative surveys might uncritically frame answers of interviewees according to particular theoretical frameworks and existing literature. During the field research, 97 people from seven provinces (in the North, Central, South and Northeastern regions of Thailand) were interviewed. However, the final draft of the book uses 86 of the interviews.[18] Semi-structured interviews were mainly used to gather information on the SAM and the LRM which are the two case studies of counter-hegemony in the agri-food system in Thailand. This is because up-to-date information from secondary sources was scarce. Interviewees associated with the movements were farmers, NGO activists, academics, civil servants and local leaders. Among 86 interviews, 12 involved government officials and five involved academics (officials were in senior positions or from local administrative offices). In addition to the interviewees, 10 organic businesses and agri-business owners were interviewed through email exchanges. In the final draft, the book uses seven of these email exchanges. The author tried to interview a larger number of government officials and representatives from agri-businesses, such as from Monsanto (Thailand), but it was not always possible to get interviews.

The SAM and the LRM were selected as case studies of counter-hegemonic movements in the agri-food system in Thailand because they can be seen as the most prominent movements which have challenged and influenced some important ideas and practices of the current corporate agri-food system for decades. Having two case studies provided more comprehensive insights of counter-hegemony in the agri-food system; while farmers in the SAM tend to have their own land or relatively easier access to land, members of the LRM tend to be landless or land-scarce farmers and marginalised population, so their priorities, goals and strategies are different. This book relies on interviews of key figures of the SAM and the LRM, as well as heads and/or representatives of private and public organisations, such as the BioThai Foundation and the Agricultural Land Reform Office, because they are persons who usually have extensive experiences and are in the positions to influence their networks. For the study of the SAM, interviews and site visits were focused in four provinces in three regions of Thailand: Bangkok (the capital city) and metropolitan area (Central), Chiang Mai (North), as well as Surin and Yasothorn (Northeast). For the study of the LRM, interviews and site visits were focused on Community Land Title Deed (CLTD) groups in Chiang Mai and Lamphun provinces in the North which is where CLTD ideas originated. Due to financial and time constraints, this research could not cover major sites in every region nor interview people in visited sites according to, for example, differences in gender, age, social and economic classes.

Chapter outline

This opening chapter has established the contemporary relevance of the book. It has also discussed the objectives, central research question, main arguments of the book, original contributions to knowledge, a summary of the theoretical framework, as well as methodology and data collection.

Chapter 2 will discuss structural problems of the global corporate agri-food system based on studies from many countries. It will then justify and elaborate on the choice of the neo-Marxist and Gramscian theoretical framework, as well as additional insights from poststructuralist and gendered perspectives. Through the neo-Marxist and Gramscian theoretical framework, the current corporate agri-food system is understood as an integral part of capitalist accumulation. However, the agri-food system is being shaped and reshaped by hegemonic as well as counter-hegemonic forces. Material and ideational structures that sustain the corporate agri-food system can be seen as part of the hegemonic forces, whereas forces which try to change and transform such mainstream ideas and practices are classified as counter-hegemonic forces.

Chapter 3 will advance the first main argument of this book that the mainstream agri-food system in Thailand has been shaped to aid capital accumulation processes by domestic and transnational hegemonic forces and is sustained through the maintenance of hegemonic agri-food production–distribution, governance structures and ideational order. Chapter 3 will use evidence from Thailand to extend the discussions of structural problems of the global corporate agri-food system in Chapter 2 and will discuss issues such as: the unsustainable industrialised production methods; land grabs; financial speculations of agri-food commodities; monopoly power in the agri-food sector; the roles of domestic and transnational forces in shaping Thai agriculture; as well as domestic and transnational hegemonic ideas which aid capital accumulation through the mainstream agri-food system in Thailand.

Chapter 4 will provide a comprehensive overview of counter-hegemony and co-optation of oppositions in the agri-food system in Thailand which serve as a foundation for the study of the SAM and the LRM in Chapter 5 and 6. This chapter will also suggest that the movements can be understood partly as a lineage of past agrarian movements in Thailand and as part of Thai civil society's search for alternative developmental paths. Moreover, this chapter will suggest that polarised political conditions and rural populist policies in Thailand hinder counter-hegemonic efforts of the SAM and the LRM, as well as opening room for co-optation of oppositions. The chapter will also explore the controversy surrounding the paddy pledging scheme.

Chapter 5 will elaborate on the SAM's counter-hegemonic ideas and discourses, production–distribution practices, and governance structures. Sustainable farmer groups to be discussed include producer rice mills in Surin and Yasothon provinces. Counter-hegemonic obstacles, grey areas, and possibilities of co-optation of oppositions will also be explored. Chapter 5 will help to advance the second and third main arguments of the book that although the mainstream agri-food system is dominated by hegemonic capitalist interests, domestic and transnational counter-hegemonic forces can influence some changes in the system even though they are faced with limitations and co-optation of oppositions. This chapter will also support the fourth main argument of the book which is that counter-hegemony should be seen as a process over a long period of time.

Chapter 6 will examine counter-hegemony and co-optation of oppositions in the case of the LRM. Similar to the preceding chapter on the SAM, Chapter 6 will support the second, third and fourth main arguments of the book. It will argue that the LRM tries to develop complementary counter-hegemonic ideas, governance structures, as well as production–distribution practices, to challenge the primacy of private individual rights and to promote de-commodification of land, as well as equitable distribution and sustainable usage of land. The concept of the complexity of rights, CLTD, and a national campaign to challenge existing legal and policy governance of land will be discussed. In addition, this chapter will explore obstacles facing the LRM and possibilities of co-optation, given the global context and contemporary Thai politics.

The concluding Chapter 7 will provide a short summary of the main arguments of this book. It will also reflect on the research experience, possible improvements, and outline areas for future research.

Notes

1 UNEP. *Towards a Green Economy Report: Pathways to Sustainable Development and Poverty Eradication.* (Geneva: UNEP, 2001), 36. Statistics on world population are based on the UN estimate in October 2011.
2 FAO, IFAD, and WFP, *The State of Food Insecurity in the World 2013. The Multiple Dimensions of Food Security* (Rome, 2013), 8.
3 Ibid., 8.
4 Poor people are classified as those who live on less than US$1.25 a day. (IFAD, *Rural Poverty Report 2011. New Realities, New Challenges: New Opportunities for Tomorrow's Generation* (Rome, 2011), 16.)
5 For example: Global Harvest Initiative, *Accelerating Productivity Growth: The 21st Century Global Agriculture Challenge. A White Paper on Agricultural Policy*, 2009, iii; Calestous Juma, 'Feeding Africa: Why Biotechnology Sceptics are Wrong to Dismiss GM', *Guardian*, 27 May 2014.
6 For example: FAO, *How to Feed the World in 2050* (Rome, FAO, 2009), 1; Global Harvest Initiative (2009), i-ii; Monsanto, 'Why Does Agriculture Need to be Improved? Growing Populations, Growing Challenges', www.monsanto.com/improvingagriculture/pages/growing-populations-growing-challenges.aspx.

7 FAO, IFAD and WFP (2013), 18.
8 Ibid., 28.
9 Ben Fine, *The Political Economy of Diet, Health and Food Policy* (London: Routledge, 1998), quoted in Michel Pimbert *et al.*, 'Global Restructuring, Agri-Food Systems and Livelihoods,' IIED Gatekeeper series no. 100, 2001, 4.
10 Philip McMichael, 'A Food Regime Analysis of the "World Food Crisis" ', *Agriculture and Human Values* 26, no. 4 (31 July 2009), 285.
11 Industry and service accounted for around 45 per cent of GDP each. (Office of Agricultural Economics, *Basic Information on the Agricultural Sector 2010* (Bangkok: Office of Agricultural Economics, 2010), 1–2.)
12 Office of Agricultural Economics, *Agricultural Economics Indicators 2010* (Bangkok: Office of Agricultural Economics, 2010), 4.
13 For instance, McMichael suggests that in the current corporate agri-food system, there are hegemonic principles and assumptions which appear as implicit natural rules, such as beliefs in efficiency over ecology. (McMichael, Philip, 'A Food Regime Analysis of the "World Food Crisis" ' (2009), 292.)
14 Angus Cameron and Ronen Palan, 'Empiricism and Objectivity: Reflexive Theory Construct in a Complex World', in *Routledge Handbook of International Political Economy: International Political Economy as a Global Conversation*, ed. Mark Blyth (London: Routledge, 2007), 123–125.
15 Jason P. Abbott and Owen Worth, 'Introduction: The "Many Worlds" of Critical International Political Economy', in *Critical Perspectives on International Political Economy*, ed. Jason P. Abbott and Owen Worth (Basingstoke: Palgrave Macmillan, 2002), 2.
16 Owen Worth, 'Reclaiming Critical IPE from the "British" School', in *Critical International Political Economy Dialogue, Debate and Dissensus*, ed. Stuart Shields, Ian Bruff, and Huw Macartney (Basingstoke: Palgrave Macmillan, 2011), 118.
17 Many books discuss the benefits of qualitative methods and semi-structured interviews such as Bruce L. Berg and Howard Lune, *Qualitative Research Methods for the Social Sciences* (New Jersey: Pearson, 2012).
18 See the list of interviewees after the bibliography.

2 Dynamics of the global capitalist agri-food system

Introduction

This chapter discusses structural problems of the global capitalist agri-food system and outlines the theoretical framework of the book to provide foundation for consequent chapters. The neo-Marxist and Gramscian theoretical framework of this book portrays the dynamics of the agri-food system as something which is continually being shaped and reshaped by hegemonic and counter-hegemonic forces. Production–distribution practices, governance structures, and ideas that sustain the mainstream agri-food system can be seen as part of hegemonic forces, while counter-hegemonic forces are those which try to challenge, reform and transform the hegemonic agri-food system toward more social and ecologically sustainable paths. The Gramscian concept of co-optation of oppositions is also used to explore hegemonic forces' attempts to integrate or subsume dissent so that it does not become a major threat to the status quo.

The first part of this chapter discusses structural problems of the global capitalist agri-food system. The second part then suggests that these problems are intertwined with neo-classical economics and neo-liberal ideologies, which makes such theoretical perspectives unsuitable for this research. An alternative neo-Marxist framework which conceptualises the mainstream global agri-food system as part of capital accumulation, riddled with structural political-economic and ecological problems, is then discussed in Part 3. Part 4 then discusses Gramscian concepts of hegemony, counter-hegemony, and co-optation of oppositions in the agri-food system, while Part 5 discusses supplementary insights from poststructuralist and feminist perspectives.

Part 1 Problems of the mainstream capitalist agri-food system

A wide range of studies suggest that the global capitalist agri-food system has some serious structural ecological and political-economic problems. This part of the chapter briefly discusses how the industrial agricultural production methods are ecologically unsustainable and work against small-scale farmers. So-called 'free trade' rules benefit countries unequally, while mono-cropping and cash-cropping for export create dependency and increase food insecurity in some countries. In addition, the supposed 'free market' conceals the power of monopolies in agri-food chains. Growing interests in agro-fuels, large-scale acquisitions of land in developing countries or 'land grabs', and financial speculations in agricultural commodity markets in recent years, are also important problems for the mainstream agri-food system.

1.1 Production

The Green Revolution, promoted around the world by institutions such as Rockefeller and Ford Foundations, the US and other Organisation for Economic Co-operation and Development (OECD) governments since the Second World War, helped transfer techniques such as plant breeding and the dissemination of High Yielding Variety seeds (HYVs) throughout the world.[1] The yield of HYVs depends on complementary capital-intensive soil management practices (fertilisers, agri-chemicals, irrigation) which often do not benefit small-scale farmers in marginal resource-scarce land.[2] The associated biological simplification and standardisation of mono-cropping and intellectual property seeds are also connected to the loss of indigenous species and biodiversity that increase genetic vulnerability, the loss of local biological knowledge in farming, and increased vulnerability to the spread of pests, weeds, fungi and disease.[3] As resistance to pesticides develops, it is likely to lead to increased economic costs in farming.[4] Chapter 3 will discuss in greater detail the Green Revolution experience in Thailand. There is evidence, for example, of environmental degradations as well as linkages between industrial agri-food production and rising debts of farmers.[5]

Repeating the experience of the Green Revolution and HYVs is the attempt to promote genetically modified (GM) seeds improvement technology as 'magic bullets' to drive change and innovation in agriculture by the corporate sector and the World Bank,[6] even though it is scientifically unproven that GM seeds are higher-yielding, better adapted to climate change, and are thus the answer to world hunger.[7] The technology and associated intellectual property rights system can help to increase monopoly power of large transnational agri-businesses[8] in addition to a possible increase in ecological, social and economic costs. Many scientists have given a variety of reasons to suggest that large-scale uses of transgenic crops pose a series of environmental risks that threaten the sustainability of agriculture.[9] In addition to the fact that farmers may have to pay inflated prices for these patent seeds, and accompanying pesticide packages, as well as bear the consequences of GM contamination and loss of export markets, GM seeds arguably have high economic and social costs as well. In addition, it has been argued that the present GM seeds and chemical intensive technological trajectories may lock out agro-ecological innovations.[10] In Thailand, even though the Thai state has not approved of the commercial-scale plantation of GM crops, news and evidence of GM papaya contaminations have already complicated Thai papaya exports to the European Union (EU),[11] as Chapter 3 will discuss in greater detail.

1.2 International trade

The World Trade Organization's (WTO) Agreement on Agriculture (AoA) implemented in 1995 established a set of binding obligations on members. These obligations include limitation and reduction of tariffs and quotas, domestic subsidies to farmers beyond market prices, and export subsidies which allow surplus production to be sold on world markets at prices below the costs of production, often referred to as 'dumping'.[12] The rules, however, have not been applied to the same extent to all countries. The EU and the US continued to give farm subsidies while many developing countries, faced with restricted access to foreign markets, were unable to protect their farm sectors from such food imports that had artificially been cheapened via subsidies.[13] Neo-liberal structural adjustment policies imposed by institutions such as the World Bank and the International Monetary Fund (IMF) also intensified the reduction in farmer-support mechanisms.[14]

Based on the belief in comparative advantage and free trade, developing countries have been encouraged to specialise and grow high-value cash-crops for export. This reduces their domestic food security and, at the same time, increases their dependence on imports of artificially cheap subsidised staple food grains such as wheat, rice, and maize from advanced capitalist countries. In many developing countries, farmland that used to grow food for domestic consumption now grows luxuries for higher-income consumers and the overseas market.[15] This problem of food dependence and insecurity is exacerbated in recent years with the growing production of agro-fuels and financial speculations, which are discussed in later sections. Even though Thailand is food sufficient at the national level, mono-cropping for export and some free trade agreements have caused a lot of economic risks and problems for small-scale farmers, as Chapter 3 will discuss.

1.3 Agri-businesses and monopoly power

There are studies which suggest that large transnational firms have monopoly power to influence agri-food chains in various ways at the expense of smaller-scale producers and consumers, namely through monopoly controls over inputs (such as seeds),[16] trade, processing and distribution channels. At the global level, agri-food trade, processing and retail are subjected to business concentration and monopoly power.[17] Large agri-businesses can also influence the agri-food system through lobbying for certain government policies and regulations. Neo-liberal policies (such as liberalisation, deregulation, and privatisation) have enabled large agri-industrial transnational corporations to increase their political and market power in many countries and to promote certain agricultural production technologies.[18] Neo-liberal policies have also helped to increase monopoly power in agri-food processing and trade industries in many countries which drive up prices at consumers' expenses. In Mexico, after the signing of the North American Free Trade Agreement (NAFTA), prices of US corn imports fell by 50 per cent but tortilla prices in Mexico tripled during the 1990s.[19] With two food processors which control over 97 per cent of the industrial corn flour market, as well as reduction of state food subsidies and wages, tortilla riots became common.[20] As Chapter 3 will discuss, transnational Thai and non-Thai agri-businesses play an important role in shaping the agri-food system in Thailand.

1.4 The food–energy complex and agro-fuels

The ecological unsustainability of the current corporate agri-food system becomes rather obvious after one look at its dependence on finite fossil fuels, principally oil and natural gas, which is needed in mechanised production methods, the production of agricultural inputs (fertilisers, pesticides and herbicides, which may be derived from petrochemicals), and transport of agri-food products.[21] It has been estimated that industrial agriculture requires an average 10 calories of fossil fuels to produce a single calorie of food.[22] Because of the food–fuel connection, rising energy costs can translate to rising costs of production and food prices.

Due to the growing fear of 'peak oil' or the scarcity of fossil fuel energy in recent years, there is increasing diversion of agri-food production resources and agri-food products from food consumption uses to the production of agro-fuels, putting upward pressures on food prices. For most forms of first generation agro-fuels (that are available in the short and medium run), the aggregate fossil energy used in the production of agro-fuels is higher than the energy contained in agro-fuel outputs, not to mention that agro-fuels output per land area is also low.[23] This suggests that first-generation agro-fuels exacerbate both the energy problems and the ecological-social unsustainability of the current agri-food system. The agri-food system in Thailand is also reliant on fossil fuels and, as Chapter 3 will discuss, it is likely that agri-food resources will be increasingly diverted to agro-fuels production.

1.5 Land grabs

Liberalisation policies have enabled captures of resources by international investors in developing countries. In recent years, many have noted the unprecedented phenomenon of 'land grabs' which usually refers to large-scale land acquisitions in land-abundant countries, especially following the 2007/2008 hikes in world food prices. Both private and public entities participate in land grabs, often with goals of securing food and energy for their own purposes or for distribution in their countries.[24] Beliefs in the benefits of large-scale farms and comparative advantages are often used to justify large-scale corporate land grabs.[25] However, there are concerns over negative environmental effects and over how small-scale farmers and the rural population might be forced off of their land, which will intensify the existing ecological and social problems of the current agri-food system. Moreover, there are opportunity costs involved in large-scale land purchases by investors as the land could have been used in alternative ways for more pro-poor effects and to benefit local farming households.[26] Land issues in the Thai context will be discussed in greater detail in Chapters 3 and 6.

1.6 Financialisation and the agri-food system

It has been suggested that the conjunction of food, energy and financial problems have prompted international capital markets to engage in speculative ventures in land, food and agro-fuels.[27] In the past few years, financial institutions have become increasingly involved at all points of the agri-food system, investing in farmland, input supplies, storage and logistics, inspection and certification, food production and processing, commodity trading, retailing and food services.[28] This potentially allows them to have the capacity to alter the conditions or to reorganise various stages of agri-food supply chains. In recent years, non-commercial speculators, such as hedge funds, have also entered futures market in large numbers to bet on rising prices of food commodities.[29] Agricultural commodity speculations partially helped to inflate a price bubble that has pushed the costs of basic foodstuffs beyond the reach of the poor in many countries between 2007 and 2008.[30] The Food and Agriculture Organization (FAO) noted that, by June 2008, a significant portion of the price volatility in international food markets was beyond what could be explained by the underlying supply and demand. Futures prices for wheat, for example, were 60 per cent beyond what the market fundamentals would dictate in March 2008.[31] While these financial actors may benefit from the boom, rapidly falling prices after the bubble bursts can harshly affect millions of food producers throughout the world.[32] Thailand is also affected by fluctuating international prices of agricultural commodities prompted by speculations, as Chapter 3 will discuss. Chapter 4 will also discuss how the speculation mentality had also inspired the Thai government's paddy pledging scheme which exacerbates problems of the mainstream agri-food system.

Part 2 A critique of neo-classical economics and neo-liberal ideologies

The diversity of the problems discussed in Part 1 may give the impressions that these are issues to be addressed separately. However, underlying threads linking these problems include neo-classical economic policy prescriptions and theoretical perspective. After the 2007/2008 hikes in prices of agri-food products, there is a renewed interest in agricultural investments. Based on ideologies of economic liberalism and free-market fundamentalism, some international finance and development institutions (such as the IMF, WTO, World Bank), major transnational agri-food monopolies (such as Cargill, Monsanto, Carrefour, Tesco, Wal-Mart), agricultural policies of the G-8 (US Farm Bill, EU's Common Agricultural Policy), and big philanthropy capital (the Bill and Melinda Gates Foundation), continue to call for the intensification of neo-liberal policies such as further deregulations of land and labour markets for large-scale investments in agro-fuels production and industrial farming.[33] The Gates Foundation, for example, advocates increasing agricultural output through corporate-led technological innovation and the expansion of global markets.[34] Calls for investments in agriculture are also often accompanied by arguments in favour of genetically modified (GM) crops.[35] However, it is argued here that such discourses and policy prescriptions over-simplify the causes of food price spikes and food insecurity while, at the same time, they neglect to address structural social-ecological problems and contradictions discussed in Part 1. This part of the chapter briefly discusses how the social, political-economic, and ecological problems of the agri-food system are intertwined with neo-classical economics and neo-liberal ideologies.[36] Therefore, the views that the intensification of such policies will be beneficial, and that neo-classical economics is an appropriate framework to analyse and solve problems in the agri-food system, are highly problematic.

There are many flaws to the neo-classical economic theoretical approach. One important flaw is how the emphasis on economic efficiency – a structural imperative imposed on firms by competitive environments where firms must combine factors of production efficiently so that consumers obtain the product at the lowest possible cost[37] – is seen as most desirable, even if efficiency does not always translate to social and ecological well-being.[38] As Part 1 has suggested, industrial agriculture does not take into account environmental and social externalities such as soil erosion and salinisation, the loss of biodiversity, and the costs to human physical and mental health.[39]

The belief in the benefits of free trade and markets as bringing competition and higher welfare is often used as an argument in favour of liberalisation and deregulations. However, such a belief conceals empirical reality where there is rarely 'perfect competition' nor 'free' trade as described in neo-classical economic textbooks, not to mention that market failures such as negative environmental externalities warrant some state interventions in the market. In effect, such rhetoric helps maintain existing unequal market and social relations. As Part 1 has suggested, large transnational agri-businesses can wield significant monopoly power, and international trade regulations also do not enforce free trade measures to all countries to equal extents. Moreover, it is doubtful that the promised benefits of specialisation in production based on comparative advantage[40] can be realised in the real world where countries compete to export agricultural commodities and also, at the same time, face unequal access to other countries' markets. Relying on few export crops and imports of other agri-food products to meet domestic food demands also increases food security risks, given the variability of climate due to global warming and other reasons that affect food price volatility. Chapter 3 will discuss these issues in greater detail using the case study of Thailand. Chapters 4 and 5 will then discuss different forms of alternative market governance structures, such as Community Support Agriculture and organic labels, which seek to embed social and ecological sustainable values in market exchanges in ways that distinguish these alternative markets from the neo-classical economic conception of free competitive markets which focuses on price competition.

Neo-classical economics' assumption that people are rational economic actors which act according to self-interests to maximise their utility,[41] as well as liberal values such as individualism and freedom, are sometimes used to justify certain consequences of the capitalist economy. They also imply that existing patterns of production, distribution, and consumption are inevitably the best outcome possible. A good example representing such views is the World Bank's development report (2008) which hides the consequences of dispossession and impoverishment through neo-liberal policies, using of terms such as 'choices' and 'free will', as well as through the assertion that rural people rationally adapt their livelihood options and strategies to their resource endowments and constraints to achieve efficiency. For example, circumstances resulting in landlessness and the movement to wage labour is interpreted as efficient adaptations (or even poverty-alleviating).[42] Such analyses neglect to take into account the importance of historical and socio-cultural contexts that shape unequal political-economic power and governance structures which conditioned choices for individuals and different groups in society. Such analytical frameworks tend to focus on individuals as the main unit of analysis without considering structural dimensions and should be critically challenged.

Similarly, technological advances under the supposedly free-market system are often seen uncritically as being political-economically neutral and desirable. However, commercial technologies are usually funded and promoted because they allow opportunities to maximise profits and rent from intellectual property rights, not because they are the best types of technologies from social and ecological perspectives. As Part 2 has discussed, GM seeds improvement technology is generally accepted in mainstream discourses and is being identified with the notion of universal progress for humanity,[43] even though there is cause to believe that it might be a socially and ecologically unsustainable technology. From neo-liberal perspectives, private intellectual property rights are important as incentives to innovate. However, it can be argued that private intellectual property rights encourage self-interested individualism as well as empower monopolies in the market. In mainstream perspectives, a lot of emphasis is put on the benefits of well-defined private property rights and intellectual property, neglecting common or community rights, public funding of research, and the benefits of common knowledge. This narrow-mindedness could be a cost to society. One could question, for example, why GM seeds' profitability should be protected through intellectual properties rights that yield monopoly rents and is fenced off as private, while in fact seeds have been developed by farmers for many generations without being patented, and can also alternatively be seen as part of the global commons. As Chapters 4 to 6 will discuss, many people in the sustainable agriculture and land reform movements in Thailand criticise such way of thinking and are also inspired by community right ideas and practices.

In summary, neo-liberal ideologies and neo-classical economic theoretical framework offer rather narrow, reductionistic and unrealistic accounts of the current agri-food system. The core beliefs, when translated into policy prescriptions, rhetoric and practices, provide ideological legitimation and support of the corporate control over the agri-food system. Such beliefs sustain problematic agri-food production–consumption practices while masking structural political-economic problems of the agri-food system. This is why the book adopted an alternative theoretical framework.

Part 3 Neo-Marxist critique of the capitalist agri-food system

Every theoretical approach could be subjected to critiques and shortcomings, but through a reading of different perspectives and evaluation of empirical evidence, this book has found neo-Marxist and Gramscian perspectives to be most convincing as a framework to understand the current agri-food system. While the neo-Marxist part of the theoretical framework helps the book to explore the dynamics of the capitalist agri-food system by bringing to light capital accumulation tendency underlying seemingly unconnected social and ecological problems of the mainstream agri-food system, the Gramscian part of the theoretical framework helps the book to analyse material as well as ideational structures of the agri-food system, as well as explore agri-food movements in different social contexts. Section 3.1 constructs a framework to explain how the general tendency of capital accumulation and hegemonic forces shape the corporate agri-food system and its socioecological problems. Section 3.2 then discusses possibilities to resolve the structural problems of the corporate agri-food system in ways that do not necessarily benefit capital accumulation.

3.1 The corporate agri-food system and capital accumulation

Marxist analysis points to the tendency that capitalists are constantly seeking new ways to increase the rate of surplus value.[44] Two main channels of surplus appropriation are often discussed, usually with the focus on the exploitation of labour in the realm of production. First, capital can increase absolute surplus value by making workers work longer hours and/or make them work harder and faster per day, while keeping wages at the same level. Second, they can increase relative surplus value by reducing wage costs or by cutting down on their subsistence needs. Cutting wages may contribute to accumulation problems stemming from over-production/under-consumption. There are, however, many ways to alleviate accumulation problems, such as through the exploitation of nature alongside the exploitation of labour, as the following paragraphs elaborate.

The exploitation of both humans and the ecological system can be observed through the study of linkages between agriculture, food and capital accumulation. Agriculture and food are linked to the accumulation process as determining factors of the value of labour power (wages) and the costs of raw materials.[45] On the one hand, lowering values of commodities consumed by workers, such as food, can reduce the value of labour and has the equivalent effects of reducing wage costs.[46] It has been argued that during the 1980s and the 1990s, the global corporate food regime was generally characterised by low prices of traded agricultural commodities, at the expense of small-scale farmers, to provide cheap food for wage earners in the North whose wages were declining.[47] On the other hand, cheaper raw materials and energy (circulating capital) has equivalent effects to that of raising labour productivity without having to increase fixed capital.[48] To keep the prices of circulating capital or raw materials down, there is a tendency for capital to continually seek new ways to appropriate 'uncapitalised nature' such as by geographically expanding the frontiers of appropriation, where nature refers to both humans and extra-human nature such as food, energy and non-energy inputs, such as metals, wood and fibers.[49] Land grabs in developing countries following the 2007/2008 hikes in food prices, as well as growing energy scarcity concerns, can be seen as manifestations of such tendency under the capitalist system.

The appropriation of extra-human nature, such as farmlands and other agricultural resources, helps to reduce the costs of raw materials and also leads to the dispossessions of small-scale farmers or 'depeasantisation', which serve to widen the pool of 'reserve army of labour'. The reserve army of labour, understood as the bulk of unemployed workers whose existence serves to discipline the employed labour force, can be one main channel to appropriate human nature (or surplus labour). If there is a large number of unemployed workers across the globe, the labour supply can be treated as almost unlimited, and there can be 'super-exploitation' where capital purchases labour power below the cost of reproduction. This is because capital no longer has to be concerned about the deteriorating health of workers and can also exploit weaker organised resistance in certain countries. Longer working hours, more intensive work per day, and wage cuts can also be imposed.[50] With contract farming and increased popularity of hiring farm managers to manage large farm estates, such as in Thailand, situations of small-scale farmers/labourers and industrial workers become more similar.

This general mechanism, which cheapens agri-food production inputs and materials to aid capital accumulation can be described as 'accumulation by dispossession' or the release of a set of assets at very low (and in some instances zero) costs for capital's benefits.[51] It is the continuation and proliferation of some processes of what Marx called 'primitive accumulation' practices.[52] Those that are related to agriculture and food include, for example, commodification and privatisation of land, forceful expulsions of peasant populations, conversions of various forms of property rights (common, collective, state, etc.) into exclusive private property rights, and suppressions of alternative (indigenous) forms of production and consumption. Moreover, new mechanisms of accumulation by dispossession have been created, which include rules on intellectual property (e.g. the Agreement on Trade-Related Aspects of Intellectual Property Rights or TRIPS agreement) that allow for the patenting and licensing of natural resources such as seeds, which have been developed by local populations over generations.[53] Commodification of nature escalates the depletion of the global environmental commons (land, air, water) and has resulted in all kinds of environmental degradations.[54] Free trade and open capital markets can also aid accumulation by dispossessions as well as give advantages to monopoly powers in advanced capitalist countries that dominate trade, production, services and finance.[55] The credit system and finance capital have also become a major method of accumulation by dispossession, most importantly through 'speculative raiding' of hedge funds and other major institutions of finance capital, which David Harvey has described as 'the cutting edge of accumulation by dispossession in recent times'.[56] These issues have been discussed in the context of the capitalist agri-food system in Part 1.

Capital can also appropriate surplus through their power in market relations, not just in the realm of production. It has been noted by many neo-Marxists that the concentration and centralisation of capital, or the rise of monopoly capital, is a natural tendency of capitalist development. For example, in a study of agriculture in Latin America in the 1970s, Andre Gunder Frank observed how 'monopoly in the modern sense refers to concentration in a universally interrelated whole', which includes the monopolisation of land, other forms of capital, labour, commerce, finance, industry and technology.[57] Part 1 has suggested how large corporations can influence agri-food chains. In many countries, including Thailand, there are small-scale farmers and/or semi-dispossessed peasantries (those who might potentially be part of the reserve labour) who still have ownership (or some access) to some of their means of production. Corporate capital and their chains of sub-contractors, through monopoly power and control over major productive resources, can appropriate their surplus via provisions of credit, seeds and other inputs, as well as market access, while labour process and partial ownership of means of production are left in the hands of direct producers.[58]

The process of accumulation by dispossession in the agri-food system in Thailand will be discussed in greater detail in Chapter 3. Important issues include: unequal distribution of land and conflicts over land use; attempts to introduce GM seeds and to patent indigenous seeds; evidence of monopoly control over productive resources, trade, distribution channels and credits; state policies which encourage large agri-businesses' monopoly control over agri-food chains; industrial agri-food production technology package; and contract farming arrangements that allow for surplus appropriation from small-scale semi-dispossessed farmers. As Chapter 3 will discuss, small-scale farmers in Thailand often rely on intensive agricultural production methods to free up time to sell their labour power to cope with short- and medium-term economic demands, even though they may be made worse off in the longer run by soil degradation and damages to health. Chapters 3 and 5 will also question the modernisation view that development occurs in linear stages and that there is (or ought to be) an on-going non-reversible transitional period where labourers move from the agricultural to industrial sectors in Thailand.

At a global level, the process of capital accumulation is filtered through competitive market relations among very unequal states and global governance structures, such as the rules of the WTO that promote the mobility of capital and intellectual property rights.[59] States, including the Thai state, often internalise neo-liberal capitalist ideologies and have a very crucial role in supporting capital accumulation. In many countries, the state shoulders the problem of rising food prices through various food stabilisation measures, such as food subsidies, price controls and export restrictions.[60] Moreover, with its monopoly of violence and definitions of legality, the state plays a crucial role in enabling accumulation by dispossession.[61] For example, the state can repress dissent, promote liberalisation through free trade agreements, privatise public assets, withdraw farm and rural subsidies, or allow land and agriculture to be accumulated in corporate hands.[62] Chapter 3 will discuss hegemonic agri-food governance while Chapters 4 to 6 will discuss suppressions of agrarian movements in Thailand.

3.2 Crisis and change?

Evidence of many social and ecological problems of the capitalist agri-food system provide grounds for some people to discuss structural contradictions which will lead to crisis and change. The food–energy connection is a good example of contradictions within the system. Cheap fuel is important for capital accumulation, but so is cheap food, because it is essential in keeping wages down and to ensure social stability. Industrial agro-fuels and value-added agriculture may solve profitability and energy scarcity problems in the short-run for political-economic elites and consumers with relatively high purchasing power, but it has been suggested that unless the need for low-carbon bio-diverse agriculture is addressed, energy, climate change and food security problems cannot be solved.[63] In addition, the acceleration of the incorporation of nature into the production process (capitalisation of nature), which intensifies the drive towards further geographical expansion, cannot go on forever as global space is 'asymptotic and finite'.[64]

Despite all these fundamental problems and contradictions, it can also be argued that there are still natural resources in many areas of the world which can be exploited in the foreseeable future. Examples include a previously closed society, such as Burma. There are also many makeshift short- and medium-run solutions to ensure the continuity of capital accumulation. This includes financial speculations on agri-food commodities, as well as many institutions and regulatory mechanisms upheld by states and international institutions, that continue to aid capital accumulations in different ways. As Chapters 3 and 4 will discuss, the Thai state implements many rural policies which enable small-scale farmers to accumulate debts without addressing structural socioecological problems. Governments also sometimes use food security concerns to subsidise agribusinesses. Moreover, even though the food price hikes of 2007/2008 exhibited problems and contradictions of the agri-food system, large transnational agribusinesses still managed to be profitable.[65]

One can argue that the general public, seeing such ecological and social problems embedded in the current agri-food system, is likely to pressure their governments and other institutions to implement some reforms and structural changes. The problems are that there are many obstacles which prevent this from happening. Utilising the insights and the concept of hegemony from Gramscian perspectives, the following part discusses how hegemonic governance structures, as well as discourses and ideas, can be used to maintain the status quo.

Part 4 Hegemony and counter-hegemony in the agri-food system

The previous part has discussed how agriculture and food fit into capital accumulation dynamics. However, to understand the capitalist organisation of agriculture, it is insufficient to look solely through the lens of capital accumulation as one should also look at 'political spaces that constitute its oppositions' which, for example, determines the existence and size of the reserve army of labour.[66]

This part of the chapter discusses Gramscian theoretical perspectives that are used in this book. Section 4.1 frames ideas, production–distribution practices, and governance structures of the capitalist agri-food system as part of the hegemonic structures. Section 4.2 discusses counter-hegemony in the agri-food system, section 4.3 discusses the concept of co-optation of oppositions with some examples, and finally section 4.4 discusses grey areas between counter-hegemony and co-optation of oppositions.

4.1 Hegemony in the agri-food system

From a Gramscian perspective, there is no simple dichotomy divide between the 'economic structure' and the 'ideological superstructure'. While the economic structure may set certain limits, so-called 'superstructural' factors have a degree of autonomy.[67] Aside from government apparatus and direct coercion, civil society consisting of private organisations such as schools, churches, clubs and the media is another channel which can be used by the ruling class to establish 'hegemony',[68] which can be defined as 'an order in which a certain way of life and thought is dominant ... informing with its spirit all taste, morality, customs, religious and political principles, and all social relations, particularly in their intellectual and moral connotations'.[69] Hegemony occurs when a leading class transcends its particular economic interests and is capable of binding and cohering diverse aspirations and general interests of various social forces.[70] It can be seen as an important tool which the ruling class uses to establish 'political leadership based on the consent of the led ... secured by the diffusion and popularisation of the world view of the ruling class'.[71] It is a method of control which helps to maintain the status quo and current social relations of production.

Hegemony could manifest itself as an international phenomenon through the outward expansion on a world scale of a particular mode of production,[72] such as the neo-liberal capitalist order promoted by political-economic elites in the US and other advance capitalist countries. Since the 1970s, there has been an increasing internationalisation of production and finance driven by a 'transnational managerial class'.[73] Aside from transnational companies, small- and medium-sized businesses as well as elements of financial capital involved in banking and insurance have also been supportive of the internationalisation of production.[74] Global governance bodies such as the IMF, the World Bank and the G-7 have also ensured the ideological osmosis and dissemination of neo-liberal policies to state agencies.[75] The role of the state is still significant despite the rising structural power of transnational capital which supported common perspectives or an 'emulative uniformity' between business, state officials and representatives of international organisations, favouring the logic of capitalist market relations.[76] From this perspective, neo-liberal capitalist hegemony has been articulated in different ways in specific national and regional contexts through a variety of political, social and cultural agents.[77] In other words, neo-liberal interests of transnational social forces of capital can be internalised into different national forms of state.[78]

In this book, hegemony specifically refers to mainstream capitalist agri-food production–distribution practices, corresponding ideas and discourses, as well as governance structures which support the continuation of the status quo. Governance structures in this book refers to both formal (such as the law) and informal (such as social relations) governance structures. Similar to many countries around the world, Thailand's agri-food system has been shaped by transnational hegemonic ideas and practices, but the Thai agri-food system also has its own local characteristics. Chapter 3 will discuss how neo-liberal ideologies and neo-classical economic ideas (previously discussed in Part 2), modernisation development world views, hierarchical patron–client mentality, and other ideas, combined to help maintain the hegemonic status quo in the agri-food system in Thailand. The state, agri-businesses, universities and other political-economic elite groups in Thai society play important roles in promoting and sustaining the hegemonic corporate agri-food system. Ideational and practical hegemony in the agri-food system, however, is not unproblematically imposed in a top-down manner on Thai society. As Chapters 4 to 6 will discuss, there are many contestations that also helped to shape the agri-food system in Thailand.

4.2 Counter-hegemony

The concept of hegemony in this book suggests that to transform the capitalist agri-food system towards more ecologically and socially sustainable paths, one should comprehensively challenge and develop alternatives to hegemonic ideas, production–distribution practices, as well as governance structures. From a Gramscian perspective, progressive social change will not happen automatically after a certain stage of economic development, but can only be produced by historically situated social agents whose actions are both enabled and constrained by their social self-understandings.[79] Hegemony is constantly being constructed and contested, and is never a static reflection of an alliance of social-class forces.[80] To build up 'counter-hegemony', it is insufficient to try to implement progressive social changes by taking over state power (war of manoeuvre), as one must also engage in what Gramsci called the 'war of position' which refers to the diffusion and mass acceptance of radical ideas about humans and society.[81] In other words, there is room to contest hegemony as existing hegemonic structures are an unstable product of a continuous process of a war of position.[82]

The level of difficulty of a war of position is determined by historical development of dominant thoughts within each nation or the 'ideological terrain'. This historical form of popular thinking forms people's 'common sense' which constitutes the realm of practical thinking for the masses of the people.[83] It is an amalgam of historically effective ideologies, scientific doctrines, and social mythologies, which can be fragmentary and contradictory, open to multiple interpretations, and hence potentially supportive of very different kinds of social visions and political projects.[84]

In the context of the agri-food system in this book, counter-hegemony consists of ideas, production–distribution practices, and governance structures which challenge and provide socio-ecologically sustainable alternatives to the hegemonic agri-food system. In Thailand, it seems like 'common sense' to believe in the superiority of large-scale high-technologies promoted by transnational agri-businesses or to see increased large-scale corporate control over the agri-food system as 'modern' and hence desirable. As the following chapter will discuss in greater detail, there are traditional cultural norms such as the 'Sakdina' patron–client attitudes that might obstruct the building up of counter-hegemony. On the other hand, as Chapters 4 to 6 will discuss, there are also other cultural and religious beliefs which aid the construction of counter-hegemonic ideas and practices. For example, Buddhist values such as moderation and self-reliance, as well as appeals to traditional wisdom and idealised versions of rural Thai community filled with generosity, are used by some people to construct counter-hegemonic ideas and practices. However, such construction is not without its problems and contradictions, as Chapters 4 to 6 will discuss.

Through a reading of Gramscian perspectives combined with field research, this book recognises the need for counter-hegemonic movements to balance between transnational and domestic dimensions and to understand the plurality and heterogeneity of contemporary social movements. On the one hand, with the transnationalisation of production and finance as well as of neo-liberalism, class struggle is now taking place not only between capital and labour at the national level, but also potentially at an international level.[85] On the other hand, hegemony at the local and national levels should also be addressed. To influence state policies and other national governance structures, counter-hegemonic movements have to take into account historical, socio-economic and cultural specificities at the local and national levels. Gramsci mentions a role for 'organic intellectuals' who can help form hegemonic or counter-hegemonic projects; by propagating certain ideas; intellectuals can perform a valuable supporting role in counter-hegemonic movements.[86] Nevertheless, inclinations toward elitist cosmopolitanism among intellectuals should be curbed and counter-hegemonic projects should consider 'national-popular' strategies which have relevance to the socio-economic needs and cultural demands of the common people.[87] Social movements should also be careful not to employ highly globalised and abstract ideological discourse that lack cultural specificity or ignore possible benefits of mobilising popular forces at a national level, using unique and particular socio-economic and cultural demands. Failure to do so could increase gaps between intellectual elites in the movements, who are likely to be more global in their outlook and the masses who might be embedded in national-popular ideological contexts.[88] Chapters 4 to 6 will discuss the role of Thai organic intellectuals that help to shape counter-hegemonic movements' ideas, strategies and actions, as well as how both sustainable agriculture and land reform movements are influenced by a combination of local, national, regional and international forces.

When speaking of social movements which try to reform the agri-food system, one may tend to focus only on rural agrarian social movements which have farmers as the majority of members. Alternatively, Marxist perspectives often discuss potentials for social changes arising from conflicts between labour and capital, assuming that small-scale farmers will eventually become part of proletarian labour. Such views may perhaps be counter-productive given complex urban–rural linkages and potentials of small-scale agro-ecological farms. In addition, problems in the agri-food system do not only concern farmers, but everyone in the society, as the consumers and as the bearers of negative socio-ecological consequences. Field research in Thailand also suggests that there are benefits to building alliances across political-economic and social groups/classes. Hence, a better approach to understand contemporary counter-hegemonic movements in the agri-food system is through the concept of the 'postmodern Prince' coined by Stephen Gill. It refers to a set of (postmodern) conditions, particularly political, material and ecological, that are giving rise to new forms of political agency with the quest to ensure human and intergenerational security on and for the planet, as well as democratic human development and human rights.[89] The postmodern Prince, as a political agency, is plural and differentiated without the institutionalised and centralised structure of representation. While many movements may appear local in nature, there is broad recognition that local problems also require global solutions.[90] Within a country such as Thailand, different agencies which may not be formally organised but are united by common goals can be seen as part of a social movement in the post-modern Prince sense.

In summary, this book aims to explore the complex local, national and global interconnections of the agri-food system, as well as accept the plurality and heterogeneity within social movements in Thailand instead of looking only at the conflicts between labour and capital or peasant and capital. The following chapters will, nevertheless, discuss possible limitations of such plural and differentiated movements.

4.3 Co-optation of oppositions and short-term fixes

One problem in the building up of counter-hegemony is that of 'co-optation of oppositions' or 'trasformismo'. The term refers to a deliberate strategy to prevent popular participation and systemic change within the policies and procedures of political institutions through ideational distortion. This can be done through the incorporation of rhetorics of radical changes and counter-hegemony into part of the hegemonic project without changing the hegemonic substance. Another method of co-optation is to include counter-hegemonic leaders and organisations in the decision-making process or integrate them into hegemonic institutions but without allowing them to affect the status quo. Such co-optation methods give impressions that hegemonic institutions have now taken into account concerns of counter-hegemonic groups and that mobilisation is no longer necessary. Hence, it can decapitate popular protests for a very long time because it is difficult to mobilise the public again around the same issues.[91]

Reassertions and intensifications of mainstream capitalist ways of managing the agri-food system, as well as implementations of various 'reform' measures that are compatible with neo-liberal ideology can also be seen as possible co-optation of oppositions, such as the construction of 'pro-poor' GM seeds image to justify investments in biotechnology, as well as to attract financial and political support.[92] Other corporate-led measures to address problems of the current agri-food system that might be problematic because they provide short-term reliefs without structural reforms include: voluntary corporate responsibility mechanisms;[93] industry-dominated certifications for sustainable soy, palm oil and agro-fuels;[94] the corporate mainstreaming faction of fair trade and of organic products;[95] as well as the World Bank, FAO, United Nations Conference on Trade and Development (UNCTAD) and the International Fund for Agricultural Development (IFAD)'s principles for responsible land investment.[96] It is doubtful that corporations would take the principles for responsible land investment into account alongside owners and shareholders' interests.[97] In addition, investors and governments in host countries have incentives to shield the deals from outside scrutiny, and voluntary guidelines may come to serve as checklists to legitimise land grabs.[98] The next section, however, discusses how boundaries between counter-hegemony and co-optation of oppositions are not always clear.

4.4 Counter-hegemony or co-optation of oppositions?

Harriet Friedmann uses the term 'corporate-environmental food regime' or 'green capitalism' to refer to the corporatisation of fair trade and organic niche markets, which can be seen as responses to concerns over food quality and safety, as well as pressures by social movements to address socio-ecological problems of the mainstream agri-food system. On the one hand, green capitalism might only benefit a few privileged consumers while obstructing the emergence of alternative agri-food systems.[99] On the other hand, market-led initiatives such as fair trade and organic markets could be seen as stepping stones to transform the mainstream agri-food system in the long run.

One main problem with the optimistic latter viewpoint is that, under the current market system, large-scale producers who can capture higher benefits of economies of scales tend to triumph over smaller-scale producers. The way highly capitalised agri-businesses and farms could out-compete smaller organic producers, such as by adopting industrial methods that play upon scale economies, is referred to as 'conventionalisation' in organic markets.[100] A good example to demonstrate this problem is in California, USA where a study in 2001 suggests that 52 per cent of sales in the California organic sector was accrued to only 1.8 per cent of growers.[101] Aside from direct economic competitions, there are also threats of lower organic standards to accommodate profit-centred agri-businesses.[102] Some studies suggest that agri-businesses in California tend to practice a shallower form of agro-ecology based on input substitutions, industrial-scale plantings of single crops, and contract farming.[103] These concerns are also relevant to Thailand, as will be explored in Chapter 5.

Literature on fair trade and local markets also suggest that there are some benefits to such initiatives, but they are not without their problems. On the one hand, there are many studies which support local and fair trade markets as a means to redistribute income to marginalised individuals.[104] For example, it is argued that fair trade shortens social distance between consumers and producers, creating networks based on trusts and fairness on a world-scale.[105] On the other hand, there are some studies which suggest that niche markets based on certified agricultural products might price out a majority of consumers and producers,[106] thereby exacerbate socio-economic inequalities at the point of production and undermine existing social norms.[107] Another critique is that fair trade is not that different from conventional businesses which use advertisements to add values to their products. For example, despite having an ethical image, a case study of fair trade shea butter produced by women in Burkina Faso suggests that female shea butter producers purchase shea nuts from female nut collectors at cut-throat prices to turn a slight profit on their own butter-production enterprise.[108] As for local markets, such as farmers market and community supported agriculture (CSA), power and privilege sometimes rest more with educated, middle-class consumers than with farmers and less-advantaged consumers. For example, if share prices of CSA are considered too high, current members may not return the following seasons while new members are difficult to recruit.[109] The influence of poststructuralist perspectives is discussed in the next part and Chapter 5 will discuss alternative green market channels in Thailand in greater detail and argue that although they may appear to provide only short to medium-term fixes, they could bear seeds of counter-hegemonic transformations.

Part 5 Insights from other theoretical perspectives

In the construction of an alternative theoretical approach to that of the neo-classical economics approach, this chapter relies mainly on neo-Marxist and Gramscian perspectives. However, it has kept in mind possible critiques of such theoretical perspectives, as well as other insights from poststructuralist and feminist perspectives. Section 5.1 discusses the poststructuralist critique of Marxism's structuralist and production-centric tendencies, as well as some main concerns regarding the importance of values and the sphere of consumption. It also argues that the Gramscian approach addresses these concerns. Section 5.2 then discusses other concerns raised by feminist/gender perspectives, particularly regarding structural oppression based on gender and the role of non-commodified work in the agri-food system.

5.1 Poststructuralism

From a poststructuralist view point, Marxist perspectives tend to see production and labour as the privileged loci of politics and social change, while consumption is seen as private, atomic and passive.[110] A Marxist analysis would suggest that what seems 'political' in the realm of consumption is just bourgeois ideology. For example, when upper income consumers buy products from niche markets, the act of buying gives an appearance of emancipation even though it is still implicated with capitalism.[111] Such view can be criticised using poststructuralist studies which suggest that knowledge and discourse can be linked to the political and material world. For example, struggles over definitions and certifications of organic food have political-economic consequences on organic production–consumption networks.[112] In sum, constructions of values and knowledge in alternative production–consumption networks, which contest normally accepted productionist values in mainstream agri-food networks, may bear 'the seeds of a political struggle' that could lead to broader political alliances.[113]

The critique of Marxism's production-centered approach is useful as a reminder not to be too narrow-minded and 'privilege the agency and power of either producers or consumers'.[114] This book values the viewpoint that struggles in the realm of ideas, values and knowledge, and which can have political implications. However, it frames the issues differently using Gramscian concepts such as counter-hegemonic ideas and war of position, in combination with a neo-Marxist analysis of the hegemonic corporate agri-food system. This is to guard against a generalisation that all kinds of supposedly 'alternative' values and knowledge in 'alternative' agri-food networks hold seeds of structural emancipatory transformations. In other words, structural analysis serves as a benchmark to evaluate these alternative ideas and practices to see if they may be able to influence and transform the hegemonic system towards more socially and ecologically sustainable directions.

5.2 Feminist/gender perspectives

There are some feminist/gender studies which indicate that women are often in disadvantaged positions in the agri-food system compared to men.[115] For example, female labour in agricultural production is often central and yet invisible (not acknowledged),[116] not to mention that women have unequal access to land compared to men in many places of the world.[117] Women also have constrained access to non-land resources such as agricultural production inputs, credit and extension services,[118] while the effects of many neo-liberal and agricultural modernisation policies have harsher consequences for women in the agri-food sector.[119] There are also empirical studies which suggest that women use their access to agricultural resources to improve household agricultural productivity and food security, as well as children's health and nutrition.[120] In addition, women might be motivated to social and political action differently than men, regarding environmental problems and crises.[121]

These gendered differences in knowledge of the environment, access, and activism should be seen as 'products of socially and culturally created structural positions', rather than something which is inherently biological.[122] Although this book uses a neo-Marxist and Gramscian theoretical framework, there is room to integrate gendered perspectives into this framework through the use of feminist socialists' critique of both capitalism and patriarchy as the two sources of structural oppression,[123] as well as perspectives on non-commodified work. Studies have noted how rural women often face 'double burden', which refers to when women are responsible for domestic tasks as well as being increasingly responsible for supplying a wage to their families. Sometimes women face a 'triple burden' when they also have to work on family farmland for partial subsistence.[124] Feminist political economy also draws attention to the importance of non-commodified work and the fluidity of the boundary between commodified and non-commodified spheres within capitalist economies. It also raises questions on how the reserve army of labour sustains itself. In Southern Africa, it has been argued that having a plot of land can be considered a form of social security against the vagaries of wage employment.[125] This is an important and useful perspective when discussing the continuing rural-urban linkages and semi-proletarian farmers in Thailand. As Chapter 5 will discuss in greater detail, the agricultural sector/rural areas in Thailand often provide social safety nets for low and semi-skilled workers who migrated to urban areas to work, as well as subsidise their costs of living, e.g. through food provision and as places to raise children.

There is not much gendered studies on the agri-food system in Thailand to build on, but the book tries to take notice of gender differences and socially differentiated groups during field research. Women can own land in Thailand and field research reveals that there are many women in the leadership positions whether in the civil service, NGOs, local politics, or business enterprises. Nevertheless, more research is needed to thoroughly examine gender differences in the agri-food system in Thailand.

Conclusion

This chapter has discussed important structural problems of the global capitalist agri-food system relating to industrial agricultural production, international trade, monopoly power of agri-businesses, the food–energy complex, land grabs, and the financialisation of the agri-food system. It has also provided a critique of neo-classical economics and neo-liberal ideas to suggest that they do not provide an appropriate framework for this research, then proceeded to outline an alternative theoretical framework based on neo-Marxists and Gramscian perspectives with some insights from poststructuralist and feminist/gender theoretical perspectives. Overall, the mainstream agri-food system is conceptualised as an integral part of capitalist accumulation, continually shaped and reshaped by hegemonic and counter-hegemonic forces.

The following chapter will build on this chapter in its exploration of hegemonic ideas and discourses, production–distribution practices and governance structures in the agri-food system in Thailand. It will also address local, national and global linkages in the Thai agri-food system. Empirical exploration in the next chapter will also support the assertion that the neo-Marxist and Gramscian theoretical framework outlined in this chapter is relevant and appropriate to the study of the agri-food system in Thailand.

Notes

1 David Goodman and Michael Redclift, 'Internationalization and the Third World Food Crisis', in *Refashioning Nature: Food, Ecology and Culture* (London: Routledge, 1991), 151–152.

2 For example, see: Vandana Shiva, *The Violence of the Green Revolution. Third World Agriculture, Ecology and Politics* (London: Zed Books, 1991), 45; Clara Ines Nicholls and Miguel A. Altieri, 'Conventional Agricultural Development Models and the Persistence of the Pesticide Treadmill in Latin America', *International Journal of Sustainable Development and World Ecology* 4, no. 2 (1997): 94.
3 Tony Weis, 'The Accelerating Biophysical Contradictions of Industrial Capitalist Agriculture', *Journal of Agrarian Change* 10, no. 3 (2010): 320; Shiva (1991), 89 and 93–95.
4 See Nicholls and Altieri (1997), 97–99, for a case study in Latin America.
5 A comprehensive study of such problems include Pattama Sittichai, Satien Sriboonrueng, Chusak Jantanopsiri, and Ukrit Marang. *A Complete Report on the Project to Compile and Analyse the Problems of Farmers and Sustainable Development* (Bangkok: National Economics and Social Development Board (NESDB), 2002) (in Thai).
6 Shelly Feldman and Stephen Biggs, 'The Politics of International Assessments: The IAASTD Process, Reception and Significance', *Journal of Agrarian Change* 12, no. 1 (2012), 146.
7 For example: D. Gurian-Sherman, *Failure to Yield: Evaluating the Performance of Genetically Engineered Crops*. (Cambridge: Unions of Concerned Scientists, 2009), quoted in Eric Holt-Giménez and Annie Shattuck, 'Food Crises, Food Regimes and Food Movements: Rumblings of Reform or Tides of Transformation?', *The Journal of Peasant Studies* 38, no. 1 (January 2011), 119; Dominic Glover, 'Is Bt Cotton a Pro-Poor Technology? A Review and Critique of the Empirical Record', *Journal of Agrarian Change* 10, no. 4 (2010): 500–503.
8 M. Blakeney, 'Recent Developments in Intellectual Property and Power in the Private Sector Related to Food and Agriculture,' *Food Policy* 36 (2011): 109–113, quoted in Colin Sage, 'The Interconnected Challenges for Food Security from a Food Regimes Perspective: Energy, Climate and Malconsumption,' *Journal of Rural Studies* (2013): 72.
9 For example, see Miguel A. Altieri and Peter Rosset, 'Ten Reasons Why Biotechnology Will Not Ensure Food Security, Protect the Environment and Reduce Poverty in the Developing World,' *AgBioForum* 2, no. 3–4 (1999): 155–162.
10 Gaetan Vanloqueren and Philippe V. Baret, 'How Agricultural Research Systems Shape a Technological Regime that Develops Genetic Engineering but Locks Out Agroecological Innovations', *Research Policy* 38 (2010): 971–983, quoted in David Wield, Joanna Chataway, and Maurice Bolo, 'Issues in the Political Economy of Agricultural Biotechnology,' *Journal of Agrarian Change* 10, no. 3 (2010): 356.
11 Bangkok Business Newspaper, 'EU Warns against GM Papaya', *Bangkok Business*, 3 July 2012 (in Thai.)
12 Bill Pritchard, 'Trading into Hunger? Trading Out of Hunger? International Food Trade and the Debate on Food Security', in *Food Systems Failure: The Global Food Crisis and the Future of Agriculture*, ed. Christopher Rosin, Paul Stock, and Hugh Campbell (London: Earthscan, 2012), 48–49.
13 Geoffrey Lawrence and Philip McMichael, 'The Question of Food Security', *International Journal of Sociology of Agriculture and Food* 19, no. 2 (2012), 135.
14 Raj Patel, *Stuffed and Starved. Power and the Hidden Battle for the World Food System* (London: Portobello Books, 2007), quoted in Lawrence and McMichael (2012), 135.
15 John Madeley, *Hungry for Trade. How the Poor Pay for Free Trade* (London: Zed Books, 2000), 54–56.
16 Wield, Chataway, and Bolo (2010), 347; ETC group, 'Global Seed Industry Concentration,' *Communiqué* 90 (2005a); ETC group, 'Concentration in Corporate Power,' *Communiqué* 91 (2005b)

17 Lawrence Busch and Carmen Bain, 'New! Improved? The Transformation of the Global Agrifood System', *Rural Sociology* 69, no. 3 (2004): 321–346; ETC group, 'Concentration in Corporate Power,' (2005b).

18 Miguel Teubal, 'Peasant Struggles for Land and Agrarian Reform in Latin America,' in *Peasants and Globalization: Political Economy, Rural Transformation and the Agrarian Question*, ed. A. Haroon Akram-Lodhi and Cristobal Kay (New York: Routledge, 2009),155–157; Zulkuf Aydin, 'Neo-Liberal Transformation of Turkish Agriculture,' *Journal of Agrarian Change* 10, no. 2 (2010), 161 and 182–183.

19 Peter Rosset, *Food is Different. Why We Must Get the WTO Out of Agriculture* (London: Zed Books, 2006), 57, quoted in Philip McMichael, 'A Food Regime Analysis of the "World Food Crisis" ', *Agriculture and Human Values* 26, no. 4 (31 July 2009), 289.

20 Patel (2007), 53 quoted in McMichael, 'A Food Regime Analysis,' (2009), 289.

21 Philip McMichael, 'Banking on Agriculture: A Review of the World Development Report 2008,' *Africa* 9, no. 2 (2009), 242; Sage (2013), 75.

22 Ross McCluney, 'Renewable Energy Limits,' in *The Final Energy Crisis*, ed. Andrew McKillop and Sheila Newman (London: Pluto Press, 2005), 153–175 and Richard Manning, 'The Oil We Eat: Following The Food Chain Back to Iraq,' *Harper's Magazine*, 2004 and Michael Pollan, 'Farmer in Chief,' *New York Times Magazine*, 2008, all quoted in Weis (2010), 321.

23 David Pimentel and Tad W. Patzek, 'Ethanol Production Using Corn, Switchgrass, and Wood; Biodiesel Production Using Soybean and Sunflower,' *Natural Resources Research* 14, no. 1 (2005): 65–76 and Tad W. Patzek and David Pimentel, 'Thermodynamics of Energy Production from Biomass,' *Critical Reviews in Plant Sciences* 24, no. 5–6 (2006): 329–364, all quoted in Weis (2010), 325.

24 For example, see: United Nations, *Foreign Land Purchases for Agriculture: What Impact on Sustainable Development?*, (United Nations, 2010); GRAIN, *Seized! The 2008 Land Grab for Food and Financial Security* (Barcelona: GRAIN, 2008).

25 P. Collier, 'Politics of Hunger: How Illusion and Greed Fan the Food Crisis,' *Foreign Affairs*, (November/December 2008), quoted in Ben White *et al.*, 'The New Enclosures: Critical Perspectives on Corporate Land Deals', *Journal of Peasant Studies* 39, no. 3–4 (July 2012), 625.

26 Olivier De Schutter, 'How Not to Think of Land-Grabbing: Three Critiques of Large-Scale Investments in Farmland', *Journal of Peasant Studies* 38, no. 2 (March 2011a), 256.

27 Philip McMichael, 'The Land Grab and Corporate Food Regime Restructuring', *Journal of Peasant Studies* 39, no. 3–4 (July 2012), 690.

28 David Burch and Geoffrey Lawrence, 'Towards a Third Food Regime: Behind the Transformation', *Agriculture and Human Values* 26, no. 4 (31 July 2009), 271.

29 Jennifer Clapp, 'Food Price Volatility and Vulnerability in the Global South: Considering the Global Economic Context', *Third World Quarterly* 30, no. 6 (September 2009), 1187.

30 Peter M. Rosset, 'Food Sovereignty and the Contemporary Food Crisis', *Development* 51, no. 4 (2008), 461.

31 FAO, *Food Outlook*, (Rome: FAO, June 2008), 55–57, quoted in Clapp (2009), 1186.

32 Rosset (2008), 461.

33 Holt-Giménez and Shattuck (2011), 119.

34 Bill and Melinda Gates Foundation, 'Agricultural Development Strategy, 2008–2011', 11 July 2008, quoted in Holt-Giménez and Shattuck (2011), 116.

35 For example, see: Mark Lynas, 'Mark Lynas Plenary Speech for International Rice Congress 2014, Bangkok, Thailand', 31 October 2014, www.marklynas.org/2014/10/mark-lynas-plenary-speech-for-international-rice-congress-2014-bangkok-thailand/; Cargill, 'Food Security: The Challenge', 2014, www.cargill.com/wcm/groups/public/@ccom/documents/document/na3059573.pdf; R. Paarlberg, *Starved for Science: How*

Biotechnology is Being Kept Out of Africa (Cambridge: Harvard University Press, 2008), quoted in Holt-Giménez and Shattuck (2011), 114.

36 For more extensive critique of neo-classical economics from scholars in the fields of political economy and economics see, for example: Frank Stilwell, 'The Ideology of the Market: Neoclassical Economics,' in *Political Economy: The Contest of Economic Ideas*, 3rd edn. (Victoria: Oxford University Press, 2012), 149–210; Herman E. Daly and Joshua Farley, *Ecological Economics: Principles and Applications* (Washington DC: Island Press, 2004); John Weeks, *The Irreconcilable Inconsistencies of Neoclassical Macroeconomics* (New York: Routledge, 2012).

37 Stilwell (2012), 178.

38 Ecological economic perspectives also criticise the neo-classical view that utility and welfare depend solely on people's preferences that are revealed through market transactions, while assuming that non-market goods contribute little to welfare (Daly and Farley (2004), 3–4).

39 Weis (2010), 316–317.

40 For an introductory discussion of these concepts, see economics textbooks such as N. Gregory Mankiw, *Principles of Macroeconomics*, 5th edn. (Mason, OH: South-Western Cengage Learning, 2009), 54–56.

41 Mankiw (2009), 3–15.

42 Kojo Sebastian Amanor, 'Global Food Chains, African Smallholders and World Bank Governance', *Journal of Agrarian Change* 9, no. 2 (April 2009), 256.

43 G. Bridge, P. McManus, and T. Marsden, 'The Next New Thing? Biotechnology and its Discontents', *Geoforum* 34 (2003), 165, quoted in Jacqui Dibden, David Gibbs, and Chris Cocklin, 'Framing GM Crops as a Food Security Solution', *Journal of Rural Studies* 29 (November 2011), 60.

44 Surplus values are understood as differences between the values of commodities produced and the values of labour power or wages.

45 Farshad Araghi, 'Food Regimes and the Production of Value: Some Methodological Issues', *Journal of Peasant Studies* 30, no. 2 (2003), 45; Jason W. Moore, 'Transcending the Metabolic Rift: A Theory of Crises in the Capitalist World-Ecology', *Journal of Peasant Studies* 28, no. 1 (2011), 23.

46 Araghi (2003), 44–45 and Moore (2011), 23.

47 McMichael, 'A Food Regime Analysis', (2009), 285.

48 Moore (2011), 21–25.

49 Ibid., 21–23.

50 Araghi (2003), 46 and 60.

51 David Harvey, *The New Imperialism* (Oxford: Oxford University Press, 2003), 149.

52 David Harvey, *A Brief History of Neoliberalism* (Oxford: Oxford University Press, 2005), 159.

53 Harvey (2003), 145–148.

54 Harvey (2005), 160.

55 Harvey (2003), 181.

56 Ibid., 147.

57 André Gunder Frank, *Capitalism and Underdevelopment in Latin America: Historical Studies of Chile and Brasil.* (New York: Monthly Review Press, 1976), 243.

58 Farshad Araghi, 'The Invisible Hand and the Visible Foot: Peasants, Dispossession and Globalization', in *Peasants and Globalization: Political Economy, Rural Transformation and the Agrarian Question*, ed. A. Haroon Akram-Lodhi and C. Kay (Oxon: Routledge, 2009), 134.

59 Philip McMichael, 'Peasant Prospects in the Neoliberal Age', *Development* 11, no. 3 (2006), 409.

60 McMichael, 'A Food Regime Analysis', (2009), 286.

61 Harvey (2003), 145 and 148.

62 Philip McMichael, 'Food Sovereignty, Social Reproduction and the Agrarian Question', in *Peasants and Globalization: Political Economy, Rural Transformation and the Agrarian Question*, ed. A. Haroon Akram-Lodhi and C. Kay (Oxon: Routledge, 2009), 304.
63 McMichael (2012), 697.
64 Moore (2011), 27.
65 See more at: GRAIN, *Making a Killing from Hunger*, 28 April 2008, 4. www.grain.org/article/entries/178-making-a-killing-from-hunger.
66 McMichael (2006), 412–413.
67 Adam David Morton, *Unravelling Gramsci* (London: Pluto Press, 2007), 96.
68 Thomas R. Bates, Gramsci and the Theory of Hegemony', *Journal of History of Ideas* 36, no. 2 (1975), 352–353; Adam David Morton, 'Social Forces in the Struggle over Hegemony Neo-Gramscian Perspectives in International Political Economy', in *Rethinking Gramsci*, ed. Marcus E. Green, 1st edn. (Oxon: Routledge, 2011), 152–153.
69 G.A. Williams, 'Gramsci's Concept of Egemonia', *Journal of the History of Ideas* 21, no. 4 (1960), 587, quoted in Ralph Miliband, *State in Capitalist Society* (London: Quartet Books, 1969), 162.
70 Morton (2011), 153.
71 Bates (1975), 352.
72 Morton (2007), 99.
73 Robert W. Cox, 'Social Forces, States and World Orders: Beyond International Relations Theory', *Millennium – Journal of International Studies* 10 (1981), 147.
74 Robert W. Cox, *Production, Power and World Order: Social Forces in the Making of History* (New York: Columbia University Press, 1987) and Stephen Gill, 'Globalisation, Market Civilisation and Disciplinary Neoliberalism', *Millennium: Journal of International Studies* 24, no. 3 (1995): 399–423 and Stephen Gill and D. Law, 'Global Hegemony and the Structural Power of Capital', *International Studies Quarterly* 33, no. 4 (1989): 475–499, all quoted in Andreas Bieler and Adam David Morton, 'A Critical Theory Route to Hegemony, World Order and Historical Change Neo-Gramscian. Neo-Gramscian Perspectives in International Relations', in *Global Restructuring, State, Capital and Labour. Contesting Neo-Gramscian Perspectives* (Basingstoke and New York: Palgrave Macmillan, 2006), 18.
75 Robert W. Cox, 'Global Perestroika', in *The Socialist Register: New World Order?*, ed. R. Miliband and L. Panitch (London: Merlin Press, 1992), 31, quoted in Morton (2011), 158.
76 Cox (1987), 298 and Gill (1995), 400–401 and Gill and Law (1989), 484, all quoted in Bieler and Morton, 'A Critical Theory Route', (2006), 18.
77 Owen Worth, 'Beyond World Order and Transnational Classes. The (re)application of Gramsci in Global Politics', in *Gramsci and Global Politics. Hegemony and Resistance*, ed. Mark McNally and John Schwarzmantel (Oxon: Routledge, 2009), 29.
78 Andreas Bieler and Adam David Morton, 'Class Formation, Resistance and the Transnational Beyond Unthinking Materialism', in *Global Restructuring, State, Capital and Labour. Contesting Neo-Gramscian Perspectives*, ed. Andreas Bieler *et al.* (Oxon: Routledge, 2006), 197.
79 Mark Rupert, *Ideologies of Globalization: Contending Visions of a New World Order* (London: Routledge, 2000), 11.
80 Morton (2007), 97.
81 Joseph Femia, 'Hegemony and Consciousness in the Thought of Antonio Gramsci,' *Political Studies* 23, no. 1 (2006), 34.
82 Rupert (2000), 11–12.

83 Stuart Hall, 'The Problem of Ideology-Marxism Without Guarantees', *Journal of Communication Inquiry* 10, no. 2 (1986), 42.
84 Rupert (2000), 11–12.
85 Bieler and Morton, 'Class Formation' (2006), 198–199.
86 Morton (2007), 92.
87 Mark McNally, 'Gramsci's Internationalism, the National-Popular and the Alternative Globalisation Movement', in *Gramsci and Global Politics. Hegemony and Resistance*, ed. Mark McNally and John Schwarzmantel (Oxon: Routledge, 2009), 62.
88 Ibid., 68–70.
89 Stephen Gill, 'Toward a Postmodern Prince? The Battle in Seattle as a Moment in the New Politics of Globalisation', *Millennium – Journal of International Studies* 29, no. 1 (1 January 2000), 131.
90 Ibid., 137–140.
91 Bill Paterson, 'Trasformismo at the World Trade Organization', in *Gramsci and Global Politics. Hegemony and Resistance*, ed. Mark McNally and John Schwarzmantel (Oxon: Routledge, 2009), 47.
92 Behrooz Morvaridi, 'Capitalist Philanthropy and Hegemonic Partnerships', *Third World Quarterly* 33, no. 7 (August 2012), 1205.
93 Holt-Giménez and Shattuck (2011), 115.
94 Annie Shattuck, 'Will Sustainability Certifications Work? A Look at the Roundtable on Sustainable Biofuels', in *Agrofuels in the Americas*, ed. R. Jonasse (Oakland: Food First Books, 2009), 75–95, quoted in Holt-Giménez and Shattuck (2011), 122.
95 Holt-Giménez and Shattuck (2011), 122.
96 World Bank, UNCTAD, FAO, IFAD, *Principles of Responsible Agricultural Investments* (Washington DC: World Bank, 2010), quoted in White *et al.* (2012), 636.
97 Saturnino M. Borras and Jennifer C. Franco, 'From Threat to Opportunity? Problems with the Idea of a "Code of Conduct" for Land-Grabbing', *Yale Human Rights and Development Law Journal* 13, no. 2 (2010): 507–523, quoted in White *et al.* (2012), 637.
98 De Schutter (2011a), 274–275.
99 Harriet Friedmann, 'From Colonialism to Green Capitalism: Social Movements and Emergence of Food Regimes', in *New Directions in the Sociology of Global Development: Research in Rural Sociology and Development Volume 11*, ed. F. Buttel and P. McMichael (Oxford: Elsevier, 2005), 230–231, 257.
100 Julie Guthman, 'Room for Manoeuvre? (In)organic Agribusiness in California', in *Agribusiness and Society. Corporate Responses to Environmentalism, Market Opportunities and Public Regulation* (London: Zed Books, 2004).
101 K. Klonsky *et al.*, *Statistical Review of California's Organic Agriculture 1995–1998* (Davis: University of California, Agricultural Issues Center, 2001), quoted in Guthman (2004).
102 T. Clunies-Ross, 'Organic Food: Swimming Against the Tide?', in *Political, Social and Economic Perspectives on the International Food System*, ed. T. Marsden and J. Little (Aldershot: Avebury, 1990), 200–214, quoted in Guthman (2004).
103 See Julie Guthman, 'Raising Organic: An Agro-Ecological Assessment of Grower Practices in California', *Agriculture and Human Values* 17 (2000), 257–266.
104 For example: Michael K. Goodman, 'Reading Fair Trade: Political Ecological Imaginary and the Moral Economy of Fair Trade Foods', *Political Geography* 23, no. 7 (September 2004); Margaret Levi and April Linton, 'Fair Trade: A Cup at a Time?', *Politics & Society* 31, no. 3 (1 September 2003), quoted in Daniel Niles and Robin Jane Roff, 'Shifting Agrifood Systems: The Contemporary Geography of Food and Agriculture: An Introduction', *GeoJournal* 73, no. 1 (26 July 2008), 6.
105 Laura T. Raynolds, 'Consumer/Producer Links in Fair Trade Coffee Networks', *Sociologia Ruralis* 42, no. 4 (October 2002), 419–420.

106 For example: Stewart Lockie, 'The Invisible Mouth: Mobilizing "the Consumer" in Food Production–Consumption Networks', *Sociologia Ruralis* 42, no. 4 (2002): 278–294; Robin Jane Roff, 'Shopping for Change? Neoliberalizing Activism and the Limits to Eating Non-GMO', *Agriculture and Human Values* 24, no. 4 (8 August 2007): 511–522.
107 For example: S. Freidberg, *The Contradictions of Clean: Supermarket Ethical Trade and African Horticulture* (London, 2003) and Christina Getz and A. Shreck, 'What Organic and Fair Trade Labels Do Not Tell Us: Towards a Place-Based Understanding of Certification', *Journal of Consumer Studies* 30, no. 5 (2006), 490–501, quoted in Niles and Roff (2008), 6.
108 Marlène Elias and Magalie Saussey, '"The Gift that Keeps on Giving": Unveiling the Paradoxes of Fair Trade Shea Butter', *Sociologia Ruralis* 53, no. 2 (1 April 2013), 159 and 173.
109 C.A. Cone and A. Kakaliouras, 'Community Supported Agriculture: Building Moral Community or an Alternative Consumer Choice', *Culture and Agriculture* 51/52 (1995), 28–31.
110 Arjun Appadurai, *The Social Life of Things: Commodities in Cultural Perspective* (Cambridge: Cambridge University Press, 1986), 31, quoted in David Goodman and E. Melanie DuPuis, 'Knowing Food and Growing Food: Beyond the Production–Consumption Debate in the Sociology of Agriculture', *Sociologia Ruralis* 42, no. 1 (January 2002), 9.
111 Goodman and DuPuis (2002), 6–9.
112 See Guthman (2000).
113 Goodman and DuPuis (2002), 17.
114 S. Lockie and L. Collie, '"Feed the Man Meat": Gendered Food and Theories of Consumption', in *Restructuring Global and Regional Agricultures: Transformations in Australasian Agri-Food Economies and Spaces*, ed. D. Burch, J. Cross, and G. Lawrence (Aldershot: Ashgate Publishing, 1999), 270, quoted in Goodman and DuPuis (2002), 15.
115 For example, see: Patricia Allen and Carolyn Sachs, 'Women and Food Chains: The Gendered Politics of Food', *International Journal of Sociology of Food and Agriculture* 15, no. 1 (2007), 1–23; Deborah Barndt, *Women Working the NAFTA Food Chain: Women, Food and Globalization* (Toronto, ON: Sumach Press, 1999); Catherine Dolan, 'On Farm and Packhouse: Employment at the Bottom of a Global Value Chain', *Rural Sociology* 69, no. 1 (2004): 99–126.
116 Allen and Sachs (2007), 5.
117 For example, see: Bina Agarwal, *A Field of One's Own: Gender and Land Rights in South Asia* (Cambridge: Cambridge University Press, 1994).
118 For example, see: A. Peterman, J. Behrman, and A.R. Quisumbing, *A Review of Empirical Evidence on Gender Differences in Non-Land Agricultural Inputs, Technology and Services in Developing Countries. International Food Policy Research Institute Discussion Paper 001003* (Washington DC, 2010).
119 Candice Shaw, 'Global Agro Food Systems: Gendered and Ethnic Inequalities in Mexico's Agricultural Industry', *McGill Sociological Review* 2, April (2011), 92–93 and 103–104.
120 For example, see: L.C. Smith *et al.*, *The Importance of Women's Status for Child Nutrition in Developing Countries. Research Report 131* (Washington DC, 2002); K. Saito, H. Mekonnen, and D. Spurling, *Raising the Productivity of Women Farmers in Sub-Saharan Africa. Discussion Paper 230* (Washington DC, 1994).
121 Paul Robbins, *Political Ecology: a Critical Introduction*, 2nd edn. (Chicester: Wiley-Blackwell, 2007), 64; Allen and Sachs (2012), 12–13.
122 Robbins (2012), 64.
123 George Ritzer, *Sociological Theory*, 5th edn. (New York: McGraw-Hill, 2005), quoted in Shaw (2011), 100.

124 Deborah Barndt, *Tangled Routes: Women, Work, and Globalization on the Tomato Trail* (UK: Rowman and Littlefield, 2008), quoted in Shaw (2011), 100.
125 Bridget O'Laughlin, 'Gender Justice, Land and the Agrarian Question in Southern Africa', in *Peasants and Globalization: Political Economy, Rural Transformation and the Agrarian Question*, ed. A. Haroon Akram-Lodhi and Cristobal Kay (New York: Routledge, 2009), 204–205.

3 Hegemony in the agri-food system in Thailand

Introduction

One of the things that Thailand is best known for is its cheap food and world-renowned cuisine. The story behind such cheap food and agricultural products, however, is one about power, inequality and ecological unsustainability. This chapter explores these issues through its discussion of the hegemonic agri-food system as it unfolded in Thailand between 1990 and 2014. It also advances the first main argument of this book which is that the mainstream agri-food system in Thailand has been shaped by transnational and domestic forces to aid capital accumulation, and is sustained through the maintenance of hegemonic agri-food production–distribution, governance structures and ideational order.

This chapter is divided into three main parts. The first part starts the discussion of the hegemonic agri-food system in Thailand by exploring hegemonic production–distribution practices. The second part of the chapter discusses hegemonic governance structures which facilitate the mainstream agri-food system in Thailand, with emphasis on the roles of domestic forces such as the Thai state and transnational forces such as global governance bodies. The last part of the chapter discusses the hegemonic ideational order: a combination of transnational neo-liberal/capitalist ideas as well as domestic historical-cultural mentality in Thailand, such as that of patron–client, which aid capital accumulation through the mainstream agri-food system in Thailand.

Part 1 Hegemonic agri-food production–distribution in Thailand

As part of the global system, hegemonic agri-food production–distribution practices in Thailand reflect many characteristics of the globalised corporate agri-food production–distribution practices that were discussed in the previous chapter. Reflections on empirical evidence in combination with the theoretical framework suggest that the hegemonic capitalist agri-food production–distribution in Thailand seems to benefit large corporations and capital accumulation at the expense of nature, small and medium farmers, as well as consumers. Issues to be discussed in sections 1.1 to 1.4 include: unsustainable industrialised production methods; land grabs; the food-fuel nexus; financial speculations of agri-food commodities; and monopoly power in the agri-food sector.

1.1 Commodification and capitalist agricultural production

From a neo-Marxist perspective, increased commodification and commercialisation of agri-food resources, as well as under-valuations of the production costs of agri-food products, help to establish conditions for cheap food and raw materials which aid global capital accumulation. Using empirical evidence from Thailand, this section illustrates how industrial agricultural production methods, genetically modified seeds and associated private property rights have been instrumental in the commodification of natural resources and agri-food products. They can also be seen as methods of accumulation by dispossessions that enable exploitations of both humans and nature in service of capital accumulation. The following paragraphs first discuss the historical roles of transnational hegemonic forces in laying the foundations of contemporary mainstream agri-food production –distribution in Thailand, then discuss the Green Revolution production paradigm in Thailand which reflect mainstream economics' disregard for ecological-social externalities in the name of economic efficiency.

Since the very beginning, transnational forces have encouraged the integration of Thailand into the global agri-food system and economy, as well as encouraged exports of Thai agricultural commodities to meet world-market demands. Commercialisation of agricultural production accelerated following the Bowring Treaty of 1855 between Thailand and Britain. In its search for cheap rice for its colonies, and raw materials, Britain encouraged Thailand to supply rice to the international market.[1] After the Second World War grains were much needed in Europe, and Thailand expanded plantations of certain commodities to meet these demands. Through the advice of the Food and Agriculture Organization of the United Nations (FAO) in 1947 and loans from the World Bank in 1952, the Thai government started to invest in infrastructures, such as, large-scale irrigation projects to help transform the agricultural sector and encourage exports of agri-food products such as rice.[2] Around 1957 and 1958, the World Bank published a report on a public development program for Thailand which became an important influence for the first Thai National Economic and Social Development plan in 1961. The plan outlined a nationwide transformation of agricultural production in different regions; rice production was to be expanded in the Chaopraya River Delta in the Central Plain while the production of sugar cane and other cash-crops was encouraged in the Northeast.[3] In the South, the spread of mono-cropping of rubber plantations was an initiative of the Thai government, but it was also encouraged by international factors such as the Korean War which increased demands for rubber. Thailand also received international loans from the World Bank and the UK Department for International Development (formerly known as the Overseas Development Administration) to implement expansions of rubber plantations between 1978 and 1982.[4]

As Chapter 2, section 1.1, discussed, the Green Revolution was promoted around the world after the Second World War by private institutions such as Rockefeller and Ford foundations, as well as by the US and other OECD governments. At the start of the adoption of Green Revolution technology in Thailand, in 1950, the US sent two agricultural science academics to train officials and students, and to collect different rice genetic materials to be developed so that they are responsive to chemical fertilisers, with aims to meet domestic demand and international trade.[5] The development of hybrid maize seeds, for example, was supported by the Rockefeller Foundation.[6]

It has been argued that the Green Revolution causes soil degradation and the reduction of biodiversity (such as loss of traditional rice, fish and plant genes) and toxins in the soil, water and food, which have negative impact on local food security.[7] However, these costs are not reflected in the costs of production of agri-food products. In addition, under the current hegemonic production, yields of mono-crops are used as measures of productivity while side effects and co-products are neglected and not seen as important even if they affect local food security, local ecologies, and potential income sources. This reflects a form of commodification of nature where agri-food products are seen in isolation as objects to be sold in markets to gain value, without considerations of how these products relate to their natural and social contexts. Intensive mono-cropping of rice and extensive use of chemicals, for example, can destroy local varieties of vegetables and fish in paddy fields which also negatively affect local food security and sources of income.[8] High Yielding Varieties (HYV) and genetically modified (GM) seeds may increase yields but prices can be rather high under corporate monopoly control.[9]

Between 1998 and 2003, the average yield of rice in Thailand was 420 kg. per rai (rai is a unit which is equal to 1,600 square metres) which was around 37.77 per cent higher than before the introduction of new HYV seeds.[10] However, as discussed previously, there were many other costs to consider. For example, new semi-dwarf rice seeds do not suit ecological realities in many areas and they also require complementary large-scale irrigation systems.[11] Intensive mono-production of rice, which does not allow paddy fields to rest, tends to lead to environmental problems such as land degradation, which is attributed for the spread of pests and the need to use increased levels of chemicals.[12] This tends to lead to vicious cycles as uses of chemicals and antibiotics increase diseases and pests.[13] Between 1994 and 2004, annual imports of agricultural chemicals in Thailand increased four-fold and chemicals usage increased by 13.2 per cent per year per rai. However, yield per rai increased, on average, only 2.5 per cent per year.[14] It has also been suggested that prices of chemical fertilisers will tend to increase in the future because they are derived from finite fossil fuels.[15]

Higher costs of production relative to revenues are often suggested as contributing factors that lead to debts and dispossessions of small-scale farmers in Thailand.[16] A study suggests that in 2009, six million farmers were in debt to a total extent of one billion baht and 30 per cent of these loans were non-performing loans.[17] There are also problems of incorrect usage of chemicals and negative consequences on health and the environment.[18] Between 2001 and 2010, there were over 1,000 cases of sickness from agricultural pesticides per year. Land in many areas of the country was also found to be contaminated.[19] A study suggests that 72 per cent of farming communities experienced soil problems such as soil erosion and lack of organic compounds in 2006.[20] A survey in 2007 from the Ministry of Health also suggests that 38.52 per cent of farmers had dangerously high levels of agricultural chemicals in their bodies.[21] Aside from dangerous toxins in agri-food products, the general population can also be negatively affected by the current production methods through other channels, such as through haze from land clearing.[22]

It can be seen that the current hegemonic production paradigm has many negative environmental and health consequences, and yet Thailand is still committed to it. By externalising socio-ecological costs, the hegemonic Green Revolution production paradigm helps capital accumulation by systematically under-valuing the costs of agri-food products. Commodification of seeds also helps capital to extract surplus or rents. Similar to the case of HYV seeds, genetically modified (GM) seeds are being portrayed in recent years as a cutting-edge technological advancement which would help solve global food security. However, as Chapter 2, section 1.1, discussed, GM seeds are scientifically unproven to be higher-yielding while many studies suggest that they have negative ecological, social and economic costs, especially when their use is coupled with strict property rights agreements that reinforce the monopoly power of biotechnology agri-businesses. From a neo-Marxist perspective, such commodification and strict intellectual property rights of seeds can be seen as a form of accumulation by dispossession. Moreover, strong reliance on finite fossil fuels suggests that the current mainstream agri-food system is not sustainable in the long run.

In Thailand, the leakage of Monsanto's genetically modified BT cottons outside experimental fields (discovered in 1999) led to widespread opposition from civil society against open-field experiments of GM seeds. In 2001, the Thai state agreed to halt GM's cultivation for commercial purposes except under laboratory and greenhouse conditions, but some contaminations have been discovered since then.[23] There have also been constant pressures, such as from some researchers, US officials, and the private sector, for the Thai state to support GM research, field tests and commercial plantation of GM plants.[24] In 2007, the Thai state finally allowed open-field experiments of GM seeds under certain conditions, such as on the state-controlled land and with the state's permission.[25] Recent attempts to introduce open-field testing of GM crops in 2014, as well as counter-movements from civil society groups, will be discussed in Chapter 5.

1.2 Land grabs and the food–fuel nexus

Section 1.4 in Chapter 2 discussed the contradictory food–fuel connections where diversions of resources to agro-fuels production threaten food security without solving finite energy problems. Even though the international prices of rice, an important food grain in Thailand, adjusted downwards in the latter half of 2008 after dramatic spikes in 2007/2008, it has been noted that agro-fuels policies and changes in prices of production inputs contributed to a new higher price level in Thailand compared to before 2007.[26] Continual increases of fossil fuel prices have also led the Thai government to support production of agro-fuels, which drives up prices of sugar cane, cassava and palm oil.[27] Sections 1.5 and 1.6 in Chapter 2 also discussed how global interests in food and agro-fuels production following the 2007/2008 spikes in global agri-food commodity prices have prompted transnational capital to engage in resource grabs and in speculations of agricultural commodity prices. From a neo-Marxist perspective discussed in Chapter 2, increased global interests in land grabs and agro-fuel investments can be seen as the capitalist system's tendency to appropriate nature to ensure continuities of capital accumulation through 'cheap' food and energy, or as a form of accumulation by dispossession, which helps turn small-scale farmers and marginalised rural populations into a reserve army of low-skilled and semi-skilled labours. As the following paragraphs discuss, both Thai and non-Thai capital, as well as other agents, actively engage in land grabs and agro-fuels production. It is also argued here that even though current land grabs for agro-fuels may be able to stimulate capital accumulation in the short- and medium-term, they are unlikely to solve the finite energy problem in the long run.

Since the 1980s there have been growing conflicts in Thailand between the state's control over forest areas, local usage of land, and the mass purchases of land all over the country by capitalists who often leave the land unutilised.[28] A study in 1999 suggests that after the Asian economic crisis of 1997, over 70 per cent of land in the country is under-utilised.[29] In the early 2010s there are many reports by farmers, real estate businesses, government officials and others which suggest that both Thai and non-Thai capital have been investing in land and at various points along vertical agri-food chains to gain integrated systemic control.[30] Although non-Thais are prohibited by the Foreign Business Act of 1999 to purchase land for agricultural purposes, in practice, there are non-Thais that manage to control land for agricultural purposes through Thai nominees. It is often difficult to gather information from farmers as they fear backlash,[31] but from what is available, it seems that land grabs in many provinces all over the country can be of various scales, such as from 10 rai to over a 1,000 rai.[32] Contrary to the typical image of land grabs for the purpose of large-scale plantations, in the case of Thailand, land grabs can also occur through networks of several small firms which were established to purchase land in different areas.[33]

There are also other arrangements similar to contract farming which allow non-Thais to control what is being produced, how it is produced and processed (for example, which company's hybrid seeds to use), and where products are distributed.[34] Thai farmers are usually hired as labour in these land plots for the production of agricultural commodities (e.g. rice) by capital from various places such as Lebanon, Taiwan and Saudi Arabia. The products are then exported to countries of origin of these capital groups.[35] There are also reports of a growing number of Thai firms that provide 'all-in-one' large-scale agricultural plantations to service non-Thai capital.[36] In the North, Northeast, Central, and South regions of the country, non-Thai capital are not only interested in land grabs for food productions, but also cash crops and energy crops.[37] Suratthani province in the South, for example, is known for having a lot of large-scale palm oil plantations owned by medium and large Thai and non-Thai (dominated by Malaysian and Singaporean capital) palm oil refinery companies.[38] There are also other forms of agricultural investment by foreign capital. For example, some Japanese capital have reportedly purchased 49 per cent shares (as limited by the Thai law) in rice mills and engaged in Japanese rice contract farming, while some Taiwanese capital have purchased shares in sugar factories in addition to their investments in sugar cane, palm oil and eucalyptus plantations.[39]

Many large land holders in Thailand are also interested in the energy sector, which further suggests the interconnections of the agri-food and energy sectors. Two of the biggest Thai transnational capital groups – Charoen Pokphand (CP) and Thai Beverage – have also joined the quest to secure agri-food production resources. They invest not only just in Thailand, but also abroad, as future profitability rises due to concerns around food security and energy scarcity. In 2008, Thai Beverage had over 100,000 rai of land in over 56 provinces.[40] In 2014, it is suggested that it has the control of over 630,000 rai of land through individual, family and company land ownerships.[41] The business group has also hired a former Director General of the Department of Agriculture, Anan Dalodom, to plan what can be grown in each area with an emphasis on key commodities such as rice, rubber, sugar cane, cassava and palm oil.[42] It is estimated that Thai Beverage has become the biggest owner of rubber and sugar cane plantations in Thailand.[43] The second largest land holder in Thailand is the CP group (over 200,000 rai)[44] which also utilises contract farming as a way to secure inputs for its biodiesel production plants. By 2017, CP plans to have over 500,000 rai of contract farms of palm oil in Thailand, Laos, Vietnam and Myanmar.[45] Other large landholders in Thailand include: United Palm Oil Industry Plc. (44,400 rai); the Crown Property Bureau (around 30,000 rai); Integrate Refinery Petrochemical Complex (IRPC) Plc. (petrochemical manufacturer which owns 17,000 rai); the Maleenont family (telecommunication business group which owns more than 10,000 rai); and Dr Boon Wanasin, Executive Managing Director of Thonburi hospital group (around 10,000 rai).[46]

The Thai state and the private sector often suggest that Thai farmers will benefit when agricultural commodities fetch higher prices due to food security concerns and the food–fuel connections (such discourses are discussed in Part 3 of this chapter). However, the influx of resource grabs in recent years contributes to higher purchase prices of land and rental prices of agricultural land in many areas, which makes it increasingly difficult for small- and medium-size farmers to continue renting land. Problems of drastic increases of land and rental prices have been reported by many people such as the BioThai Foundation,[47] Dr Permsak Mokarapirom (an academic and member of the

National Reform Committee),[48] journalists' local sources,[49] and civil servants.[50] For example, Mr Phraiwal Choomai from the Agricultural Office in Patlung province suggests that recent waves of land grabs have pushed the price of rubber plantations from 120,000 to 200,000 baht per rai.[51] At the national level, between 2008 to 2011 and 2012 to 2015, the average price of land increased 5 per cent (8 per cent in the South).[52] In areas with good access to public utilities, prices could double. Such increases in the prices of land also further stimulate large-scale purchases for speculation purposes.[53] In another new practice, rent is now charged, not per year, but per round of production, as landlords see that agri-food products can fetch higher prices.[54] In Chainat the rental price more than tripled from 500 baht per rai per year (before 2007) to 1,500 baht per rai per round of production (as reported in 2009).[55] Landlords also sometimes decide to stop renting and engage in agricultural production themselves.[56] Chapter 4 will also discuss the paddy pledging scheme which contributed to the increase in rental prices of farmland.

The recent spurs of land grabs in Thailand can increase the scale of dispossession of small- and medium-scale farmers, or transform them into semi-farmers/semi-workers through contract farming arrangements. Some farmers have become farm managers to manage large-scale plantations to meet non-Thai capital's export orders.[57] As Chapter 2 suggested, their situations become similar to that of workers in the industrial sector. Farmers who still have their own land might also be increasingly tempted by short-term monetary gains and sell their land even though future prospects as low or semi-skilled workers, or as part of the 'reserve army of labour', can be rather bleak. In addition, even though Thailand is still a net exporter of food, recent waves of land and other forms of resource grabs have raised concerns over food security, environmental degradation, and reduction of biodiversity. After 2002, domestic prices of food and energy crops increased substantially and many farmlands switched their production from food crops to energy crops. In total, energy crop plantation area increased from 18.6 million rai in 2002 to 22.3 million rai in 2007.[58] A regression study also suggests that fossil fuel prices positively correlate with prices of energy crops in Thailand and to a lesser extent with prices of food crops. This suggests a future trend where more resources are devoted to energy crop production due to price incentives, which could result in rising costs of agri-food production and potential domestic food security problems.[59]

As discussed in Chapter 2, given current technology, aggregate fossil energy used in the production of first-generation agro-fuels is higher than the energy contained in agro-fuel outputs.[60] Hence, the growth of large-scale production of agro-fuels is unlikely to solve the finite energy problem. Many agricultural inputs such as fertilisers and chemicals are also derived from fossil fuels and it can be seen that, for example, fertiliser costs increased dramatically in 2008 as a result of higher fossil fuel prices.[61] In addition, there are also opportunity costs to consider with regard to agro-fuels production, as land could perhaps be used in other ecologically sustainable ways to benefit the majority of the population.[62]

1.3 Commercial crops, volatile prices and speculations

Concerns over food and energy scarcities have prompted not only the recent waves of land and other resource grabs, but also financial speculations on agricultural commodities which exaggerate prices beyond supply–demand fundamentals. This section explores how financial speculations on agri-food products can contribute to increasingly volatile prices, which have dispossession effects on small- and medium-scale producers by making their revenues uncertain. Moreover, as will be discussed below using empirical evidence from Thailand, speculations can sometimes increase prices of food within a short period of time, which has similar effects to reductions in real wages of average consumers and can lead to forced under-consumption. However, price increases do not necessarily proportionately benefit producers.

Important commercial agricultural products in Thailand include rice, rubber, cassava, maize, palm oil, and top major export products in terms of value include rubber, rice, shrimps, fish and their products, as well as sugar and cassava.[63] As discussed in Chapter 2, in the past few years, non-commercial speculators have entered futures markets in large numbers, betting on rising prices.[64] For example, hedge funds saw sugar as 'the new crude oil'.[65] These artificially high prices send problematic market signals to producers. When prices are high, producers are often encouraged to expand production, which then leads to higher supply and lower prices. Increased financial speculations amplifies these problems. In Thailand, sugar cane prices reached the highest level in 28 years in 2009 and the price level was estimated by Thai sugar mill associations to remain high for many years due to world demand (such as from India and China) and due to speculations by hedge funds. Thai sugar cane producers then increased production to respond to the higher prices.[66] However, producers in other countries also increased their production. In early 2014, prices of sugar cane dropped to near or below break-even prices for producers in Thailand, mainly because of increased world supply of sugar cane and sugar from India, China and Brazil.[67] Maize producers in Thailand have faced similar problems. For example, there was an expansion of maize production in Naan province after the high prices in 2007 and 2008.[68] However, the costs of production (seed, fertiliser and herbicide prices) doubled during the same period while there was no significant increase in yield. Later on, prices received by producers dropped significantly (almost by half) due to increased supply and also due to imports of maize from neighbouring countries.[69]

Such cycles of 'low supply-high price' and 'high supply-low price' are common for agricultural commodities under current market arrangements, although this does not mean that such market arrangements cannot be changed or should be accepted as natural. Speculations also further complicate the situations. Some commercial plants such as palm oil, rubber, and other garden plants require some fixed investments over a period of time before produce can be harvested, which means that producers could harshly be affected economically by fluctuating prices. Similar to the case of sugar, rubber in Thailand is grown mostly for export, and prices depend on various factors such as world supply and demand (particularly demand from large industrialised economies such as China, Japan, the US and the EU), as well as on speculations in Japanese and Singapore markets.[70] In early March 2011, prices of rubber in Thailand dropped drastically in the same direction as in futures markets of Tokyo and Singapore, as a response to concerns in the Middle East and other factors. This caused further speculations and a downward spiral in prices. Drastic drops in prices (22 US dollars/ton in one week) caused small and medium rubber co-operatives and other players in Thailand to lose over 10,000 million baht.[71]

By relying on one or few of these commodities, small-scale or semi-dispossessed farmers face increased economic risks as volatile prices make their revenues uncertain. They also face increased food insecurity due to reductions of biodiversity and food crops in their land.[72] Global financial speculations on basic food grains, such as rice, can also affect the agri-food system and well-being of the majority of people in Thailand. The price spikes of 2007/2008 drove up domestic prices of rice which negatively affected (especially low-income) consumers, while small- and medium-scale producers were not the main beneficiaries of the higher prices, as discussed below.

Thailand produces around 20 million tons of rice per year. Roughly half of it is used for domestic consumption and the other half is exported.[73] Due to linkages with the global market, domestic price movements in Thailand closely follow world market prices. Between 1985 and 2011, the movements of domestic paddy and rice prices were in the same directions as export market prices.[74] A study from FAO also suggests that although Thailand has some government interventions in terms of procurement and storage, domestic prices nevertheless follow world prices very closely (except in the 1960s and 1970s) such as between 2003 and 2007.[75] After 2008, prices of rice in important export markets became increasingly volatile[76] and the paddy pledging scheme in recent years also makes the situation more complicated (to be discussed in Chapter 4). When international prices of rice surged from an average of $378 per ton in December 2007 to more than $700 per ton by the end of March 2008, domestic rice prices in Bangkok increased 17 per cent between January and February 2008.[77] Between April and May 2008, a few food commodity prices in Bangkok became significantly higher, particularly Jasmine rice (103 per cent), followed by brown sugar and meat.[78] This negatively affected not only low income and poor people in the city, but also the general population, as a field research in 2010 suggests that spending on food accounted for 30 to 50 per cent of total household income across the country.[79] Interestingly, a study in 2003 suggests that despite proximity to agricultural production resources, around 17.8 per cent of households in rural areas spends more than 80 per cent of their income on food.[80]

Rice producers in Thailand have occasionally benefited from increased prices, but not as much as intermediaries and large-scale corporations operating along the rice export supply chain. It has been noted that the increase in prices received by farmers tends to be proportionately less than the increase in wholesale and export prices.[81] A study based on interviews of rice mill operators and rice exporters, as well as figures from the Office of Agricultural Economics (OAE), suggests that during the global food price spikes of 2007/2008 (between 2007 and 2008), farmers' average costs of paddy production increased around 60 per cent; variable costs (labour, seeds and other inputs) increased around 44 per cent while other fixed costs, such as rent, increased over 108 per cent.[82] Profits accrued to farmers, however, increased 52 per cent between 2007 and 2008, which accounted to around 18.5 per cent of total profits in rice export supply chains – a reduction from 21 per cent in 2007.[83] Profits accruing to middlemen, on the other hand, increased 440 per cent, which amounted to 8.5 per cent of total profits in 2008, which was a massive increase compared to their share of 2.8 per cent in 2007.[84] Profits accruing to rice mills increased 16 per cent between 2007 and 2008 (profits of rice mills were already substantially increasing by 128 per cent between 2005 to 2008) and, most importantly, exporters' profits increased 134 per cent, which amounted to 42.7 per cent of total profits in rice export supply chains in 2008.[85]

Rice mills and exporters had the lion's share of total profits in the late 2000s. Between 2005 and 2008, rice mills and exporters' profits amounted to around 73 to 77 per cent of total profits of rice exports.[86] Such distribution of profits is likely to be, at least partially, the result of monopolistic/monopsonistic structures of the paddy and rice markets, as well as the result of the paddy pledging scheme (to be discussed in Chapter 4). In 2009, there were various news reports that rice mills often hoard rice to bargain for higher prices from exporters when international market prices were expected to be higher. Such actions help to push up prices of rice in Thai domestic markets without yielding higher economic benefits to small-scale farmers.[87]

As the next section elaborates, farmers whose revenues are already uncertain due to volatile prices of agri-food commodities can also be subjected to monopoly power in the markets, which dictate prices and pass on the burden of depressed prices to smaller players. The next section also discusses contract farming arrangements in Thailand which, in theory, seem to provide some certainty and less risks for producers, with fixed guaranteed channels to sell products and pre-agreed prices. However, in reality, there are some inequitable contract farming arrangements in Thailand which enable surplus appropriations from producers to agri-businesses through market exchanges of agri-food inputs and outputs.

1.4 Monopoly power, large agri-businesses and surplus appropriation

As Chapter 2 discussed, the neo-Marxist critique of the corporate agri-food system suggests the tendency for monopoly capital to emerge in the capitalist system, and that monopoly capital can use their power to appropriate surplus through their monopoly controls, such as over production inputs, trade channels, and credits. The previous sections have briefly suggested that there are certain degrees of monopoly control over production inputs such as seeds and land in

Thailand. As for agricultural chemicals, a study suggests that the 10 biggest importers of agricultural chemicals (out of around 200 companies) controlled 52.64 per cent of market shares in Thailand in 2007.[88] The following paragraphs also discuss monopoly power and appropriations of surplus in the agri-food system in Thailand, in greater detail.

Agri-businesses and contract farming: integrated monopoly control

One of the largest and most influential agri-businesses in Thailand is the Charoen Pokphand (CP) group which started out as a seed company and grew into a leading transnational company based in Thailand with over 100 companies around the world, including in Asia, Europe, North America and the Middle East, with businesses in many sectors aside from agro-industry, such as petro-chemical, communications, real estate, etc.[89] CP has considerable power in some agri-food commodity chains in Thailand. It holds a large amount of land and also engages in contract farming of many products such as poultry, pork, and fish. In Thailand, CP controlled over 20 per cent of the market in chicken production, 20 per cent in the pork retail sector, 40 per cent in animal feed, and 20 per cent of the total export markets in the broiler sector in 2001.[90]

According to the FAO Integrated Pest Management regional programme, contract farming is becoming the most dominant export production system in Thailand.[91] Some contract farming arrangements in Thailand can be seen as the amalgamation of monopoly control over productive resources, processing, trade channels, and credit. Studies suggest that many contract farming arrangements yield lower benefits to small-scale farmers compared to contracting companies, such as the 2003 report by the Thai Senate Committee on Agriculture and Co-operatives.[92] Many contract farming arrangements also encourage commodification and capitalist agriculture, and it has been suggested that farmers are often converted into mere 'workers in a vast agro-industrial assembly line' who perform specialised production skills.[93] Nevertheless, as will be discussed in Chapter 5, there are also some contract farming arrangements for sustainable agri-food products where companies try to give producers fair prices.

Contract farmers tend to have low bargaining power and usually have to carry the production risks, while the returns that they receive can sometimes be lower than the income received by non-agricultural sector labourers.[94] Aside from having to carry disproportionate parts of production risks, small-scale farmers usually have to purchase their inputs only from the agri-businesses they are selling their products to.[95] A study in 2011 found that over 70 per cent of small-scale contract farmers' costs of production were in different forms of payment to agri-businesses.[96] In the case of fish and chicken contract farming, payment for production inputs can be as high as 85 to 90 per cent of total costs.[97]

Signing up to contract farming might seem like a matter of individual choice, but farmers do so under structural limitations where monopoly influence over production inputs, trade channels, and access to credits in the agri-food system, limits options and choices of small-scale producers. As suggested by a field research in 2004 of pig and chicken farmers in three provinces of the Central and Northeastern regions, farmers signed the contracts because they had no capital to set up independently as it was difficult for them to receive loans from other sources. If they signed contracts with the company, the company would provide inputs and access to bank loans. In addition, there was no market for independent farmers who want to raise chicken broilers as contracting companies controlled the majority of trade channels.[98]

Contract farming arrangements of some commodities require large sums of fixed capital investments, often financed through bank loans, which discourage farmers from breaking off their contracts when they find the contracts to be inequitable. For example, egg contract farmers at Ampur Banpong community, in Chiang Mai province, had to invest a lot in production equipment and often used their land as collateral. In addition, there were a lot of negative externality problems in terms of pollution and unhygienic conditions which caused grave conflicts in the community.[99] The author's interviews of a few egg contract farmers at Romphothong village in Chiang Mai province in 2012 also support these points.[100]

Agri-businesses and monopoly control over agri-food processing and trade

This subsection uses examples of rice, fruits and vegetables to demonstrate how participants in some agri-food chains in Thailand tend to have unequal market power. In the case of rice, a study found that in the late 1990s and early 2000s, some farmers had to sell their paddy to rice mills even though they knew the rice mills were cheating them, or that they were paid less than what they should had received. This was because they lacked other channels to sell their paddy, and it would cost just the same to transport the paddy to other mills.[101] This study also found that gross revenues and net profits of Jasmine rice traders were quite high compared to that of farmers.[102] Rice trade in Thailand, before the implementation of the paddy pledging scheme in recent years, was dominated by only a few big firms. In 2007, the 10 biggest companies exported 70 per cent of total Thai rice export. The biggest company was Nakhon Luang or Capital Rice, which exported 17.6 per cent of the total rice export.[103] In 2010, five companies exported 50 per cent of the total export.[104] Chapter 4 will also discuss how the paddy pledging scheme has helped to increase the power of large rice mills and traders.

In the case of fruits, it has been suggested that the monopoly power of around four to five longan traders in the North help to depress prices received by smaller-scale traders and farmers. Moreover, it is very difficult to export to China – the main export market – without connections; delays at Chinese customs, which may spoil the products, can be used to eliminate competition or to force collaborations, not to mention that Chinese importers prefer to deal with large-scale middlemen.[105] As for domestic fruits and vegetable central/wholesale markets in Thailand, at first glance they might appear to be competitive with many players.[106] However, it has been suggested that there are some well-established 'networks' backed by large capital or influential individuals who wield considerable power along some commodity chains. The BAAC in Chiang Mai had tried to directly collect products from farmers and find channels to sell them to reduce the power of middlemen. However, even when they sold the products at lower prices at a central market, virtually nobody bought the products. This is because traders only buy from their usual networks. If they buy products from someone else, such as from the BAAC, they might face retributions. Smaller-scale traders are, overall, more concerned about maintaining good long-term relationships with these monopoly networks and influential individuals who have extensive controls over many agri-food product supply chains, rather than with short-term price competitiveness.[107] Such informal rules of the market are compatible with the widespread acceptance of patron–client relationships in Thai society, which are discussed in the next part of the chapter as part of the hegemonic governance structures. Smaller players are allowed to enter some small retail markets, such as on the streets or markets in front of hospitals, but not the central wholesale markets which determine nationwide retail prices.[108]

There are also monopolies in the modern retail trade sector where agri-food products are important components. Studies suggest that, with increased vertical concentrations along agri-food chains in both developed and developing countries, supermarkets now play a huge role in product development, branding, supplier selection and distribution. They can use their market power to exercise control along the chains. For example, they can specify how products should be grown, harvested, transported, processed and stored.[109] In Thailand, a few companies which developed through alliances of Thai and non-Thai capital have been able to control major market shares in the national modern retail sector. Supermarkets in Thailand have approximately a 40 to 50 per cent share of the national fruit and vegetable market,[110] and many agri-food products are now being sold through modern trade channels of varying scales, ranging from large hypermarkets to village-level convenience stores.

At the time of writing, three of the largest Thai capital groups dominate the modern retail sector; the CP group, the Central group, and the TCC (Thai Charoen Corporation) group associated with Thai Beverage.[111] CP's annexation of Siam Makro (the biggest wholesale and retail company in Thailand) in 2013 further reaffirms the status of the CP group as one of the most powerful monopoly transnational agri-business and agri-food retail giant operating in Thailand. In addition to having partial ownership and management interests in Tesco-Lotus, the biggest hypermarket-supermarket company in Thailand which is largely owned by Tesco (the British supermarket giant), CP also owns 7–11 and CP Fresh Mart convenient stores in Thailand which have numerous branches throughout the country. This means that CP has some control and influence over three out of the four biggest retail companies operating in Thailand (7–11, Tesco-Lotus, Makro, Big C).[112]

The growth and development of modern trade in Thailand have largely been influenced by advanced capitalist countries' transnational retail companies' business models and management techniques, implemented through co-operations and joint investments with transnational companies based in Thailand. The CP group, for example, learned and imported management techniques from transnational businesses in advanced capitalist countries.[113] It has also been noted that before 1997, the Central group did not play a major role in the management of Big C and Carrefour even though they were major shareholders.[114] After the Asian economic crisis of 1997, CP and Central groups sold most shares of their hypermarkets (Lotus, Big C, and Carrefour) to non-Thai transnational companies.[115] Joint co-operations seem to be mutually beneficial to both non-Thai and Thai transnational companies. For example, CP tried to learn from Tesco as it expanded its operations in countries such as China and also used connections with Tesco to export its poultry products to the UK,[116] while Tesco benefited from CP's cultural and political linkages in Thailand and China.[117]

Theoretically, monopolies in the agri-food retail sector can use their market power to extract favourable trade deals from small- and medium-size suppliers with less bargaining power. Indeed, some suppliers reported to the Ministry of Commerce in 2002 that they were charged unfair fees by retail giants who used these fees to cover their losses from predatory pricing.[118] Often, agricultural products such as rice were sold at low prices to promote sales of other products, which depressed rice prices.[119] In addition, there were various reports from small and medium retail businesses in many provinces that they were being squeezed out of the market.[120]

The monopolistic market power of large hypermarkets can further support the dominance of large agri-businesses and large-scale middlemen in agri-food supply chains, which further reduces the power and choices of both consumers and producers. The CP group, for example, uses their retail outlets as market channels for their agri-food products such as poultry and frozen food.[121] In addition, as a few studies suggest, hypermarket giants prefer to deal with large-scale suppliers who can meet their standards.[122] Smaller-scale producers and suppliers may not be able to gain significant profits after having to pay fees charged by large retailers. Naso producer rice mill in Yasothon province (to be discussed in Chapter 5), for example, had tried to supply rice to many hypermarket companies only to discover that huge fees imposed by the companies did not make the sales worthwhile.[123] At the same time, monopoly control over retail channels will make it increasingly difficult for smaller-scale producers and suppliers to sell their products through alternative channels, especially if they need to sell perishable agri-food products in large volumes.

Part 2 Governance structures of the hegemonic agri-food system in Thailand

The previous part of the chapter has discussed how the mainstream agri-food production–distribution practices in Thailand aid capital accumulation. Production–distribution practices, however, are only parts of the hegemonic agri-food system in Thailand. From a Gramscian theoretical perspective discussed in Chapter 2, hegemony encompasses more than just the economic structure, but also governance and ideological structures. It can be argued that important problems of the global mainstream agri-food system partially arise from deficiencies of current agri-food governance, including the lack of effective global governance structures to regulate transnational capital from land grabs and excessive speculations on food prices. Governance structures relating to private intellectual property rights and trade liberalisation, as well as regulations (or the lack of them) on market monopolies and contract farming, can also be used as means to facilitate accumulation by dispossession.

This part of the chapter discusses the hegemonic governance structures of the agri-food system in Thailand while Part 3 discusses the hegemonic ideological order that helps to sustain the hegemonic agri-food system. The conceptualisation of agri-food governance takes into account public, private, formal and informal frameworks – or rules and norms – that affect the agri-food system in Thailand. Section 2.1 explores the role of domestic forces in shaping hegemonic agri-food governance structures in Thailand and section 2.2 focuses on the role of transnational forces in shaping hegemonic agri-food governance in Thailand.

2.1 Hegemonic domestic forces' influence on the governance structures

This section focuses on the central role of the Thai state in the maintenance of hegemonic agri-food governance structures. However, Chapters 4 to 6 will discuss how some smaller parts of the Thai state are open to alternative agri-food projects, which suggests that the Thai state should not be seen as a monolithic entity. This section also discusses the privileged position of the Crown Property Bureau which is a large holder of land, as well as patron–client relations – important informal norms underlying the crony capitalist nature of the Thai state – that help to sustain the hegemonic agri-food system.

Policies to aid capital accumulation through the agri-food sector

The Thai state has consistently promoted capital accumulation through the agri-food sector and also favoured large agri-businesses at the expense of small-scale farmers and consumers. When the Green Revolution production paradigm was first introduced, the Thai state encouraged Thai farmers to stop using traditional seeds and to purchase new seed varieties or high-yield variety (HYV) seeds from the state and corporations.[124] Markets for maize seeds, for example, are now dominated by a few agri-businesses.[125] The Thai state has also favoured the industrial sector at the expense of the agricultural sector. For example, the Thai state depressed prices of some agricultural commodities to keep industrial workers' wages low in the past,[126] such as through rice premium or ad valorem tax on rice exports.[127] It has been suggested that the Thai state's policy to use agriculture to subsidise industry was not a transitory policy like in some other countries. Instead, it is a permanent policy, as substantial parts of government revenues do not go back to improve agriculture.[128]

Since the early 1960s, agri-businesses could secure packages of tax breaks, duty privileges and other promotional measures,[129] and agricultural export promotion policies were clearly adopted since the 1970s.[130] In the fifth National Economic and Social Development (NESD) plan (1982–1986), agri-businesses were given high priority.[131] It has been suggested that the domination of agri-businesses in Thailand, starting in the 1970s and 1980s, can partially be seen as a 'symbolic political victory' of the elites, following violent repressions of agrarian movements in the 1970s which weakened the rural population politically (to be discussed in Chapter 4). Farmers were also weakened, economically, due to the decline of primary commodity prices in the 1980s.[132]

Vertical integrations of farming, processing and high value-added exports were encouraged by the state, such as through the Office of Agricultural Economics (OAE) and the Department of Agricultural Extensions (DAE).[133] On the other hand, as discussed in the previous part, little has been done to ensure fair and equitable contracts between agri-businesses and farmers. The Thai state also supports contract farming in neighbouring countries such as Myanmar, Laos and Cambodia through the Ayawadee-Chaopraya-Mekong Economic Co-operation (ACMECS) agreement, and transnational Thai agri-business investors receive tax exemptions when they import raw agricultural commodities into Thailand from these countries.[134] These tax-exempted imports from lower-cost countries aid capital accumulation by Thai agri-businesses, but they are also likely to depress domestic prices received by domestic producers.

Despite concerns over the recent global rush for food–energy land grabs, by 2014 there is still no clear Thai state policy to safeguard agricultural land for food production. The Thai state, however, started to promote agro-fuels since the early 2000s. It also supports conversions of agricultural land for the production of ethanol and bio-diesel inputs such as sugar cane, cassava and palm oil. Ethanol production has been promoted through many measures, such as machinery and corporate tax exemptions from the Board of Investment (BOI). Exports of ethanol to countries such as Japan, China, and the US are also encouraged by the Thai Ministry of Commerce.[135] Land surrounding ethanol production plants have been purchased by private entities, and local farmers were also encouraged by the state and private sector to grow energy crops.[136]

Crony capitalism: the Thai state and politically connected agri-businesses

Generally, the Thai state subscribes to the usual modernisation policy prescriptions and neo-classical economic beliefs. Nevertheless, the Thai state hardly promotes textbook-style free competition. It has been suggested that policies which subordinate agriculture to industrial needs also selectively benefited Thai urban-industrial interests that had ties to the bureaucracy.[137] This is a reflection of the crony capitalist nature of the Thai state. Through both direct and indirect participations in politics, some large businesses manage to influence policies and state apparatus for their interests, as the following paragraphs elaborate.

It is common practice for businesses in Thailand to give a lot of financial contributions to help political parties and individual politicians (from all parties) with their election campaigns (and vote buying), so that they can call in favours at later dates.[138] Moreover, large agri-businesses in Thailand have built connections with political parties, educational institutions, the bureaucracy, and other prominent institutions in Thailand through financial support and by giving other aids. These businesses, in turn, benefit from state concessions and public research.[139] CP, for example, has been noted to have strong political linkages with the Thai state since the late 1970s partially because CP helped establish relations between Thai and Chinese government leaders, which allowed CP to gain the trust of both the Chinese and Thai governments.[140] CP currently has strong ties with various institutions in Thailand such as the bureaucracy, political parties, and educational institutions,[141] and seems to be managing well despite polarised politics in Thailand.

After the 1997 Asian economic crisis, debt-ridden Thai conglomerates' struggles for survival, combined with the 1997 Constitution which gave much power to the executive branch, provided conditions for strong alliances of politicians and large business conglomerates which come to assume leading roles in Thai politics.[142] Thaksin Shinnawatra, whose business was in the area of telecommunications, headed the newly established Thai Rak Thai (TRT) party in 1998 which came to power in 2001. Funds to create TRT came from pooled resources of various large capital groups[143] and Bangkok-based business-politicians emerged as the most powerful group of state managers, although provincial business politicians were still able to exert some influence.[144] In 2001, the proportion of members of parliament with business backgrounds was 30 per cent.[145] Thaksin had also appointed businessmen to the boards of government agencies and state enterprises,[146] and some studies suggest that capital groups associated with politics benefit economically from their direct linkages with the Thai government.[147] The early Thaksin Cabinet also included big business representatives such as Mr Pitak Intarawitayanunt and Mr Wattana Muangsuk from the CP group. [148] Moreover, during the first Thaksin administration (2001 to 2005), CP received several tax exemptions from the BOI.[149] Some state offices such as local branches of the Bank of Agriculture and Co-operatives also encourage farmers to join projects to grow CP hybrid rice seeds.[150]

Patron–client relationships

The cronyist nature of the Thai state can be seen as part of the tendency for capital to try to become larger and more powerful to survive, but in addition to that, patron–client mentality lends a helping hand to support and justify crony capitalism. Patron–client relationships can be seen as historical-cultural legacy of the Sakdina absolute monarchical Thai state. It infers an understanding that those higher up in the hierarchy maintain power through the support of those below them, while those lower down in the hierarchy in turn expect tangible benefits from their patrons.[151] Patron–client as a hegemonic mentality in Thai society is discussed in Part 3 of this chapter while this section discusses patron–client relations in Thai politics.[152]

Many scholars have discussed the central role of patron–client relationships in Thai politics.[153] Patron–client relationships infer that members are unequal and hence undermine a democratic principle of equality in Thailand.[154] Patronage roles in pre-1990s Thailand were typically filled by state officials, middlemen and politicians,[155] and many studies have linked patron–client relations with vote-buying[156] where vote buying goes beyond monetary exchanges[157] and can be defined to include many measures that help to sustain patron–client networks. For example, local canvassers may try to provide special development budgets for certain communities or to promise other benefits.[158] Many scholars suggest that, owing to patron–client relations, elections are often seen by Thais as a means to support their patrons or leaders to gain national political power. The leaders are then expected to share the spoils of political victory within their patron–client networks, rather than to prioritise national policies that would benefit the whole country.[159] Political parties also reinforce patron–client relationships by selecting candidates based on the criterion that they have large patron–client networks.[160]

The Thai state, under the TRT and Phua Thai administrations, provides good examples of the most successful political patron–client networks in recent years.[161] On the one hand, TRT, under the command of Thaksin Shinnawatra, adopted many pro-capital and many seemingly neo-liberal friendly policies such, as privatisation and free trade agreements. Thaksin is also known to be a fan of neo-liberal economists such as Hernando de Soto and Michael Porter.[162] On the other hand, it has been argued that Thaksin used his political power to build massive-scale patron–client networks around himself and his allies, which consist of several large business conglomerates, political parties, the National Assembly, the military and the police.[163] Moreover, many of TRT and Phua Thai's agri-food policies reinforced hierarchical patron–client relations and exacerbated structural problems in the agri-food system, as will be discussed in detail in Chapter 4.

The Crown Property Bureau and the lèse majesté law

Another notable capital group relevant to the discussion of the agri-food system is the Crown Property Bureau (CPB), previously named the Privy Purse Bureau, which was established in 1890 under the absolute monarchy regime.[164] It has been estimated that in the early 1970s, the CPB's landholdings included almost one-third of pre-war Bangkok and estates in 22 provinces.[165] The CPB has been given some special privileges by the state. For example, the 1948 Crown Property Act absolved the CPB from tax on its income.[166] As of around 2008, the CPB was worth around US$41 billion.[167] However, the extent of influence and privilege of the CPB, as well as its exact relationships with the Thai monarchy, have not been clearly and widely studied. This is related to the lèse majesté law in Thailand that tends to prevent research and public discussions on the CPB, which is problematic to the study of the agri-food system in Thailand because the CPB owns vast amounts of land and many other businesses.[168] As Part 3 discusses, Sakdina patron–client mentality and royal nationalist sentiments in Thailand also help to limit discussions on the CPB. In effect, such sentiments support the continuing existence of the lèse majesté law and the privileged position of the CPB.

2.2 Hegemonic transnational forces' influence on the governance structures

As discussed in Part 1, transnational forces have been instrumental in the shaping of physical infrastructures and hegemonic agri-food production–distribution in Thailand. This section continues to discuss how they have also influenced the hegemonic governance structures of the agri-food system in Thailand, particularly the governance of trade and intellectual property rights of agri-food products. Domestic actors do not only support transnational hegemonic forces just because their interests are aligned but also because they have internalised globalised hegemonic ideologies, as discussed in greater detail in Part 3 of the chapter.

After the Asian economic crisis of 1997, the IMF imposed many austerity measures on Thailand as part of the conditions for its loan, resulting in cutbacks of public investments in the agricultural sector which further reinforced the status of agri-businesses as the 'nexus point' between the world market and farms.[169] In 1999, the Asian Development Bank (ADB)'s $300 million loan for agricultural sector restructuring in Thailand, which accounted for 10 per cent of the Agriculture Ministry's budget, also included measures explicitly designed to introduce market relations into previously state-subsidised activities, particularly the provision of water resources, which helped to increase the power of agri-businesses in the agri-food system.[170]

Hegemonic domestic and transnational forces often help each other to influence the governance structures of the agri-food system in Thailand, such as by lobbying the Thai state to sign free trade agreements (FTAs) and accept strict property rights regime that, as discussed in Part 1, can enhance monopoly controls over seeds. Representative groups of the Thai population are usually not involved in FTA negotiations, and the Thai state tends to involve representatives from industries and agri-businesses in FTA negotiations.[171] Pressures to sign FTAs with China and the US in the early 2000s, for example, have been argued to come from some domestic and transnational companies.[172] The Thailand–EU FTA negotiations in the early 2010s, which have been criticised for their lack of transparency,[173] put pressures on Thailand to modify domestic laws to enforce a stricter property rights regime on plant genetic materials in accordance with the International Union for the Protection of New Varieties of Plants (UPOV) of 1991. This means, for example, eliminating a clause on sharing benefits of genetic materials, arguably making it easier for seed and biotechnology companies to patent genetic materials in Thailand. In addition, patent protection might be extended from 12 years to 20 years.[174] A study by FTA Watch

(Thailand) suggests that the signing of the Thai–EU FTA is likely to lead to monopoly control of seeds which results in six times higher prices, which will cost Thailand 1.4 trillion baht per year in addition to another 1.2 trillion baht per year cost of medicine.[175] The costs arguably outweigh the benefits of 30,000 to 40,000 million baht gained from exporting agri-food products through the EU's generalised system of preferences (GSP),[176] which would be accrued to a few transnational Thai agri-businesses.[177]

Another good example to demonstrate how the combined power of hegemonic domestic and transnational forces can shape agri-food governance structures to aid capital accumulation is in the case of the modern retail industry in Thailand. As discussed briefly in the previous section, giant supermarkets in Thailand have adopted commodity standards, management and distribution practices from their transnational non-Thai partners. In addition to that, public governance structures have been lenient to large retail transnational capital. As one of the conditions to receive financial aid from the IMF after the Asian economic crisis of 1997, Thailand had to pass the Foreign Business Act of 1999 which made foreign investments easier in many areas.[178] It has also been suggested that the Thai state generally does not directly challenge large monopoly transnational capital. Instead, it initiates some secondary policies and supports retail giants' training programmes to help small- and medium-size Thai retailers to increase their competitiveness.[179]

Part 3 Hegemonic ideational order of the agri-food system in Thailand

Underlying hegemonic governance structures and production–distribution practices is the hegemonic ideological order that supports the mainstream agri-food system in Thailand. The hegemonic ideological order of the agri-food system in Thailand is propagated and reproduced by transnational and domestic hegemonic forces through different channels, such as educational institutions and the media. Internalised by the majority of the Thai population, the hegemonic ideational framework helps to establish consent and acceptance of the status quo in the agri-food system in Thailand, including even by those who are disadvantaged by it. Section 3.1 discusses hegemonic transnational neo-liberal ideologies and neo-classical economic ideas, modernisation development theory, and compartmentalised knowledge as hegemonic ideas that aid capital accumulation through the agri-food system. As pointed out in the Gramscian theoretical perspective in Chapter 2, neo-liberal capitalist ideologies can be seen as global hegemonic ideas promoted by political-economic elites in advance capitalist countries as well as other transnational forces, and are mediated within specific national-local contexts through various agencies such as by state officials, businesses and academics. Section 3.2 then discusses more locally specific hegemonic ideas of Sakdina patron–client mentality and nationalist sentiments.

3.1 Neo-classical economics, modernisation and compartmentalised knowledge

Food–energy scarcity concerns which put upward pressures on energy crop prices are often portrayed by the state and the private sector as economic opportunities for both agri-businesses and small-scale farmers in Thailand. For example, high sugar cane and sugar prices in world market in 2009 were presented as a golden opportunity for growers in Thailand.[180] The state's support of the production of ethanol, which is made from cassava and sugar cane, is also argued by some state officials and the private sector to be opportunities to improve income levels and the economic stability of farmers.[181] However, these purported suggestions that the food–energy scarcities provide 'win-win' opportunities for agri-businesses, and farmers alike doubtful and need to be critically evaluated. As Part 1 has discussed, higher prices tend to lead to higher supply and future reductions in prices. This might be good from capital accumulation's perspective, but it can be economically destructive to small-scale producers that invested to increase their production. Volatile prices, fuelled by speculations in recent years, also make it difficult for producers to plan their productions. In addition, the existence of monopolies and unequal market power relations suggest that large players tend to benefit more from higher prices compared to smaller-scale players, as with the case of rice exports between 2007 and 2008 that was discussed in Part 1. Mainstream neo-classical economic views, however, tend to simply suggest that volatile prices are inevitable outcomes of supply–demand. Aside from some short-term government interventions to help stabilise or support prices, mainstream neo-classical economists are not very concerned with governance mechanisms to curb speculations nor with other types of structural reforms. In effect, such discourses, which are often propagated by state officials, private sectors, and academics, help to establish the acceptance of the hegemonic agri-food system.[182]

The Thai state and the private sector have also used the rhetoric of competitive and efficient free markets that benefit everyone to rally the public's acceptance of few regulations of large monopoly corporations. Hegemonic arguments in support of retail giants usually refer to their purportedly higher standards which force Thai suppliers to improve, benefits that consumers receive from lower prices, and that there can be 'win-win' situations where small- and medium-sized retailers can buy their products from retail giants.[183] A few studies have suggested that such 'win-win' situations are doubtful.[184] In addition, these arguments do not address the problem of how increased concentration and centralisation of control over retail channels and agri-food supply chains reduce choices and the power of both consumers and producers in the longer-run.

Beliefs in market mechanisms and efficiency are also related to the modernisation development worldview which tends to see development as having linear stages where industrial and service sectors' economic activities are seen as having higher values or as the 'next steps' of development compared to agricultural economic activities. Such a view tends to see it as a desirable progress when more labourers move from the agricultural sector to the industrial sector, even through dispossessions by market forces. It has been suggested that some Thai bureaucrats believe most of the agricultural workforce would eventually be absorbed into the industrial sector if left to market forces, so perhaps they do not feel much need to intervene and to solve problems facing small-scale farmers.[185] The private sector and some academics also help to promote the views that it is unquestionably normal and desirable to increase mechanisation in agriculture to reduce the number of farm labourers and move them to the industrial and service sectors.[186]

The views discussed above reflect mechanistic understanding of development and also did not take into account the unsustainability of current industrial agri-food production methods. Similar to the position adopted by the World Bank's development report (2008) previously discussed, such views reduce humans to labour commodities that, 'rationally' speaking, should be able to move around freely across economic sectors to gain the highest returns. However, in reality, farmers often have to move to other economic sectors not by choice but because they are forced to or are 'dispossessed' by hegemonic forces in the agri-food system. From a neo-Marxist theoretical perspective, dispossessed farmers can be seen as part of the reserve army of labour which benefits capital accumulation. In addition, there are other factors that mainstream economic views do not take into account, such as the importance of access to agricultural resources to marginalised people in terms of maintenance of family ties, local and national food security, as well as other components of quality of life.[187] Overall, it seems that mainstream neo-classical economic views help to legitimise the current hegemonic agri-food system that serves capital accumulation at the expense of nature and labour. The argument here is not to maintain the current number of labourers in the agricultural sector, but to encourage critical explorations of development alternatives which can increase bargaining power and choices of agricultural producers and rural labourers.

The specialisation and compartmentalisation of agricultural production knowledge, which reflects the commodification of nature and natural resources, also underlies industrial/Green Revolution agricultural production methods discussed in section 1.1 of this chapter.[188] It has been suggested that the compartmentalisation of knowledge of agricultural science in Thailand is responsible for the specialised departmental organisational structure of the Ministry of Agriculture and Co-operatives, and that it is a result of modern education that trains people to become specialists in certain agricultural components or products.[189] The problem is that these specialists tend not to be able to analyse the agri-food production system as part of the socio-ecological system.[190] Such compartmentalised hegemonic knowledge paradigm also plays a part in preventing alternative production methods such as agro-ecology from emerging. In Chapter 5, sustainable agricultural production knowledge will be discussed as part of counter-hegemony in the agri-food system in Thailand.

3.2 Sakdina patron–client mentality and nationalist sentiments

This section discusses the deeply rooted Sakdina patron–client mentality in Thai society which underlies informal norms of patron–client relations discussed in Part 2. It also discusses some forms of nationalist sentiments which have been used to aid capital accumulation through the current agri-food system, particularly royal nationalism and crony capitalist nationalism, which give support to the special status of the Crown Property Bureau and some large Thai agribusinesses.

Thailand used to be under the rule of the absolute monarchy in which the 'Sakdina' system had regulated the social order since the late fifteenth century. Essentially, the basic hierarchical cleavage in the Sakdina society was between the royalty and aristocracy on the one hand, and the peasantry or 'Phrai' on the other.[191] Under this system, there are different hierarchical levels of masters–followers who were bound to each other through informal norms and ethical rules, and were expected to fulfil certain obligations according to their social hierarchies. People's mentality and political consciousness were narrowly based on loyalty to groups and individual leaders.[192] Even when the Sakdina and corvee system were abolished, traditional personal linkages between people of different classes persisted as patron–client relationships, as discussed in Part 2. The Sakdina attitude – the consciousness of hierarchical social structures – affect all kinds of social relations in Thai society[193] and can hinder the development of a more equitable agri-food system in many ways. Notably, the Sakdina attitude has become infused in the working culture of the Thai bureaucracy as can be seen from top-down nature of rural development and agrarian promotion policies discussed in Part 2 of the chapter.

Sakdina influence in Thai society is also reflected in the prominent status of the royal family in contemporary Thailand, as well as the lèse majesté law and the special position of the CPB which were discussed in Part 2. The importance and popularity of the monarchy in Thailand can partially be explained as a political construct, which started in the 1940s when the military built up the role of the monarch as the symbolic head of the nation through various means.[194] The promotion of royalism in Thailand is arguably not a continuous and consistent process, but most recently, the coups d'état in 2006 and 2014 seem to open up new opportunities for the military to promote royalism agenda in Thailand. Another notable reason for the monarchy's popularity, which is related to the agri-food system in Thailand, was the special personality of King Bhumiphol Adulyadej. King Bhumiphol was widely admired for his dedication to rural development projects. He was also instrumental in the promotion of sufficient philosophy and economic ideas that aim to help counter-balance negative effects of the globalised capitalist economy. As the following chapters will discuss, such ideas and philosophy often provide positive inspirations to some people in counter-hegemonic movements in the agri-food system in Thailand, although such ideas are not without problems. It has also been suggested that King Bhumipol donated 44,000 rai of his own land to small-scale farmers and encouraged the development of rural groups and co-operatives in Thailand.[195] However, the CPB, with its holding of around 30,000 rai of land, is still considered one of the largest landholders in the country.[196] Overall, regardless of the role of King Bhumiphol in rural development, royal nationalism reinforces Sakdina mentality and aids the maintenance of some aspects of hegemonic agri-food governance; in addition to the lèse majesté law, loyalty to the King tends to restrain Thais from discussing the power and influence of the CPB.

Nationalist sentiments can also be used to rally public support for Thai capital. For example, the CP group, with the help of the Director-General of the Department of Internal Trade, had used the fact that CP is a Thai capital group to gather public tolerance and support for CP's expansion and monopoly power in the retail market.[197] Nevertheless, there is no reason to believe that Thai capital's drive to accumulate profits is any different from non-Thai capital. It should be noted, however, that aside from such crony capitalist nationalism, there can be other forms of nationalism such as the more radical populist nationalism of non-governmental organisations (NGOs) and people's organisations in Thailand.[198]

In sum, this part of the chapter has discussed the hegemonic ideological order underlying hegemonic production–distribution practices and governance structures of the mainstream agri-food system in Thailand. The hegemonic ideological order's most important function is to help establish consent or acceptance among the Thai population of the hegemonic status quo. As the following chapters will discuss, counter-hegemonic movements in the agri-food system in Thailand have tried to tackle the hegemonic ideational order but it is not an easy task.

Conclusion

This chapter has advanced the first main argument of the book; that the mainstream agri-food system in Thailand has been shaped by transnational and domestic forces to aid capital accumulation, and that the system is sustained through a combination of hegemonic agri-food production–distribution, governance structures and ideational order.

Through an exploration of the hegemonic agri-food system in Thailand which is operating within the global agri-food system, this chapter has brought interesting insights which are locally distinctive and are globally relevant. For example, the chapter has explored the many ways in which domestic and transnational forces can collaborate to facilitate land grabs in Thailand, such as through the use of nominees. The chapter has also discussed how monopoly power in the agri-food system in Thailand can come in many forms, ranging from formal contract farming to informal monopoly networks. Hegemonic agri-food governance structures and ideational order which are locally specific to Thailand have also been discussed in relation to and as part of the hegemonic global agri-food system. In addition, this chapter's analysis of the hegemonic agri-food system in Thailand has yielded support to some main arguments in global corporate agri-food system literature, such as regarding negative consequences of excessive financial speculations on agri-food commodities and of the Green Revolution production paradigm.

This chapter has discussed some of the Thai state and transnational companies' actions and discourses as being part of the hegemonic forces. However, it should be noted that there can be discrepancies and heterogeneities within these institutions which might allow some room for counter-hegemony. The next chapter will give an overview of counter-hegemony and co-optation of oppositions in the agri-food system in Thailand. It will also provide a foundation for the discussions of sustainable agriculture and land reform movements in Chapter 5 and 6.

Notes

1 Walden Bello, Shea Cunningham, and Li Kheng Pho, *A Siamese Tragedy. Development and Disintegration in Modern Thailand* (New York: Zed Books, 1998), 168.
2 Witoon Lienchamroon and Suriyon Thankitchanukit, *From the Green Revolution to Bio-Engineering. Lessons for the Future of Thai Agriculture.* (Nonthaburi: BioThai, 2008), 61; Sayamon Kraiyoorawong *et al.*, *Traditional Wisdom: Community and Nature's Ways* (Bangkok: Duan-tula Printing, 2008), 101 (all in Thai).
3 Sukran Rojanapraiwong *et al.*, *Local Genes and Sustainable Agriculture: A Document for the Third Alternative Agriculture Assembly 18–21 November 2004, Kasetsart University* (Nonthaburi: Pim-dee Printing, 2004), 46–48 (in Thai).
4 Lienchamroon and Thankitchanukit (2008), 80 and 88–89.
5 Ibid., 49–51.
6 Rojanapraiwong *et al.* (2004), 50–59.
7 Lienchamroon and Thankitchanukit (2008), 156.
8 Ibid., 148–149. The field study was conducted in the early 2000s.
9 BioThai, 'Report on the Problems of Hybrid Rice Seeds: Case Study of Hybrid Rice Owned by the Charoen Pokphand Group', 2009, 18–20. www.biothai.net/node/150 (in Thai).
10 Calculation based on FAO STAT (2004) in Lienchamroon and Thankitchanukit (2008), 114–117.
11 Ibid., 124.
12 Assoc. Prof. Juthatip Patrawart, Director of an academic study of co-operatives, Kasetsart University, quoted in Yupin Hongthong, 'The State Pushes to Solve Farmer Crisis: Open Smart Farmers School in 6 Provinces' *Bangkok Business News*, 11 August 2013 (in Thai); Kookiet Sroythong, 'Pesticides Usage and the Spread of Brown Planthoppers among Rice Crops in the Central and Lower North Regions', in *An Academic Conference to Monitor Agricultural Chemicals 1, 16–17 June 2011*, ed. National Committee to Plan for Food Security, 2011 (in Thai).
13 Lienchamroon and Thankitchanukit (2008), 185–187.
14 National Health Committee, *Report of the Meeting 1/2008 on the Topic of Policies and Strategies to Reduce Negative Health Effects from Chemical Pesticides on 14 January 2008* (Bangkok, 2008), quoted in Sajin Prachason, 'A Draft Document for the Meeting "Agriculture and Food in Time of Crisis", 22 July 2008', in *Progress Report to the National Health Commission on Developments of Proposals from the National Health Assembly 2008*, 40 (in Thai).
15 Lienchamroon and Thankitchanukit (2008), 118–120.
16 For example, see Pattama Sittichai *et al.*, *A Complete Report on the Project to Compile and Analyse the Problems of Farmers and Sustainable Development* (Bangkok: NESDB, 2002) (in Thai).
17 Dr Sansit Piriyarangsan's interview (head of the Farmers' Reconstruction and Development Fund) in Thairath Newspaper, 'The Economics Team's Editorial', *Thairath*, 15 June 2009 (in Thai).

18 Over-usage of agricultural chemicals are often attributed to incorrect usage of chemicals by farmers (this view is shared by Songpun Kuldilokrat, Managing Director at Arysta LifeScience Co., Ltd, email correspondent date 21 January 2013 and Dr Kriengsak Suwantharadol, Syngenta (Thailand), email correspondent date 14 March 2013), uncontrolled advertising and imports of dangerous types of chemicals (Phuttina Nontaworakarn, 'Summary of the Current Status of the Revised Dangerous Chemical Acts 2008', in *An Academic Conference to Monitor Agricultural Chemicals 1, 16–17 June 2011*, ed. National Committee to Plan for Food Security (Bangkok, 2011), 100–101 (in Thai)).

19 National Committee to Develop Strategic Plan to Manage Chemicals, *National Strategic Plan to Manage Chemicals 4 (2012–2021)* (Nonthaburi: Integrated Programme for Chemical safety, Food and Drugs Administration, Ministry of Public Health, 2011), 8 (in Thai).

20 Office of Natural Resources and Environmental Policy and Planning, 'Situation on State of Environment', 2006, quoted in Sajin Prachason, *Food Security in Thai Society: A Report Submitted to UNDP Thailand, January 2009* (Bangkok, 2009), 37 (in Thai).

21 Dr Pibul Issarapan, Vice Deputy Director Bureau of Occupational and Environmental Diseases, Ministry of Health, 'Farmers' Risks from Using Agricultural Chemicals and Sudden Illness', in *An Academic Conference to Monitor Agricultural Chemicals 1, 16–17 June 2011*, ed. National Committee to Plan for Food Security (Bangkok, 2011), 60 (in Thai).

22 Assoc. Prof. Dr Phongthep Wiwattanadech, the Department of Community Medicine, Faculty of Medicine, Chiang Mai University, interviewed in Thai Publica, '"Phongthep Wiwattanadech", Medical Doctor at Chiang Mai University Suggests "Contract Farming" to be the Cause of Haze Pollution in Northern Thailand. Revealed Statistics Suggesting Peaked Dangerous Chemicals – Lung Cancer', *Thai Publica*, 1 September 2012 (in Thai).

23 Prachason (2009), 44 and Natwipa Iewskul, '18 Years Track Records of GMOs: Threats to Thailand's Food Sovereignty', 2 April 2013, www.greenpeace.org/seasia/th/PageFiles/505377/18-year-of-gmo.pdf (in `1Thai)

24 Iewskul (2013) and Lienchamroon and Thankitchanukit (2008), 266–269.

25 Isra news, 'Judiciary Declared the State Was Not Guilty for GM Papaya Contamination, Greenpeace Feared Monsanto Monopoly', *Isra News*, 2 April 2013 (in Thai).

26 Somporn Isawilanont and Sanit Kao-ian, *Dynamics of Thailand's Rice Production Economy and the Future Outlook* (Bangkok: Thailand Research Fund, 2009), 33 (in Thai).

27 Ibid., 33 and 35.

28 Sittichai *et al.* (2002), 69–71.

29 See the abstract of Warin Wongharnchao and Land Institute Foundation *et al.*, *A Study of Ownership and Usage of Land, as Well as Economic and Legal Measures to Maximise Land Usage* (Bangkok: Thailand Research Fund, 2001) (in Thai).

30 For example, Dr Weerachai Narkwibulwong, Secretary General of ALRO, interviewed 14 February 2013, Bangkok. For interviews of state officials from DSI and Ministry of Commerce, as well as vice mayor of Phichit province, see Post Today Newspaper, 'Foreign and Thai Capital's Purchases of Foundations of Agriculture', *Post Today*, 20 February 2010. Other examples include: Manager Newspaper, 'Foreign Force's Land Grabs in 25 provinces. Land Sold in Massive Volume by Farmers and Brokers', *Manager Newspaper (weekly)*, 17 September 2009; Matichon Newspaper, 'Village Leader Tells of Capitalist Land Grabbing of Rice Fields', *Matichon*, 4 April 2012 (in Thai).

31 Mr Prasit Boonchuey, President of Thai Rice Farmers' Association, quoted in Dailynews, 'Foreign Force Swallows Million Rai of Paddy Field. President of Thai Farmers' Association Exposed Dangerous Sign; Foreign Force's Land Grab Goals in Central and Northeastern Regions', *Dailynews*, 4 August 2009 (in Thai).

32 DSI and Ministry of Commerce's preliminary investigation of foreign land grabs, quoted in Post Today, 'Foreign and Thai Capital, (2010); Prasit Boonchuey quoted in Dailynews, 'Foreign Force' (2009); BioThai and local informants quoted in Manager Newspaper (weekly), 'Foreign Force's Land Grabs in 25 Provinces' (2009).
33 Local Act Organisation's study based on the database of the Department of Land, quoted in Prachachat Turakij Newspaper, 'Famous Business Families Stocking up Land All over Thailand, Jareon Riched with 6.3 Hundred Thousand Rai, Land Tax in Consideration', *Prachachat Turakij*, 18 June 2014 (in Thai).
34 See Dailynews, 'Foreign Force', (2009) and Bangkok Business Newspaper, 'President of Thai Farmers' Association Reports to DSI about Foreign Land Grabs of Rice Fields', *Bangkok Business*, 6 August 2009 (in Thai).
35 Summary from interviews of Prasit Boonchuey in Dailynews, 'Foreign Force' (2009) and Bangkok Business Newspaper, 'President of Thai Farmers' (2009).
36 For example, see Manager Newspaper, 'Foreign Force's Land Grabs' (2009).
37 For example, in the South there are reports of land grabs by Thai and Malaysian capital for palm oil plantations (Prachachart Turakij Newspaper, 'Wave of Land Grabs for Speculations and Agro-Fuels Inputs due to Low Interest Rates and Rising Agricultural Commodity Prices', *Prachachart Turakij*, 14 May 2008). According to the BioThai Foundation's investigation with help from farmer networks in over 19 provinces, the top 6 provinces for foreign land grabs are in the Central plain including Ayuthya where there are Middle East capital investing in rice production (Witoon Lienchamroon from BioThai, quoted in Manager Newspaper, 'Foreign Force's Land Grabs' (2009)).
38 Land Reform Network and Local Act, *A Report on the Study "Land Management and Social Justice: A Case Study of the Land Reform Network"* (Bangkok: Chulalongkorn University Social Research Institute, 2010), 106–108 (in Thai).
39 Manager Newspaper, 'Foreign Force's Land Grabs' (2009).
40 According to a manager at TCC Agro which is part of the Thai Beverage group, quoted in Business Thai, 'Thanin-Jaroen: 2 Rich Men are Revolutionising Thai Agriculture!', 8 May 2008 (in Thai).
41 Local Act Organisation's study based on the database of the Department of Land, quoted in Prachachat Turakiij Newspaper, 'Famous Business Families Stocking up Land' (18 June 2014).
42 Manager Newspaper, 'Foreign Force's Land Grabs' (2009).
43 Business Thai, 'Thanin-Jaroen' (8 May 2008).
44 Local Act Organisation's study based on the database of the Department of Land, quoted in Prachachat Turakiij Newspaper, 'Famous Business Families', (18 June 2014).
45 Manager Newspaper, 'CP Advances on Biodiesel Business, Contract Farming of Palm Oil in Indochina', *Manager Newspaper (weekly)*, 21 March 2008 (in Thai).
46 Local Act Organisation's study based on the database of the Department of Land, quoted in Prachachat Turakiij Newspaper, 'Famous Business Families' (18 June 2014).
47 Quoted in Manager Newspaper, 'Food Crisis Increases Pressure on Landless Farmers. Watch out for CP's Monopoly Control over 100,000 Million Baht Rice Seeds Market', *Manager*, 1 May 2008 (in Thai).
48 Quoted in Matichon Newspaper, 'National Reform Committee Suggests Land Reform to Take Advantage of Food Crisis', *Matichon*, 16 March 2011 (in Thai).
49 Manager Newspaper (weekly), 'Foreign Force's Land Grabs' (17 September 2009).
50 For example, complaints received from farmers were reported by Minister of Agriculture and Co-operatives (MOAC) in MOAC, 'Ministry of Agriculture and Co-operatives Tries to Stop Capitalists from Increasing Rent and Exploiting Farmers, Using Legal Means according to the Agricultural Land Rent Act', 21 April 2008. www.moac.go.th/ewt_news.php?nid=1911&filename=wimol (in Thai).

51 Reported in Prachachart Turakij Newspaper, 'Wave of Land Grabs' (14 May 2008).
52 Assistant Professor Dr Duangmanee Laowakul, Faculty of Economics, Thammasat University, research presentation at the Food Security Assembly 2014 in Thailand, quoted in Isra News, 'Macro View of Land in Thailand Reveals Inequality and Highly Concentrated Land: Wealth in Poor People's Tears', *Isra News*, 14 July 2014 (in Thai).
53 Ibid.
54 MOAC (2008).
55 Manager Newspaper (weekly), 'Foreign Force's Land Grabs' (17 September 2009).
56 Witoon Lienchamroon quoted in Manager Newspaper (online), 'Food Crisis Increases Pressure on Landless Farmers' (1 May 2008) (in Thai).
57 During the author's field research in Thailand, a few farmers in the Central and Northeastern regions discussed having been offered positions as farm managers of certain agri-food commodities, or that they know of other farmers who took such jobs. One example is Ms Nanta Haitook, President of Baan Tanon organic group, interviewed 20 December 2012, Surin.
58 Isawilanont *et al.* (2009), 35.
59 Ibid., 33 and 36.
60 David Pimentel and Tad W. Patzek, 'Ethanol Production Using Corn, Switchgrass, and Wood; Biodiesel Production Using Soybean and Sunflower', *Natural Resources Research* 14, no. 1 (2005): 65–76 and Tad W. Patzek and David Pimentel, 'Thermodynamics of Energy Production from Biomass', *Critical Reviews in Plant Sciences* 24, no. 5–6 (2006): 329–364, quoted in Weis (2010), 324–327.
61 Isawilanont *et al.* (2009), 47.
62 An analysis of land grabs using the concept of opportunity costs has been used by Olivier De Schutter, 'How Not to Think of Land-Grabbing: Three Critiques of Large-Scale Investments in Farmland', *Journal of Peasant Studies* 38, no. 2 (March 2011a): 249–279.
63 Office of Agricultural Economics (Thailand), *Agricultural Statistics of Thailand 2010*, 168.
64 Jennifer Clapp, 'Food Price Volatility and Vulnerability in the Global South: Considering the Global Economic Context', *Third World Quarterly* 30, no. 6 (September 2009), 1187.
65 Paul Tharp, 'Hedge Funds Find New Sweet Spot in Sugar', *New York Post*, 30 September 2009.
66 Matichon Newspaper, '3 Sugar Plants Associations Believe in the Long Bright Future of Sugar Cane and Sugar Industries, Pushing the State to Support Ethanol', *Matichon*, 25 September 2009 (in Thai).
67 Thai Post Newspaper, 'World Supply of Sugar Pulls down Prices of Sugar Cane. Thai Producers Ask the State for Help', *Thai Post*, 6 December 2013; Than Settakit Newspaper, 'Many Factors Cause Sugar Cane Prices to Drop', *Than Settakit*, 5 January 2014 (in Thai).
68 Muanfan Ratsongkwae, 'CP Maize: Naan Case Study', in *CP and Thai Agriculture*, ed. CorpWatch-Thailand and BioThai (Nonthaburi: BioThai, 2009), 133 and 135 (in Thai).
69 Ibid., 135–139.
70 SATHAI (Sustainable Agriculture Thailand), *Interesting Knowledge about Commercial Garden Plants: Case Studies of Rubber and Palm Oil* (Nonthaburi: SATHAI, 2009), 39 and 42; Post Today Newspaper, 'Yanyong Reveals That Low Prices of Rubber is due to Depressed Economic Conditions', *Post Today*, 6 September 2013; Naew Na Newspaper, 'Warn the State to Revise Measures for Rubber Prices. Three Strategies to Develop the Rubber Industry', *Naew Na*, 13 December 2012; President of the Thai Rubber Association, *Rubber Market Situation in 2013*, December 2013; Office of the Rubber Replanting Aid Fund quoted in Prachachat Turakij Newspaper,

'Speculations Causes Rubber Prices to Plummet and for Rubber Co-Operatives', *Prachachat Turakij*, 16 March 2011; Rubber Research Institute of Thailand quoted in Than Settakit Newspaper, 'Rubber Prices Adjust Upwards According to Speculations in Tokyo', *Than Settakit*, 12 October 2013 (in Thai).

71 Mr Pherk Lertwangpong, President of the Rubber Co-operatives' Association of Thailand, quoted in Prachachart Turakit (16 March 2011).

72 SATHAI (2009), 11–18 and 64–65.

73 Somporn Isawilanont and Prue Santithamrak, *A Report on Global and Thai Rice Production and Trade Situation 2011 and Future Tendency (KNIT Agricultural Policy No. 2012–1)* (Bangkok: KNIT, 2011), 2–3 (in Thai).

74 Isawilanont and Kao-ian (2009), 30–31 and Isawilanont and Santithamrak (2011), 12.

75 David Dawe, 'Have Recent Increases in International Cereal Prices Been Transmitted to Domestic Economies? The Experience in Seven Large Asian Countries' (Rome: Agricultural Development Economics Division, FAO, 2008), 6–7.

76 Isawilanont and Santithamrak (2011), 12.

77 Dawe (2008), 8.

78 Foundation for Labour and Employment Promotion, Four Regions Slum Network, and Committee of Thai labour solidarity, *A Survey of 9 Consumer Products Prices and Effects on the People* (Bangkok, 2008), quoted in Prachason (2008), 44.

79 Field research by the National Planning Committee for Food Security in 2010, quoted in Witoon Lienchamroon, 'Suggestions to Avoid Food Crisis for Thailand', in *Reform the Agricultural Sector for Food Security: Analysis and Practical Policies* (Nonthaburi: BioThai, 2011e), 262 (in Thai).

80 Ministry of Public Health, *A Survey on Food and Nutrition of Thailand, 5th Assessment* (Bangkok, 2003), 60, quoted in Prachason (2009), 19–20.

81 Isawilanont and Kao-ian (2009), 33.

82 Nattakarn Rodmua, *An Analysis of Costs and Process of Thai Rice Export. A Dissertation for a Master's Degree in Economics, Thammasat University* (Bangkok: Thammasat University, 2009), 42–43 (in Thai) (author's calculation).

83 Ibid., 42–43 (author's calculation).

84 Ibid., 42–43 (author's calculation).

85 Ibid., 42–43 (author's calculation).

86 Ibid., 42–43.

87 For example, see Thairath Newspaper, 'Rice Mills Slowly Sell Their Rice to Speculate on Prices While Exporters Ask the Government to Sell its Rice Stock. Ministry of Commerce Also Threatens to Sell its Own Brand of Rice', *Thairath*, 14 December 2009 (in Thai).

88 Rapijan Phurisamban, 'Basic Information on the Market and Usage of 4 High-Priority Agricultural Chemicals in the Monitoring List', in *An Academic Conference to Monitor Agricultural Chemicals 1, 16–17 June 2011*, ed. National Committee to Plan for Food Security (Bangkok, 2011), 15 (in Thai).

89 CP's website www.cpthailand.com/; CorpWatch-Thailand and BioThai, *CP and Thai Agriculture* (Nonthaburi: BioThai, 2008), 11–20 (in Thai).

90 FAO, *Project on Livestock Industrialisation. Trade and Social-health-Environment Impacts in Developing Countries*, July 2003, quoted in Isabelle Delforge, *Contract Farming in Thailand: A View from the Farm, A Report for Focus on the Global South*, (Bangkok: Focus on the Global South Group, 2007), 11.

91 Delforge (2007), 4–5.

92 Senate Committee on Agriculture and Co-operatives, *Report on the Investigation on Contract Farming of the Senate Committee on Agriculture and Co-operatives* (Bangkok, 2003), quoted in Delforge (2007), 5.

93 Sompop Manarangsan, 'Contract Farming and Thailand's Agricultural Development', in *Our Lands, Our Lives*, ed. Buddhadeb Chaudhuri (Bangkok: ACFOD, 1992), 156, quoted in Bello, Cunningham and Li (1998), 164.

94 Bootsara Limnirandkul, Cho-paka Muangsuk and Pratanthip Kramol, and Pruek Yipmantasiri 'Contract Farming and the Opportunity of Development of Small-scale farmers', A paper presented at the Multiple Cropping Centre Seminar, Faculty of Agriculture, Chiang Mai University, 22–23 September 2006, 99 (in Thai).
95 Interviews with Scott Christensen, 31 March 1994 and Taweekiat Prasertcharoensuk, Bangkok, 18 June 1993, quoted in Bello, Cunningham, and Pho (1998), 164.
96 Witoon Lienchamroon, 'The Role of Agri-Businesses and the Changes in Rural Thailand and Thai Society', 25 November 2011, 8. www.biothai.net/node/10889 (in Thai).
97 Ibid., 8.
98 Delforge (2007), 9 and 12.
99 Jirawat Rakchat, 'From Farming to Contract Eggs Chicken: The Growth of Agri-Business', in *Thai Countryside: Medium Size Farmers and Landless Agricultural Labourers*, ed. Jamari Chiengthong *et al.* (Chiang Mai: University of Chiang Mai, 2011), 245–246 and 284–287 (in Thai).
100 Mr Kampol Kongsathan, Ms Amporn Suyakomol and Ms Pimlada Pheekaew, interviewed 31 October 2012, Chiang Mai.
101 Narong Phetprasert, 'Rice Politics under State-Capital Monopoly', in *Journal of Political Economy (for the Community)* (Bangkok: Edison Press, 2006), 117–118 (in Thai).
102 Ibid., 94–95.
103 Than Settakit Newspaper, 'Fat Rice Traders! 6,000/ton Profit Export to Malaysia', *Than Settakit*, 12 June 2008 (in Thai).
104 The information was reported by the Thai Rice Export Association. Asia Golden Rice was the number one exporter (1.7–1.8 million tons), followed by Capital Cereals and Capital Rice which are companies in the same group (1.1–1.2 million tons), then CP Inter-rade and Chai-porn rice (another 700,000–800,000 tons) (Prachachat Turakij Newspaper, 'Top Rice Exporter, Asia Golden Rice, Received Right to Purchase Government's Stock at Low Price – Medium/Small Size Companies at a Disadvantaged', *Prachachat Turakij*, 13 January 2011 (in Thai)).
105 Mr Pitak Saengsin, Vice President of the BAAC's Chiang Mai branch, interviewed 2 November 2012, Chiang Mai.
106 For example, a study in 2002 by TDRI suggests that there was high competition in fruits and vegetable central/wholesale markets in Thailand (Niphon Puapongsakorn *et al.*, *The Retail Business in Thailand: Impact of the Large Scale Multinational Corporation Retailers* (Bangkok: TDRI, 2002) (in Thai)).
107 Pitak Saengsin, interviewed 2 November 2012, Chiang Mai.
108 Ibid.
109 John Humphrey, 'Policy Implications of Trends in Agribusiness Value Chains', *The European Journal of Development Research* 18, no. 4 (2006): 574–575; Lawrence Busch and Carmen Bain, 'New! Improved? The Transformation of the Global Agrifood System', *Rural Sociology* 69, no. 3 (2004): 321–346.
110 Yanee Srimanee and Jayant Kumar Routray, 'The Fruit and Vegetable Marketing Chains in Thailand: Policy Impacts and Implications', *International Journal of Retail and Distribution Management* 40, no. 9 (2012), 660.
111 In 2010, Big C hypermarkets owned by Casino Guichard Perrachon from France and Jiratiwat family (Central group) took over Carrefour hypermarkets which were owned by French capital (Than Settakit Newspaper, 'Close the Deal Carrefour and Big C, Strategic Take Over', *Than Settakit*, 22 November 2010). Then, in 2013, CP ALL company took over one of the biggest wholesale and retail company, Siam Makro, from HSV Netherlands company (Manager Newspaper, 'CP Took over Makro, Swallowed Thailand, Advancing on Asian Markets', *Manager*, 27 April 2013). In 2016, the TCC group associated with Thai Beverage Plc. purchased the majority of shares in Big C (Thairath Newspaper, 'Tycoon Jaroen Invested 1.2 Hundred Million in Big C Purchasing the Majority of Shares', *Thairath*, 8 February 2016).

112 Makro has 58 branches in Thailand in over 50 provinces while 7–11 has over 6,000 branches in Thailand (Manager Newspaper, 'CP Took over Makro', (27 April 2013)).
113 For example, when it opened its first supermarket in Thailand in 1990, CP invited two managers from Wal-Mart to be its management consultants (Athiwat Sapphaitoon, *6 Mega Retail Business Empire: Various Marketing Techniques for Modern Trade, Case Study and Lessons from Thailand* (Bangkok: Phueng-ton, 2002), 241 and 291–292 (in Thai)).
114 Suthichart Jirathiwat, a manager in the Central group, interviewed in Wirat Sangthongkam *et al.*, *70 years Jirathiwat: Central's Competition and Growth*, (Bangkok: Manager Classic, 2003), 126, quoted in Weerayuth Karnchuchat, 'Thai Retail Business: Two Cities Divide', in *The Struggles of Thai Capital 2: Politics, Culture and Survival*, ed. Pasuk Phongpaichit (Bangkok: Matichon, 2006), 238 (in Thai).
115 Karnchuchat (2006), 217 (in Thai).
116 Than Settakit News, 27–30 August 2000, quoted in Karnchuchat (2006), 239 and Arunee Pholnoi, *Retail and Wholesale Trade's Strategies* (Bangkok: Pansan, 2003), 137 (in Thai).
117 Pholnoi (2003), 55 and Karnchuchat (2006), 237.
118 Pholnoi (2003), 71, 76, 78, 81–82.
119 Parliament's Committee of Commerce, *Report on the Study of Problems and Effects of Modern Trade* (Bangkok, 2003), 9 (in Thai).
120 Ibid., 7.
121 Pawida Pananont and Weerayuth Karnchuchat, 'Thai Capital Expands Abroad', in *The Struggles of Thai Capital 1: Adaptation and Dynamics*, ed. Pasuk Phongpaichit (Bangkok: Matichon, 2006), 329 (in Thai) and Pholnoi (2003), 65.
122 Srimanee and Routray (2012), 665; Pholnoi (2003), 69.
123 Ms Chutima Muangman, manager of Naso producer rice mill, interviewed 25 December 2012, Yasothon.
124 Rojanapraiwong *et al.* (2004), 50–59.
125 Lienchamroon (25 November 2011), 6.
126 Apichai Puntasen and Paradorn Preedasak, 'Agriculture in Thailand at the Cross-Road', *ASEAN Economic Bulletin* 15, no. 1 (1998), 90–92.
127 Bello, Cunningham and Li (1998), 135.
128 Ibid., 136.
129 Pasuk Phongpaichit and Chris Baker, *Thailand: Economy and Politics* (New York: Oxford University Press, 1995), 59–60.
130 Jasper Goss and David Burch, 'From Agricultural Modernisation to Agri-Food Globalisation: The Waning of National Development in Thailand', *Third World Quarterly* 22, no. 6 (2001), 978; Puntasen and Preedasak (1998), 92; Bello, Cunningham, and Li (1998), 133–135.
131 Tirawuth Senakham and Witoon Panyakul, 'The State and Agri-Businesses: From "See-Prasan" to Agricultural Council', in *Analysis and Policy Suggestions to Develop Alternative Agriculture: A Book for the Assembly of Alternative Agriculture 10–15 November 1992, Thammasat University* (Bangkok: Alternative Agriculture Network, 1992), 158–163 (in Thai) as well as Goss and Burch (2001), 979.
132 Goss and Burch (2001), 979.
133 Songsak Sriboonchitta, *Overview of Contract Farming in Thailand: Lessons Learned. ADBI Discussion Paper 112.* (Tokyo: Asian Development Bank, 2008), 1–2; the OAE's strategies for agricultural commodities (2002–2006) and DAE's 'Plan to Encourage Safe and up to Standard Agricultural Commodities', (2006), quoted in Prachason (2008), 41.
134 Prachason (2008), 41.
135 Department of Industrial Promotion, *A Study of the Feasibility of Ethanol Production from Cassava 2009* (Bangkok: Ministry of Industry, 2009), 10–12 (in Thai).

136 Ibid., 20.
137 For example, Bello, Cunningham and Li (1998), 136.
138 Pricha Oopayokin and Suri Karnchanawong, *Business/tradesmen and Thai Parliamentary System: A Study Funded by the Secretariat of the House of Representatives* (Bangkok, 1999), 263–264 (in Thai).
139 Lienchamroon (25 November 2011), 12–13.
140 Duncan McCargo and Ukrist Pathmanand, *The Thaksinization of Thailand* (Copenhagen: Nordic Institute of Asian Studies (NIAS) Press, 2005), 33. In China, the CP group is known as the Chia Tai group (Zheng Da Ji Tuan) and it is the first transnational company to invest in China's agri-business (CP website www.cpthailand.com/).
141 CorpWatch-Thailand, 'Connections between CP, Politicians and Thai Bureaucracy', in *CP and Thai Agriculture* (Nonthaburi: BioThai, 2008), 27–31 (in Thai).
142 McCargo and Pathmanand (2005), 215–216. For a study which suggests how the 1997 Constitution empowers the executive, particularly the Office of Prime Minister, see Rangsan Thanapornpan, *The Political Economy of the 1997 Constitution* (Bangkok: Thailand Research Fund, 2003) (in Thai).
143 McCargo and Pathmanand (2005), 219–220 and 234.
144 Ukrist Pathmanand, 'Globalisation and Democratic Development in Thailand: The New Path of the Military, Private Sector, and Civil Society', *Contemporary Southeast Asia* 23, no. 1 (2001), 31.
145 Kitti Prasertsuk, 'From Political Reform and Economic Crisis to Coup D'état in Thailand: The Twists and Turns of the Political Economy, 1997–2006', *Asian Survey* 47, no. 6 (2007), 882.
146 Ibid., 888.
147 For example, see: Ammar Siamwalla, *Politics and Business Interests under the 1997 Constitution: A Complete Report for Prapokplao Foundation* (Bangkok, 2003) (in Thai); Masami Imai, 'Mixing Family Business with Politics in Thailand', *Asian Economic Journal* 20, no. 3 (September 2006): 241–256.
148 Others include Adisai Bodharamik of the Jasmine Group, Pracha Maleenont from a TV and entertainment conglomerate, and Suriya Jungrungruangkit from the largest local auto parts maker (Thai Summit) (Prasertsuk (2007), 881).
149 Examples include an exemption from the payment of import duty on machinery and the exemption from the payment of income tax for certain operations for 5–8 years (CP Foods, *Kitchen of the World: Annual Report 2003*, quoted in Delforge (2007), 4).
150 BioThai, 'Report on the Problems of Hybrid Rice Seeds' (2009).
151 Charles F. Keyes, *Thailand: Buddhist Kingdom as Modern Nation-State* (Bangkok: Westview Press, 1987), 136.
152 This section focuses on patron–client relations during electoral democracy periods in Thailand in recent years. It would be interesting to explore patron–client relations and mentality in the context of brief periods of military governments in Thailand (after the 2006 and 2014 coups d'état), but it is beyond the scope of this research because the situation is still developing at the time of writing.
153 For example, see the discussion in Elin Bjarnegård, 'Who's the Perfect Politician? Clientelism as a Determining Feature of Thai Politics,' in *Party Politics in Southeast Asia: Clientelism and Electoral Competition in Indonesia, Thailand and the Philippines*, ed. Dirk Tomsa and Andreas Ufen (London and New York: Routledge, 2013), 145.
154 Seksan Prasertkul, *Citizen Politics in Thai Democracy* (Bangkok: Amarin, 2005), 10 and 15 (in Thai).
155 Keyes (1987), 136.
156 Jeremy Kemp, *Community and State in Modern Thailand (Working Paper no. 100)*, Southeast Asia program, University of Bielefeld, 1988, quoted in Anek Laothamatat, *Thai Democracy as a Tale of Two Cities: Paths to Reform Politics and Economy for Democracy*, 5th edn. (Bangkok: Wipasa, 2000), 26 (in Thai).

157 Sombat Jantarawong, *Election Crisis* (Bangkok: Kopfai, 1993), 111–167 and Rangsan Thanapornpan, *Transient Characteristics of Thai Politics* (Bangkok: Manager News Group, 1993), 113–116, quoted in Laothamatat (2000), 26.
158 For example, see: Prasertkul (2005), 14; Pricha Oopayokin and Suri Karnchanawong, *Business/tradesmen and Thai Parliamentary System: A Study Funded by the Secretariat of the House of Representatives* (Bangkok, 1999), 273 (in Thai); the interview with constituency candidate for the TRT party, Constituency 5 March 2006 (similar views were also put forward by Democrats), and the interview with Director of Provincial Election Commission, Constituency One, May 2006, in Bjarnegård (2013), 148–149, and 158.
159 Prasertkul (2005), 17.
160 Bjarnegård (2013), 142. The study was an in-depth field research (around the year 2006) which focused on campaigns and political networks of the two major Thai political parties – Democrat and Thai Rak Thai.
161 Pasuk Phongpaichit and Chris Baker suggest that the TRT populist rural policies can be seen as attempts to replace old local patron–client relationships with direct loyalty to the TRT party (Pasuk Phongpaichit and Chris Baker, *Thaksin: The Business of Politics in Thailand* (Chiang Mai: Silkworms Books, 2004), 188–189).
162 Jim Glassman, 'Economic Nationalism in a Post-Nationalist Era: The Political Economy of Economic Policy in Post-Crisis Thailand', *Critical Asian Studies*, 36, no. 1 (2004), 59–60, quoted in McCargo and Pathmanand (2005), 181.
163 McCargo and Pathmanand (2005), 212–215.
164 Porphant Ouyyanont, 'The Crown Property Bureau in Thailand and the Crisis of 1997', *Journal of Contemporary Asia*, 38, no. 1, February 2008, 166.
165 *Investor*, February 1971, 124–125 and *Business in Thailand*, February 1973, 20–22, quoted in Phongpaichit and Baker (1995), 282.
166 Ouyyanont (2008), 171.
167 Ibid., 184.
168 Paisal Sricharatchanya, 'Thailand's Crown Property bureau mixes business with social concern', *Far Eastern Economic Review*, 30 June 1988, 140 (26), 61 and Ouyyanont (2008), 174.
169 Goss and Burch (2001), 981.
170 Ibid., 981–982.
171 Thammawit Terd-udomsap, *The Political Economy of Thai FTAs, Research Document 8* (Bangkok, 2008), 140 (in Thai).
172 Witoon Lienchamroon and Supha Yaimuang, 'Alternative Agriculture: From Individual Farmers to Social Movements', in *Reform the Agricultural Sector for Food Security: Analysis and Practical Policies*, ed. Witoon Lienchamroon (Nonthaburi: BioThai, 2011), 307–309 (in Thai).
173 For example, criticisms were made by Assoc. Prof. Dr Jirapon Limpananont, member of the NESDB, quoted in Prachathai news, 'NESDB Warns the Government the Unconstitutional Risk of Not Listening to Public Opinions Regarding Thai-EU FTA', *Prachathai*, 16 January 2013 (in Thai).
174 BioThai, 'Effects of Thai-EU FTA on Plant Genes, Biodiversity, and Food Security', 26 February 2013. www.biothai.net/node/16573 (in Thai).
175 Kannikar Kitwetchakul, FTA Watch (Thailand), quoted in Isra News, 'Against Section 190 Modification. NGOs against an Increase in the Power of the Executive – Elites, and a Reduction of Civil Society's Spaces', *Isra News*, 18 November 2013 (in Thai).
176 Ibid.
177 Post Today Newspaper, 'Draft of Thai-EU FTA: Thai Loses More than Gain', *Post Today*, 10 December 2012 (in Thai).
178 Karnchuchat (2006), 234.
179 Ibid., 236 and Pholnoi (2003), 181.
180 Matichon Newspaper, '3 Sugar Plants Associations' (2009).

181 Department of Industrial Promotion (2009), 15 and Sitiwuth Siempakdee, Vice President of Thai Sugar Miller company, quoted in Matichon Newspaper, '3 Sugar Plants Associations' (2009).

182 There are also some reformist views among economists. Dr Ammar Siamwalla, for example, suggested that Thailand's agri-food products are inevitably dependent on global markets so government interventions, such as those which aim to maintain prices, can only be temporary measures. Nevertheless, Ammar also suggested that if Thailand refuses the global markets, there must be clear alternatives which take into account competitiveness as well as global warming (Siamwalla's speech at 'The future of Thai agriculture in the global context', 29–30 August, Mahidol University, Nakhon Pathom, Thailand, quoted in Prachathai News, 'Ammar's Speech "The Future of Thai Agriculture Under Changing Circumstances"', *Prachathai*, 29 August 2013 (in Thai)).

183 Pholnoi (2003), 96, 133–134 and Manager Newspaper, 'CP Took over Makro', 2013.

184 For example, see: Puapongsakorn *et al.* (2002); The Parliament's Committee of Commerce (2003); and interview with Dusit Nonthanakorn, Vice President of Thai Chamber of Commerce, in Thailand Industry News, 'The Private Sector Pushes for the Birth of Retail Business Act, Concerns over Foreign Monopoly and Destruction of Traditional Thai Shops', *Thailand Industry News*, 16 June 2008 (in Thai).

185 Interview with an Agriculture and Cooperatives Ministry official, anonymity requested, September 1993, in Bello, Cunningham and Li (1998), 167.

186 For example, Viroj Naranong's presentation from an economics perspective at a public conference: 'Rice, Fish, Food: Menu of Inequalities Facing Thai Farmers', 14 January 2013, Thammasat University, Bangkok, Thailand. In 2008, Mr Thanin Jiarawanont of the CP group proposed in a television show that Thailand should reduce farmers to only 1 to 2 per cent (probably referring to percentage of the labour force or population) while the rest should work in the service sector in Thailand or abroad (quoted in BioThai, *People's Handbook about Food (In)security and Thailand's Solutions* (Nonthaburi: BioThai, 2010), 27 (in Thai)).

187 Such views are also advanced by farmers and agri-food activists interviewed (see Chapter 5).

188 Transfers of specialised/departmentalised Green Revolution production knowledge from Western academics and international organisations are also discussed in, for example, Lienchamroon and Thankitchanukit (2008), 38–49.

189 Mr Chanuan Rattanawaraha, former Deputy Director General of the Department of Agriculture who held a position at the Office of Department of Agriculture (DOA) Technical Advisor, interviewed 17 January 2013, Nonthaburi.

190 Ibid.

191 Keyes (1987), 135.

192 Prasertkul (2005), 11–13.

193 Duncan McCargo, *Politics and the Press in Thailand: Media Machinations* (London: Routledge, 2000), 136, quoted in McCargo and Pathmanand (2005), 173.

194 For example, various ceremonies have been used to raise the monarchy's profile. Controls over royal properties were also returned to the monarchy (Phongpaichit and Baker (1995), 281–282).

195 Weerachai Narkwibulwong, '37 Years of Land Reform and the Adaptation of Sufficiency Economy', in *37 Years of the Agricultural Land Reform Office* (Bangkok: ALRO, 2012) (in Thai).

196 Prachachat Turakiij, 'Famous Business Families Stocking up Land' (18 June 2014).

197 See the interviews in Manager Newspaper, 'CP Took over Makro' (27 April 2013).

198 Crony capitalist nationalism and a different variant of radical populist nationalism are discussed in Kasian Tejapira, 'Post-Crisis Economic Impasse and Political Recovery in Thailand: The Resurgence of Economic Nationalism', *Critical Asian Studies* 34, no. 3 (2002): 323–356.

4 Counter-hegemony and co-optation of oppositions in the agri-food system in Thailand

Introduction

This chapter, as well as the following Chapter 5 and 6, advance the second and third main arguments of the book, which are that although the mainstream agri-food system is dominated by hegemonic capitalist interests, domestic and trans-national counter-hegemonic forces can, to certain extents, influence some changes in the system. As the previous chapter has discussed, the hegemonic structures of the current agri-food system consists not only of production–distribution practices, but of hegemonic ideas and governance structures. The discussion of counter-hegemony, then, should take into account these three dimensions, which is consistent with the Gramscian approach adopted by this book where counter-hegemony is conceptualised as practical and ideological challenges to the hegemonic status quo.

Part 1 of this chapter briefly discusses historical development of Thai agrarian movements and alternative development ideas between the 1970s and 1990s. It then provides an overview of counter-hegemonic ideas, production–distribution practices, and governance structures of the sustainable agriculture movement (SAM) and the land reform movement (LRM). Part 2 of this chapter discusses co-optation of oppositions, controversial agrarian policies, as well as polarised political situations and their divisive effects on agrarian social movements in the 2000s and early 2010s.

Part 1 Counter-hegemony in the agri-food system in Thailand

To a certain extent, the SAM and the LRM build themselves on past agrarian movements and influential alternative development ideas in Thai society. The first organised agrarian movement in Thailand was the Peasants' Federation of Thailand (PFT) which was established in November 1974 to protect the interests of farmers.[1] Even though the PFT was violently suppressed in the late 1970s, some of the PFT's ideas and sympathisers survived. Many activists, local leaders, farmers, academics and civil servants who helped to advance the SAM's and the LRM's counter-hegemonic projects were partly involved or were inspired by the PFT and the spirit of activism of that era. Examples include Mr Rangsan Sansongkwae who is a farmer leader of Raidong Community Land Title Deed (CLTD) project in Lamphun province and Mr Boonsong Martkhao from Kammad Organic Agriculture group in Yasothon province.[2] Despite violent repressions, the Thai state made some attempts to appease the rural population in the 1970s.[3] As Chapter 6 will discuss in greater detail, the Agricultural Land Reform Office (ALRO) was established in 1975 as a response to demands for land reform. The ALRO has generally been perceived as ineffective in distributing land to small-scale farmers and to a certain extent, CLTD ideas and practice can be seen as reactions to the limitations of ALRO. Nevertheless, Chapter 6 will suggest that ALRO's counter-hegemonic potential should not be completely ruled out.

In the 1980s, non-governmental organisations (NGOs) and their rural development projects were starting to be seen in a better light by the state, and NGOs also started to develop linkages with other sectors such as the media and the middle class.[4] Alternative development ideas, often referred to as 'the community culture school of thought', was also popularised by Thai academics such as Chatthip Nartsupha and Prawase Wasi.[5] Localist ideas are closely associated with concepts of sufficiency, self-reliance and community rights. The concept of 'grassroots democracy', which is widely promoted by Thai NGOs, also has great resonance with localist ideas; it infers wide-ranging reforms of the bureaucracy and decentralisation of power to allow local communities and people's organisations to take part in the decision-making process, and to restore their rights to manage local natural resources.[6] Owing to pressures from NGOs and public intellectuals in the community school of thought, the 1997 and 2007 Constitutions recognise the importance of community rights in the sustainable management of natural resources.[7] However, practical implementation of community rights is very limited.[8] As Chapter 6 will discuss, the lack of supporting subsidiary laws which support community rights is problematic for the LRM.[9] Chapter 5 and 6 will also discuss in greater detail Thai localism, sufficiency economy, as well as their influence on the SAM's and LRM's counter-hegemonic ideas and practice.

From the late 1980s onwards, conflicts between citizens, the state, and capital over use rights of land and other natural resources have intensified.[10] As reactions to the problems facing small-scale farmers in the agricultural sector, many grass-root rural organisations emerged in the early 1990s, such as the Small-scale Farmers of the Northeast (So Ko Yo Oo) and the Northern Farmers Network. Through the mid-1990s, rural organisations used protests to attract attention and negotiations to gain concessions from the state. On the International Human Rights day, 10 December 1995, a new umbrella organisation called the Assembly of the Poor was formed in Thailand. It encompassed agricultural groups, such as the Alternative Agriculture Network (AAN), which is the core group of the SAM, as well as other marginalised people's groups and their urban middle-class allies.[11] As Chapter 5 will discuss, the AAN received the budget for its pilot programme to promote sustainable agriculture in Thailand as part of the concessions made to the Assembly of the Poor. Many other concessions, however, were revoked by Chuan Leekpai's Democrat government in 1998.[12] Chapter 6 will also discuss the Assembly of the Poor and the Northern Peasants Federation as Thai members of La Vía Campesina – the largest transnational agrarian social movement – and how they help to spread transnational counter-hegemonic ideas within their networks.

1.1 An overview of the sustainable agriculture movement (SAM) in Thailand

SAM supporters in Thailand try to provide alternatives to the mainstream agri-food system and prioritise health, social ties, self-reliance and ecological sustainability over profit maximisation.[13] Some promoters of sustainable agriculture use religion and traditional cultural beliefs to inspire counter-hegemonic ideas and to promote sustainable agriculture, while others prefer transnational ideas and terms such as those from the food security and food sovereignty discourses.

As the name suggests, SAM groups promote various forms of sustainable agriculture such as organic agriculture and integrated farming, partly to reduce economic and food insecurity risks of small-scale farmers. They learned from international experiences, such as that of organic farming in Europe, and have also formed transnational trade linkages as well as other forms of co-operation.[14] Instead of being fixated on only small-scale farms, there are also practical examples of many different sizes of agricultural farms and arrangements, such as organic contract farming, which are accepted as long as they embodied counter-hegemonic principles.[15] There are also many types of distributional channels of sustainable agri-food products in Thailand ranging from local green markets to large-scale exports of organic and fair trade products. Most groups that were interviewed try to expand their activities so that members can benefit from value-added opportunities along agri-food chains, as well as from job creations that come with processing and marketing agri-food products.[16]

SAM members also recognise the importance of fostering counter-hegemonic individual behaviours and informal social relations to support their sustainable agricultural production and distribution practices.[17] Moreover, the AAN also tries to shape the policy and legal structures governing the agri-food system in Thailand at the local, national and (to a limited extent) global levels, such as those relating to the governance of seeds, intellectual property rights, and free trade agreements. Due to limited success, some people in the SAM prefer to concentrate on developing alternative production–distribution practices without much engagement with the Thai state,[18] as Chapter 5 will explore in greater detail.

1.2 An overview of the land reform movement (LRM) in Thailand

The LRM criticises the primacy of private individual rights and are inspired by community rights ideas, particularly the concept of 'the complexity of rights' put forward by Anan Ganjanapan from Chiang Mai University. To put it simply, complexity of rights suggests that different forms of rights can overlap within a geographical unit.[19] For example, one may have an ownership right over a piece of land, but others may use some by-products of the land.[20]

Land occupations in the 1990s and early 2000s led to the call for land reform and redistribution of land to marginalised people in the form of CLTD. CLTD reflects the complexity of rights concept as land is owned collectively, such as by a co-operative, while individual members receive usage rights over individual plots of land.[21] Generally, members can use individual plots of land for agricultural and housing purposes but land exchanges are controlled so that, for example, land cannot be sold to people outside of the community for speculation purposes.[22] Other parties such as the state and civil society can be involved in the governance of local natural resources in a form of checks and balances.[23] This general principle is established to prevent land grabs by capital groups and to encourage small-scale farmers' access to land. By encouraging democratic participations, CLTD projects encourage the spirit of solidarity and provide counter-hegemonic challenges to hierarchical social structures and mentality in Thailand. At the leadership level, additional goals include safeguarding agricultural land for domestic food security and the promotion of sustainable agriculture.[24] Participations in international conferences organised by La Vía Campesina, as well as exchanges with other civil society groups in Thailand and abroad, also help to promote LRM members' interests in food security and food sovereignty.[25]

The LRM also recognises that it is important to address macro-level legal and policy governance structures to challenge and transform the hegemonic status quo. In 2014, the LRM started pushing for 'four laws for the poor' which include laws regarding land taxation, land banks and community rights in the management of land and natural resource (CLTD law), as well as a law to support the establishment of a Justice Fund for marginalised citizens who need help with their legal fees.[26] However, there are many obstacles, as Chapter 6 will elaborate.

Part 2 Co-optation of oppositions in the agri-food system in Thailand

There are many forms of opposition and intimidation which discourage counter-hegemony in the agri-food system in Thailand. For example, some LRM land occupiers have faced legal suits, while the Thai state often tries to discredit and suppress rural social movements.[27] These measures are rather obvious compared to 'co-optation of oppositions' – a Gramscian concept which refers to strategies of ideational and practical distortion to subsume and hinder counter-hegemony in the agri-food system. As Chapter 2 has discussed, methods of co-optation of oppositions include, for example, the incorporation of the rhetoric of radical change without changing hegemonic principles or substance, as well as the incorporation of leaders and organisations in the decision-making process without allowing them to influence the status quo.[28]

This part of the chapter provides some background information regarding the contemporary political situation in Thailand and possibilities of co-optation of oppositions relating to the SAM and the LRM. Section 2.1 discusses co-optation of agrarian movements through patron–client relations, polarised political discourses, and what could arguably be described as rural populist policies which serve as distortions of counter-hegemony in the agri-food system. Section 2.2 then discusses Phua Thai government's paddy pledging scheme and its co-optive consequences; although it is being presented as a major solution, this section argues that the scheme intensifies and exacerbates structural problems of the agri-food system.

2.1 Co-optation, rural populist policies and polarised political discourses

Patron–client relations, discussed in the previous chapter, have been used as a tool to co-opt agrarian movements; by providing political patronage and some concessions to selected marginalised population and farmer groups, political-economic elites can exert influence over them and control their agenda. It has been noted that in most provinces where there were viable profit-making state promoted co-operatives, local and national politicians were usually behind them as advisers.[29] In addition, many rural leaders and AAN activists point to the prevalence of patron–client relations and co-optation of rural groups by politicians and local notables, such as through offers and promises of short-term gains.[30] If agricultural co-operatives and farmers' groups have to rely on patron–client relationships, they may only be able to develop as cases of 'special concessions' from the state, and might not seek to expand on their own initiatives or to challenge the hegemonic status quo.

The Thai Rak Thai (TRT) party and its successor Phua Thai were in power most of time between 2001 and 2014, and they are arguably two of the most powerful patrons, at a national level, in recent years.[31] Before he came to power, TRT leader Thaksin Shinnawatra had enlisted many activists, academics, and local leaders as advisors. However, during the first Thaksin administration, social movements rarely mobilised or were quickly dispersed, while some NGO and academic activists were portrayed as middlemen who exploited poverty.[32] Many scholars have noted how rural policies of the first Thaksin administration (2001 to 2004) reinforced hierarchical patron–client attitude in Thai society.[33] By creating feelings of personal gratitude, such policies also manage to bound many Thais to Thaksin Shinnawatra, his family and his political party, as well as encourage them to overlook policies which support and intensify exploitative political-economic structures in the agri-food system. It has been suggested that many farmers and marginalised people feel very defensive of rural populist policies because, for many decades, they felt neglected and weakened by the state.[34] Grassroots support also allows Thaksin and his allies to expand their political and economic influence.[35] Moreover, Thaksin, his family and close associates have been accused of many corruption charges and of using political positions to increase the family fortune.[36]

From a quick glance, TRT policies such as the debt moratorium for small-scale farmers and the scheme to provide a one million baht fund for each village, or to give money to rural villages in general, would benefit the rural population such as small-scale farmers. The fine prints, however, often suggest that these policies reinforce hegemonic capitalist agriculture.[37] Phua Thai party – a political successor to the TRT party after it was abolished under a court order in 2007 – has not departed much from such agricultural policies. It is beyond the scope of this chapter to discuss all of Phua Thai's rural policies in detail, but section 2.2 discusses one famous example which is the paddy pledging scheme of the Yingluck Shinnawatra's administration (2011 to 2014).

After the 2006 coup d'état in Thailand, which ousted the second Thaksin administration from power, polarised political conflicts and accompanying discourses in Thailand have escalated and also hindered counter-hegemony in the agri-food system in Thailand. Contemporary political polarisation in Thailand is often simplified as having two sides; the yellow shirts or the People's Alliance for Democracy (PAD) and more recently (2013 to 2014) the People's Democratic Reform Committee (PDRC), versus the red shirts or the United Front for Democracy Against Dictatorship (UDD). PDRC and PAD supporters are often perceived as those who oppose Thaksin Shinnawatra, his family and political party, and are also seen by the red shirts as being pro-monarchy and elitist. UDD supporters, on the other hand, present themselves as those who oppose the military and feudal elites, but they are perceived by others as being pro-Thaksin and pro-Phua Thai. Despite the stereotypes, it is not necessarily the case that all of those who protest against Phua Thai government are conservative royalists. Many see themselves as activists and reformers or as socially conscious citizens. Likewise, some people sympathise with the red shirts, not because they support Thaksin, but because of other reasons, such as to express their disagreements with coups d'état.

The popularity and legitimacy of Phua Thai's agricultural policies are being supported by discourses which present Phua Thai and red-shirt leaders as being on the side of 'peasants' or 'phrai' who are fighting for marginalised people's causes, to defend democracy, and to challenge elitist Sakdina or the 'ammart' influence in Thai society. The red shirts' claim to represent the peasants, however, is questioned by many Thais as well as some academic studies which suggest that Thaksin and his associates help to orchestrate and benefit from the red shirts' political mobilisation.[38] The definition of the 'ammart' is also problematically vague and has come to include not only the groups of people directly associated with the monarchy and the 2006 coup d'état, such as the privy council, but also whatever institutions and people (often portrayed as the middle/upper class) that criticise Phua Thai government, including some senators, academics, and the Supreme Court.[39] Even some civil-society networks which have built themselves up over the past two to three decades are often dubbed by red-shirt intellectuals as being part of the 'ammart's network'.[40]

Such polarised 'phrai' versus 'ammart' discourses can be seen as a form of co-optation of oppositions, engineered by political-economic elites to solicit support from the people by directing their attention and attributing some grievances arising from the hegemonic agri-food system to the vaguely defined 'ammart' class. This helps to mask structural problems of the hegemonic agri-food system and to distract the public's attention away from the social and ecological threats posed by the hegemonic agri-food system. Such discourses also undermine counter-hegemonic ideas in the agri-food system and hinder rational debates in Thai society. This is because polarised political discourses often lead to the narrow framing of rural development issues, where rural development is portrayed as having only two opposing paths. Rural populist policies of TRT and Phua Thai parties are generally portrayed by the red shirts as modern globalised choices compared to the backward path of development offered by those who utilise terms associated with Thai localism and the King's sufficiency economy concept, such as community rights and self-reliance. Justifiable environmental concerns from increased usage of pesticides to produce rice and other attempts to promote sustainable agriculture are also sometimes ridiculed as middle/upper-class elitist concerns.[41] Those who criticise the paddy pledging scheme have been portrayed as being unsympathetic to farmers, while protests and oppositions to the Phua Thai government are often portrayed as being motivated by disingenuous political gains.[42]

There are also some academics who suggested that: (1) electoral results which allowed TRT and Phua Thai parties to come into power serve to legitimise the modern capitalist developmental path and other major policies that these parties pursue, and that; (2) the electoral results also delegitimises Thai localist alternatives which are seen as the opposite (anti)development path. For example, Hall, Hirsch and Li (2011) discusses the Assembly of the Poor as an advocate of community-based resource management and pitches it against Thaksin and his party's modern capitalist development approach.[43] Since the Shinnawatra's political party received a lot of electoral support from the North and Northeast despite failing to follow through the Assembly of the Poor's demands, the book suggests that this represents a 'betrayal' of the Assembly and that the rural population had no objection to capitalism or modernity, nor quarrel with the concept of development.[44] However, there are many problems with such an assessment. Some members of the Assembly of the Poor support Thaksin and the red shirts while others do not.[45] Although the Phua Thai party won the election in 2011, the percentage of votes in the 2011 election in the North and Northeast (supposedly Phua Thai's stronghold) actually indicates the rural population to be rather politically fragmented. For example, Phua Thai received only 54.9 per cent of party-list votes in the North.[46]

For the sake of argument, even if one assumes that there are no patron–clients and vote buying that distort the principles of electoral democracy in Thailand, people's decisions to vote for TRT and/or Phua Thai can be based on many reasons, e.g. as a second-worse choice, because they approve of a few policies, or because of their appreciations of local candidates. In other words, voting for TRT and/or Phua Thai does not necessarily imply complete endorsement of all dimensions and consequences of capitalism and modernity, nor does it imply that voters have critically evaluated structural problems of capitalism and are ideologically consistent. As Chapter 6 will discuss, some members of the LRM sympathise with the red shirts even though they promote community rights to manage local natural resources.[47] In addition, both the Democrat and Phua Thai parties advocated CLTD projects in their 2011 election campaigns.[48] Overall, it seems that using electoral results to legitimise the capitalist development approach of the Phua Thai party and delegitimise community rights ideas are problematic and could consequently serve to benefit elites as well as maintain the hegemonic status quo. Chapter 5 will also discuss how the assumption that capitalism and modernity represent 'development' is problematic and that it can be considered part of the hegemonic ideological order.

Some NGO activists suggest that agrarian social movements have been weakened due to political polarisation and the lack of unity partly makes large-scale mobilisation difficult.[49] After the coup d'état in 2006, many NGO activists were uncertain about their political beliefs and future strategies, so their projects suffered as a consequence.[50] The situation has improved at the time of writing in 2013 and early 2014, but it is still difficult for agrarian social movements to try to expand their networks and alliances without being labelled as either red or yellow. Red-shirt intellectuals and supporters sometimes perceive demands by other social movements as 'minor' and that Phua Thai party's policies alone are rather sufficient.[51] To make matters worse, hard-core red-shirt groups sometimes mobilise to stop other social movements' demonstrations, to defend the Phua Thai government. For example, the Rak Chiang Mai 51 group – a branch of the red shirts – tried to obstruct demonstrations to oppose the 3,500 million baht water management plan at the Second Asia-Pacific water summit in Chiang Mai province between 14 and 20 May 2013.[52] In early 2014, some farmers who had not received payment from the paddy pledging scheme for over half a year also claimed that they were threatened by local red shirts and community leaders to stop their protests against the government.[53]

The critique of the red shirts movement in this book does not intend to suggest that red shirts are fully co-opted or that they completely lack counter-hegemonic potential, because many red shirts are genuinely interested in bringing about a more egalitarian and democratic social order. This book also certainly does not suggest that all anti-red shirt groups should be considered as part of counter-hegemony in the agri-food system because they encompass a variety of groups with different agendas. The intention of the critique is mainly to point out that the red shirts' 'phrai-ammart' political discourse currently have problematic implications toward counter-hegemony in the agri-food system in Thailand, and that relationships between people's movements and established political authorities deserve critical scrutiny. Worryingly, some anti-red shirt groups ignore inequality problems in Thai society and blindly accept the domination of other elite groups as long as they are not from the Shinnawatra family, while many red shirts refrain from criticising Phua Thai and the Shinnawatra. At the time of writing, the Thai military recently staged the 12th successful coup d'état in Thailand on 22 May 2014 and suspended the 2007 Constitution, so it is unclear how such new development in Thai politics will affect civil society and counter-hegemony in the agri-food system in Thailand. Chapter 6 will discuss some recent developments as well as how the LRM's activities are often obstructed by the military after the coup d'état in 2014.

2.2 A case study of the paddy pledging scheme

The paddy pledging scheme is a subject of fierce debate in Thailand which also fuels polarised political conflicts. This section discusses the paddy pledging scheme with a focus on its implementation under Phua Thai government between 2011 and 2014. It argues that the scheme is a co-optive rural policy that presents itself as a pro-poor policy aiming to help marginalised farmers, and as a solution to problems in agriculture, while actually failing to do both. Not only did it have a dubious record on raising the material well-beings of rice farmers, the scheme also exacerbated structural problems in the agri-food system. The scheme was a massive drain on the government budget,[54] but as the following paragraphs elaborate, there is little evidence to suggest that the scheme did truly benefit small-scale rice farmers. One could also question why rice producers were hugely subsidised while other types of farmers, such as rubber producers in the South (which is not the electoral base of Phua Thai), did not receive equal treatment. As the following paragraphs elaborate, the scheme intensifies problematic industrial production methods as well as increases the power of monopolies and large capital in rice commodity chains. At the time of writing in early 2014, many management problems are being revealed and the Thai National Anti-Corruption Commission (NACC) is also investigating corruption practices in the scheme.[55]

The first paddy pledging programme was introduced in Thailand in the 1981/1982 cropping season to provide soft loans for farmers who wanted to delay sales of their crops. However, since around 2001, the scheme has been used to support price and to increase farmers' income.[56] A study of the paddy pledging programme in year 2005/2006 suggests that most of the benefits (55 per cent) did not go to farmers and that the scheme tends to benefit well-to-do farmers in irrigated areas and large-scale exporters.[57] During the global agri-food commodity, price spikes of 2007/2008, the Thai government did not sell any portion of its 2.1 million tons of rice stock but increased the guaranteed price for its paddy pledging programme to a high record of 14,000 baht per ton for the 2008 dry-season crop.[58] The share of pledged paddy in total production then increased dramatically to 44.8 per cent for the 2007/2008 dry season paddy, making the government the country's largest trader of rice.[59]

Phua Thai government under the leadership of Prime Minister Yingluck Shinnawatra, which came into power in August 2011, continued to support the paddy pledging scheme which offered to buy rice at significantly higher prices than the market. Phua Thai government officials had often explained that they intended to speculate and sell rice in the international market at high prices.[60] The nature of the rice market makes that wish rather impossible as high prices of rice inevitably tend to increase production in other countries, and as large stockpiles of perishable rice in warehouses keep prices low because buyers could predict that the Thai government eventually has to sell.[61] The Office of the Ombudsman report in 2014 also suggests that the scheme is a failure as huge stocks of deteriorating rice are left unsold and the government has to borrow money to pay farmers for their paddy.[62]

A study of the paddy pledging scheme between October 2011 to October 2012 found that around 52 per cent of the country's total rice production was under the control of the government through the pledging scheme, and that benefits were accrued mostly to middle and high income farmers rather than poor farmers.[63] This could be because, for example, small-scale farmers did not have the means to transport their rice to the mills so they had to sell to middlemen at lower prices.[64] Moreover, those who benefit most live around irrigated areas which allow them to grow rice several rounds per year, whereas more marginalised farmers in the North and Northeast could only grow rice once a year.[65]

Another main problem of the paddy pledging scheme is that it has increased the monopoly power of large rice mills.[66] A study in 1997 suggests that rice farmers sold paddy through three main channels: (1) local middlemen (50.9 per cent); (2) central markets (23.8 per cent), and (3) rice mills (19.0 per cent).[67] However, since 2004, rice mills became more influential after becoming paddy collectors in the government's paddy pledging scheme. By 2007/2008, 90 per cent of paddy was sold to rice mills and most central markets throughout the country had been closed.[68] The rice pledging scheme has also benefited monopolistic large-scale rice mills in particular; around 53 per cent of medium-scale rice mills closed down between 2000 and 2008, while the number of large-scale rice mills increased by 32 per cent.[69] The geographical distribution of each rice mill throughout the country allows them to establish 'few-buyers' markets where they have monopsony power over rice paddy, especially with the destruction of relatively more competitive central markets which used to be the main trading hubs of paddy.[70] It has also been argued that some rice mills do not use fair and up-to-standard measuring equipments.[71]

Owing to the paddy pledging scheme, Thai rice supply chains have been reorganised in ways that seem to benefit large rice mills that have a good relationship with government officials.[72] As will be discussed in greater detail in Chapter 5, the scheme has also been criticised for destroying smaller-scale operators along rice supply chains and for discouraging the production of quality and organic rice.[73] Producer rice mills, such as in Tambol Jedihak, Ratchaburi province, which used to mill 100 tons of paddy per month, had to reduce production and milled only 10 tons of paddy per month due to the effects of the scheme.[74] Other community enterprises that used to sell rice seeds (that may take longer to grow but are of better quality) are also negatively affected.[75]

The paddy pledging scheme also exacerbates environmental problems because it encourages the intensification of hegemonic industrial agri-food production methods that were discussed in Chapter 3. Under the paddy pledging scheme, the government buys rice from all farmers without discriminating against low quality (the criteria is based only on the general type of rice, dampness and impurity), so farmers have incentives to only care about increasing the quantity of paddy in order to increase their revenues. This has pushed them to increase their usage of chemical fertilisers, pesticides, and also to use seeds which have a short harvest time that will result in a lower quality of rice.[76] A lot of farmers tried to intensify their production to increase quantity, such as by harvesting rice three to five times a year (instead of just one or two) without resting the land,[77] which contributed to serious spreads of aphis.[78]

The paddy pledging scheme also produces a lot of opportunity costs which greatly affect the agri-food system in Thailand. Due to distorted higher prices of rice, a lot of resources have been switched to the production of rice which puts upward pressures on the costs of production. There are, for example, reports that some landlords in Ayuthya and Lopburi provinces have increased land rents (50 to 100 per cent), stopped renting to landless farmers, or bought up more land as responses to this policy.[79] A study suggests that rent in the Central Region increased from 800 to 1,000 baht per year to 1,000 baht per rai per harvest, and fertiliser costs also increased despite stagnations in the level of yields.[80] There were also over-expansions of rice mill capacity (currently Thailand has 90 million tons per year capacity even though it needs only 35 million tons),[81] not to mention that there are huge opportunity costs of alternative public investments in other socially beneficial projects and infrastructures.[82] The Ombudsman's study in 2014 criticises the paddy pledging scheme for not improving farming productivity and also suggests that the scheme has not helped secure a higher farmer's income because of corresponding increases in production costs. Moreover, the scheme cannot provide sufficient income for farmers to purchase important factors of production such as land.[83] Landless farmers also have to pay higher land rents and are likely to be transformed into farm labourers with little occupation security.[84]

In early 2014, there were protests in many provinces by farmers who sold their paddy to the government almost half a year ago but had not received payment.[85] The delayed payment caused significant negative repercussions throughout the rural economy and Thai agri-food sector as purchasing power in rural areas dipped. In mid-February 2014, more than one million farmers had not been paid the total value of 130 billion baht for the paddy they pledged to the government.[86] Many farmers had to borrow money through informal channels with high interest rates to invest in a new round of production or just to sustain themselves.[87]

Conclusion

This chapter has provided an overview of counter-hegemonic ideas, production–distribution practices, and governance structures of the SAM and the LRM. It has also discussed the SAM and the LRM in relation to the historical development of agrarian social movements and alternative development ideas in Thailand. This chapter also discussed co-optation of agrarian movements, as well as how agrarian policies and polarised politics in Thailand open up room for co-optation of oppositions. In particular, the paddy pledging scheme is discussed as an example of a co-optive policy that is claiming to help improve the situations of small-scale farmers and the agricultural sector, while actually masking and exacerbating structural problems of the mainstream agri-food system.

The following chapters will explore counter-hegemonic ideas, production–distribution practices, and governance structures of the SAM and the LRM. The chapters will also discuss their obstacles as well as how the lines between counter-hegemony and co-optation of oppositions can be quite blurred, especially given that predominantly hegemonic and counter-hegemonic forces continually interact and evolve.

Notes

1 Kanoksak Kaewthep, 'The Struggle of Thai Farmers 1989–1999', in *The Path of Thai Farmers* (Bangkok, 1999), 41–42 (in Thai).
2 Interviewed 30 October 2012 and 25 December 2012, respectively.
3 Pitch Pongsawat, 'The Relationship Between the Economic and Political Changes and Farmers Movement in the Present Thai Society: A Critical Observation', *Fah-Diewkan*, Year 1, Vol. 1 (January–April 2005), 67 (in Thai).
4 Naruemon Thabchumpon, 'NGOs and Grassroots Participation in the Political Reform Process', in *Reforming Thai Politics*, ed. Duncan McCargo (Copenhagen: NIAS Press, 2002), 189.
5 Pasuk Phongpaichit and Chris Baker, *Thailand: Economy and Politics* (New York: Oxford University Press, 1995), 386–388.
6 Thapchumphon (2002), 196–197.
7 Wich Jeerapat, 'Reflection on Thai Community Right Ideas', *Julniti Journal*, vol. 3, no. 38 (2010), 40 (in Thai).
8 Chatthip Nartsupha, *Modernisation and the "Community" School of Thought* (Bangkok: Sangsan Publishing, 2010), 160 (in Thai).
9 For example, see Ittipol Srisaowalak *et al.*, *A Study Project on the Law to Manage Local Areas* (Bangkok: Thailand Research Fund, 2001), Abstract page II and III (in Thai).
10 Kaewthep (1999), 71–72.
11 Chris Baker, 'Pluto-Populism: Thaksin and Popular Politics', in *Thailand Beyond the Crisis*, ed. Peter Warr (New York: RoutledgeCurzon, 2005), 119.
12 Phongpaichit and Baker (1995), 408–411.
13 For example: Mr Pat Apaimool, sustainable farmer, interviewed 1 November 2012, Chiang Mai; Mr Pakphum Inpan, sustainable farmer, interviewed 20 December 2012, Surin; Mr Decha Siripat, Khao Kwan Foundation, interviewed 14 October 2012, Nonthaburi.
14 Mr Witoon Lienchamroon, BioThai, interviewed 5 April 2012, Nonthaburi; Mr Ubol Yoowah, NGO activist, interviewed 22 December 2012, Yasothon; Dr Chomchuan Boonrahong, lecturer at Mae-Jo University, interviewed 3 November 2012, Chiang Mai.
15 For example, there is an organic contract farming arrangement in Suphanburi which is a result of collaborations between Khao Kwan Foundation, local rice mills and local farmers.
16 Mrs Supha Yaimuang, president of SATHAI, interviewed 3 October 2012, Nonthaburi.
17 Mr Arpakorn Krueng-ngern, Mae-ta organic farmer, interviewed 1 November 2012, Chiang Mai; Sajin Prachason *et al.*, *Market Options of Farmers: Structural Effects on Unfairness and Benefit Distribution* (Bangkok: BioThai and the Social Research Foundation, Chulalongkorn University, 2012), 285 (in Thai).

18 Such as Mr Kankamkla Pilanoi, Thamma-ruamjai moral rice network, interviewed 23 December 2012, Yasothon.
19 Anan Ganjanapan, 'Community Rights in Development', in *The Community Dimension: Local Way of Thinking Regarding Rights, Power and Natural Resource Management* (Bangkok: Thailand Research Fund, 2001), 241 and 243 (in Thai).
20 For example, see Prayong Doklamyai, 'From Discourse to Practical Innovation: Land Reform by Communities. Transcript of the Presentation at a Conference on Anan Ganjanapan's Complexity of Rights, 8 March 2008', in *"I Don't Have the Answer": 60 Years Professor Dr. Anan Ganjanapan and 20 Years of Social Movement on Community Rights and Natural Resources Management* (Chiang Mai: Sustainable Development Foundation, 2008), 251 (in Thai).
21 Anan Ganjanapan, lecturer of Sociology and Anthropology, Chiang Mai University, interviewed 29 October 2012, Chiang Mai.
22 Pongthip Samranjit, 'A Summary of Research on Ground-up Land Reforms by Communities', 22 July 2011, www.landreformthai.net (in Thai).
23 Anan Ganjanapan, interviewed 29 October 2012, Chiang Mai.
24 Prayong Doklamyai, interviewed 1 November 2012, Chiang Mai; The Land Reform Network, *CLTDs – We Can: a Handbook* (Bangkok: Land Reform Network, 2012), 14 (in Thai).
25 Mr Direk Kong-Ngern, Baan Pong CLTD, interviewed 31 October 2012, Chiang Mai.
26 Acharawadee Buaklee, 'The North Pushes for 4 Land Laws', *ThaiPBS*, 4 April 2014, www.citizenthaipbs.net/node/4015.
27 For example, between 1998 and 1999 the second Chuan Leekpai government (Democrat party) had tried to portray rural protesters as development obstructers (Kaewthep (1999), 81).
28 Bill Paterson, 'Trasformismo at the World Trade Organization', in *Gramsci and Global Politics. Hegemony and Resistance*, ed. Mark McNally and John Schwarzmantel (Oxon: Routledge, 2009), 47.
29 Nipon Puapongsakorn and Ammar Siamwalla, 'Rural Villagers' Economic Group: Success and Survival, 51', in *A Report for the Annual Seminar 1995 of Thailand Development Research Institute (TDRI), 9–10 December* (Cholburi, Thailand, 1995), 51 (in Thai).
30 Mr Praderm Damrong-jaroen, former Farmer Network Party, phone interview on 17 October 2012; Decha Siripat, interviewed 14 October 2012, Nonthaburi; Mr Samrueng Roopsuay and Mr Arunsak Ocharos, veterans in rural social movements from Sri-saket, Northeast of Thailand, interviewed 6 April 2012, Bangkok.
31 In this book, 'populist policies' refer to policies which might be popular with the people and may solve short-term problems but do not solve structural problems.
32 Witoon Lienchamroon and Supha Yaimuang, 'Alternative Agriculture: From Individual Farmers to Social Movements', in *Reform the Agricultural Sector for Food Security: Analysis and Practical Policies*, ed. Witoon Lienchamroon (Nonthaburi: BioThai, 2011), 309–311 (in Thai).
33 Pasuk Phongpaichit and Chris Baker suggest that the TRT populist rural policies are attempts to replace old local patron–client relationships and transfer the rural people's loyalty directly to the TRT party (Pasuk Phongpaichit and Chris Baker, *Thaksin: the Business of Politics in Thailand* (Chiang Mai: Silkworms Books, 2004), 188–189).
34 Former high-ranking TRT politician, Mr Prapat Panyachatrak, interviewed 29 January 2013, National Farmer Council, Bangkok.
35 Duncan McCargo and Ukrist Pathmanand, *The Thaksinization of Thailand* (Copenhagen: Nordic Institute of Asian Studies (NIAS) Press, 2005), 217.
36 For a discussion of how Thaksin used his political power to benefit his family's business empire, see Chapter 7 'Power and Profit' in Phongpaichit and Baker (2004).
37 There are quite a few studies of the TRT rural development policies such as Ammar Siamwalla and Somchai Jitsuchon, *Tackling Poverty: Liberalism, Populism or Welfare*

State. A Paper Presented at the Annual Thailand Development Research Institute Academic Seminar, 10–11th November 2007 (Cholburi, Thailand, 2007) (in Thai).

38 For example, see: Tim Forsyth, 'Thailand's Red Shirt Protests: Popular Movement or Dangerous Street Theatre?', *Social Movement Studies*, vol. 9, no. 4 (November 2010): 461–467; Yoshinori Nishizaki, 'Peasants and the Redshirt Movement in Thailand: Some Dissenting Voices', *Journal of Peasant Studies* vol. 41, no. 1 (30 January 2014), 1–28.

39 Also see the discussion in Nishizaki (2014), 2.

40 Prapart Pintoptang, Political Science lecturer who specialises in Thai social movements, interviewed 16 October 2012, Nonthaburi.

41 For example: Nithi Iewsriwong, 'Changing Thailand with the Rice Mortgage Scheme', *Matichon*, 5 November 2012; Nithi Iewsriwong, 'Changing Thailand with the Rice Mortgage Scheme (One More Time)', *Matichon*, 3 December 2012; Kam Pakha, 'Morality Leads Thailand Towards Destruction', *Matichon (weekly)*, 14–20 January 2011 (all in Thai).

42 For example, see: Bangkok Business Newspaper, 'Thida Condemns Doctors for Joining PDRC', *Bangkok Business*, 21 January 2014 (in Thai).

43 Derek Hall, Philip Hirsch, and Tania Murray Li, *Powers of Exclusion: Land Dilemmas in Southeast Asia* (Singapore: NUS Press, 2011), 187–188.

44 Andrew Walker, 'Beyond the Rural Betrayal: Lessons from the Thaksin Era for the Mekong Region'. Paper presented at the International Conference on Critical Transitions in the Mekong Region. Chiang Mai, Thailand, 29–31 January 2007, quoted in Hall, Hirsch, and Li (2011), 188.

45 Prapart Pintoptang, interviewed 16 October 2012, Nonthaburi.

46 For further discussion see Nishazaki (2014), 5.

47 Direk Kong-ngern and Montri Bualoi, Baan Pong CLTD leaders, interviewed 31 October 2012, Chiang Mai.

48 Mr Prayong Doklamyai, Northern Peasants Federation, interviewed 1 November 2012, Chiang Mai; P-move, *Declaration number 18*, 26 April 2013.

49 Mr Witoon Lienchamroon, BioThai, interviewed 5 April 2012, Nonthaburi.

50 Ms Sawitta Teerowattanakul, Northern Peasants Federation, interviewed 29 October 2012, Chiang Mai.

51 Prapart Pintoptang, interviewed 16 October 2012, Nonthaburi.

52 Manager Newspaper, 'Rak Chiang Mai 51 Shows Support to "Plod" – Threathens NGOs Causing Chaos at the Water Summit – Prepares to Mobilise Thousands to Resist', *Manager*, 16 May 2013 (in Thai).

53 Bangkok Post, 'Farmers End Protest in Phitsanulok', *Bangkok Post*, 28 January 2014.

54 Estimated costs of the scheme for the year 2011/2012 was 179,314 million baht (Nipon Puapongsakorn, *Thai Rice Strategy: Research and Development on Thai Rice and Looking Forward* (Bangkok: Thailand Research Fund, 2013), Chapter 7, p. 6 and Chapter 7, p. 7 (in Thai)).

55 For example, see: Bangkok Post, 'NAAC Decides to Impeach Yingluck', *Bangkok Post*, 8 May 2014; Bangkok Business Newspaper, 'Yingluck Government Lied about G-to-G Rice Deal – Damages to the Budget and Rice Stock', *Bangkok Business*, 17 January 2014 (in Thai); David Eimer, 'Burmese Smugglers Get Rich on Yingluck Shinawatra's £13 Billion Thai Rice Subsidies', *The Telegraph*, 4 February 2014; Thai Post Newspaper, 'Hand over to DSI to Deal with Corruption in Rice Mortgage Scheme. Threaten to Blacklist-Boonsong Organised the Team', *Thai Post*, 24 February 2012 (in Thai); Patsara Jikkham, 'Rice Stockpile to be Audited', *Bangkok Post*, 13 June 2014.

56 Nipon Puapongsakorn, 'The Political Economy of Thai Rice Price and Export Policies in 2007–2008', in *The Rice Crisis Markets, Policies and Food Security*, ed. David Dawe (London and Washington DC: FAO and Earthscan, 2010), 192.

57 Nipon Puapongsakorn and Jittakorn Jarupong, *Rent Seeking Activities and the Political Economy of the Paddy Pledging Market Intervention Measures* (Bangkok: Office of the National Anti-Corruption Commission, 2010), Executive Summary (v) and 41 (in Thai).

58 Puapongsakorn (2010), 191 and 214 and Somporn Isawilanont, *Thai Rice: Changes in Production and Distribution Structure* (Bangkok: Thailand Research Fund, 2010), 66–68 (in Thai).
59 Puapongsakorn (2010), 194.
60 Mr Kittirat Na-Ranong, Vice Prime Minister and Minister of Finance, quoted in Post Today Newspaper, 'Expensive Lesson: From Paddy Pledging to Rubber Price Speculations', *Post Today*, 19 July 2012 (in Thai).
61 Post Today Newspaper, 'Expensive Lesson' (2012) and Nipon Puapongsakorn quoted in Thai Publica, 'An Interview with Niphon Puapongsakorn, Academic Master on Rice, on Things He Did Not Want to See in Paddy Pledging Scheme and Fear of Politics Destroying the Thai Rice Market', *Thai Publica*, 21 September 2011, http://thaipublica.org/2011/09/nipon-rice/ (in Thai).
62 Sriracha Jaroenpanich *et al.*, *A Study of the Effects of the Paddy Pledging Scheme on Thai Farmers' Quality of Life* (Bangkok: Office of the Ombudsman Thailand, 2014), 13–14.
63 Puapongsakorn (2013), Chapter 7, p. 1 and Chapter 7, p. 4 (in Thai).
64 Khaosod Newspaper, 'Grassroot Voices Regarding the Rice Mortgage Scheme', *Khaosod*, 16 April 2012 (in Thai).
65 Jaroenpanich *et al.* (2014), 9.
66 For example, see Jaroenpanich *et al.* (2014), 3–4 and 12–13.
67 Research unit on agri-businesses at Kasetsart University, *Strategic Commodity: Rice Department of Agricultural Economics and Natural Resource* (Kasetsart University, 1997), quoted in Iswilanont (2010), 83.
68 Isawilanont (2010), 83.
69 Makasiri Chaowakul, *Revision of Thai Rice Market Structure: A Complete Report for Thailand Research Fund* (Naresuan University, 2009), quoted in Isawilanont (2010), 83.
70 Isawilanont (2010), 91–92. The discussion of central markets for paddy, as well as usage of studies from economic perspectives in this part of the book, do not intend to suggest that these central markets nor the (appearance of or ideal) free markets in the neo-classical economics conception which are concerned with price competitiveness are the same as counter-hegemonic markets embedded in counter-hegemonic ideas and governance structures which reflect concerns for social and ecological sustainability.
71 Chaowakul (2009) quoted in Isawilanont (2010), 92.
72 See the discussion in Puapongsakorn (2013), 7–24.
73 Based on many interviews with farmers, civil servants, community rice mills managers and NGOs in the AAN such as Ms Sompoi Jansang, manager of the Rice Fund Surin Organic Agriculture Co-operative, 19 December 2012, Surin. Also, see Jaroenpanich *et al.* (2014), 4, 12, 14 and 31–32.
74 Puapongsakorn and Siamwalla (2012).
75 Ibid.
76 Mr Sittiporn Bangkaew, Director of the Office of Commercial Affairs in Surin, interviewed 21 December 2012, Surin; Ms Sompoi Jansang, Rice Fund Surin Organic Agriculture Co-operative, interviewed 19 December 2012, Surin.
77 Puapongsakorn (2013), 7–15; Jaroenpanich *et al.* (2014), 5 and 12.
78 Puapongsakorn (2013), iv.
79 Post Today Newspaper, 'Farmers Complain to the Government about Exorbitant Land Rents', *Post Today*, 3 October 2011 (in Thai).
80 Puapongsakorn (2013), iv.
81 Ibid., 7–14.
82 Nipon Puapongsakorn and Ammar Siamwalla, 'Transform Thailand with the Paddy Pledging Scheme: Facts for Ajarn Nithi and the Public', 24 November 2012, http://tdri.or.th/tdri-insight/responses-to-nidhi/ (in Thai).

83 Jaroenpanich *et al.* (2014), 7–8, 10–11 and 30–31.
84 Ibid., (9)–(10).
85 Bangkok Post, 'Farmers End Protest in Phitsanulok', (2014) and The Nation, 'Stress Drives Another Farmer to Suicide', *The Nation*, 16 February 2014.
86 Pitsinee Jitpleecheep and Piyachart Maikaew, 'Delayed Scheme Payments Lead to Higher NPLs', *Bangkok Post*, 17 February 2014.
87 For example, see: Post Today Newspaper, 'Farmers Complained that Late Payment Made them Turn to Informal Loans', *Post Today*, 8 January 2014 (in Thai); Manager Newspaper, 'Farmers Bittered from Discriminatory Payment as the Government Only Paid their Supporters', *Manager*, 29 January 2014 (in Thai).

5 The sustainable agriculture movement in Thailand

Introduction

To many people in the sustainable agriculture movement (SAM) in Thailand, sustainable agriculture is not merely just production methods, but also a way to help reform social relations and humans' relationship with nature. Promoters of sustainable agriculture and green market channels in Thailand adopt different sources of ideas, discourses and practices, so there are often confusions about what sustainable agriculture means and what difference it can make to the mainstream agri-food system.

This chapter provides an in-depth exploration of the SAM which supports the second and third main arguments of the book, which are that although the mainstream agri-food system is dominated by hegemonic capitalist interests, domestic and transnational counter-hegemonic forces can influence some changes in the system even though they are faced with limitations and co-optation of oppositions. This chapter also argues that counter-hegemonic ideas, production–distribution practices, and governance structures of the SAM are all vital integral components of counter-hegemony, and that the Thai SAM can be seen as part of global counter-hegemonic forces in the agri-food system. In addition, this chapter helps to support the fourth main argument of the book, which is that transformations of the agri-food system should be seen as an on-going, non-linear evolutionary process over a long period of time where counter-hegemonic forces may sometimes retain hegemonic elements or be partially co-opted, which suggests that they should continually refine and develop clear counter-hegemonic ideas and practices.

Secondary sources in English and Thai are used in this chapter as well as interviews of 54 people which includes farmers, activists, social entrepreneurs and civil servants. Interviews and site visits for this chapter were based in four provinces in three regions of Thailand where there is a strong SAM presence: Bangkok and metropolitan area (Central), Chiang Mai (North), Surin and Yasothon (Northeast). In particular, the focus is on sustainable farmer groups and producer rice mills in Surin and Yasothon provinces. In Yasothon, these groups include the Naso Rakthammachart group, Bak-rua rice farmer group, Nam-oom enterprise, Kammad sustainable agriculture group, and Thamma-ruamjai moral rice network. In Surin, the focus is on the Rice Fund Surin Organic Agriculture Co-operative and its members, particularly Tamor, Ta-toom, and Taptai groups. A few interviews were also collected from the Mae-ta sustainable agriculture group in Chiang Mai.

This chapter is divided into four main parts. The first three parts discuss the SAM's counter-hegemonic ideas and discourses, production–distribution practices, and governance structures. Part 4 of this chapter then discusses some grey areas between hegemony, counter-hegemony, and co-optation of oppositions which are relevant to the SAM.

Part 1 Counter-hegemonic ideas and discourses

This part of the chapter explores counter-hegemonic ideas and discourses of SAM supporters in Thailand. Section 1.1 discusses these actors' critique of the hegemonic agri-food system while section 1.2 discusses Thai and non-Thai sources of counter-hegemonic inspirations, such as localism, food sovereignty, and natural farming principles. Lastly, section 1.3 discusses main counter-hegemonic ideas and discourses of the SAM in Thailand, as well as attempts to construct the counter-hegemonic identity of farmers.

1.1 The SAM's critique of the mainstream agri-food system

Sustainable agriculture promoters in Thailand generally criticise negative health and environmental consequences of the mainstream agri-food system as well as low nutritional quality of agri-food products produced in this system.[1] Sometimes these criticisms arose from personal experience and observations, such as of farmers' health problems arising from usage of agricultural chemicals.[2] Similar to the critique of the hegemonic agri-food system provided in Chapter 3, many people in the movement are concerned about monopoly and political power of large agri-food businesses and retailers in Thailand and at the global level.[3] Sustainable agriculture supporters in Thailand often criticise what they see as exploitative relations in the agri-food system where farmers lose their control over factors of production and household food security to market forces.[4] Agri-food products under the current hegemonic system are also seen as embodiments of exploitation of small-scale farmers. As Dr Chomchuan Boonrahong, main founder of sustainable agriculture movement based in Chiang Mai described: 'Thai consumers are used to buying cheap agri-food products but these cheap prices are artificial ... and are based on the exploitation of farmers' sweat and labour through monopoly power in the markets'.[5] Changing eating habits in favour of fast food is also seen as having negative effects on local markets, negligence of traditional crops and reductions of biodiversity.[6]

Sustainable agriculture discourses in Thailand frequently involve criticisms of large transnational agri-businesses and their patents of seeds.[7] However, supporters of sustainable agriculture do not simply attribute negative effects of the hegemonic agri-food system to particular companies. Many SAM activists, farmers and a developmental monk explain the problems in conventional agriculture as stemming from the globalised capitalist system, as well as the belief in one-track modernisation and neo-liberalism[8] which allow large transnational Thai and non-Thai capital to exploit the Earth.[9] From Buddhist perspectives, capitalist agriculture is criticised for encouraging farmers to see 'plants merely as products' and select which crop to grow based on monetary gains in robotic and mechanistic manners.[10] Such agri-food production methods are seen as violent,[11] greedy, and as lacking in mercy because farmers do not hesitate to kill pests in their farms by using agricultural chemicals.[12] Moreover, they tend not to be concerned about toxin residues in agri-food products that may harm consumers.[13] Globalised capitalism is also seen as being responsible for hegemonic cultural norms and social relations, such as the 'culture of individualism', which prevent people from forming groups to empower themselves.[14]

The Thai state has also been criticised for its focus on promoting consumerism and the production of cash crops for export and economic growth[15] without much concern for whether small-scale farmers will be in debt or whether prices will plunge downwards due to excessive supply,[16] and also for being bias in favour of large-scale enterprises.[17] Many sustainable farmers who were interviewed also criticise the paddy pledging scheme which, as discussed in the previous chapter, supports conventional rice production and hinders sustainable agriculture. Some sustainable farmers view the scheme as the Thai state's attempt to keep farmers and farmer groups weak[18] and as a method to re-enforce direct patron–client relations between politicians and farmers.[19] Other policies are also criticised for being supportive of problematic production methods, such as policies to provide free agricultural chemicals in some provinces,[20] or are criticised as encouragements for farmers to accumulate debt.[21]

1.2 The SAM's sources of counter-hegemonic ideas

Dissatisfactions with the mainstream agri-food system have led many people to experiment with alternatives and promote sustainable agriculture. Some existing literature have noted that many strands of thoughts such as Buddhism, Christianity, political economy and community culture school, have influenced the SAM in Thailand.[22] This section gives a more comprehensive overview of how the SAM in Thailand has been influenced by many domestic, regional and transnational sources of counter-hegemonic ideas. This helps to suggest that although the movement may seem local and national oriented, it is nevertheless part of global counter-hegemonic forces which try to challenge and transform the hegemonic agri-food system.

The Thai SAM's ideas and discourses are quite similar to those in the progressive and radical trends of global agri-food counter-hegemonic movements. Notably, the progressive trend which supports sustainable and community supported agriculture, as well as the more radical concept of food sovereignty which emphasises democratic control over food resource and redistributive land reforms among other things.[23] Global counter-hegemonic forums such as the

NGO Forum for Food Security in 1996, in Rome, have also produced ideas and concepts that have influenced and helped to legitimise the Thai SAM. Examples include the emphasis on human rights to food, support of decentralised governance structures, and promotion of farmer rights to genetic resources.[24] A manifesto of a sustainable farmer group in Thailand in 2009, for example, utilises similar terms and calls for the state to protect rights of farmers and communities.[25] Global social movements against genetically modified seeds and global social movements' concerns over the WTO's Agreement on Trade-Related Aspects of Intellectual Property Rights (TRIPS) have also influenced counter-hegemonic ideas of the SAM in Thailand.[26] Other sources of ideas include the Occupy movement which inspired the 'Occupy Your Life' manifesto of Mekong Youth Alliance for Organic Agriculture and Agro-ecology that calls on young farmers to reclaim their roles in food production.[27] Thai NGOs (non-governmental organisations) and sustainable farmer groups also exchange ideas with civil society groups in other countries through seminars and other forms of collaborations. Examples include La Vía Campesina (an umbrella body that encompasses more than 120 small-scale farmers' and peasants' organisations in 56 countries),[28] Biodiversity for Sustainable Agriculture Asia, Genetic Resources Action International in Spain,[29] fair trade movements in the US[30] and Europe,[31] as well as organic agriculture movements from countries such as Canada, Germany, Philippines and Bhutan.[32]

Many promoters of sustainable agriculture in Thailand utilise transnational counter-hegemonic ideas and discourses or develop them further. The 'agri-food resource base' concept discussed by some Thai academics, for example, brings to attention the importance of social and natural foundation of agri-food production and distribution which should be locally situated and are based on self-reliance, diversity and democratic participation in agri-food governance structures. The concept was developed from many sources of ideas such as food security and food sovereignty, cultural ecology, and human rights[33] but with some differences: whereas the food sovereignty discourse is perceived as having a focus on small-scale farmers, agri-food resource base discourse emphasises the need for the Thai SAM to build broad cross-class alliances.[34]

Many middle-class Thais also help to shape ideas and strategies of the SAM in Thailand. Examples include public intellectuals and activists such as Rapee Sakrig, Saneh Jamarik, Prawase Wasi, and Rosana Tosritrakul, as well as green entrepreneurs who founded the Green Net Co-operative, Lemon Farm supermarkets,[35] and green urban consumer networks such as the ones spearheaded by Suan-ngern Meema Publishing. Some people from the health and medicine professions also help to promote sustainable agriculture,[36] while some urban-based Thais seek sustainable agricultural lessons from foundations such as Khao Kwan because they want alternatives to office jobs and for ways to live off their own land for the sake of freedom and food security.[37]

Many SAM supporters are inspired by writings of E.F. Schumacher, Buddhist economics, and ideas regarding small-scale technologies.[38] They are also inspired by Ghandi[39] and natural farming principles of Masanobu Fukuoka from

Japan[40] who visited Thailand and inspired many farmers groups such as Naso in Yasothon province in the early 1990s.[41] Fukuoka's principles of natural farming extend beyond agricultural production to a way of life based on Zen Buddhism which received a lot of interests especially among the Thai middle class. Natural farming principles have also inspired the Santi Asoke movement in Thailand which engages in sustainable agricultural production in Buddhist communes.[42] As Part 2 of this chapter elaborates, many sustainable production–distribution practices in Thailand are also inspired by the Japanese Tekei system or community supported agriculture (CSA)[43] and effective micro-organism (EM) soil improvement technology of the Sekai Kyusei Kyo group.[44] The SAM has also been influenced by other social movements in Thailand, such as the left-wing student movement in the 1970s[45] and the environmentalism current of other social movements. At times, people organisations' desire to develop sustainable agriculture in their local areas can be seen as manifestations of their disapproval of negative environmental effects of industrial development projects that they see in their communities or in other communities, such as in Maptaputh, Rayong province.[46]

Another main source of counter-hegemonic ideas regarding alternative development which has significant impact on Thai civil society and the SAM is the community culture or localism school of thought. Main founder of Thai localism or the community culture school of thought, Chatthip Nartsupha, criticises the capitalist way of thinking associated with consumerism that it is lacking in morality and generosity.[47] He suggests that communities are basic foundations of Thai society, argues for an ideal utopian vision of a society based on generosity within and between communities in contrast to individualistic culture, and proposes a model of national development based on self-reliance and dignity which he thinks would correspond to the wishes of the people.[48] Chatthip also rejects the view that there is one path to modernisation or that it is the same as Westernisation, and proposes that Thailand ought to find its own path to modernisation. This is to be done, not through conservative ideals, but through the concept of communities based on generosity where Thailand chooses to embrace only useful aspects of Western modernisation and of other civilisations.[49] Generally speaking, the community culture school of thought can be seen as a strategy to offer a long-term way to integrate everyone into the national and international economy from the bottom up, where communities would build on their own wisdom and resources, but not statically and not in isolation, and with help from modern ideas and technology.[50] The state is seen as an agent of capitalism and oppositions to the state can be done through withdrawal into self-reliance or by endeavouring to change the state's character.[51] As section 1.3 discusses, some of the SAM's counter-hegemonic ideas and discourses, such as the focus on building strong self-help groups at local levels, resemble the community culture's ideas and discourses.

Thai localism is also associated with the concept of sufficiency which has gained more attention after the Asian financial crisis of 1997 and after King Bhumipol's speech of the same year, which urged for a sufficient economy.[52]

Sufficiency ideas have a foundation in Buddhist philosophy of moderation or the Middle Way.[53] Generally, the core of a sufficiency economy is about moderation, reasonableness and self-immunity, where self-immunity is an ability to cope with shocks using knowledge and integrity.[54] Although they are narrowly perceived as being limited to the King's New Theory of agriculture, which emphasises the importance of diversified farms, sufficiency ideas are broad ideas that are supposedly applicable to all levels of the economy.[55] When the concept of sufficiency is applied to economic development, a main concern is to be able to cope with possible negative effects of globalisation.[56] It has also been interpreted as a path towards ecological sustainability.[57] A few people in the SAM who were interviewed for this book discuss how their experience led them to support sufficiency ideas[58] or suggest that sufficiency philosophy is compatible with their visions of sustainable agriculture based on self-reliance, diversified farms and local food security.[59]

Thai localist writings often give the impression that their development ideas are inspired by traditional essence of 'Thai-ness' which infers a sense of nationalistic exclusivity. As Part 4 discusses, this can be interpreted as conservative sentiments, which are anti-globalisation and are not relevant to the future progress of Thailand. However, it should be pointed out that localist ideas in Thailand resonate with ideas of many people and social movements around the world which try to find paths to alternative globalisation. For example, scholars have used counter-hegemonic localist terms and concepts such as 'localization',[60] 'eco-localism',[61] and 'relocalization'[62] to envision alternatives to capitalist globalisation, not to mention that there are many localist movements around the world. Ideas associated with transnational terms such as 'food miles' also support the localism of agri-food production and distribution using environmental reasoning.[63] From this light, localism in Thailand can be seen as more than just isolationist nationalistic ideas and as part of the global counter-hegemonic trend that tries to transform the hegemonic capitalist system from the ground-up, not to mention that many localist-inspired SAM groups strive to make transnational alliances.

Another problem of Thai localism is that sometimes there is a tendency to insist that ideal local communities who govern by co-operation and generosity do (or did) exist in Thailand, rather than to suggest that such ideal is something to strive toward. Similarly, it has been suggested that there has been a conceptualisation of peasant 'communities' in food sovereignty discourse, which suggests that peasant communities embody principles such as co-operation, reciprocity, and egalitarianisms[64] can potentially be problematic. This is because such conceptualisation obscure contradictions within communities such as with regards to inequality, gender and intergenerational relations.[65] Such potential problems should be guarded against, and many localist scholars have come to recognise such problems. For example, as Chapter 6 will discuss in further detail, the conceptualisation of communities in Thailand by Anan Ganjanapan does not insist on the intrinsic and static nature of Thai communities.[66]

1.3 Counter-hegemonic ideas of the SAM

This section elaborates more clearly how the SAM draws on various sources of inspirations to build their own counter-hegemonic ideas regarding alternative agri-food systems. Due to the diversity of people and groups in the SAM in Thailand, this book is cautious not to engage in over-simplication and generalisation of the SAM's counter-hegemonic ideas and discourses. Nevertheless, some unifying goals, values, main ideas and discourses of the SAM can be identified. The following paragraphs discuss the movement's visions of alternative production–distribution channels, supporting counter-hegemonic ideas and discourses, as well as cultural identity struggles to empower small-scale farmers.

As the name suggests, the main unifying goals of the SAM are to promote sustainable agricultural production, more equitable distribution of surpluses through alternative green market arrangements, and to ensure fair economic returns and treatment of producers.[67] As Part 2 discusses in greater detail, some people in the movement prefer larger-scale trade arrangements as a way to promote sustainable agri-food production while some people prefer to promote diversified production, local markets and local food security goals compared to longer-distance trading in bulk or export market channels. However, benefits of multi-level market channels are generally recognised.[68]

There are also differences in SAM supporters' uses of counter-hegemonic terms and discourses. Many groups, such as the BioThai and SATHAI foundations, tend to adopt transnational counter-hegemonic terms such as food security, food sovereignty and farmer rights. However, there are those who prefer terms and discourses which have more local and cultural appeals. Such differences in discourses have strategic values in enabling the movement to appeal to different groups of people in Thailand. However, depending on the audience, uses of certain terms can create misperceptions and alienate some people from the SAM. A few social critics, for example, are quick to rail against sustainable farmers who advocate simple self-reliant lifestyles or use Buddhist concepts in their discourses.[69] Despite different ideas and adoption of counter-hegemonic terms, what people in the movement generally agree on is the importance of sustainable agricultural production, supportive and fair market channels, as well as the promotion of partnership producer-consumer social relations and collaboration with other groups in society.

Promoters of sustainable agriculture in Thailand have used their criticisms of the current system, discussed in section 1.1, as a basis to legitimise their counter-hegemonic ideas and discourses. The term 'self-reliance', for example, is promoted as a counter-hegemonic concept to challenge farmers' over-dependence on conventional market relations and large agri-businesses. Self-reliance can be achieved through, for example, practices such as biodiversity preservation, diversified agro-ecological production methods, fair markets,[70] and seed saving.[71] As a response to the commodification of agri-food resources under the capitalist agri-food system,[72] some supporters of sustainable agriculture have appealed to traditional Thai beliefs, culture and non-price aspects of agri-food products to aid their counter-hegemonic discourses and the building of producer-consumer relations. For example, Decha Siripat insists that for Thai people 'rice is a core of life, not just food' because it embodies culture, a belief system and ecological balance which have been developed through many generations.[73] Others also try to promote nutritious and preventive medicinal values of agri-food products.[74]

Discourses which portray farmer consciousness under the hegemonic agri-food system as being greedy and lacking in mercy[75] have also been used as negative contrasts to the main values of sustainable agriculture which are seen as compatible with Buddhist virtues such as generosity.[76] It has been suggested that farmers can practice Buddhist teachings or Dhamma in their everyday lives through sustainable agricultural practices because, for example, they refrain from killing other living beings by using pesticides.[77] The Thamma-ruamjai moral rice network discusses in Part 2, for example, embedded Buddhist teachings in their sustainable agricultural practices.[78] In a related manner, some SAM supporters see sustainable agriculture as a way to cultivate new consciousness,[79] to challenge the hegemonic capitalist system and patron–client relations,[80] to give individuals a sense of peacefulness,[81] freedom and independence,[82] as well as to transform society towards a better one that is based on sharing and environmental sustainability.[83] Some sympathisers of agro-ecology in other countries similarly perceive agro-ecology not only as technical production techniques, but also as being related to counter-hegemonic social transformations.[84]

The SAM in Thailand also engages in cultural identity struggles where counter-hegemonic images of agriculture and of small-scale farmers are reconstructed to raise the latter's negotiating power and importance. Farming is generally perceived as a low-income profession in Thailand, and younger generations of Thais who were born in agricultural households tend to seek employment opportunities in other sectors of the economy in the hope of higher wages, partially resulting in a higher average age of Thai farmers and a lack of farm labourers.[85] Coupling this with Sakdina mentality, these reasons help to explain rather widespread condescending attitudes toward agriculture and farming as a profession in Thai society, which concerns the SAM. Rural households in Thailand are also generally having what some call 'hybrid livelihoods' where they divide their time between farm and non-farm activities.[86]

The SAM recognises the importance of the agricultural sector beyond monetary contributions and is generally concerned about food security and the disintegration of social structures in rural communities. Some SAM supporters also argued that if farmers are not confident of themselves, it will be difficult for them to empower themselves and seek alternatives.[87] To challenge condescending attitudes, the SAM tries to create counter-hegemonic images of agriculture and farmers, arguing that the knowledge-intensive nature, as well as the social and environmental benefits of sustainable agriculture, can help to rejuvenate the agricultural sector and give farmers back their dignity.[88] The preservation and development of local traditional rice strands by farmers[89] as well as the term 'local sage', which describes successful sustainable farmers who can pass on their production knowledge to other farmers, for example, are used to establish a new cultural identity that commands respect and dignity for these farmers, which further supports SAM's cause.[90] Some people in the Thai middle and upper class, including urban farmers and white-collar workers, also help to promote the counter-hegemonic identity of farmers.[91] In a way, middle class support of sustainable agriculture can also be seen as a rejection of mainstream middle-class identity associated with materialism and consumerism because embracing the identity associated with sustainable agriculture infers free, independent and self-reliant livelihoods.[92]

Some people who believe that development occurs through stages might tend to look down on agriculture while seeing industrialisation and the service sector as higher forms of development. However, aside from food security and other benefits, SAM supporters point out that the agricultural sector has proven to help alleviate economic problems in times of economic crisis.[93] Agriculture and rural households in Thailand acted as social safety nets for migrated labour forces after the Asian economic crisis of 1997 where a lot of Thai workers who had been laid off returned to their original or familial homes in rural areas.[94] Following the 2008 global financial crisis, a dry-season survey in 2009 by the National Statistical Office found that 74 per cent of the most recently migrated rural migrants was to return home.[95] Moreover, sometimes those who work in the cities or other sectors of the economy find it necessary to send their children to live in the family farms.[96] In these cases, the agricultural sector seems to be subsidising labour reproduction and the reserve army of labour. Aside from typical seasonal migrants, when agricultural prices are high, some migrants (such as taxi drivers) also return to their rural family farms to help with agricultural production.[97]

There are also other reasons why some people want to choose farming as a profession despite occupational difficulties. Many farmers interviewed for this book suggest that sometimes, over a certain age (around 45 years or higher), low-skilled migrant labourers would like to return to rural areas and agriculture because their work in the industrial and service sectors were becoming detrimental to their health or because it was getting difficult to gain employment.[98] Some people also suggest they prefer farming as a profession because they feel that they have more freedom and that it is important in terms of maintaining healthy family ties.[99] Therefore, helping to rejuvenate the agricultural sector through sustainable agriculture could help increase their life options.

The SAM generally believes in incremental changes over time through dissemination of counter-hegemonic ideas and values that would not only challenge hegemonic agri-food ideas but also transform identities, social relations and informal norms. Some SAM supporters also point out the importance of promoting value changes, to alter the patterns of food consumption, in favour of sustainable and fair agri-food products,[100] and that a paradigm shift towards sustainable agriculture is not merely a technical issue because it requires a social transformation based on understanding and collaboration between producers and consumers.[101] The movement tries to promote counter-hegemonic ideas through many channels such as books, newspaper articles, television programmes, public seminars, and by holding public events with invited speakers from sustainable agriculture movements in other countries.[102] Thammasat University and Sukothai Thammathirat Open University have also opened sustainable agriculture courses.[103] Local attempts to spread counter-hegemonic ideas include, for example, the Thamma-ruamjai moral rice network's local radio station which covers areas in five provinces (estimated audience of around 20,000 people).[104] Nevertheless, it is not always easy to promote counter-hegemonic ideas. Middle-class forces in the SAM are sometimes ridiculed or seen as hypocritical while sustainable farmers are often mocked or seen as crazy by other farmers in their areas.[105] SAM activists have even compared weaning farmers off of agricultural chemicals to that of weaning off an addiction.[106] It is also important to point out, however, that counter-hegemonic ideas discussed in this part of the chapter are not problem-free as there are different interpretations and corresponding practices which allow room for co-optation of oppositions, as Part 4 discusses in greater detail.

Part 2 Counter-hegemonic production–distribution practices

There are some misperceptions about sustainable agricultural production–distribution in Thailand; that it infers reverting to traditional production methods without the use of modern technologies and that sustainable agricultural products are only meant for high-income consumers and niche export markets. As this part of the chapter discusses, sustainable agricultural production is knowledge intensive and there are many forms of production, processing and distribution channels of sustainable agri-food products. Section 2.1 discusses sustainable agricultural production while section 2.2 discusses the processing and retailing of sustainable agri-food products in Thailand. Section 2.3 then focuses on producer rice mills and sustainable farmer groups in Surin and Yasothon. Lastly, section 2.4 evaluates counter-hegemonic potential and the current problems of sustainable agricultural practices in Thailand. It should be noted that the realms of counter-hegemonic ideas and practice are not mutually exclusive. On the contrary, they seem to have evolved together as counter-hegemonic forces accumulate their experience. For example, successful sustainable farms reaffirm farmers' beliefs in agro-ecology based on sharing and natural balance.

2.1 Sustainable agricultural production in Thailand

In Thailand, notable promoters of sustainable agricultural production include those in the Alternative Agriculture Network (AAN) which was formed as a loose network in 1989 by NGOs and small-scale farmers. By 1997, the AAN consisted of 84 member organisations.[107] An important regional AAN group is the AAN of the Northeast which includes 40 farmer organisations in 14 provinces.[108] Main founders of the AAN include, for example, Mr Witoon Lienchamroon of the BioThai Foundation in Nonthaburi, Mrs Supha Yaimuang of the Sustainable

Agriculture Foundation (SATHAI) in Nonthaburi, Mr Decha Siripat of Khao Kwan Foundation in Suphanburi, Dr Chomchuan Boonrahong, who was former director of the Institute for a Sustainable Agriculture Community (ISAC) in Chiang Mai, and the Community of Agro-ecology Foundation (CAE) in Surin. The AAN promotes different forms of sustainable agriculture in Thailand, such as organic, agro-forestry, natural and integrated farming.[109] Most organic products in Thailand are primary products, such as rice, vegetables and fruits.[110] Aside from the AAN, there are also other individuals and groups in Thailand that promote sustainable agriculture in their own ways, such as the Santi Asoke movement.[111]

Sustainable agricultural production in Thailand is concerned with the restoration and preservation of the ecological and environmental balance, as well as fair economic and social returns that increase the quality of life of farmers, consumers, and local social institutions.[112] Generally speaking, sustainable agricultural production is interpreted as methods which preserve and encourage biodiversity and varieties of agri-food crops in farms. It is also seen as a way to reduce economic and food insecurity risks for small-scale farmers as they can rely on sales (and personal consumption) of a few crops instead of just one. In this sense, sustainable agricultural practices in Thailand challenge hegemonic commodification of agri-food resources, as well as the conventional profit-led agri-food system discussed in Chapter 3.

Many sustainable agriculture practitioners were inspired by some traditional methods of diversified farming such as fish farming in paddy fields and the use of ecological balance to control predators and parasital insects.[113] Some notable sustainable farmers (or 'local sage') who have developed successful techniques include Mahayoo Sunthornchai in Surin province who started to develop his diversified farming techniques in 1973[114] and Mr Tool Sayamol who developed agro-forestry techniques.[115] Although sustainable agricultural practices in Thailand have developed before the popularisation of the King's sufficiency economy ideas and his New Theory of Agriculture, following the 1997 Asian economic crisis,[116] there are also those who were inspired by the New Theory, such as the one rai-100,000 baht training group. [117]

As discussed in Part 1, farmers' control over seeds is seen as part of farmer rights, independence, and counter-hegemonic identity. Preservation and development of traditional seeds can also be seen as a challenge to commodification of seeds and agri-food products because nutritional quality and local tastes are given a priority, whereas the hegemonic agri-food system tends to encourage the development of chemical-responsive rice seeds with short harvest time. Many SAM groups are inspired by traditional practices of free seed exchanges which encourage biodiversity and counteract monopoly control over seeds. Some also promote production practices where different types of seeds are planted so that the products can be harvested at different times to reduce risks from drastic weather changes due to global warming[118] and to reduce labour costs.[119] Notable groups engaging in seed saving and development in Thailand include, for example, Khao Kwan Foundation, Tamor natural farmer group in Surin,[120] and

Kammad sustainable agriculture group in Yasothon where there are 12 core households which have developed over 15 traditional strands with help from academics from the Rice Center at Ubonratchathani province.[121] Aside from seeds, soil is also treated with respect and not as a static container of elements, but as a place containing interacting living micro-organisms.[122] There is a wide-spread usage of the effective micro-organism (EM) soil improvement technology among SAM supporters,[123] such as by Mr Kittithanet Rangkaworaset of the one rai-100,000 baht training project[124] and Mr Suchit Nokham of the Maeping Organic Company in Chiang Mai whose experimentation with probiotic micro-organisms in his own farm since 1992 has enabled him to diversify production to include many organic agri-food products.[125]

Sustainable farmer groups in Thailand have developed varieties of techniques and production patterns to suit different local contexts. For example, the Mae-ta sustainable agriculture group in Chiang Mai is located near well-preserved forest areas so they use agro-forestry techniques as well as knowledge of micro-organisms in their organic farms.[126] For the Taptai group in Surin province, where members tend to have small farm areas, members are encouraged to diver-sity their production from rice to organic pork to make use of small plots of land, as advised by a lecturer at Ratchamongkol Esaan University of Technology, Surin.[127] In urban areas, there is a growing movement of low income consumers, supported by the Thai Health Promotion Foundation and SATHAI's urban agri-culture projects, who grow their own pesticide-free vegetables for health and economic reasons since the early 2010s.[128] It should be noted, however, that although a lot of emphasis of the SAM is on helping small-scale farmers, many SAM members do not only support small sustainable farms and are open to other forms of production arrangement, such as organic farming arrangements organ-ised by Khao Kwan Foundation which is discussed in Part 3.[129]

2.2 Processing and retailing of sustainable agri-food products

Promoters of sustainable agriculture in Thailand tend to recognise that it is insuffi-cient to only promote sustainable agricultural production and that there should also be complementary development of sustainable agri-food processing, as well as multi-level market channels (local, national and international) which respond to different production volumes and help to diversify sales opportunities. This is to help producers to earn higher income from sustainable premiums and to capture value-added from moving up along agri-food chains.[130] Well-developed processing and market channels which help to guarantee short- and medium-term sources of income for producers, with premium prices for producing sustainable products, are seen as crucial incentives for producers to make transitions towards sustainable agri-food production. Some have also emphasised, however, that sustainable pro-duction should lead the market and not the other way round. This means that altern-ative markets should accommodate agro-ecological practices, such as, by supporting sales of seasonal agri-food products, usage of environmentally friendly packaging, and also try to limit distribution radius as much as possible.[131]

In the late 1980s, some NGOs and academics in Thailand started to promote processing and marketing activities of sustainable agri-food products,[132] but there were a lot of difficulties due to the lack of interests from domestic consumers.[133] In the mid-1990s, civil society groups such as the Green Net Co-operative, Puan-thammachart group, Asoke group, and Imboon Center in Chiang Mai (established in 1994) managed to expand the number of green shops and consumer interests in Thailand. Such expansion was made possible by health concerns prevalent among Thai middle-class consumers.[134] This suggests that consumer support is crucial and that it is important to promote counter-hegemonic ideas in wider society to aid counter-hegemonic practices. By 1996, there were around 33 green shops in many big cities such as Bangkok (18 shops), Chiang Mai and Songkla.[135] A lot of green shops closed down after the Asian economic crisis of 1997 but the movement did not die off completely. By the early 2000s, modern trade players in the organic market became prominent, such as, Lemon Farm supermarkets.[136]

There are those who believe in the benefits of large-scale distribution of sustainable agri-food products. For example, Mr Witoon Panyakul, one of the founders of the Green Net Co-operative in Thailand (established in 1993), argues for the importance of having centralised bodies to professionally manage logistics and distribution of agri-food products in a large scale.[137] Green Net is a member of the Fairtrade Labeling Organization International (FLO) and exports to many European countries. With its sister Earth Net Foundation, Green Net helps to promote the expansion of organic production in Thailand, such as in Yasothon province, and acts as a distribution centre of many organic products in Thailand and abroad.[138] On the other hand, some main figures in the AAN prefer developing local markets and more direct forms of marketing channels, as well as to encourage smaller-scale farmer groups to produce different varieties of agri-food products and move up along agri-food chains.[139] Notable local green markets in Thailand include the ones in Chiang Mai, Surin and Yasothon provinces, but there are also green alternative markets in other provinces such as Chachoeng-sao and Bangkok.

In Surin, the main green market began to operate in 2003. In the early 2010s, there were around 65 to 70 sellers of various products, such as, rice, vegetables, fish and organic pork.[140] Organic farm visits are often organised and are seen as opportunities for consumers to learn more about production costs, process, and quality of organic agriculture.[141] Active participants in the market include those from the Taptai community in Surin. With quite secured market channels, the group is able to purchase organic pork from members at 50 per cent higher prices than in conventional markets, and also has a long-term plan to invest in small-scale industrial machineries to produce other organic pork products and develop their own brand.[142] There are also smaller green markets in Surin and also in Yasothon, which started to become more popular in the 2000s because of growing consumer support of organic products.[143] In Chiang Mai, aside from green local markets, such as the JJ Organic Market, the Mae-ta sustainable agriculture group also engages in Community Support Agriculture (CSA) with a direct selling of pre-paid vegetable boxes to around 16 to 50 consumer households (depending on the season).[144] Counter-hegemonic market governance structures are discussed in greater detail in Part 3.

2.3 Producer rice mills and sustainable farmer groups in Surin and Yasothon

Producer rice mills in Surin and Yasothon provide interesting examples of counter-hegemony in the agri-food system because they are widely networked and established groups, with a long history of learning from experience, which allows them to develop different varieties of practical counter-hegemonic alternatives. First, this section discusses relatively large-scale producer rice mills and sustainable production of their member groups. These rice mills include Rice Fund Surin Organic Agriculture Cooperative in Surin province, as well as rice mills of the Naso Rakthammachart group, Bak-rua organic farmer group, and Nam-om community enterprise in Yasothon province. To give a fuller picture, smaller-scale producer rice mills with distinct characteristics are also discussed, namely Kammad Sustainable Agriculture group and Thamma-ruamjai moral rice network in Yasothon.

Alternative agriculture movements in Surin and Yasothon started in the 1980s. In 1995, the AAN of the Northeast was formed to promote production, processing, and marketing of sustainable agri-food products, as well as to create venues for member groups to exchange their ideas and knowledge.[145] Farmer founders in many groups became interested in alternative agriculture because they experienced unfair trading practices and felt exploited by middlemen and rice mills due to the lack of bargaining power. In addition, they had also observed negative health and environmental effects of Green Revolution agricultural methods.[146] Founders of Naso Rakthammachart group, for example, were inspired to find alternatives to the mainstream agricultural production after seeing a large number of fish had died in the paddy field due to agricultural chemicals. Moreover, they also experienced rising costs of production while paddy prices, determined by powerful middlemen and rice mills, seemed to stagnate.[147] Such instances ignite many people's interests in herbal medications and sustainable agriculture.[148] They were also inspired by Fukuoka's visit and his ideas of natural farming, and developed their own techniques further to suit local conditions.[149]

In Surin, the Farmer Rice Seller Network was formed in 1987 to collect paddy in bulk from Sahatham for Development, Ta-toom Natural Agriculture, and Surin Natural Agriculture groups. It was hoped that this would increase market power of farmers in relation to rice mills and middlemen. The network received support from many groups and people such as NGOs, Green Net Cooperative, Saneh Jamarik,[150] as well as Luang-po Naan – a monk from Tasawang temple, who helped to raise funds from the locals and state development programmes to build a producer-controlled rice mill. Through a Swiss NGO, the network started to export pesticide-free rice to European and fair trade markets for the first time in the early 1990s.[151] In 2002, it received funding from the state-funded pilot programme (discussed in Part 3) to build a 24-ton per day capacity rice mill and to build a warehouse that could hold 500 tons of rice. In 2003, the rice mill was registered as a co-operative with smaller producer groups named according to the areas such as Tamor, Ta-toom, and Taptai.[152] In 2012, the Rice Fund Surin Organic Agriculture Co-operative had 250 out of 326 members who passed organic certification.[153] Since 2005, it was certified a Fairtrade producer group by FLO[154] and took over marketing activities from Green Net Co-operative.[155] In 2012, the Surin rice mill sold its rice through its retail store in Surin ('Khao-hom') and directly to consumers in Bangkok (around 40 per cent), while the rest was exported to France, the US, the UK and Australia (around 60 per cent).[156]

In Yasothon, Naso Rakthammachart and Bak-rua groups seem to have some similar experiences in the building up of their counter-hegemonic ideas and practices. Naso group thought that members' economic situations would improve if they could bypass middlemen by having their own rice mill to process and sell their own rice.[157] Between 1991 and 1993, the group lobbied for a budget from the state to build their own producer rice mill and encouraged other farmer groups in the province to do the same.[158] Similar to the case of Naso, some farmers in Bak-rua community started to form a group in 1976 to increase their bargaining power in relation to paddy middlemen.[159] In 1994, Bak-rua group managed to use community savings and provincial budget to build a community rice mill.[160] In 2012, Naso rice mill had 243 members and milled around 650 to 700 tons of rice (conventional and organic) per year.[161] Bak-rua rice mill also had around 200 members and milled 600 tons of rice per year (400 out of 600 tons were organic rice).[162] Both Bak-rua and Naso producer rice mills export their organic and fair trade rice through Green Net Co-operative since the mid-1990s. Naso also sells directly to consumers in local and urban areas through many brands, shops and Yasothon local markets.[163] It also tries to establish linkages with other co-operatives, such as a fruit-selling co-operative in Jantaburi province, as well as socially conscious companies and organisations in Thailand, which purchase rice from the group.[164] Both Naso and Bak-rua require members to invest some shares in the rice mills. In return, members will receive dividends. In addition, both groups have community saving banks which help with the rice mills' cash flow, especially with paddy payment.[165] There are also collaborations between community rice mills in Yasothon with regards to cash flow, price setting, and to develop other rice products such as rice bran capsules.[166]

A relatively newer Nam-oom sustainable farming group in Yasothon was established around 1999 and was aided by an academic, Dr Seri Phongpit, who helped to facilitate discussions between 12 villages regarding problems facing farmers. The discussions encouraged many people, including village leaders, to turn to organic rice production as a partial solution.[167] The group registered as a community enterprise in 2008 and received some funding from the Bank of Agriculture and Agricultural Co-operative (BAAC) to expand their rice mill capacity. The number of members has grown from 100 to 538 people by 2012.[168] The enterprise exports organic rice to fair trade and organic markets in Europe with the help of the Aden company. By 2012, the mill processed over 700 to 800 tons of rice a year on average.[169] The enterprise is managed by a 15-member committee and also has a profit sharing scheme according to members' shares in the enterprise.[170] Nam-oom community enterprise, as well as Naso and Bak-rua community rice mills, are usually considered 'success' cases of community rice mills in Thailand but as section 2.4 discusses in detail, such success is based on certain conditions that might not be available to other groups. In addition, the rice mills sometimes face financial and management problems as well as other limitations.

Kammad and the moral rice network are relatively newer producer rice mill groups in Yasothon, which learned from the development experience of older groups and adapted their practices to suit their particular conditions. Kammad group, for example, branched out from Naso in 2010 even though some members still sell some paddy to Naso rice mill. This is because most of the land in that area (around 6,000 rai[171] in 4 Tambol) falls under the jurisdiction of the Agricultural Land Reform Office (ALRO) so members could receive some support from ALRO. The group also receives help from some academics and some companies' corporate social responsibility projects. By 2012, the group had around 100 organic farmer members in total.[172] One distinctive feature of the group is that they focus on producing traditional rice strands and direct domestic sales, such as to individuals and restaurants. The group preserves over 100 strands of traditional rice and 12 households produce organic rice seeds.[173]

Kammad members reflected on their experience during the pilot programme (discussed in Part 3) and concluded that to reduce risks and costs they should shorten management chains. In addition, since Kammad is a relatively small group, members prefer using a decentralised management system where there is no centralised space to hold the paddy. Instead, members hold paddy in their own barns. When there are orders from consumers, paddy is milled at the central mill and then directly transported to the consumers. One main benefit of such an arrangement is that the group does not have to borrow from banks to purchase paddy, and hence does not have to pay interest rates.[174] Similarly, Thammaruamjai moral rice network in Yasothon has a central headquarters which relies on small-scale rice mills in different communities to reduce costs. In 2012, the group had nine small rice mills and were going to build another 12 mills to service 20 of their centres. Meetings are held to plan organic rice production according to consumer demands, and the headquarters also checks the quality of rice before distribution.[175] Some members also engage in the preservation and development of traditional rice strands with the aim to provide good quality, inexpensive, and nutritious organic rice for domestic consumers rather than to export.[176]

Most organic farmers interviewed in Yasothon tend to employ secular terms and discourses to describe their counter-hegemonic ideas and practices. However, as the name suggests, those in the moral rice network explicitly adopt Buddhist ideas and incorporate them in their sustainable agricultural practices. In 2006, the groups' farmer manifesto was written to set some guidelines of how members would agree to adopt some moral standards such as to give up on liquor, smoking and gambling. In 2006, around 100 people joined the group, but only 38 people passed both organic and morality standards. By 2012, there were around 100 members who met the standards.[177] The group has established 16 learning centres in the area to promote sustainable agricultural production and facilitate knowledge-sharing[178] as well as 16 saving funds in the area.[179] Monks from Thamma-ruamjai temple also help to promote morality standards while the groups' radio station helped to promote their ideas and sustainable agricultural knowledge in Yasothon and nearby provinces.[180]

The moral rice network also collaborated with researchers from the Institute of Co-operative study at Kasetsart University in Nonthaburi which had helped the group with setting-up capital and retail channels. Burapha television company also helped by establishing a consumer network which pre-orders organic rice to help producers with production planning and cash flow situation.[181] In 2009, the Moral rice group managed to set their organic rice price higher than the prices of organic jasmine rice in the same area by 25 per cent.[182] In 2012, the group also started to search for other distribution channels such as through postal service and other forms of direct sales.[183]

2.4 Counter-hegemonic potential of sustainable agri-food practices

This section explores the counter-hegemonic potential of sustainable agri-food production–distribution practices and producer rice mills discussed in the previous sections. First, some evidence of viability and benefits of sustainable agri-food practices are discussed, followed by a discussion of current limitations of sustainable agri-food practices.

Evidence in support of counter-hegemonic potential

There is evidence to suggest that sustainable agri-food practices, if properly managed and implemented under supportive conditions, can yield many material and non-material benefits. Sustainable agriculture activists and farmers suggest that sustainable agricultural production leads to lower costs of production and similar levels of yield as conventional production,[184] especially after a few transitional years.[185] Many individual success stories where sustainable farmers managed to raise their quality of life are used to back up these arguments.[186] In many cases, the costs of organic production can roughly be the same as conventional production due to higher labour costs.[187] A study of the harvest year 2005/2006 of 80 farmers in Surin, for example, suggests the organic jasmine rice farming can help to improve economic situations of farmers because of a higher yield (an average of 411 compared to 379kg. per rai) and higher price (around 10 compared to 7 or 8 baht per kg.) while the costs of production are roughly the same (2,662 baht per rai for organic compare to 2,619 baht per rai for conventional production).[188] Another study in 2009 of 80 people in five producer groups in Chiang Mai, who grow products such as longan and rice also suggests that organic farmers in the transitional period received a higher level of income per year on average compared to conventional farmers.[189]

Interviews of sustainable farmers in Surin and Yasothon also suggest that the average organic rice paddy yield is comparable to that of conventional production. Farmer members of Tamor and Ta-toom in Surin reported their average yield to be between 350 and 500 kg. per rai, which is similar to the conventional yield in the same region.[190]Average rice paddy yield in other parts of the country, such as in the Central plain, tends to be higher due to better irrigation and soil quality. In Chiang Mai, Maeping Organic Company's rice paddy fields reportedly produce an average yield of 600 kg per rai.[191] For those who sell their products through organic and fair trade channels in Yasothon and Surin, a study in 2011 of around 145 households suggests that they had significantly lower costs of production for organic rice paddy (a difference of around 7,600 baht per ton of paddy), and hence net profit for sustainable farmers (revenue minus production and marketing costs) was 5,533 baht per ton of paddy on average, while conventional farmers in the same areas loses an average of 2,293 baht per ton of paddy (–2,293).[192] Sustainable farmers also received additional benefits from a wider range of agri-food products and from fair trade premiums,[193] not to mention that the diversity of output throughout the year can also help to reduce production risks and costs of living.[194]

One main difference between conventional and sustainable agricultural practices is how sustainable producers have opportunities to increase their bargaining power in the market and embed values in their agri-food products. For example, Mr Thamma Sangkalee of Ta-toom Natural Farmer group in Surin suggests that when farmers grow cash crops they lack power to influence prices but with sustainable agri-food products and alternative market channels, farmers have more say in price setting.[195] Kammad group also wants to be able to discuss with consumers the setting of fair prices, and chooses to deal with consumers they can discuss the setting of fair prices with and understand the value of their work.[196] By selling through socially conscious enterprises such as Green Net Co-operative, members of Naso Rakthammachart group can discuss their production problems and participate in price setting which give them more power compared to selling through conventional business channels.[197] Similarly, at the Surin rice mill, members can participate in paddy measuring and other activities which makes the paddy selling process more transparent compared to some private rice mills.[198] In addition, multi-channel alternative markets provide more options for producers.[199] For example, farmers in Yasothon and Surin can be members of more than one group and can sell their organic rice directly to consumers in green markets or to the rice mills.[200]

Alternative green markets have also been credited as positive forces for job creations and as important additional sources of income. For example, CSA and green market initiatives in Chiang Mai create jobs for young people in Mae-ta community.[201] Individual situations differ, but many Naso farmers who sell their produce at the Yasothon local green market receive around 10,000 to 20,000 baht per month,[202] while some farmers from the Taptai group reportedly earn

100,000 baht per person per year from the local green market in Surin.[203] For Taptai, income from the local green market is comparable to that which is gained from selling organic and fair trade rice. In addition, drought could reduce a person's earning from organic rice to 50,000 baht per year[204] which suggests that selling diversified products through local green markets help to reduce economic risks. The earnings from local green markets are not insignificant, considering that in 2011 the average monthly income per household in the Northeast was 18,217 baht per month.[205] A farm operator household in the Northeast earned around 14,300 to 14,400 baht per month (excluding those in forestry and fishery activities), while farm workers earned 9,437 baht per month of monetary income.[206] Taptai group's plan to produce other organic pork products[207] and Nam-oom enterprise's plan to encourage younger members to learn English to help with marketing[208] are also examples of how sustainable agri-food production –distribution channels could be used to create jobs. Moreover, NGO activists point to the benefits of local markets in fostering interactions and understanding between consumers and producers.[209]

Some discussions and evaluations of sustainable agriculture in Thailand only focus on a few aspects, such as monetary returns, costs of production, and yield. However, since the SAM's goals and values extend beyond these issues and cover other non-material aspects of life, it is important to evaluate sustainable agri-food practices on these criteria, as well. Aside from monetary rewards, it has been noted that sustainable agriculture has many positive benefits, such as in terms of local food security from diversified farming methods,[210] improved health conditions, and social ties.[211] Some farmers who used to work as low-skilled labourers and faced health problems, for example, suggest that green markets and organic farming in Surin gave them options not to have to continue working as low-skilled labourers.[212] Sustainable farmer groups can also create positive externalities which benefit not only their members but local communities. Aside from providing production support, some producer rice mills such as Bak-rua and Naso provide welfare benefits and monetary aids to their members and local communities.[213] For example, Naso uses some of its earning from the fair trade premium to fund farmers who are making transitions toward organic agriculture, and also contribute to the natural disaster relief fund.[214]

Some promoters of sustainable agriculture suggest that for a farming household to successfully make a transition to sustainable agriculture, it is important to provide sustainable agriculture training for both men and women in the household.[215] Moreover, it has been noted that women are particularly active in the marketing and processing of sustainable agri-food products.[216] An average female seller in Chiang Mai green market, for instance, could earn an income of 15,000 baht per month.[217] Women also managed to gain leadership positions in many organisations such as in Naso, Bak-rua, and Surin producer rice mills,[218] as well as in Baan Taptai organic farmer group and Baan Tanon organic herb and vegetable processing group in Surin.[219] Nevertheless, at other sustainable agriculture groups leaders were mostly men.

Current problems and counter-hegemonic limitations

Despite some progress, sustainable agricultural development in Thailand is still very limited from a national perspective. In 2012, the share of organic farmland in total agricultural land in Thailand was estimated to be only around 0.2 per cent.[220] In a well-known organic rice production area such as Surin, it is estimated that organic agricultural practices constitute only 1 per cent of all agricultural activities in the province.[221] The following paragraphs explore some important problems associated with sustainable agri-food production, processing and marketing channels which limit their counter-hegemonic potential. In sum, problems include how farmers can be deterred from changing their production methods to sustainable agriculture because of the knowledge-intensive nature of sustainable production, as well as many technical problems they will face in the first few years which can lower their income. Migration to urban areas and the lack of farm labourers also contribute to high costs of production. The problems are also connected to the governance structures of sustainable agri-food products. As Part 3 discusses, the costs of certification of sustainable agri-food products can alienate some farmers and also add significant costs to producer groups.

In the first few transitional years toward sustainable agriculture, there can be many technical problems and yield will tend to drop before soil quality improves.[222] Some farmers who are deeply convinced of the benefits of creating sustainable agri-food alternatives will accept such risks and persevere, but most farmers are motivated by short- and medium-term monetary gains due to necessity. Since sustainable agriculture requires a lot of time and labour to change the whole production system, farmers tend to back out when they start to face serious obstacles.[223] It has also been suggested that in local Surin/Khmer culture, some farmers care a lot about 'losing face' if their rice or paddy fields are not as physically pleasing as other farmers', which deters them from organic rice farming.[224]

Difficulties in changing the production system to a more sustainable one can also be attributed to the lack of agro-ecological knowledge and research in Thailand. There are very few academic courses which teach sustainable agricultural practices.[225] Contrary to some mainstream perceptions that sustainable agriculture means 'doing nothing' to the farm or simply just applying some standard techniques and organic fertilisers, many people in the movement point to the need to develop new and more extensive knowledge of agro-ecology which meet distinct needs of different areas.[226] For example, some farmers think that applying home-made organic fertilisers are sufficient to improve soil, but such practice can be improved by using laboratory analyses and other types of technology to develop probiotic micro-organisms in the soil.[227] In addition, many practitioners suggest that research in universities should be more relevant to real farming conditions and should perhaps be in joint-cooperation with farmers.[228] As Part 3 discusses, there is no comprehensive national plan to encourage research in sustainable agricultural methods in Thailand, although a few state offices provide some support.

The lack of farm labourers in the agricultural sector also affects the expansion of sustainable agricultural production because it tends to require more effort compared to conventional production. The problem is partly accrued to the growing average age of farmers and migration of younger generations, previously discussed, which add significantly to the costs of sustainable agricultural production.[229] Some have argued that agro-ecological production and diversified farms, where different varieties of crops aid each other's growth, can help reduce labour requirement and costs.[230] Kammad group also tries to promote interests in organic agri-food production among the younger generation, such as, by working with local schools to open organic agriculture courses.[231]

Owing to limited expansion of agri-food production and other production problems, sustainable agri-food processing industry in Thailand is not well-developed. It has been argued that certain scales need to be reached for efficiency[232] and there are still few processed organic agri-food products in Thailand due to insufficient and inconsistent supply.[233] Part 3 discusses in greater detail how some forms of pre-arranged planning and co-operation between producers, processors, and retailers, whether through formal contract or informal long-term social relations based on trusts, are important to develop value-added agri-food products in larger scales. Without such arrangements, farmers might be more reluctant to expand their production. On the other hand, if organic farmers suddenly refuse to sell to green retail shops because short-term prices in the conventional market are exceptionally high, it will damage the retailers.[234]

Aside from sustainability certifications, retailers and consumers in domestic and international markets also tend to impose physical appearance standards on agri-food products and their packaging[235] which can be rather unrealistic at times. When coupled with contract farming arrangements, unrealistic physical standards can negatively affect sustainable agricultural production. For example, it has been suggested that some organic contract farmers in the Northern part of Thailand face strict appearance standards in addition to organic standards, which causes many producers to lose profits because when they could not pass the appearance standards, so they received much lower prices. Because of this, many farmers were discouraged from producing in a larger scale and decided to grow organic vegetables only for their own consumption or for local markets.[236] Nevertheless, there seems to be some retailers which form long-term relations with producer groups, such as Lemon Farm, and try to be flexible with regards to physical appearances of agri-food products. In addition, due to the unpredictability of the weather and production conditions, sometimes Lemon Farm purchases more than it initially planned to so as to help reduce economic problems of producers that they have long-term relations with.[237] Part 3 discusses in greater detail the importance of social relations as a form of informal counter-hegemonic agri-food governance, while Part 4 discusses problems with retailers that sell organic agri-food products but do not necessarily share counter-hegemonic ideas and goals of the SAM.

There are also some mainstream hegemonic perceptions on the side of consumers which provide obstacles to the expansion of sustainable agriculture. Due to globalised consumption patterns, urban consumers in Thailand tend to prefer cold-climate vegetables, such as broccoli, which can be problematic for producer groups because they do not have control over these seeds, and local farm conditions might not be suitable.[238] Some of these vegetables also require a lot of water to produce which makes them risky choices for producers, given erratic weather patterns due to climate change.[239] Moreover, it has been suggested by green retailers that Thai consumers generally are accustomed to cheap food and are not willing to pay for organic products which have higher prices due to sustainability premiums.[240] Nevertheless, consistent promotion of counter-hegemonic ideas (discussed in Part 1) and exchanges of ideas through producer-consumer networks, as well as other types of relationships (discussed in Part 3), may help to overcome these perceptions.

Some sustainable agri-food producers and retailers suggest that there are insufficient interests from domestic consumers to accommodate the expansion of sustainable agri-food production in Thailand,[241] so they try to solve the problem by exporting to organic and fair trade markets in the US and in Europe.[242] These alternative market channels, however, are not without their problems. Some have criticised mono-crop production of organic products for not focusing on ecological balance[243] and for adopting a Ricardian comparative advantage mentality similar to the mainstream agri-food system.[244] Thai organic and fair trade exporters also have to engage in price competitions with lower-costs countries (e.g. lower labour costs or special trading privileges) which provide limits to price premiums.[245] This is not too dissimilar to conventional international trading channels where price competitions between developing countries to export agri-food commodities put downward pressures on prices. It has been suggested that in some cases, buyers from Europe manage to negotiate prices of organic products down significantly.[246] Minimum fair trade prices are also criticised for not being flexible enough to take into account fluctuations in mainstream market prices, so sometimes fair trade prices are lower than conventional market prices.[247] Moreover, a study suggests that even though fair trade rice value chain in Thailand benefits all actors along the chain, it is insufficient to elevate small-scale farmers from poverty and that other activities, such as vegetable and fish production or value-added projects should be used to generate additional income.[248]

Interviews of producer rice mills managers in Surin and Yasothon also suggest some limitations of organic and fair trade markets. Rice Fund Surin, Bak-rua, and Nam-oom rice mills report that, despite the premiums, they do not retain much profit, and their cash flow problems led them to borrow from banks, so the interest rates add to even higher costs of production.[249] Nam-oom enterprise, for example, had to borrow around 11 million baht from the BAAC at 6 per cent interest rate to pay for paddy in 2011.[250] Leading members suggest that it will take them another few years to be able to purchase second-hand equipment and machineries that they needed,[251] and that it is unlikely for them to negotiate for higher prices due to the concern that foreign buyers will purchase from organic producer groups in other countries with lower costs of production, such as Vietnam.[252] Moreover, as Part 4 discusses in greater detail, in the early 2010s, producer rice mills in Yasothon and Surin face significantly higher costs of production due to the government's paddy pledging scheme and were at even greater risks of losing foreign organic and fair trade buyers. Some trade partners help the producer rice mills with their cash flow problems by agreeing to pay 50 to 80 per cent of the total costs of rice in advance and[253] there are also other attempts to improve cash flow, such as, by asking members to purchase more shares in the mills.[254] Rice Fund Surin, for example, has a four-year contract with fair trade Swiss buyers but admits that such relationships are rare even in fair trade markets.[255] Quoting the manager of Rice Fund Surin: 'what we learn is that business is just business'.[256]

High production and management costs of producer rice mills can be linked back not only to high labour costs (compared to some other developing countries), but also to current technologies, which are not suitable for small-scale production. As suggested by relatively larger-scale rice mills such as Naso and Bak-rua, the mills have high fixed costs due to the scale of the mills. However, they had to invest in large-scale mills in the first place to meet export quality standards, such as to reduce the volume of broken rice. Naso, for example, has a 7,000 tons per year capacity but could only purchase 3,000 tons of paddy so their costs of production are higher than bigger rice mills in conventional markets. Out of this amount, only one-third is organic rice which receives a high premium.[257] In the case of Bak-rua, around 10,000 baht worth of organic rice (referred to as 'cleaning costs') needs to be counted as conventional rice when the mill changes from processing conventional paddy to organic paddy.[258] As discussed previously, newer groups such as Kammad and the moral rice network in Yasothon try to avoid such problems by using smaller rice mills and decentralised management.

Overall, it seems that although exports of widely-traded agri-food products, such as rice in organic and fair trade markets have some benefits, there are still certain limitations. Counter-measures include using the Organic Thailand standard to meet slowly blooming domestic (and regional) demands, develop Thailand's own fair trade standards,[259] and rely on sales based on reputation.[260] At times, producer rice mills face rather serious management and financial problems. In early to mid-1990s, the Rice Fund Surin group struggled as a business which was partially due to low quality of produce. However, after the national Organic Thailand label was established in 1996, there was a renewed attempt to export organic rice in 1999.[261] Naso group also faced financial difficulties around 2006 and 2007 because of unpredictable rice prices and also because the group could not sell off a large supply of rice while having to pay a high interest rate from bank loans that they took out to purchase paddy, resulting in four consecutive years of negative profits.[262] This further serves to explain why many NGO activists think that farmers do not earn enough income from organic rice selling to improve their livelihoods and try to develop local markets for sustainable agri-food products, as well as encourage producers to diversify their production and produce value-added products.[263]

Part 3 Counter-hegemonic agri-food governance structures

Part 2 has discussed different forms of direct and indirect market arrangements which give importance to values such as ecological balance and fairness.[264] What distinguishes these production–distributional channels from conventional market channels, based on price competitiveness, are the different forms of governance structures which ensure that agri-food practices are embedded in counter-hegemonic values. First, section 3.1 discusses counter-hegemonic market regulations and informal social relations which govern sustainable agri-food production–distribution. Section 3.2 then discusses counter-hegemonic movements' attempts to challenge hegemonic agri-food policy and legal governance structures at local, national and global levels. This section also argues that their extent of success is dependent on the political situation and the strength of civil society at that particular period of time.

3.1 Governance structures of sustainable agri-food production–distribution

There are local, national and international labels that have been used to govern alternative agri-food production–distribution in Thailand. In 1993, the AAN collaborated with the private sector and the International Federation of Organic Agriculture Movements (IFOAM) to develop an organic certification system in Thailand to help export Jasmine rice to Europe, Canada, Australia and Japan.[265] The Thai state also developed the 'Organic Thailand' national standard and by 2008, there were seven types of alternative agri-food certifications in Thailand, but it was estimated that over 50 per cent of all organic land in Thailand was certified by international non-Thai private bodies.[266] In 2012, representatives from the Green Net Co-operative in Thailand were also invited to join the committee to develop a new standard for the World Fair Trade Organization.[267] The benefits of sustainability certifications, such as in helping to establish consumer trusts, are well recognised. However, as Part 4 discusses in greater depth, relatively high costs of certification and lack of participation in the setting of standards can obstruct the expansion of SAM in Thailand and open room for co-optation of oppositions.

Aside from international and national standards, there are also local standards, such as the one being used in Chiang Mai since 2001, which was developed by the Northern Organic Standard – an independent organisation founded by ISAC (Institute for a Sustainable Agriculture Community) in 1995. The standard was inspired by Canadian and German organic standards, experience of the Thai SAM, and exchanges of ideas with farmers in Malaysia and Indonesia.[268] Local sustainable markets have an advantage over long-distance trade in terms of making it easier for both producers and consumers to engage in continuous dialogues and to participate more equally in regulation and price setting. For Surin green market, a committee consisting of people from different areas and professions discuss fair prices for both producers and consumers based on the costs of production.[269] Selling quotas are also used to ensure that producers with high production capacity do not disproportionately benefit from the market.[270] In the case of the moral rice network, members are required to follow the Buddhist Five Precepts and refrain from three main vices, which include alcohol, cigarette and gambling in addition to organic standards.[271] As for Santi Asoke, a well-known religious group in Thailand, some consumers tend to trust that their agri-food products are pesticides-free even without organic certifications.[272]

Many have suggested that farmers need certainty that there are markets for their organic products before they produce[273] and hence there are some merits to contract farming arrangements for sustainable agri-food products. Unfortunately, the term 'contract farming' receives a rather negative image among some groups in civil society in Thailand due to many problematic examples of contract farming arrangements, as discussed in Chapter 3. The lack of contract farming regulations in Thailand also does not inspire confidence that producer rights are sufficiently protected. Nevertheless, there are some promising contract farming arrangements of sustainable agri-food products that aim to be fair to both producers and buyers. For example, Khao Kwan Foundation agreed to work with local rice mills to develop a contract farming system to create Suphanburi province's own brand of organic rice. Rice seeds that are used were developed and selected by Khao Kwan and farmers in the programme. It has been argued that all sides benefit: (1) the foundation can promote organic production, give advice on production methods and inspects the quality; (2) farmers receive a price that is higher than the market price and can also rely on the foundation for technical advice and for ensuring fair contracts with the local rice mills; (3) the local rice mills can create a unique marketing identity which will enable them to compete with larger rice mills; (4) price setting also takes into account fairness for consumers.[274] The first batch of organic rice was sold in October 2012 and the costs of production was reportedly less than 3,000 baht per ton, allowing farmers the profit of 10,000 baht per ton.[275] Another example is Maeping Organic Company in Chiang Mai's rice contract farming arrangement where the company advises farmers on production methods using probiotic micro-organisms and ensures high farm prices. The company distributes organic rice domestically and also exports to Singapore.[276]

There are also informal social relations and behaviours which can be seen as an important part of counter-hegemonic agri-food governance. In addition to pre-payment arrangements in the form of CSA, Mae-ta group also organises farm visits and other activities to foster understanding and good relations between farmers and consumers[277] which encourage continual support of the CSA scheme. Producer rice mills in Yasothon and Surin allow members to participate in the paddy purchasing process and pay dividends according to member shares, which encourage an equitable sense of partnership and horizontal social relations. Another example is how Lemon Farm tries to go beyond contractual business arrangements by establishing long-term supportive relations with producer groups, and also work to raise consumer awareness about organic agriculture and sustainable farmer groups.[278] In this sense, consumption can be seen as having the potential to introduce changes in society through altering social relations.

As Part 1 has discussed, some people in the movement see sustainable agriculture's way of thinking not only as counter-hegemonic ideas regarding agricultural production, but also as counter-hegemonic ideas which re-think relationships between humans, society and the ecological system. A few other people in the movement also emphasise the importance of introducing counter-hegemonic changes at the individual level, not just for farmers but also consumers, which lead to changes in how individuals conduct social relations which then affect society as a whole.[279] For example, Phra Promma who helps the moral rice network in Yasothon argues that to challenge the capitalist system and patron–client relations, one needs knowledge and mindfulness so that one can use technology appropriately and also not be led by consumerism.[280]

It is not an easy task to alter an individuals' way of thinking and form counter-hegemonic social relations due to deep-rooted hegemonic ideas and conventional practices. It has been noted by sustainable agriculture promoters how individualistic culture and mainstream market relations deter most farmers from seeking alternatives. However, in some areas, social relations such as community and family ties can still play significant roles to ignite interests in sustainable agriculture.[281] Another point to note is that sustainable producer groups are in different positions to establish supportive social relations with other groups in society. As Part 2 has discussed, relatively successful groups benefited from building alliances with other groups in society, such as academics and the media. The moral rice network and Kammad group, for example, benefited from the national media's attention on their leading members which helps them to establish relationships with consumers that help their economic situations. In the case of the moral rice network, TV Burapha has interviewed and given an award to Mr Kankamkla Pilanoi – a relatively young farmer who works to develop traditional rice strands – as well as helped to find market channels for the moral rice producer group. [282] As for Kammad, aside from receiving help from ALRO, one of its leading members also sometimes receives media coverage which helps the group to find new customers.[283] Some producer groups, however, may not be as fortunate in terms of their ability to build supportive networks.

3.2 Counter-hegemonic agri-food policy and legal governance structures

The previous section has discussed the importance of counter-hegemonic market regulations and social relations governing agri-food production–distribution. However, these governance structures are insufficient if one wants to promote sustainable agriculture in larger scales and transform the hegemonic agri-food system, as hegemonic agri-food policy and legal governance structures also need to be addressed. This section first discusses the Thai state's promotion of sustainable agriculture before focusing on the pilot programme to promote sustainable agriculture which was under the control of the AAN. Then, it discusses counter-hegemonic attempts to shape the legal structures governing the agri-food system, particularly relating to the governance of seeds, intellectual property rights and the signing of free trade agreements.

The Thai State's promotion of sustainable agriculture

There are some state offices at national and local levels, as well as civil servants, who are sympathetic to diversified farms and sustainable agriculture.[284] In the early 2010s this includes ALRO which works with the Kammad group in Yasothon to expand sustainable agricultural production,[285] as well as the Thailand Research Fund (TRF) which gives some funding to participatory research projects, such as to preserve and develop traditional rice strands.[286] TRF funding, however, is inconsistent and is dependent on the government's policy direction. Some sustainable farmer groups, such as Tamor in Surin, also recognise the benefits of building alliances with local administration offices to promote organic farming.[287] One former governor of Surin implemented serious sustainable agriculture development policies for six years[288] and had a lot of positive influence on the SAM in the Northeast,[289] but after he retired there was a change in policy.[290]

Mae-ta group in Chiang Mai interestingly managed to create a supportive political space that greatly enhanced their work by supporting one of its members towards a local administrative position. This political space, however, is available because of more than a decade of civil society's pressure for the Thai state to decentralise power.[291] By 2012, Mr Kanoksak Duangkaewruan from Ampur Mae-ta was elected three times as Chief Executive of the Sub-district Administrative Organisation (SAO) and had used his nine years in office to promote sustainable agriculture and implement policies to curb negative social and environmental effects of conventional farming, such as to form five- to 10-year development plans and zoning maps to manage negative externalities from conventional agriculture.[292] In addition, the SAO provides funding for farmers to adjust their production towards sustainable agriculture and to promote agri-food processing activities, with the goals to promote local food security and job creations.[293] The case of Mae-ta is interesting because, from past experience, many in the SAM found that expansions of sustainable agricultural activities tend to depend on government and other private external organisations' budget and projects which can be rather inconsistent.[294] With the support of the SAO which receives a budget of 15 million baht per year, Mae-ta is able to implement longer-term plans.[295]

There have also been attempts to introduce sustainable agriculture as part of Thailand's national development agenda, notably in the eighth National and Economic Social Development (NESD) plan written in 1996. The plan was steered by public intellectuals such as Dr Prawase Wasi to reflect people-centred development philosophy and incorporated some ideas from civil society groups such as the AAN.[296] The plan explicitly suggests that 20 per cent of agricultural land in the country or at least 25 million rai should be transformed to sustainable agricultural areas[297] but there was some resistance from the bureaucracy and the plan was never effectively implemented. As the next sub-section discusses, this led the AAN to demand for the national pilot programme for sustainable agriculture to be managed by civil society groups in the network.[298]

It is not uncommon in Thailand for some national policy plans to be announced, but they are not seriously followed through. In 2001, the Thai Rak Thai government announced a policy to develop Thailand as a centre of organic agricultural production but without significant practical plans of implementation.[299] Another state-led plan was the first National Strategic Plan to Develop Organic Agriculture (2008–2011) which was criticised for not involving civil society and other organic agriculture stakeholders.[300] An evaluation at the end of the plan suggests that there are still a lot of unaddressed problems such as insufficient knowledge on organic farming in the country and the lack of databases on organic agriculture.[301] The Thai state sometimes show interests in sustainable agriculture because of transnational influence. However, such interests are limited to special projects to promote sustainable agriculture, usually in collaboration with organisations such as the United Nations Development Programme (UNDP), NGOs and farmer groups, and are based in marginalised land areas rather than prime agricultural land areas.[302] Other important criticisms include how the state does not provide support for farmers during the transitional period to sustainable agriculture nor promote consumer demands for organic products in the country.[303]

Another reason why the Thai state gives some funding to promote sustainable agriculture is because of King Bhumipol's support of diversified agriculture and sufficiency ideas. For example, after the 2006 coup d'état (2006 to 2007) the royalist government tried to follow some sufficiency economy ideas and provided budget for sustainable agricultural projects, as well as local sage centres which help to propagate sustainable agricultural techniques.[304] The King also founded the Chaipattana Foundation which aims to help citizens through development projects in ways that are more flexible and faster than the bureaucracy, in line with the King's sufficiency philosophy and his other development ideas.[305] The overall effects of the monarchy's involvement in the promotion of sustainable agriculture are rather complicated, as Part 4 of the chapter discusses in greater detail.

It has been suggested that when the Thai bureaucracy has to promote sustainable agriculture, it tends to focus on quantifiable outcome, such as the number of households that they can claim to be covered by their projects,[306] but does not care to encourage farmers to form self-help sustainable agriculture groups nor to do post-training follow-ups.[307] Whether farmers choose to adopt sustainable agricultural methods after training or not is seen as a matter of individual choice.[308] In addition, it has been noted that civil servants tend to look at the promotion of organic agriculture as being the same as promoting certain organic inputs, rather than to change the system as a whole or to study agro-ecological methods. Hence, they tend to adopt a one-day training approach in organic agricultural methods and provide organic input handouts, instead of devising a more effective longer-term participatory training process.[309] Such an approach can also partly be attributed to compartmentalised agricultural education and knowledge, internalised by Thai civil servants, which was discussed in Chapter 3.

The previous part of the chapter has discussed how organic agriculture is a knowledge-based production which requires a lot of research support from the state[310] as the private sector and civil society in Thailand tend to have limitation in terms of funding.[311] However, the Thai state generally spends little in research – only 0.24 per cent of GDP according to a study in 2008 – in comparison to 2 per cent in developed countries.[312] Research on organic agriculture accounted for 20 million baht or 0.12 per cent of the research budget of the whole country.[313] The TRF, for example, funded Ratchapat Utaradit University to research on low-cost machineries suitable for the production of organic rice.[314] Aside from some examples of promising research projects, criticisms remain that there is still no national-level research network which equitably distribute benefits or guarantee access to all types of stakeholders,[315] and not enough attention is being paid to participatory technological research.[316]

The Thai state's half-hearted promotion of sustainable agriculture is revisited in Part 4 of this chapter, which discusses some attempts by the state to promote sustainable agriculture as possible co-optation of oppositions. In the next sub-section, the discussion is shifted to civil society groups' attempt to wrestle for control of some of the government's budget to promote sustainable agriculture in Thailand by themselves.

The AAN's national pilot programme to develop sustainable agriculture

As previously discussed, the eighth NESD plan supports the transformation of 20 per cent of agricultural land in the country to sustainable agricultural areas. Nevertheless, practical plans and implementation of the goal were under the full control of the bureaucracy.[317] Some civil servants in the Ministry of Agriculture and Co-operatives clearly suggested that they disapproved of the goal and tried to resist by not putting the agenda in practical plans.[318] The AAN tried to follow up on this issue and joined the Assembly of the Poor – a loosely structured umbrella organisation established in 1995 to represent voices and demands of different marginalised groups of people in Thailand – to increase its bargaining power.[319]

In early 1997, the Assembly of the Poor staged a much larger protest than usual where 20,000 people camped outside of the Government House for 99 days. They presented 125 demands to the government, mostly regarding conflicts over the usage of land and forests. The Assembly of the Poor managed to gain some concessions from the Thai state but some of these concessions were revoked later on.[320] As part of the Assembly of the Poor, the AAN proposed the establishment of a fund to promote sustainable agriculture to the Chavalit Yongchaiyut government in December 1996.[321] However, the establishment of a national fund to support sustainable agriculture is a lengthy process which requires subsidiary laws to be passed, so the AAN changed its demand and asked for a fund for a 'pilot programme' to develop sustainable agriculture instead[322] because according to the eighth NESD plan, citizens have the right to propose development projects and manage the budget themselves.[323] In addition, the AAN thought it would be more efficient to operate outside of conventional bureaucratic structures.[324]

The Chavalit government approved a 950 million baht budget for a four-year pilot programme to promote sustainable agriculture to be implemented between 1998 and 2001.[325] Nevertheless, the succeeding Democrat government led by Chuan Leekphai (November 1997 to February 2001) revoked most of the concessions made to the Assembly of the Poor and it took three years for the cabinet to finally approve the funding of 633 million baht for the sustainable agriculture pilot programme to be implemented between 2001 and 2003.[326] The pilot programme operated in nine areas in 37 provinces and covered 27,100 rai of land.[327] It aimed to encourage self-reliance of small-scale farmers through sustainable agriculture and sustainable management of coastal resources to ensure food security, environmental sustainability, and economic security at household and community levels. The fund received was used to develop production, processing and marketing techniques of sustainable agri-food products, as well as to support the organisation of small-scale farmer networks and to campaign for the public's support.[328] Depending on local needs, the funds were used to, for example, sponsor farmer trainings, to build small-scale irrigation,[329] and to sponsor research on traditional rice strands.[330] Surin green market also received some funding from the pilot programme between 2002 and 2003 and started to become more established by 2003.[331] Rice Fund Surin Organic Agriculture Co-operative also received some funding from the pilot programme in 2002 to build a 24-ton capacity rice mill and 500 tons capacity warehouse.[332] A self-evaluation report suggests that the pilot programme yielded positive benefits and allowed more farmers to make transitions to sustainable agriculture. For example, surveys indicated that after the programme, farmers in the network used less chemical fertilisers (from 65.6 per cent to 36.7 per cent) and instead used organic fertilisers. In addition, households had greater food security due to diversified farms.[333]

The pilot programme should be credited as a significant step for the SAM as it is the first time the movement was able to push for some decentralisation of the state's developmental budget to civil society. In addition, the funding has helped to propagate counter-hegemonic ideas and sustainable production–distribution, at least in the AAN circles and within the limits of the budget. However, the pilot programme had limitations not only in terms of budget but also in terms of implementation time and personnel, not to mention that they were closely monitored by the Thai government for any slight mistakes that would allow the pilot programme's work to be discredited.[334] Arguably, the pilot programme which focused on funding small practical projects, rather neglected macro-level hegemonic governance structures. The next sub-section, however, discusses other attempts by the AAN to challenge hegemonic legal governance structures.

Counter-hegemonic attempts to shape legal agri-food governance

In the 1990s and early 2010s, AAN core groups and other environmental movements, such as BioThai and Greenpeace, engage in national and international campaigns to hinder legal governance structures which support the hegemonic agri-food system. The following paragraphs discuss a few important examples of such campaigns which are related to the governance of seeds, intellectual property rights, and the signing of free trade agreements (FTAs). There are also other initiatives to pass, such as, Farmer Rights law and laws to protect contract farmers,[335] but they are beyond the scope of this book. These examples suggest that the SAM has tried to challenge some hegemonic governance structures at domestic as well as at global levels, although there are other hegemonic governance structures which the movement have not addressed.

The SAM in Thailand has strong interests in the issues of biodiversity and patents of seeds since the early 1990s. Spurred by the signing of the Convention on Biological Diversity (CBD) in 1992 and attempts to patent a traditional Thai plant by a Japanese firm, NGOs and academics formed a Network of the Right of Thai Local Wisdom in 1994 to support farmer and community rights over biological resource and traditional wisdom.[336] In 1998, there was also a movement against the patent of Jasmine rice strand (Jasmati) by an American company.[337] Owing to strong interests from civil society on the issues of seeds and intellectual property rights, a committee was set up by the Ministry of Commerce in 1998 to gather public opinions, such as from academics and NGOs, regarding the intellectual property rights regime of the TRIPS agreement that would be in effect in 1999.[338] As a result, on 30 November 1998, a formal letter from the Department of Intellectual Property, Ministry of Commerce, was submitted to the Thai representative at the WTO (World Trade Organization) to object to clause 27.3b of TRIPS, which supports property rights regime of seeds along the lines of the International Union for the Protection of New Varieties of Plant in 1991 (UPOV 1991).[339] Moreover, through India's leadership, Thailand was among a group of countries, which included Brazil, Bolivia, Peru and Venezuela, that submitted a paper to the TRIPS Council of the WTO calling for amendments in TRIPS to harmonise it with the CBD.[340]

The attempts to amend the TRIPs agreement was unsuccessful. However, at the domestic level, the AAN and the Assembly of the Poor successfully pushed for a law to protect local plant genetics in 1999.[341] This law is seen by the AAN as a compromise which balances between the interests of agri-businesses to commercialise seeds, and farmer rights to seeds along the lines of UPOV 1978 and CBD.[342] There were also collaborations with people from countries such as India and the Philippines to develop Community Intellectual Right law.[343]

As both hegemonic and counter-hegemonic forces operate continuously to shape their terrains, counter-hegemonic gains should not be considered permanent. Chapter 3, section 1.1 briefly discussed civil society's successful attempts to block the commercial plantation and open-field testing of genetically modified (GM) seeds but also suggested that there are renewed attempts to introduce pro-GM agri-food regulations in Thailand, as recently as in 2014.[344] Even though civil society groups managed to halt open-field testing of GM seeds before a biosafety law can be put in place, at the time of writing, there are still some concerns that agri-businesses and the Thai bureaucracy will rush to pass a careless biosafety law.[345] In 2013, the Department of Agriculture also proposed a new law to replace the 1999 law governing the use of plants genetics, which will be more in accordance with UPOV 1991 and will help increase the power of agri-businesses.[346] Events are still unfolding at the time of writing but historical experience suggests that counter-hegemonic gains can be reversed depending on the strength of counter-hegemonic forces and political space at particular periods of time. For example, it has been noted that before 2005 civil society groups were not strong enough to inspect agri-food related clauses in Thailand's FTAs with China and Australia. However, in 2005 civil society groups consisting not only of the AAN but also 11 other networks, such as human immunodeficiency virus (HIV) patients and four-region slum network, were strong enough to successfully block the US–Thailand FTA in Chiang Mai which would have imposed a strict pro-business property rights regime in Thailand.[347] As of early 2010s, Part 4 of this chapter argues that political polarisation in Thailand has helped to weaken counter-hegemonic forces in the agri-food system in Thailand.

Many attempts to lobby for counter-hegemonic changes at the national governance structures have so far been rather unsuccessful, such as the campaign to increase tax and control over agricultural chemicals. AAN activists believe that this is due to lobbying power of Thai and non-Thai agri-businesses whose influence extend to all governments and all political parties.[348] Some activists have admitted that the AAN needs to expand their allies to further increase their bargaining power.[349] Other reactions, however, include the perception that perhaps it is better to spend time and effort on building alternative agri-food production–distribution channels rather than hoping to change the Thai state's policies and legal structures.[350] On the one hand, this sounds like a rational strategy for individuals, but on the other hand, it implies the acceptance that sustainable agriculture is just an 'alternative' to serve niche markets, rather than a counter-hegemonic possibility that can lead to the transformation of the mainstream agri-food system.

As previously discussed, there were some attempts to challenge global governance structures, such as TRIPS, in collaboration with other countries. However, other aspects of hegemonic global governance are rarely discussed, such as the lack of regulations over speculations of agricultural commodities and the World Bank's framework regarding land investments in developing countries. Although these issues might seem rather far-removed from immediate problems in the agri-food system in Thailand, they are nevertheless significant elements of the hegemonic global agri-food order which Thailand is a part of, as discussed in Chapter 3. One may suggest that the SAM in Thailand can try to affect changes at the global governance level through transnational social movements such as La Vía Campesina. However, as the next chapter will discuss, Thai members of La Vía Campesina, which include the Assembly of the Poor and the Northern Peasants Federation (part of the land reform movement), face some difficulties participating in the international arena due to language barriers and other reasons.[351] In the next part of the chapter, grey areas between hegemony, counter-hegemony, and co-optation of oppositions are also explored as obstacles which limit the counter-hegemonic potential of the SAM.

Part 4 Grey areas and co-optation of oppositions

This part of the chapter focuses on examples of co-optation of oppositions which are relevant to the SAM, as well as grey areas between hegemony and counter-hegemony. First, section 4.1 evaluates some critiques of localism and sustainable agriculture which portray them as conservative forces. This section argues that while it is important to guard against conservative interpretations and practices, looking beyond the modernisation world view allows one to see that there can be some counter-hegemonic potential to localism and sustainable agriculture. Section 4.2 discusses grey areas and co-optation of oppositions by the private sector in sustainable agri-food markets. Lastly, section 4.3 considers the Thai state's promotion of sustainable agriculture from the light of co-optation of oppositions.

4.1 Counter-hegemonic extent of localism and sustainable agriculture

Thai localism and sufficiency ideas have been criticised by some academics as backward conservative forces. Such interpretation is sometimes mapped onto the SAM and also aids polarised political and rural development discourses in Thailand which, as this section discusses, distract the population from structural problems underlying the mainstream agri-food system. This section first evaluates some main critiques of Thai localism and suggests that while they tend to over-simplify Thai localist ideas, these critiques serve as useful tools to warn against conservative interpretations and practical translations of localist ideas that limit their counter-hegemonic potential. This section then argues that despite some conservative examples and elements, Thai localism should still be credited as attempts to build national-popular strategies to rally Thais behind counter-hegemonic projects. In addition, the SAM can more appropriately be seen as part of global counter-hegemonic forces, rather than as an insular movement that tries to retreat to the past.

Some scholars have suggested that Thai localism and sufficiency philosophy imply advocacies of autarkic closed communities that are hostile to market relations.[352] However, as discussed in Part 1, Thai localists' advocacy of using local wisdom and resources to help people integrate into national and international economy does not imply that they have to develop in isolation without help from modern ideas and technology.[353] Despite the emphasis on community and local-level development, it is argued that localist ideas do not oppose trade and collaborations with other parts of society[354] while the King's speeches also suggest that full sufficiency – that every family must produce all the basic needs for themselves – is impossible.[355] Practical interpretations of these ideas, however, can be very different.

Another related and popular critique is that Thai localism infers anti-globalisation, anti-outsiders, anti-urban and anti-industrialisation sentiments. Rigg and Nattapoolwat (2001), for example, contrasted NGO activists, journalists and academics sympathetic to localism, who have 'fears of globalization', with ordinary Thais' enthusiasm with globalisation[356] which open up economic opportunities for rural people.[357] Similarly, Hewison (2002) suggests that localist discourses draw both conservative and radical Thais together to oppose 'globalization, neo-liberalism, and capitalist industrialisation'[358] and that 'there is no place for large-scale industrialization or urbanization'[359] for localists. Moreover, the study suggests that anti-urban bias can and does preclude political alliances across the supposed rural–urban split.[360] On the contrary, localist scholars, such as Prawase Wasi, clearly advocate building alliances with other sectors in Thai society, including the state and the private sector.[361] Anan Ganjanapan, for example, emphasises how communities can adapt over time and are not necessarily geographically based. In addition, communities should also establish alliances with other groups in civil society, such as progressive middle-class Thais.[362]

When Thai localism is portrayed as being backward and anti-development, it often reflects underlying assumptions regarding the nature of development as having to follow more or less a single one-directional path. In Hewison (2002), a quote from Prawase Wasi suggesting that self-reliance entails standing on one's own feet to achieve sustainable development from one's own initiatives is somehow interpreted as a perspective which can be 'anti-development'.[363] Another example is Rigg, Promphaking and Le Mare (2014) which suggests that localist discourses and their focuses on villages and rural communities as places to return to, or as places of retirement and refuge, are obstacles for Thailand's economic progress and for Thais to reach their human potential.[364] Needless to say that criticising the globalised capitalist economy does not simply equate to anti-globalisation, anti-industrialisation, anti-Western, or anti-progress sentiments. Localist discourses understandably place a lot of emphasis on the development of sustainable agricultural production, community enterprises and self-help groups, because they are basic economic activities based on natural resources that marginalised people can gain easier access to compared to industrial production, which require more capital. Previous parts of the chapter have discussed how the SAM's critique of the market-led capitalist agri-food system and Western-dominated globalisation is used as foundations to envision better forms of globalisation embedded in values, such as sustainability, fairness and partnership, to ensure that the majority of people benefit from globalisation in more equitable manners. In addition, Part 2 has discussed how promoters of sustainable agriculture do not object to industrial production and they encourage producers to move up along agri-food chains. The SAM also puts a lot of emphasis on building alliances with other groups in Thailand and abroad. Moreover, sustainable markets help to alter conventional market relations and provide alternatives, but they do not encourage farmers to be fully self-sufficient.[365]

Thai localism's appeal to traditional wisdom and Buddhist values, as well as the King's support for self-reliance and sufficiency concepts, have also led critics to conflate Thai localism with the King's concept of sufficiency and to see such ideas and discourses as being fundamentally conservative, nationalist and royalist. For example, McCargo (2001) suggests that localism is a call to return to Thai agrarian roots which is conservative, nostalgic, and closely resembles the official Thai nationalism which is elitist and statist.[366] Another study by Hewison (2002) suggests that Thai localism resembles right-wing nationalist trinity in Thailand of Nation, Religion and King.[367] This, however, is arguably the opposite of localist views. As discussed in Pasuk and Baker (1995), Thai localists are sceptical of the centralised Thai state and oppose conservative views which imagine rural Thailand as a society of contented peasants owing allegiance to the state, epitomised by the trinity of Nation, Religion and King.[368] This research also finds that localist discourses clearly emphasise the need to decentralise power and to build democratic horizontal social relations. Nartsupha, for example, was inspired by some strands of anarchist thoughts and explicitly states his concerns with Sakdina mentality and top-down co-optation by the state of Thai communities, as well as argues in favour of encouraging the spirits of freedom, international understanding, equality, generosity and democracy to undermine the power of the state and hierarchical culture.[369] His conception of communities does not infer hierarchical social structures nor violent intimidation within households or within communities.[370] Other Thai scholars who share similar views include Seksan Prasertkul who suggests that self-organised people's groups can be used to counter-balance the power of the state and market forces, and Anek Laothamatat who suggests that self-organised community groups and their networks can help people to break free from patron–client relations and hierarchical social structure.[371] As previous parts have discussed, sustainable producer groups encourage partnership social relations within and between groups rather than to support unequal vertical social relationships.

Some authors have gone further to interpret sufficiency ideas and discourse as determined efforts by conservative forces to repress the aspirations of poor Thais for political inclusion and material well-being, although Unger (2009) suggests that there is little evidence to support such an interpretation.[372] While section 4.3 of this chapter discusses some conservative sufficiency programmes implemented by the bureaucracy and, as discussed in Chapter 3, a large amount of land holding by the Crown Property Bureau undermines counter-hegemonic images of the monarchy, these instances do not suggest that sufficiency *as ideas* should fundamentally be generalised as attempts to repress the aspirations of poor Thais or that they are devoid of counter-hegemonic potential. Sustainable agricultural groups are sometimes portrayed as being co-opted by conservative forces and indeed there are some sustainable agriculture groups which adopt rather royalist discourses such as the Agri-Nature Foundation.[373] However, as Part 1 has discussed, there are many sources of ideas not exclusively limited to

Thailand that give rise to varieties of practices within the SAM, which have started before the popularisation of sufficiency ideas and King Bhumipol's New Theory of Agriculture following the 1997 economic crisis. There are also different interpretations of sufficiency and self-reliance which suggest that they are not completely monopolised by elite groups. Previous parts of the chapter have also discussed similarities of the Thai SAM with those in other countries which suggest that it is more appropriate to view the SAM in Thailand as localised counter-hegemonic responses to structural problems in the global agri-food system. Understandably, vehement rejection (as well as uncritical embrace) of localism and sufficiency ideas often reflect evaluations of King Bhumipol and perception of his role in Thai politics at least as much as the content of the ideas.[374] To further complicate the situation, polarised political conflicts in Thailand in recent years also add fuel to conservative interpretations of Thai localism, sufficiency ideas, and sustainable agricultural practices because of their perceived association with the King.

By pointing out that Thai localism and SAM should not be treated simply as the opposite end of development and progress nor generalised as royalist conservative attempts to suppress the people's aspirations, this book does not suggest that Thai localism and SAM are unproblematically counter-hegemonic, but that they deserve just and careful consideration. Suggestions that sustainable agriculture groups in Thailand are generally part of conservative forces, ignoring structural political-economic causes which gave rise to these groups, serve to depoliticise and undermine the SAM, which tries to challenge the hegemonic capitalist agri-food system.

As discussed in Chapter 2, a Gramscian perspective suggests that social agents can draw on materials from their social and cultural contexts to build counter-hegemonic ideas. Such ideas can be fragmentary and contradictory, open to multiple interpretations and hence potentially supportive of emancipatory social visions and political projects.[375] For example, on the one hand, religions can be used as a key component in the construction of hegemony, but on the other hand, religions can also be used to advance the counter-hegemonic project.[376] Brazil's Landless Rural Workers' Movement (MST) – an important member of La Vía Campesina – has made use of religious ideas as well as socialist, nationalist and communitarian ideas to build up their counter-hegemonic movement ,which both practically and ideologically challenge the hegemonic status quo.[377] Therefore, similar to many social movements around the world, localist and sustainable agriculture ideas and practices in Thailand, which employ stereotypically conservative elements, such as those relating to Buddhism, should be seen as national-popular strategies or as attempts to build locally situated counter-hegemony based on various sources of inspirations.

As Part 1 has argued, SAM members use different types of terms and discourses to aid their counter-hegemonic project. To a certain extent, such varieties help to encourage different groups of people in Thai society to become interested in sustainable agriculture. Some people use localist and Buddhist terms, while some people prefer transnational counter-hegemonic terms and practices, such as food sovereignty and community supported agriculture, which appeal more to younger generations and middle-class Thais. What they generally agree on, however, is the importance of developing a sustainable and fair agri-food system. Some promoters of sustainable agriculture have been seen as subscribers of the community culture school of thought even though they suggest that it is their experience, rather than social theories, which led them to work on developing alternative agri-food production–consumption networks at local levels.[378]

There are benefits to having different varieties of counter-hegemonic discourses and practices, but it is also important to have critical reflections and non-judgmental discussions to evaluate counter-hegemonic potential of these ideas and practices, to find room for improvement and to guard against co-optation of oppositions. Such discussions can also be enriched by other perspectives, new sources of counter-hegemonic ideas and practices, as well as by encouraging the participations of diverse groups in society. The SAM's use of the term 'local sage', for example, is meant to help construct counter-hegemonic identity of sustainable Thai farmers, but critique from a gender perspective pointed out that the term can be problematic because it tends to be associated with male farmers who have their own land.[379] Other potential problems include how, as Part 1 has discussed, localist ideas allow for challenges to the state and capitalism to include withdrawal into self-reliance at local levels.[380] This can potentially be problematic if macro-level hegemonic governance structures are left unchallenged because, although developing alternative agri-food production–distribution channels is useful, it is unlikely to lead to large-scale transformation of the current agri-food system by itself. Another issue to consider is whether some people in the SAM embrace sufficiency ideas because of their counter-hegemonic potential or because of their loyalty to the King. In the latter case, such loyalty can affect critical evaluations and hinder attempts to improve on sufficiency ideas and practices.

4.2 Grey areas and co-optation of oppositions by the private sector

Concerns over transformative counter-hegemonic potential and co-optation of oppositions of alternative agri-food production–distribution channels, such as organic agriculture and fair trade, are well documented in existing literature, as discussed in Part 4 of Chapter 2. Some people welcome increased involvements of large agri-businesses in organic markets because it implies that organic products will be traded in larger scales, or suggest that large agri-businesses can co-exist with smaller-scale producers in organic markets.[381] However, there are those who argue that increased domination of large agri-businesses opens up opportunities for a hijacking of organic agriculture[382] as large agri-businesses have power to push out smaller competitors.[383]

Reflecting the trends in other parts of the world, some corporations in Thailand have adopted counter-hegemonic terms such as sustainable agriculture and also try to enter the organic market, even though they are still major players which sell chemical inputs and engage in hegemonic agri-food production and distribution. Charoen Pokphand (CP), for example, has many corporate social responsibility programmes which involve agricultural projects that claim to be inspired by King Bhumipol's integrated farms and sufficiency ideas.[384] Many large agri-businesses have also started organic contract farming programmes where farmers ought to purchase seeds and organic fertilisers from the companies in exchange for production loans. In many of these cases, it has been argued that farmers lack the freedom and power to negotiate terms.[385] Some large-scale distributors and retailers of sustainable agri-food products also engage in both conventional and alternative agri-food markets. By 2007, Capital Rice (Nakhon Luang) had also become one of the largest organic rice exporters, alongside Green Net Co-operative.[386] Many supermarkets allow a few organic items on their shelves even though they might not have a further interest to promote sustainable agriculture.[387] Naso group had supplied their rice to a supermarket in the past but found that the supermarket charged many fees so it was not profitable to continue supplying to the supermarket.[388]

To a certain extent, developing clear counter-hegemonic ideas, production–distribution practices, as well as supportive governance structures can help to ameliorate problems of co-optation of oppositions. This is a difficult task even in supposedly counter-hegemonic organic and fair trade markets where there also seem to be grey areas between hegemony and counter-hegemony. As Part 2 has discussed, there are those in the SAM who criticise large scale exports of mono-crops through organic and fair trade channels because such an approach retains some similar ideas and practices as that in the hegemonic agri-food system. Some academic studies have voiced similar concerns, arguing that organic agriculture regulations should understand organic agriculture as production and distribution processes which encompass social and ecological dimensions, rather than mere usage of organic inputs or 'cookie-cutter' organic practices which allow large corporations to engage in large scale mono-crop plantations of organic agri-food products.[389]

Private sustainability and fairness standards can also be seen as potentially problematic governance structures. Understandably, to sell to distant markets, it is necessary to pass sustainability standards, such as organic and fair trade which are accepted in those countries.[390] However, the certification process can be complicated and prices can be high, which imply a bias in favour of large-scale farms, while small-scale farmers are likely to require external help, such as from export or distribution companies. For example, Bak-rua producer rice mill pays aproximately a 300,000 baht certification fee for 100 of their members, which means that even though organic producers have low costs of production, the mill has rather high management costs.[391] As Part 2 has discussed, even if farmers managed to receive certifications, there is no guarantee that their products can be sold in international markets. There is a great deal of competition from producers in other developing countries[392] who have advantages over Thai producers due to cheaper labour costs and historical colonial ties with European countries.[393]

Other problems facing sustainable farmer groups which were discussed in Part 2 include: (1) difficulties in establishing long-term consumer–producer relations and to explain local problems to distant buyers; (2) profits received from the sales of one or two items are still insufficient to raise living standards of producers and of farmer groups, and; (3) unavailability of appropriate production technology for small-scale enterprises. These problems also call into question the counter-hegemonic extent of current organic and fair trade production–distribution practices. There are studies which also voice similar concerns, suggesting that private sustainability and fair trade standards require a high level of investments that favour large-scale producers[394] and can act as non-tariff trade barriers.[395] In addition, there is also a question of participation and democratic legitimacy in setting such private standards.[396] On the other hand, local and national market channels, such as green markets and CSA also have limited counter-hegemonic potential as they are constrained by smaller market size, smaller transaction volumes, and limited geographical coverage.

4.3 Grey areas and co-optation of oppositions by the Thai state

As Part 3 has discussed, the Thai state makes some attempts to promote sustainable agriculture. However, it has been noted that the bureaucracy tends to promote diluted versions of alternative agriculture with only mild changes in the production system.[397] In some publications, the definition of alternative agriculture still allows for the use of some chemical inputs[398] and there is no emphasis on helping farmers to reduce the costs of production nor to use resource as efficiently as possible.[399] In addition, some have observed that the bureaucracy tends to promote growing different crops in a farm, but is not concerned with how each crop aids one another in an ecological manner, which is not very different from promoting a few mono-crops in one farm.[400]

Since the Thai state's publications often conflate sustainable agriculture with King Bhumipol's sufficiency economy philosophy,[401] one might expect the bureaucracy's interests and acceptance of the King's sufficiency concept to be a positive motivating factor. However, it has been argued that the bureaucracy's mechanical promotion of sufficiency economy and sustainable agriculture has become a tool of bureaucratic ideological control[402] where the bureaucracy uses sufficiency programmes to impose some moral values on the locals, uses the people's fear of authority to force them to co-operate, or uses the King's name to legitimise their projects.[403] Often, standardised sustainable agriculture or sufficiency programmes are implemented on every region without taking into account local differences nor involve local farmers in the decision-making process,[404] which suggest a markedly different understanding of sustainable agriculture and sufficiency as discussed in the previous parts of this chapter. These can be seen as examples of co-optation of oppositions where the bureaucracy subsumes potentially counter-hegemonic ideas into Sakdina patron–client top-down mentality through implementations of their development projects.

There are some interests in the Ministry of Commerce to promote organic agriculture but this is mainly because the Ministry sees opportunities to export organic products to serve growing niche markets in advanced capitalist countries,[405] not because the Ministry is motivated to transform the agri-food system in Thailand as a whole. As a national policy, the Thai state is more interested in food safety and good agricultural practice (GAP) standard which allow the use of some pesticides.[406] In 2004, the Thai government declared a year of food safety and introduced a public standard for GAP called Q-GAP which is fully managed by the government. By 2010, Q-GAP certificates were issued to around 212,000 farmers, covering 3.7 per cent of the country's farm households and 1.2 per cent of the country's arable and permanent cropland.[407] Q-GAP, however, becomes one of many competing alternative state and private agri-food labels with different sustainability criteria that serve to confuse consumers. A survey of 848 respondents in Bangkok in 2005, for example, suggests that consumers who purchase organic vegetables cannot clearly differentiate between various pesticide-safe labels and organic labels, and are unsure of the differences in production methods.[408] Some have also argued that Q-GAP and other safe food labels increase market competitions, which hinder development of organic agriculture and other forms of agro-ecological production organic products.[409] In addition, Q-GAP may not lead to safer food or more sustainable agricultural practices as a study in Northern Thailand suggests that Q-GAP fruit and vegetable producers did not use fewer nor less hazardous pesticides due to many reasons, such as poor implementation of farm auditing and rapid expansion of the Q-GAP programme.[410]

As the previous chapter discussed, the paddy pledging scheme can also be seen as a form of co-optation of oppositions; the scheme claims to help solve rice farmers' economic problems and portrays the government as being on the side of small-scale producers, even though the scheme intensifies problems of the hegemonic agri-food system. Interviews of producer rice mill managers in Yasothon and Surin also suggest that the paddy pledging scheme hinders organic rice production and undermines small-scale rice enterprises.[411] The scheme significantly raised the purchase price for paddy which reduced the difference between prices of organic and ordinary paddy. In 2011, the price of Jasmine paddy under the scheme was higher than organic Jasmine paddy price (20 baht per kg. compared to 17 to 18 baht per kg.).[412] The producer rice mills in Yasothon and Surin had to increase their purchase price for organic paddy to be able to fulfil their export orders. If they did not raise their purchase price, some of their farmer members might chose to sell elsewhere or even switch back to intensive conventional production.[413] In the case of Bak-rua rice mill in 2011, only around 130 members out of the usual figure of 200 sold their paddy to the rice mill.[414] With lower volumes of paddy to process, the rice mills lose more profits due to costs.[415] Raising paddy purchase price, however, was problematic because of cash flow problems and because the rice mills could not receive higher export prices from buyers who tended not to understand domestic situations in Thailand[416] and are also searching for suppliers in other countries.[417]

This section has discussed lingering hegemonic influence in the Thai state's promotion of sustainable agriculture and possibility of co-optation of oppositions. However, it is important to stress that the Thai state should not simply be seen as a monolithic hegemonic entity, and that within the state apparatus there is also tension between hegemonic and counter-hegemonic forces, similar to some large corporations which engage in both hegemonic and counter-hegemonic practices. As previously discussed, there are some state managers and offices which seem genuinely supportive of SAM. The support, however, also depends on policy direction at the top-levels and can be inconsistent. Moreover, even though some state officials embrace some counter-hegemonic agri-food ideas, their positions in the Thai state's apparatus force them to find compromises because they have to follow policy directions of the ruling political parties, such as with regards to the paddy pledging scheme,[418] or because many people in their local districts (and many Thais, in general) still believe that agricultural chemicals are necessary as organic agriculture cannot produce enough food to ensure Thai and global food security.[419]

Conclusion

This chapter has discussed the SAM's counter-hegemonic ideas and discourses, production–distribution practices, governance structures, as well as grey areas between hegemony, counter-hegemony, and co-optation of oppositions. Exploration of the SAM in this chapter supports the book's main argument that counter-hegemony should be seen as a heterogeneous and evolving process over a long period of time. It is unrealistic to assume or to expect that counter-hegemonic movements should embody purely counter-hegemonic elements because counter-hegemony is an ongoing process, not to mention that movements often have to compromise as short- to medium-term strategies so that they can survive in the dominantly hegemonic agri-food system. Moreover, as hegemonic forces try to adapt and subsume dissenting forces which challenge the status quo, it is important that counter-hegemonic forces continuously try to develop clear ideas, practices and governance structures to guard against co-optation.

The next chapter will discuss the land reform movement in Thailand to give a fuller picture of counter-hegemony in the agri-food system in Thailand. Members of the land reform movement tend to be marginalised farmers and workers, whereas sustainable farmers discussed in this chapter tend to have their own land.

Notes

1 Mr Samrit Boonsuk, president of the Community of Agro-Ecology Foundation, interviewed 19 December 2012, Surin; Decha Siripat, 'Present and Future of Alternative Farmers in Thailand (first Published in 1987)', in *The Path of Sustainable Agriculture*, 2nd edn. (Samut-Sakorn: BioThai, 2011), 87 (in Thai).
2 Mr Pakphum Inpan, Tamor group, interviewed 20 December 2012, Surin; Mr Thamma Sangkalee and Mr Bood-dee Piengprom, Ta-toom group, interviewed 22 December 2012, Surin.
3 Mr Witoon Lienchamroon, BioThai Foundation, interviewed 5 April 2012, Nonthaburi; Mr Decha Siripat, Khao Kwan Foundation, interviewed 14 October 2012,

Nonthaburi; Mrs Supha Yaimuang, SATHAI, interviewed 3 October 2012, Nonthaburi; Mr Pat Apaimool, Mae-ta organic farmer, interviewed 1 November 2012, Chiang Mai; Mr Chanuan Rattanawaraha, Agricultural Advisor Office, Department of Agriculture, interviewed 17 January 2013, Nonthaburi; Mr Prapat Panyachatrak, Chairman of National Farmer Council, interviewed 29 January 2013, Bangkok.

4 Decha Siripat, interviewed 14 October 2012, Nonthaburi.

5 Dr Chomchuan Boonrahong, lecturer at Mae-Jo University and one of AAN founders, interviewed 3 November 2012, Chiang Mai.

6 Supha Yaimuang, interviewed 3 October 2012, Nonthaburi; Chomchuan Boonrahong, interviewed 3 November 2012, Chiang Mai; Thamma Sangkalee, interviewed 22 December 2012, Surin; Boonsong Martkhao, Kammad group, interviewed 25 December 2012, Yasothon.

7 Krisda Boonchai *et al.*, *Ideas and Policies Regarding Agri-Food Resource Base* (Nonthaburi: BioThai, 2007), 25; AAN farmer groups, 'Kaen-Nakhon Manifesto: Local Rice, Secure Food and Farmer Livelihoods', E-Saan Local Rice Expo, 14–15 March 2009 (in Thai).

8 Nattapong Pattanapanchai, *Food – Life or Commodity? Marketable Culture under the Control of Corporations*, ed. Ubol Yoo-wah (Nonthaburi: SATHAI, 2008), 40–41 (in Thai); Decha Siripat, interviewed 14 October 2012, Nonthaburi; AAN farmer Groups, 'Kaen-Nakhon Manifesto', (2009); Southern Alternative Farmer Group, 'Manifesto of the Southern Alternative Farmer', 6 June 2009, Patlung (in Thai).

9 Phra Promma Suphatto, a monk at Thamma-ruamjai forest temple, interviewed 23 December 2012, Yasothon.

10 Decha Siripat, interviewed 14 October 2012, Nonthaburi; Mr Adisorn Puangchompoo, main founder of one rai-100,000 baht project, interviewed 13 January 2013, Nonthaburi.

11 San Saeng-arun Magazine, 'In the Water There are Fishes, in the Paddy Field There is Rice: Farmer Livelihoods, Disintegration and Survival', *San Saeng-Arun Magazine* (Bangkok, 2012), 24–25 (in Thai).

12 Decha Siripat, interviewed 14 October 2012, Nonthaburi; Pat Apaimool, interviewed 1 November 2012, Chiang Mai.

13 Mr Ubol Yoowah, NGO activist based in Yasothon, interviewed 22 December 2012; Mr Kankamkla Pilanoi, Thamma-ruamjai moral rice network, interviewed 23 December 2012, Yasothon.

14 Phra Promma Suphatto, interviewed 23 December 2012, Yasothon.

15 Adisorn Puangchompoo, interviewed 13 January 2013, Nonthaburi.

16 Pat Apaimool, interviewed 1 November 2012, Chiang Mai; Supha Yaimuang, interviewed 3 October 2012, Nonthaburi; Phra Promma Suphatto, interviewed 23 December 2012, Yasothon; Mr Jirapan Meesap, Thamma-ruamjai network, interviewed 23 December 2012, Yasothon; Chomchuan Boonrahong, interviewed 3 November 2012, Chiang Mai; Samrit Boonsuk, CAE, interviewed 19 December 2012, Surin.

17 Prapat Panyachatrak, interviewed 29 January 2013, Bangkok.

18 Pakphum Inpan, Mitr Boontawee, Som Sadomsuk, Rungroj Kajadroka and Samrach Thong-iam, Tamor group, interviewed 20 December 2012, Surin.

19 Rungroj Kajadroka, interviewed 20 December 2012, Surin.

20 Kankamkla Pilanoi, interviewed 23 December 2012, Yasothon.

21 Thamma Sangkalee, interviewed 22 December 2012, Surin.

22 Anusorn Unno, *Sustainable Agriculture Movement in Thailand and the Politics of Sustainable Agriculture Narratives* (Nonthaburi: Sustainable Agriculture Foundation Thailand (SATHAI), 2003), 106 (in Thai).

23 Eric Holt-Giménez and Annie Shattuck, 'Food Crises, Food Regimes and Food Movements: Rumblings of Reform or Tides of Transformation?', *The Journal of Peasant Studies* 38, no. 1 (January 2011), 125 and 128.

24 Nora Mckeon, 'The FAO, Civil Society and the Global Governance of Food and Agriculture', in *The United Nations and Civil Society: Legitimating Global Governance – Whose Voice?* (New York: Zed Books, 2009), 36–37.
25 AAN farmer groups, 'Kaen-Nakhon Manifesto', (2009).
26 Supha Yaimuang, interviewed 3 October 2012, Nonthaburi.
27 Mekong Youth Alliance for Organic Agriculture and Agro-Ecology, 'Occupy Your Life Manifesto', obtained at an academic form on agro-ecology, farmer rights, food sovereignty and farmer movements, 12 November 2012, Chulalongkorn University, Bangkok. It is an alliance of young small-scale diversified farmers from various Asian countries namely Bhutan, Cambodia, Myanmar, Thailand, Vietnam, Laos.
28 Annette Desmarais, *Globalization and the Power of Peasants: La Vía Campesina* (London: Pluto Press, 2007), 34.
29 Witoon Lienchamroon, interviewed 5 April 2012, Nonthaburi.
30 Pakphum Inpan, interviewed 20 December 2012, Surin.
31 Ubol Yoowah, interviewed 22 December 2012, Yasothon and Green Net Co-operative, 'About Green Net Cooperative', www.greennet.or.th/about/greennet.
32 Chomchuan Boonrahong, interviewed 3 November 2012, Chiang Mai.
33 Boonchai *et al.* (2007), 23–27 (in Thai).
34 Ibid., 49.
35 Paranat Suksut and Wanna Jarusomboon, 'The Identity of Sustainable Agriculture: A Case Study of the Middle Class', in *Sustainable Agriculture: Cultural Identity, Agricultural Problems and the Identity of Thai Farmers*, ed. Anusorn Unno (Nonthaburi: Sustainable Agriculture Assembly Committee and Heinrich Böll Foundation, 2004), 198 (in Thai).
36 For example, Ms Pattarawan Jansiri, professional nurse and director at Kamkhuenkaew hospital, helps to promote organic agriculture in Yasothon, interviewed 24 December 2012. Also, many hospitals in Thailand become sites of local green markets.
37 Decha Siripat, interviewed 14 October 2012, Nonthaburi.
38 Chomchuan Boonrahong, interviewed 3 November 2012, Chiang Mai; Decha Siripat, interviewed 14 October 2012, Nonthaburi; Anusorn Unno, *Sustainable Agriculture Movement in Thailand and the Politics of Sustainable Agriculture Narratives* (Nonthaburi: SATHAI, 2003), 104 (in Thai). Schumacher's influential book, first published in 1973, is called *Small Is Beautiful: A Study of Economics as if People Mattered* and has been translated into Thai.
39 Samrit Boonsuk, interviewed 19 December 2012, Surin.
40 Samrit Boonsuk, interviewed 19 December 2012, Surin; Pakphum Inpan, interviewed 20 December 2012, Surin; Chomchuan Boonrahong, interviewed 3 November 2012, Chiang Mai.
41 Unno (2003), 130.
42 Ibid., 128.
43 Chomchuan Boonrahong, Witaya Jantawongsri, and Tassanee Palee, *Appropriate Alternative Markets for Sustainable Agricultural Products* (Bangkok: Thailand Research Fund, 2000), 14 (in Thai).
44 Unno (2003), 131; Mr Kittithanet Rangkaworaset, one rai-100,000 baht project, interviewed 13 January 2013, Nonthaburi.
45 Boonsong Martkhao, interviewed 25 December 2012, Yasothon.
46 Supha Yaimuang, interviewed 3 October 2012, Nonthaburi.
47 Chatthip Nartsupha and Wanworn Ja-noo, 'Editorial', in *Community Culture School of Thought in Thai Society*, ed. Chatthip Nartsupha and Wanworn Ja-noo (Bangkok: Sangsan Publishing, 2012), 10 (in Thai).
48 Chatthip Nartsupha, *Modernisation and the "Community" School of Thought* (Bangkok: Sangsan Publishing, 2010), 163–165 (in Thai).
49 Ibid., 166–167 and 174, 177.

50 Pasuk Phongpaichit, 'Developing Social Alternatives. Walking Backwards into a Khlong', in *Thailand Beyond the Crisis*, ed. Peter Warr (New York: Routledge-Curzon, 2005), 138.
51 Pasuk Phongpaichit and Chris Baker, *Thailand: Economy and Politics* (New York: Oxford University Press, 1995), 388.
52 Phongpaichit (2005), 162.
53 Peter Warr, 'The Economics of Enough: Thailand's "Sufficiency Economy" Debate', *International Conference on "Happiness and Public Policy", Organized by PPDO, Prime Minister's Office, UNESCAP, UNCC, Bangkok, 18–19 July 2007* (2007), 8–9.
54 See UNDP, *Thailand Human Development Report 2007: Sufficiency Economy and Human Development* (Bangkok: UNDP, 2007), quoted in Danny Unger, 'Sufficiency Economy and the Bourgeois Virtues', *Asian Affairs: An American Review* 36, no. 3 (2009), 143.
55 Thanwa Jitsanguan, 'Sustainable Agricultural Systems for Small-Scale Farmers in Thailand: Implications for the Environment', paper at Kasetsart University, Bangkok, 12 January 2001, quoted in Unger (2009), 143.
56 Self-sufficiency philosophy of King Bhumiphol Adulyadej published by the National Economic Development Board (NESDB) and other agencies in 1999, quoted in Suthep Udomrat, 'Self-sufficiency Philosophy', in *Safety and Stability Through Self-sufficiency Economy*, ed. Pitaya Wongkul, Withithat. Institute (Bangkok, 2008), 72 (in Thai).
57 Saneh Jamarik, 'Self-Sufficient Economy in the Globalisation Current', in *Safety and Stability Through Self-Sufficiency Economy*, ed. Pitaya Wongkul (Bangkok: Withithat Institute, 2008), 120 (in Thai).
58 Pat Apaimool, interviewed 1 November 2012, Chiang Mai; Ms Kanya Onsri, village leader and leader of Baan Taptai Organic Agriculture group, interviewed 22 December 2012, Surin; Adisorn Puangchompoo, interviewed 13 January 2013, Nonthaburi.
59 Boonsong Martkhao, interviewed 25 December 2012, Yasothon.
60 Colin Hines, *Localization: A Global Manifesto* (London: Earthscan, 2000), quoted in Amory Starr and Jason Adams, 'Anti-Globalization: The Global Fight for Local Autonomy', *New Political Science* 25, no. 1 (March 2003), 22.
61 Fred Curtis, 'Eco-Localism and Sustainability', *Ecological Economics* 46, no. 1 (August 2003): 83–102.
62 Tim Lang and Colin Hines, *The New Protectionism: Protecting the Future Against Free Trade* (New York: New Press, 1993), quoted in Starr and Adams (2003), 22.
63 Clare Hinrichs, 'The Practice and Politics of Food System Localization', *Journal of Rural Studies* 19, no. 1 (January 2003), 35.
64 Henry Bernstein, 'Food Sovereignty via the "Peasant Way": A Sceptical View', *The Journal of Peasant Studies* 41, no. 6 (8 January 2014), 1045.
65 Ibid., 1046.
66 See Anan Ganjanapan, 'Village in Thai Society: Conceptual Critiques', in *The Community Dimension: Local Way of Thinking Regarding Rights, Power and Natural Resource Management* (Bangkok: Thailand Research Fund, 2001), 56 (in Thai).
67 Boonrahong, Jantawongsri and Palee (2000), 35–37.
68 Sajin Prachason *et al.*, *Market Options of Farmers: Structural Effects on Unfairness and Benefit Distribution* (Bangkok: BioThai and the Social Research Foundation, Chulalongkorn University, 2012), 285 (in Thai); Decha Siripat, 'Diversified Farms: Solutions for Farmers (first Published in 1987)', in *The Path of Sustainable Agriculture*, 2nd edn (Samut-Sakorn: BioThai, 2011), 82 (in Thai).
69 For an example, see: Kam Pakha, '"Life Must Be Easy" Is Just a Propaganda', *Matichon*, 18 September 2014; Kam Pakha, 'Morality Leads Thailand towards Destruction', *Matichon (weekly)*, 14–20 January 2011 (in Thai).
70 AAN farmer groups, 'Kaen-Nakhon Manifesto' (2009) and Southern Alternative Farmer Group, 'Manifesto of the Southern Alternative Farmer' (2009).
71 Boonsong Martkhao, interviewed 25 December 2012, Yasothon.

72 Krisda Boonchai *et al.*, (2007), 25.
73 Decha Siripat, interviewed 14 October 2012, Nonthaburi.
74 Boonsong Martkhao, interviewed 25 December 2012, Yasothon; Adisorn Puangchompoo, interviewed 13 January 2013, Nonthaburi.
75 Ubol Yoowah, interviewed 22 December 2012, Yasothon.
76 Pakphum Inpan, interviewed 20 December 2012, Surin; Kittithanet Rangkaworaset, interviewed 13 January 2013, Nonthaburi.
77 Phra Promma Suphatto, interviewed 23 December 2012, Yasothon; Rungroj Kajadroka and Pakphum Inpan, interviewed 20 December 2012, Surin.
78 Mr Nikhom Pechpa, Thamma-ruamjai network, interviewed 23 December 2013, Yasothon.
79 Prachathip Kata, *Civil Society and the Path of Self-Reliance: Lessons from the Organic Agriculture Network in Yasothon* (Bangkok: Society and Health Institute, 2005), 42 (in Thai).
80 Phra Promma Suphatto, interviewed 23 December 2012, Yasothon.
81 Unno (2003), 118–119.
82 Pat Apaimool, interviewed 1 November 2012, Chiang Mai.
83 Nikhom Pechpa *et al.*, *A Complete Report of the Research Project on the Moral Rice Network* (Bangkok: Thailand Research Fund, 2009), English and Thai Abstract (in Thai); Pakphum Inpan, interviewed 20 December 2012, Surin.
84 For example, see: Steve Gliessman, 'Agroecology and Sustainable Food Systems Agroecology: Growing the Roots of Resistance', *Agroecology and Sustainable Food Systems* 37, no. 1 (2013): 19–31; Eric Holt-Giménez and Miguel A. Altieri, 'Agroecology, Food Sovereignty and the New Green Revolution', *Agroecology and Sustainable Food Systems* 37, no. 1 (4 September 2013): 90–102.
85 Dr Weerachai Nakwiboolwong, Director of Agricultural Land Reform Office (ALRO), quoted in Yupin Pongthong, 'Solving Farmers Crisis through Professional Schools in 6 provinces', *Bangkok Business News*, 11 August 2013 (in Thai).
86 For example, see Jonathan Rigg and Sakunee Nattapoolwat, 'Embracing the Global in Thailand: Activism and Pragmatism in an Era of Deagrarianization', *World Development* 29, no. 6 (June 2001): 945–960.
87 Prachason *et al.* (2012), 283.
88 Southern Alternative Farmer Group, 'Manifesto of the Southern Alternative Farmer' (2009) and AAN farmer groups, 'Kaen–Nakhon Manifesto' (2009).
89 Prachason *et al.* (2012), 232–233.
90 Chalita Bantuwong, 'Local Sage: Creation of Identity through Sustainable Agriculture', in *Sustainable Agriculture: Cultural Identity, Agricultural Problems and the Identity of Thai Farmers*, ed. Anusorn Unno (Nonthaburi: Sustainable Agriculture Assembly Committee and Heinrich Böll Foundation, 2004), 238–239 (in Thai).
91 An example is Mr Wilit Thechapaibul (see Bangkok Business Newspaper, 'Wilit Techapaibul ... Revolutionary Farmer', *Bangkok Business News*, 11 August 2008 (in Thai)).
92 Suksut and Jarusomboon, (2004), 199.
93 Supha Yaimuang, interviewed 3 October 2012, Nonthaburi.
94 Wanna Prayukvong, 'A Buddhist Economic Approach to the Development of Community Enterprises: A Case Study from Southern Thailand', *Cambridge Journal of Economics* 29 (2005): 1172.
95 J.W. Huguet, A. Chamratrithirong, and K. Richter, 'Thailand Migration Profile', in *Thailand Migration Report 2011: Migration for Development in Thailand – Overview and Tools for Policymaker*, ed. J.W. Huguet and A. Chamratrithirong (Bangkok: International Organization for Migration, 2012), 7–15, quoted in Jonathan Rigg, Buapun Promphaking and Ann Le Mare, 'Personalizing the Middle-Income Trap: An Inter-Generational Migrant View from Rural Thailand', *World Development* 59 (July 2014): 190.

96 Adisorn Puangchompoo, founder of the one rai-100,000 baht training programme, also discussed how some high school students joined the sustainable agriculture training programme in hope to earn enough income so that their parents can stop working in factories (interviewed 13 January 2013, Nonthaburi).
97 Witoon Lienchamroon, interviewed 5 April 2012, Nonthaburi.
98 A few interviewees mention these issues such as Mr Jai Kiti, a farmer from Mae-Aow village, Lamphun, interviewed 30 October 2012 and Mr Boonlue Jaroenmee, President of Klongyong co-operative, interviewed 10 October 2012, Nakhon Pathom.
99 Many sustainable farmers suggest this such as Pakphum Inpan and Samrach Thong-iam from Tamor group, interviewed 20 December 2012, Surin. Samrach, for example, used to work in a factory and in a company before he migrated back after the economic crisis of 1997. He decided to stay on due to relatively higher freedom and independence as a farmer compare to his previous jobs.
100 Krisda Boonchai *et al.*, (2007), 25; Supha Yaimuang, interviewed 3 October 2012, Nonthaburi.
101 Chomchuan Boonrahong, interviewed 3 November 2012, Chiang Mai.
102 See Suan-ngern mee-ma's website: www.suan-spirit.com/.
103 Chanuan Rattanawaraha, *Organic Agriculture* (Nonthaburi: Biotech Center, Department of Agriculture, 2007), 65 (in Thai).
104 Nikhom Pechpa, interviewed 23 December 2013, Yasothon.
105 Ms Sompoi Jansang, Manager of the Rice Fund Surin Organic Agriculture Co-operative Ltd., interviewed 19 December 2012, Surin; Mr Witoon Panyakul, main founder of Green Net Co-operative, interviewed 23 January 2013, Bangkok; Pakphum Inpan, interviewed 20 December 2012, Surin; Thamma Sangkalee, interviewed 22 December 2012, Surin.
106 Decha Siripat, interviewed 14 October 2012, Nonthaburi; Samrit Boonsuk, interviewed 19 December 2012, Surin.
107 Decha Siripat, 'The Assembly of the Poor and Alternative Agriculture Policies', in *The Path of Sustainable Agriculture*, 2nd edn. (Samut-Sakorn: BioThai, 2011), 96 (in Thai).
108 Unno (2003), 133.
109 Witoon Lienchamroon, 'Alternative Agriculture: A Path of Free and Independent Agriculture', in *Reform the Agricultural Sector for Food Security: Analysis and Practical Policies* (Nonthaburi: BioThai, 2011a), 167–173 (in Thai).
110 Green Net Co-operative's research quoted in National Committee to Develop Organic Agriculture, *National Strategic Plan to Develop Organic Agriculture 1 2008–2011 and National Practical Plan to Develop Organic Agriculture 2008–2011* (Bangkok: Sahamit Printing, 2008), 9 (in Thai).
111 Unno (2003), 145.
112 Witoon Lienchamroon and Supha Yaimuang, 'Alternative Agriculture: From Individual Farmers to Social Movements', in *Reform the Agricultural Sector for Food Security: Analysis and Practical Policies*, ed. Witoon Lienchamroon (Nonthaburi: BioThai, 2011), 269 (in Thai).
113 Siripat, 'Diversified Farms: Solutions for Farmers' (2011), 79–82.
114 Unno (2003), 109–111.
115 Ibid., 118.
116 Witoon Lienchamroon, interviewed 5 April 2012, Nonthaburi.
117 Adisorn Puangchompoo, interviewed 13 January 2013, Nonthaburi.
118 Dr Permsak Mokarapirom, President of Thammakaset Community in Prajeenburi province and Mr Wiwat Salyakamthorn, President of the Agri-Nature Foundation, quoted in Bangkok Business Newspaper, 'Natural Rice Production Method to Survive Flood', *Bangkok Business News*, 13 October, 2011 (in Thai).
119 Sukran Rojanapraiwong *et al.*, *Local Genes and Sustainable Agriculture: A Document for the Third Alternative Agriculture Assembly 18–21 November 2004, Kasetsart University* (Nonthaburi: Pim-dee Printing, 2004), 38–44 (in Thai).

120 Prachason *et al.* (2012), 187 and 190.
121 Ibid., 135.
122 San Saeng-Arun Magazine, 'From Way of Life and Cultural Roots to Machine-like Farmers: Problems and Solutions in the View of Witoon Lienchamroon', *San Saeng-Arun Magazine* (Bangkok, 2012), 79 (in Thai).
123 Unno (2003), 131.
124 Kittithanet Rangkaworaset, interviewed 13 January 2013, Nonthaburi.
125 Suchit Nokham, interviewed 2 November 2012, Chiang Mai.
126 Mr Arpakorn Krueng-ngern, Mae-ta organic farmer, interviewed 1 November 2012, Chiang Mai.
127 Sukran Rojanaphraiwong, *A Mission in Self-Reliance: Report of the Study on Tap-Tai Community Way of Life, Surin, by Natpong Pattanapanchai and Arat Saeng-Ubol* (Nonthaburi: Alternative Agriculture Network, 2008), 61 (in Thai).
128 Supha Yaimuang, interviewed 3 October 2012, Nonthaburi.
129 Decha Siripat, interviewed 14 October 2012, Nonthaburi. Similar suggestion include Ben White *et al.*, 'The New Enclosures: Critical Perspectives on Corporate Land Deals', *Journal of Peasant Studies* 39, no. 3–4 (July 2012), 626.
130 Prachason *et al.* (2012), 285.
131 Boonrahong, Jantawongsri and Palee (2000), 35–37.
132 Unno (2003), 145–146.
133 Supha Yaimuang *et al.*, *Alternative Markets: Partnership for a New Society* (Bangkok: Pim-dee Printing, 1996), 35 (in Thai).
134 Witoon Panyakul and Jade-sanee Sukjirattikarn, *Organic Market: Opportunities and Paths to World Organic Markets* (Bangkok: Earth Net Foundation/Green Net Co-operative, 2003), 131–132 (in Thai); Ms Pornpilai Lertwicha, researcher on Thai rural communities, skype interview 17 October 2012; Supha Yaimuang, interviewed 3 October 2012, Nonthaburi.
135 Unno (2003), 147.
136 Panyakul and Sukjirattikarn (2003), 133.
137 Ibid., 147
138 See: www.greennet.or.th/en for more detail.
139 Supha Yaimuang, interviewed 3 October 2012, Nonthaburi and Chomchuan Boonrahong, interviewed 3 November 2012, Chiang Mai.
140 Prachason *et al.* (2012), 178–179 and 182.
141 Ibid., 183.
142 Kanya Onsri, interviewed 22 December 2012, Surin.
143 Ubol Yoowah, interviewed 22 December 2012, Yasothon.
144 Arpakorn Krueng-ngern, interviewed 1 November 2012, Chiang Mai.
145 Rojanapraiwong *et al.* (2004), 67.
146 Prachason *et al.* (2012), 160–161.
147 Kanoksak Kaewthep, 'Rakthammachart Rice Mill: Naso Community, Ampur Kudchum, Yasothon Province', in *Journal of Political Economy (For the Community) 18* (Bangkok: Chulalongkorn University, 2001), 124–125 (in Thai).
148 Man Samsri, interviewed 25 December 2012, Yasothon.
149 Kata (2005), 21.
150 Sompoi Jansang, interviewed 19 December 2012, Surin.
151 Prachason *et al.* (2012), 165 and Rattanawaraha (2007), 11.
152 Prachason *et al.* (2012), 167–168.
153 Sompoi Jansang, interviewed 19 December 2012, Surin.
154 Rice mill manager's interview, 6 November 2012, quoted in Prachason *et al.* (2012), 168.
155 Sompoi Jansang, interviewed 19 December 2012, Surin.
156 Prachason *et al.* (2012), 172.

157 Ms Chutima Muangman, Manager of Naso rice mill, interviewed 25 December 2012, Yasothon.
158 Kata (2005), 21.
159 Ms Somwang Chomchuen, manager of Bak-rua rice mill, interviewed 24 December 2012, Yasothon.
160 Ibid.
161 Chutima Muangman, interviewed 25 December 2012, Yasothon.
162 Somwang Chomchuen, interviewed 24 December 2012, Yasothon.
163 Ibid.
164 Chutima Muangman, interviewed 25 December 2012, Yasothon.
165 Ibid. and Somwang Chomchuen, interviewed 24 December 2012, Yasothon.
166 Somwang Chomchuen, interviewed 24 December 2012, Yasothon.
167 Mr Boonyuen Arj-arsa, a committee member of Nam-oom Sustainable Agriculture Social Enterprise, interviewed 23 December 2012, Yasothon.
168 Mr Kamnueng Maneebool, advisor and former president of Nam-oom Sustainable Agriculture Social Enterprise, interviewed 23 December 2012, Yasothon.
169 Kamnueng Maneebool and Boonyuen Arj-arsa, interviewed 23 December 2012, Yasothon.
170 Ibid.
171 Rai is a Thai unit equals to 1,600 square metres.
172 Boonsong Martkhao, interviewed 25 December 2012, Yasothon.
173 Ibid.
174 Interviews of group leaders and members, quoted in Prachason *et al.* (2012), 139–140.
175 Ibid., 240.
176 Nikhom Pechpa, interviewed 23 December 2013, Yasothon.
177 Juthatip Patrawart, 'Branding as the Marketing Strategy for Organic Products: A Case Study on Moral Rice', *Asian Journal of Food and Agro-Industry* (2009), 256.
178 Ibid., 256.
179 Pechpa *et al.* (2009), English and Thai abstract.
180 Ibid.
181 Prachason *et al.* (2012), 131.
182 See the Abstract of Patrawart (2009).
183 Ibid.
184 Sompoi Jansang, interviewed 19 December 2012, Surin; Decha Siripat, interviewed 14 October 2012; Mr Kiatsak Chatdee, co-ordinator at the Institute for a Sustainable Agriculture Community (ISAC), interviewed 31 October 2012, Chiang Mai.
185 Decha Siripat, interviewed 14 October 2012 and Thamma Sangkalee, interviewed 22 December 2012, Surin.
186 Pat Apaimool, interviewed 1 November 2012, Chiang Mai.
187 Suchit Nokham, interviewed 2 November 2012, Chiang Mai.
188 Manus Losirikul and Prasit Karnchan, *The Possibility of Hom Mali Rice Production in Organic Farming Systems as an Alternative Farming Career with Poverty Alleviation Potential for Lower-Northeastern Farmers: A Case of Surin Province* (Bangkok: Thailand Research Fund, 2006), Executive Summary (in Thai).
189 Sukhum Pannarong and Pimolna Boonyasena, *A Study of Development Opportunity and Direction of Organic Crop Production System* (Chiang Mai: Research and Development Center for Community Economy, Economics Department, Chiang Mai University and the National Research Council of Thailand (NRCT), 2009), 140 (in Thai).
190 Pakphum Inpan, interviewed 20 December 2012, Surin; Thamma Sangkalee, interviewed 22 December 2012, Surin. During drought, yield could fall to 100 kg./rai.
191 Suchit Nokham, interviewed 2 November 2012, Chiang Mai.
192 Prachason *et al.* (2012), 277.

193 Ibid., 278.
194 Suphajit Manopimok *et al.*, *A Complete Report on the Research Project on the Possibility of Alternative Agriculture in Thailand: An Economics Analysis* (Bangkok: Thailand Research Fund, 2001), 24–25 (in Thai).
195 Thamma Sangkalee, interviewed 22 December 2012, Surin.
196 Prachason *et al.* (2012), 151–152.
197 Ibid., 151.
198 Ibid., 195.
199 Ibid., 195.
200 Ibid., 147 and 149 and 1164. Example includes Mr Uthai Juansang, Bak-rua organic farmer who has a household-scale mill and sells organic rice in local markets in addition to selling through Bak-rua rice mill (interviewed 24 December 2012, Yasothon).
201 An example include Arpakorn Krueng-ngern, interviewed 1 November 2012, Chiang Mai.
202 Chutima Muangman, interviewed 25 December 2012, Yasothon.
203 Kanya Onsri, interviewed 22 December 2012, Surin.
204 Ibid.
205 Quoted in TABLE 2: average monthly income per household by source of income and socio-economic class, Northeastern region: 2011 (in Baht), cited from the National Statistical Office (NSO), Thailand www.nso.go.th/.
206 Ibid.
207 Kanya Onsri, interviewed 22 December 2012, Surin.
208 Kamnueng Maneebool, interviewed 23 December 2012, Yasothon.
209 Triyada Trimakka and Ubol Yoo-wah, *A Study on Alternative Markets in Thailand: Market Access of Small-Scale Farmers* (Nonthaburi: SATHAI, 2008), quoted in Prachason *et al.* (2012), 185.
210 Suggestions based on personal experience by, for example: Kanoksak Duangkaewruen, interviewed 1 November 2012, Chiang Mai; Uthai Juansang, interviewed 24 December 2012, Yasothon.
211 For example, see Manopimok *et al.* (2001), 24–25.
212 Nattapong Pattanapanchai and Arat Saeng-ubon, *A Report on the Taptai Community Way of Life, Surin* (Surin: Alternative Agriculture Network, 2007), 43, quoted in Prachason *et al.* (2012), 186.
213 Somwang Chomchuen, interviewed 24 December 2012, Yasothon; Prachason *et al.* (2012), 148–149.
214 Prachason *et al.* (2012), 133.
215 Chomchuan Boonrahong, interviewed 3 November 2012, Chiang Mai.
216 Ibid.; Supha Yaimuang, interviewed 3 October 2012, Nonthaburi.
217 Chomchuan Boonrahong, interviewed 3 November 2014. In 2011, the average monthly income per household in the North was 17,350 baht per month (Table 2: average monthly income per household by source of income and socio-economic class, Northern region: 2011 (in Baht), cited from the National Statistical Office (NSO), Thailand www.nso.go.th/).
218 In 2012 managers of these rice mills were all female.
219 Ms Nanta Haitook, President of Baan Tanon Organic Herb and Vegetable Processing Group, interviewed 20 December 2012, Surin.
220 Research Institute of Organic Agriculture (FiBL) and International Federation of Organic Agriculture Movements (IFOAM), *The World of Organic Agriculture. Statistics and Emerging Trends 2014*, ed. Helga Willer and Lernoud Julia (Frick and Bonn: FiBL and IFOAM, 2014), 186.
221 Sompoi Jansang, interviewed 19 December 2012, Surin.
222 Kiatsak Chatdee, interviewed 31 October 2012, Chiang Mai; Nanthiya Hutanuwat and Narong Hutanuwat, *Before a Community Rice Mill Business Can Be Established:*

A Case Study of Bakrua Farmer Group, Yasothon Province (Ubolratchathani: Local Development Institute (LDI), 2000), 91–92 (in Thai); Assistant Professor Ampapan Pongpladisai, science lecturer at Ratchapat Surin University, interviewed 21 December 2012, Surin.

223 Ms Suwonasart Konbua, Green Net Co-operative officer, interviewed 24 December 2012, Yasothon.
224 Assistant Professor Ampapan Pongpladisai, interviewed 21 December 2012, Surin.
225 Witoon Lienchamroon, interviewed 5 April 2012, Nonthaburi.
226 Kiatsak Chatdee, interviewed 31 October 2012, Chiang Mai.
227 Suchit Nokham, interviewed 2 November 2012, Chiang Mai.
228 Examples: Mr Nichai Taipanich, Agricultural Advisor Office, Department of Agriculture, interviewed 17 January 2013, Nonthaburi; Arpakorn Krueng-ngern, interviewed 1 November 2012, Chiang Mai.
229 Sompoi Jansang, interviewed 19 December 2012; Uthai Juansang, interviewed 24 December 2012, Yasothon.
230 From experiences of farmers such as Arpakorn Krueng-ngern, interviewed 1 November 2012, Chiang Mai.
231 Boonsong Martkhao, interviewed 25 December 2012, Yasothon.
232 Mr Witoon Panyakul, Green Net Co-operative, interviewed 23 January 2013, Bangkok.
233 Panyakul and Sukjirattikarn (2003), 135; Ms Archinya Ourapeepattanapong, Managing Director at Chiangmai Organic and Spa Company, email exchange date 16 January 2013; Mr Paladisai Jinapak, All Be One Thailand, email exchange date 18 January 2013.
234 Witoon Panyakul, interviewed 23 January 2013, Bangkok.
235 Prachason *et al.* (2012), 172; Panyakul and Sukjirattikarn (2003), 135.
236 Kiatsak Chatdee, interviewed 31 October 2012; Pat Apaimool and Arpakorn Krueng-ngern, interviewed 1 November 2012, Chiang Mai; Aarat Sang-ubol, interviewed 19 December 2012, Surin; Bood-dee Piengprom, interviewed 22 December 2012, Surin.
237 Ms Suwanna Langnamsank, Managing Director of the Health Society Company Ltd (Lemon Farm Supermarkets), interviewed 11 February 2013, Nonthaburi.
238 Arpakorn Krueng-ngern, interviewed 1 November 2012, Chiang Mai.
239 Kiatsak Chatdee, interviewed 31 October 2012, Chiang Mai.
240 Suwanna Langnamsank, interviewed 11 February 2013, Nonthaburi; Witoon Panyakul, Green Net Co-operative, interviewed 23 January 2013, Bangkok.
241 Mr Pisit Werawaitaya, Earth Born Co. Ltd. (virgin coconut oil), email exchange date 18 January 2013 and Mrs Piyanat Na-Nakhon, Southeast Asia Organic Co. Ltd., email exchange date 16 January 2013.
242 Sompoi Jansang, interviewed 19 December 2012, Surin.
243 Kittithanet Rangkaworaset, interviewed 13 January 2013, Nonthaburi.
244 Chomchuan Boonrahong, interviewed 3 November 2012, Chiang Mai.
245 Ibid.; Pisit Werawaitaya, email exchange date 18 January 2013; Archinya Ourapeepattanapong, email exchange date 16 January 2013.
246 Paladisai Jinapak, email exchange date 18 January 2013.
247 Witoon Panyakul, interviewed 23 January 2013, Bangkok.
248 Rebec A. Fernandez, 'Agricultural Value Chain Financing in Thailand', in *Financial Access and Inclusion in the Agricultural Value Chain*, ed. Benedicto S. Bayaua (Bangkok: APRACA, 2008), 88–89.
249 Prachason *et al.* (2012), 171; Sompoi Jansang, interviewed 19 December 2012, Surin; Somwang Chomchuen, interviewed 24 December 2012, Yasothon; Kamnueng Maneebool, interviewed 23 December 2012, Yasothon.
250 Kamnueng Maneebool, interviewed 23 December 2012, Yasothon.
251 Boonyuen Arj-arsa, interviewed 23 December 2012, Yasothon.
252 Kamnueng Maneebool, interviewed 23 December 2012, Yasothon.

253 Sompoi Jansang, interviewed 19 December 2012, Surin; Boonyuen Arj-arsa, interviewed 23 December 2012, Yasothon.
254 Prachason *et al.* (2012), 171.
255 Ibid., 173.
256 Sompoi Jansang, interviewed 19 December 2012, Surin.
257 Chutima Muangman, interviewed 25 December 2012, Yasothon.
258 Somwang Chomchuen, interviewed 24 December 2012, Yasothon.
259 Chomchuan Boonrahong, interviewed 3 November 2012, Chiang Mai.
260 Rattanawaraha (2007), 68.
261 Manager's interview, 6 November 2012, quoted in Prachason *et al.* (2012), 168.
262 Chutima Muangman, interviewed 25 December 2012, Yasothon.
263 Supha Yaimuang, interviewed 3 October 2012, Nonthaburi; Kiatsak Chatdee, interviewed 31 October 2012, Chiang Mai; Chomchuan Boonrahong, interviewed 3 November 2012, Chiang Mai; Aarat Sang-ubol, interviewed 19 December 2012, Surin; Suwonasart Konbua, interviewed 24 December 2012, Yasothon.
264 For a comprehensive overview, also see Prachason *et al.* (2012) which covers groups from four provinces of Thailand (Nakhon Sawan, Karnchanaburi, Yasothon, Surin).
265 Rattanawaraha (2007), 11.
266 National Committee to Develop Organic Agriculture (2008), 12.
267 Green Net Co-operative, 'About Green Net Cooperative', www.greennet.or.th/about/greennet.
268 Akrapong Aanthong, 'Organic Product Standards: Symbolic Declaration from Civil Society', in *NGOs for Social Benefits ... and Social Processes Based on Knowledge and Wisdom*, ed. Sombat Hesakul, Supaporn Worapornpan, and Akrapong Aanthong (Bangkok: National Health Foundation, 2004), 60 (in Thai).
269 Nanta Haitook, interviewed 20 December 2012, Surin.
270 Prachason *et al.* (2012), 195.
271 Ibid., 130.
272 This view is also supported by Nikhom Pechpa, interviewed 23 December 2013, Yasothon.
273 Chutima Muangman, interviewed 25 December 2012, Yasothon.
274 Decha Siripat, interviewed 14 October 2012, Nonthaburi.
275 Ibid.
276 Suchit Nokham, interviewed 2 November 2012, Chiang Mai.
277 Arpakorn Krueng-ngern, interviewed 1 November 2012, Chiang Mai.
278 Summary from the interview of Suwanna Langnamsank, 11 February 2013, Nonthaburi.
279 Ibid.; Decha Siripat, interviewed 14 October 2012, Nonthaburi; Phra Promma Suphatto, interviewed 23 December 2012, Yasothon.
280 Phra Promma Suphatto, interviewed 23 December 2012, Yasothon.
281 Suwonasart Konbua, interviewed 24 December 2012, Yasothon.
282 Kankamkla Pilanoi, interviewed 23 December 2012, Yasothon.
283 Boonsong Martkhao, interviewed 25 December 2012, Yasothon.
284 An example include Dr Pratueng Narintarangkul Na Ayuthya, Chief Executive of Farmers' Reconstruction and Development Fund in Chiang Mai, interviewed 2 November 2012, Chiang Mai.
285 Boonsong Martkhao, interviewed 25 December 2012, Yasothon.
286 See Daoruang Puechphol *et al.*, *A Complete Report of the Research Project to Study Traditional Rice Genetics to Expand Organic Rice Production in Baan Kudhin, Baan Kammad, Baan Nonyang in Tambol Kammad, Ampur Kudchum, Yasothon Province* (Bangkok: Thailand Research Fund, 2010) (in Thai).
287 Pakphum Inpan, interviewed 20 December 2012, Surin.
288 Mr Kasemsak Sanpoch, former Surin governor, interviewed 21 December 2012, Surin.
289 Aarat Sang-ubol, interviewed 19 December 2012, Surin.

290 Kasemsak Sanpoch, interviewed 21 December 2012, Surin.
291 Kanoksak Duangkaewruan, interviewed 1 November 2012, Chiang Mai.
292 Ibid.
293 Ibid.
294 Ibid. and Rungroj Kajadroka, interviewed 20 December 2012, Surin.
295 Kanoksak Duangkaewruen, interviewed 1 November 2012, Chiang Mai.
296 Decha Siripat, interviewed 8 August 2001, quoted in Unno (2003), 157–158.
297 Siripat, 'The Assembly of the Poor' (2011c), 96–97.
298 Ibid., 96–97.
299 Rattanawaraha (2007), 217.
300 Witoon Panyakul and Pattarawadee Poomsak, *A Report on the Status of Research and Innovation Relating to Organic Agriculture in Thailand* (Bangkok: National Innovation Agency, 2008), 30 (in Thai).
301 'National Strategic Plan to Develop Organic Agriculture 2 2013–2016' draft, Received from Ms Wibulwan Wannamolee, Senior Specialist on Agri-Food Standards, National Bureau of Agricultural Commodity and Food Standards Office, 31 January 2013, 12–15 (in Thai).
302 Unno (2003), 185.
303 Nanthiya Hutanuwat, 'A Strategy to Expand Organic Jasmine Rice Production. A Paper for the 5th National Academic Conference on Agricultural System 5: Alternative Energy and Food Security for Humanity, 2–4 July 2009, Ubol International Hotel, Ubolratchathani Province' (Ubolratchathani, 2009), 129 (in Thai).
304 Rattanawaraha (2007), 217.
305 In 2014, the King was the Honorary President of the foundation and the crown princess was the committee chair, www.chaipat.or.th/chaipat/index.php/th/about-the-chai-pattana-foundation/about-us.
306 For example, see: Sompan Techa-artik, *Diversified Farms Save Lives and Dhamma: Self-Reliance and Growing Wealth in the Soil Sustainably* (Bangkok: Research and Development Institute, Khon-Kaen University, 1995), 174–175 quoted in Unno (2003), 186.
307 Mr Lun Saneh-ha, Naso member who was often invited by the bureaucracy to train other farmers, interviewed 25 December 2012, Yasothon.
308 Mr Somchai Wisartpong, Organic Agriculture and Development Group, Department of Agricultural Extension, phone interview on 21 January 2013.
309 Panyakul and Sukjirattikarn (2003), 145.
310 Ibid., 145.
311 For example, Ms Akinee Jiwattanapaiboon, Marketing Manager of Xondur Thai Organic Food Co. Ltd., discussed the company's limitations and inability to train producers in a larger scale (email exchange date 21 February 2013).
312 Panyakul and Poomsak (2008), 2.
313 Ibid., 3.
314 Karnda Boonthuan, 'Technology That Changes Paddy Fields', *Bangkok Business News*, 2 January 2014.
315 Panyakul and Poomsak (2008), 4–6.
316 Panyakul and Sukjirattikarn (2003), 145.
317 Lienchamroon and Yaimuang (2011), 295.
318 Decha Siripat, interviewed 8 August 2001, quoted in Unno (2003), 159.
319 Siripat, 'The Assembly of the Poor' (2011c), 96–97.
320 Phongpaichit and Baker (1995), 408–411.
321 Summary of initial demands of the Assembly of the Poor, 14 January 1997 and Decha Siripat, interviewed 8 August 2003, quoted in Anusorn Unno, *Social Movements for Common Resource Rights in the Thai Society: Alternative Agriculture in the Context of Property Rights System* (Nonthaburi: Alternative Agriculture Fair Committee, 2004), 231–232 (in Thai).

322 The Pilot Project to Develop Sustainable Agriculture for Small-Scale Farmers, *Lessons and Experiences of Sustainable Agricultural Development by Farmers and Community Organisations* (Nonthaburi: Sustainable Agriculture Foundation Thailand (SATHAI), 2004), 6 (in Thai).
323 Decha Siripat, interviewed 8 August 2001, quoted in Unno (2003), 159.
324 Ibid.; The Pilot Project to Develop Sustainable Agriculture for Small-scale Farmers (2004), 5.
325 Unno (2004), 233.
326 Ibid., 237; Decha Siripat, interviewed 8 August 2003, quoted in Unno (2004), 238.
327 The Pilot Project to Develop Sustainable Agriculture for Small-Scale Farmers (2004), 12.
328 Ibid., 11.
329 Ibid., 35.
330 Rojanapraiwong *et al.* (2004), 73.
331 Prachason *et al.* (2012), 177.
332 Ibid., 167–168.
333 The Pilot Project to Develop Sustainable Agriculture for Small-Scale Farmers (2004), 89–90.
334 Decha Siripat, interviewed 14 October 2012, Nonthaburi.
335 Paisit Panichkul, law lecturer at Chiang Mai University, interviewed 7 November 2012, Chiang Mai.
336 Tasnee Weerakan, NGO activist, interviewed 27 July 2003, quoted in Unno (2003), 161–162.
337 Witoon Lienchamroon, 'Lessons from the Struggle over Plant Genetics Protection under the WTO's TRIPS', in *Reform the Agricultural Sector for Food Security: Analysis and Practical Policies* (Nonthaburi: BioThai, 2011d), 73 (in Thai).
338 Ibid., 73.
339 Ibid., 73.
340 Vandana Shiva, 'The Future of Food: Countering Globalisation and Recolonisation of Indian Agriculture', *Futures* 36 (2004), 718.
341 Tasnee Weerakan, NGO activist, interviewed 27 July 2003, quoted in Unno (2003), 161–162.
342 Lienchamroon, 'Lessons from the Struggle' (2011d), 69.
343 Anusorn Unno, *Farmer Rights in Thailand: Learning Process and Agricultural System Development. A Research Under Thai Human Rights Project.* (Bangkok: Thailand Research Fund, 2002), 70, quoted in Unno (2004), 280.
344 Bangkok Post Newspaper, 'Fresh Struggle Kicks off to Halt GM Crops', *Bangkok Post*, 24 October 2014.
345 BioThai, 'Civil Society Is on Guard against the Passing of GMO Law That Will Benefit Transnational Seed Companies', 21 January 2015, www.biothai.net/node/25705. (in Thai)
346 From many news report and Witoon Lienchamroon's interview in Prachathai, 'Civil Society Disagrees with Changing of the Law to Aid Seed Companies', *Prachathai*, March 1, 2013 (in Thai).
347 Witoon Lienchamroon, 'Fighting FTA: the Thai Experience', in *Reform the Agricultural Sector for Food Security: Analysis and Practical Policies* (Nonthaburi: BioThai, 2011c), 311–314 (in Thai).
348 Decha Siripat, interviewed 14 October 2012, Nonthaburi. Also see: Witoon Lienchamroon, 'Behind the Movement to Extend Agricultural Chemicals Registration', in *Reform the Agricultural Sector for Food Security: Analysis and Practical Policies* (Nonthaburi: BioThai, 2011b), 55–58 (in Thai).
349 Lienchamroon and Yaimuang (2011), 296.
350 Witoon Panyakul, interviewed 23 January 2013, Bangkok; Kankamkla Pilanoi, interviewed 23 December 2012, Yasothon.

351 Arat Sang-ubol, interviewed 19 December 2012, Surin; Mr Direk Kong-ngern and Mr Montri Bualoi, Baan Pong CLTD, interviewed 31 October 2012, Chiang Mai.
352 For example: Andrew Walker, 'Environmental Issues in Thailand: A Rural Perspective', in *Thailand's Economic Recovery: Proceedings of the National Thai Studies Centre Annual Thailand Update 2004*, ed. Cavan Hogue (Singapore: ISEAS, 2006), 78–80; Kevin Hewison, 'Responding to Economic Crisis: Thailand's Localism', in *Reforming Thai Politics*, ed. Duncan McCargo (Copenhagen: NIAS Press, 2002), 149 and 156–157.
353 Phongpaichit (2005), 138.
354 Apichai Puntasen, 'Applying Self-Sufficient Economy to Systematically Solve Poverty', in *Dhamma Economics: A Collection of Speeches of Distinguished Professors from the Economics Department, Thammasat University* (Bangkok: OpenBooks, 2010), 93 (in Thai).
355 The King's birthday royal speech in 1998, quoted in Warr (2007), 3; Royal speeches in 2007, 2008, and 2011 quoted in Suthep Udomrat, 'Self-Sufficiency Philosophy', in *Safety and Stability Through Self-Sufficiency Economy*, ed. Pitaya Wongkul (Bangkok: Withithat Institute, 2008), 74 and 77.
356 Rigg and Nattapoolwat (2001), 946.
357 Ibid., 957.
358 Hewison (2002), 148.
359 Ibid., 158.
360 Ibid., 155–156.
361 Prawase Wasi, *Ideas and Strategies for Equality between State, Power and Society, and for Wisdom* (Bangkok: Komolkeemthong, 1993) and Prawase Wasi, *Buddhist Agriculture and Peaceful Happiness for Thai Society* (Bangkok: Mo-chaoban, 1987), quoted in Nartsupha (2010), 159 (in Thai).
362 Anan Ganjanapan, *Dynamics of Communities in Resource Management: Ideological Framework and Policies* (Bangkok: Thailand Research Fund, 2000) and Anan Ganjanapan, *Economic Culture in an Economy of No Culture* (Bangkok: Kopfai, 2001), quoted in Nartsupha (2010), 159–160 (in Thai).
363 Hewison (2002), 149.
364 Rigg, Promphaking and Le Mare (2014), 186 and 195.
365 Prachason *et al.* (2012), 285.
366 From the Abstract of Duncan McCargo, 'Populism and Reformism in Contemporary Thailand', *South East Asia Research* 9, no. 1 (2001): 89–107.
367 Hewison (2002), 157 and also see Thongchai Winichakul, 'Nationalism and the Radical Intelligentsia in Thailand', *Third World Quarterly* 29, no. 3 (April 2008): 575–591.
368 Phongpaichit and Baker (1995), 388.
369 Nartsupha (2010), 170–172
370 Ibid., 168.
371 Seksan Prasertkul, *Citizen Politics in Thai Democracy* (Bangkok: Amarin, 2005) (in Thai); Anek Laothamatat, *Progressive Locality: Political Theories to Build the Local as a Foundation for Democracy* (Bangkok: Thai Health Organisation, 2009) (in Thai); Anek Laothamatat, *Changing Areas and Foundation: Building Local Administration and a Foundation for Democracy* (Bangkok: Thammasart University, 2009) (in Thai), all quoted in Nartsupha (2010), 175–176 (in Thai).
372 Unger (2009), 145.
373 See: www.agrinature.or.th/node/1.
374 Unger (2009), 145.
375 Mark Rupert, *Ideologies of Globalization: Contending Visions of a New World Order* (London: Routledge, 2000), 11–12.
376 Owen Worth, 'Beyond World Order and Transnational Classes. The (Re)application of Gramsci in Global Politics', in *Gramsci and Global Politics. Hegemony*

and Resistance, ed. Mark McNally and John Schwarzmantel (Oxon: Routledge, 2009), 29–30.

377 Abdurazack Karriem, 'The Rise and Transformation of the Brazilian Landless Movement into a Counter-hegemonic Political Actor: A Gramscian Analysis', *Geoforum* 40, no. 3 (May 2009), 323–324.

378 Lienchamroon and Yaimuang (2011), 294.

379 Bantuwong (2004), 268.

380 Phongpaichit and Baker (1995), 388.

381 Brad Coombes and Hugh Campbell, 'Dependent Reproduction of Alternative Modes of Agriculture: Organic Farming in New Zealand', *Sociologia Ruralis* 38, no. 2 (1998): 127–145, quoted in Julie Guthman, 'Room for Manoeuvre? (In)organic Agribusiness in California', in *Agribusiness and Society. Corporate Responses to Environmentalism, Market Opportunities and Public Regulation* (London: Zed Books, 2004), 118.

382 Daniel Buck, Christina Getz and Julie Guthman, 'From Farm to Table: The Organic Vegetable Commodity Chain of Northern California', *Sociologia Ruralis* 37, no. I (1997): 3–20.

383 Guthman (2004).

384 CorpWatch-Thailand, 'Connections Between CP, Politicians and Thai Bureaucracy', in *CP and Thai Agriculture* (Nonthaburi: BioThai, 2008), 38 (in Thai).

385 Witoon Lienchamroon, 'Alternative Agriculture' (2011a), 177–178.

386 Panyakul and Sukjirattikarn (2003), 134.

387 Nikhom Pechpa, interviewed 23 December 2013, Yasothon.

388 Chutima Muangman, interviewed 25 December 2012, Yasothon

389 For example: Peter M. Rosset and Miguel A. Altieri, 'Agroecology Versus Input Substitution: A Fundamental Contradiction of Sustainable Agriculture', *Society and Natural Resources* 10, no. 3 (1997): 283–295; Julie Guthman, 'Regulating Meaning, Appropriating Nature: The Codification of California Organic Agriculture', *Antipode* 30, no. 2 (1998): 135–154.

390 Prachason *et al.* (2012), 172.

391 Somwang Chomchuen, interviewed 24 December 2012, Yasothon.

392 Many interviewees pointed out this issue such as: Supha Yaimuang, interviewed 3 October 2012, Nonthaburi; Chomchuan Boonrahong, interviewed 3 November 2012, Chiang Mai.

393 An observation by Sompoi Jansang, Manager of the Rice Fund Surin mill, 19 December 2012, Surin.

394 For example, see: Laura DeLind and Philip Howard, 'Safe at Any Scale? Food Scares, Food Regulation, and Scaled Alternatives', *Agriculture and Human Values* 25, no. 3 (2008): 301–317; Yuichiro Amekawa, 'Reflections on the Growing Influence of Good Agricultural Practices in the Global South', *Journal of Agricultural and Environmental Ethics* 22, no. 6 (2009): 531–557, quoted in Pepijn Schreinemachers *et al.*, 'Can Public GAP Standards Reduce Agricultural Pesticide Use? The Case of Fruit and Vegetable Farming in Northern Thailand', *Agriculture and Human Values* 29 (2012), 520.

395 For example, see: C. Chen, J. Yang and C. Findlay, 'Measuring the Effect of Food Safety Standards on China's Agricultural Exports', *Review of World Economics* 144, no. 1 (2008): 83–106, quoted in Schreinemachers *et al.* (2012), 520.

396 For example, see: Lawrence Busch, 'The Private Governance of Food: Equitable Exchange or Bizarre Bazaar?', *Agriculture and Human Values* 36, no. 3 (2009): 1–8, quoted in Schreinemachers *et al.* (2012), 520.

397 Anusorn Unno, 'Alternative Agriculture: Indigenous Knowledge Advances and Counter-Attack', in *Knowledge and Politics of Natural Resources. Academic Series Number 43*, ed. Darin Inmuan (Bangkok: Princess Maha Chakri Sirindhorn Anthropology Centre, 2005), 228 (in Thai).

398 Ibid., 237–249.
399 Ibid., 228.
400 Ibid., 229.
401 An example include the 'National Strategic Plan to Develop Organic Agriculture 2 2013–2016 draft', received from Ms Wibulwan Wannamolee, Senior Specialist on Agri-Food Standards, National Bureau of Agricultural Commodity and Food Standards Office, 31 January 2013, 1 and 11.
402 Pruek Thaotawil, 'Self-Sufficiency Project at the Village Level: Elitist Control over the Rural Sector', *Fah-Diewkan Academic Magazine* 6, no. 2 (2008), 71 and 73 (in Thai).
403 Ibid., 86.
404 Ibid., 86. Similar points are also made by Decha Siripat, 14 October 2012, as well as by Adisorn Puangchompoo and Kittithanet Rangkaworaset, interviewed 13 January 2013, Nonthaburi.
405 Mr Sittipon Bangkaew, Director of the Office of Commercial Affairs in Surin, interviewed 21 December 2012, Surin.
406 Ms Wibulwan Wannamolee, senior officer at the Office of Agricultural Standards and Accredition, interviewed 31 January 2013, Nonthaburi.
407 Schreinemachers *et al.* (2012), 521–522.
408 Birgit Roitner-Schobesberger *et al.*, 'Consumer Perceptions of Organic Foods in Bangkok, Thailand', *Food Policy* 33 (2008), Abstract, 114 and 115.
409 Panyakul and Sukjirattikarn (2003), 136.
410 Schreinemachers *et al.* (2012), 519, 523–526.
411 Examples: Sompoi Jansang, 19 December 2012, Surin; Somwang Chomchuen, interviewed 24 December 2012, Yasothon; Boonsong Martkhao, interviewed 25 December 2012, Yasothon.
412 Prachason *et al.* (2012), 237.
413 Ibid., 237; Sompoi Jansang, interviewed 19 December 2012, Surin; Thamma Sangkalee, interviewed 22 December 2012, Surin.
414 Somwang Chomchuen, interviewed 24 December 2012, Yasothon.
415 Prachason *et al.* (2012), 124.
416 Ibid., 122–123; Suwonasart Konbua, interviewed 24 December 2012, Yasothon; Chutima Muangman, interviewed 25 December 2012, Yasothon.
417 Sompoi Jansang, interviewed 19 December 2012, Surin; Sittiporn Bangkaew, interviewed 21 December 2012, Surin; Kamnueng Maneebool, interviewed 23 December 2012, Yasothon.
418 Sittipon Bangkaew, interviewed 21 December 2012, Surin
419 Mr Thaspong Tonklang and Mr Thanachote Jaikla, Director and Vice Director of the local administration office in Tambol Tamor, Surin, interviewed 20 December 2012, Surin; Mr Songpun Kuldilokrat, Managing Director at Arysta LifeScience Co. Ltd., email correspondent 21 January 2013; Dr Kriengsak Suwantharadol, Syngenta (Thailand), email correspondent 14 March 2013.

6 The land reform movement in Thailand

Introduction

Compared to the sustainable farmers discussed in the previous chapter, members of the land reform movement (LRM) in Thailand tend to consist of relatively more marginalised farmers and labourers without or with insufficient land. The contemporary LRM can be seen as partially a legacy of the Peasants Federation of Thailand, which was brutally suppressed by the military and right-wing groups in the 1970s and 1980s, but it also found inspirations from community rights ideas as well as the transnational food sovereignty discourse and land movements in other countries. This chapter discusses the LRM's counter-hegemonic ideas, governance structures, and production–distribution practices. It also suggests that the LRM can be seen as part of global counter-hegemonic forces consisting of transnational, national, and local movements which try to de-commodify and promote equitable distribution of land. Similar to the previous chapter, this chapter helps to support the second and third main arguments of the book: although the mainstream agri-food system is dominated by hegemonic capitalist interests, domestic and transnational counter-hegemonic forces can influence some changes in the system even though they are faced with limitations and co-optation of oppositions. This chapter also supports the fourth main argument of the book and suggests that even though the LRM faces some difficulties, its hegemonic project should be seen as an on-going process that evolves over time, constrained by political-economic structural conditions, and that lingering hegemonic elements should be addressed rather than sentenced as failures.

Empirical information in this chapter is based on secondary sources in English and Thai, as well as interviews of 27 people, such as land occupiers, activists, civil servants, and academics. In this chapter, the LRM is conceptualised as broad and unstructured networks consisting of different groups and individuals from all regions of Thailand who are united by similar ideas and goals. Notable groups include the Northern Peasants Federation, Esaan Land Reform Network, Southern Peasants Federation, and Bantad Mountain Land Reform Network. Interviews and site visits for this chapter were based in five provinces in two regions of Thailand, including Bangkok, Nonthaburi, and Nakhon Patom in the Central region, as well as Chiang Mai and Lamphun in the Northern region, with focuses on Community Land Title Deed (CLTD) projects. Interviews of LRM members from the South were conducted during the LRM protest in front of Government House in Bangkok in October 2012.

The first part of this chapter discusses the LRM's critique of hegemonic land governance and its counter-hegemonic ideas. Counter-hegemonic governance structures and production–distribution practices are discussed in Parts 2 and 3 respectively. Part 4 then discusses some important obstacles facing the movement such as violence, legal suits, political polarisation, as well as possibility of co-optation of oppositions.

Part 1 Counter-hegemonic ideas and discourses

LRM members use terms, such as 'commodification of land' and 'community rights' in their discourses, but these terms often cause confusions to those outside the movement. Some Thais are also sceptical of the term 'community rights' because for them it invokes conservative backward images of closed and hierarchical social structures. This part of the chapter provides an overview of the LRM's counter-hegemonic ideas which help to shed light on these issues. First, section 1.1 discusses the LRM's critique of hegemonic land governance structures which give primacy to private individual rights and encourage the commodification of land. This section also discusses the LRM's ideas in relation to current academic literature and transnational land movements. Section 1.2 then discusses counter-hegemonic ideas of the LRM that inspire CLTD practices, particularly ideas regarding the complexity of rights.

1.1 The LRM's critique of hegemonic land governance

Between 1982 and 1986, the Thai state started to implement a formal titling programme, with encouragements from the World Bank and other international institutions, which gave loans to Thailand.[1] Formal titling increased land values throughout the country.[2] There were also more land transactions and increased borrowing against land from formal financial institutions, as well as increased fiscal revenues from land, which all led to the Thai formal titling programme's receipt of the World Bank Award for Excellence in 1997.[3] The World Bank also promoted similar market-led agrarian reform schemes in other countries in the 1990s, such as in Brazil, South Africa, and the Philippines.[4]

Some academics and members of the LRM point out that formal land titling resulted in increased land speculation. Some people used land as collateral to take out loans from commercial banks to purchase more land,[5] which were then often left under-utilised.[6] After the Asian economic crisis of 1997, fallen land prices led to a lot of non-performing loans. Many land plots were confiscated by banks and left unused.[7] Similar to the situations in many other countries, dispossessions of relatively poorer parts of the population, such as farmers, become notable effects in Thailand because land sales favour those who have access to capital and greater ability to purchase land.[8] Some academic studies and members of the LRM also point to widespread corruption in the issuing of formal titling documents,[9] as well as transparency problems in the rental and usage of state-owned land. In Suratthani province, Thai and foreign companies continued to use 60,043 rai[10] of reserved forest land even though their licence had already expired, and 68,500 rai of palm oil plantations also continued their operations even though their licenses had expired.[11] The capturing of the titling process by elites is, however, not specifically unique to the Thai context.[12]

LRM members often use the term 'commodification of land' to describe the consequences of market-led governance of land[13] or sometimes as the work of Neo-liberalism.[14] Commodification of land is also criticised as being responsible for over-usage of land. One frequently cited example is eucalyptus plantations which lead to land and water degradation in nearby areas.[15] Even though they did not use academic terms, some interviewed LRM members express feelings of alienation from the legal system and from state land policies,[16] criticise the centralisation of political power in Bangkok,[17] as well as linkages between large capital and the Thai state which stop land reform issues from being taken seriously.[18] Although the Constitution (1997 as well as 2007) accepts principles of community rights in resource management, legally there can only be either state or private land.[19] In addition, forestry laws encourage the Forestry Ministry's control over many sites of land whose ownerships are being contested.[20] These issues are discussed in greater detail in section 2.2.

To be fair, the Thai state has made some attempts to redistribute land and to promote equitable ownership of land. Owing to pressures from social movements in the 1970s, which called for land reform, the Thai state passed the Land Reform Act and established the Agricultural Land Reform Office (ALRO) in 1975.[21] The Land Reform Act stipulated a maximum holding of 50 rai of land with surplus land liable to expropriation and distribution to peasants after compensation at market value.[22] In practice, however, the law is generally not enforced on the landlords.[23] As for ALRO, most land that it managed to redistribute to small-scale farmers were state owned or deforested public land. Only 383,760 rai of farmland had been purchased from private landowners by 1993.[24] By 2012, ALRO claimed to redistribute 34 million rai of land to 2.26 million farmers in 70 provinces.[25] However, data in 2010 suggests that only 29 per cent of farmers own land.[26] ALRO is also haunted by the Sor Por Kor 4–01 scandal during the Chuan Leekpai administration, which came into power in 1993, where some ALRO land were believed to have been given to rich and influential allies of the government in the South.[27] A few studies also suggest that redistributed state land given to small-scale farmers have changed hands despite prohibitive laws.[28] As the next section discusses in greater detail, the LRM also suggests that individual titling deeds manoeuvre for dispossessions of small-scale farmers through market forces. Moreover, exchanges of ideas with transnational social movements, such as La Vía Campesina, also increase LRM members' awareness of the new wave of global land grabs which partly arises from food–energy scarcity concerns.

1.2 Counter-hegemonic ideas regarding land governance

The LRM has developed its counter-hegemonic ideas and practices over time by learning from experience and through discussions between local farmers, NGOs and academics. Many people in the contemporary LRM in the North were inspired by the leftist Peasants Federation of Thailand (PFT)[29] which mobilised to pressure for land reform in the 1970s, but was brutally suppressed by the military and right-wing groups in the late 1970s and early 1980s.[30] Discussions among Northern farmer networks, which led to the establishment of the Northern Peasants Federation on 22 October 1999, concluded that many problems facing farmers, such as those relating to land, water, forest, agricultural prices and debt, are similar to the problems back in 1972.[31] Members of the LRM also suggest that one failure of the ALRO is that it distributes land in the form of individual title deeds, which allows these land to be sold off to non-farmers and enables relatively easy appropriation by businessmen and landlords who have higher economic power.[32] As a potential solution to this problem, many people in the LRM are drawn to community rights ideas, which, as discussed in previous chapters, are seen by many NGOs and activists in Thailand as inspirations to alternative development paths. In addition, Anan Ganjanapan's work on the 'complexity of rights' are often referred to by the LRM.

Some scholars warn against romanticising the community-based governance of natural resources where community is conceptualised as territorially fixed, small, and homogenous.[33] Anan Ganjanapan also points out that communities should not be seen as a static ideal or essentialised units which remain unchanged over time, nor as isolated units with no relations to wider society, the state, or market. Instead, it is important to see communities as changeable and recreatable, as well as to recognise power ideologies and social relations in the constructions of communities which can be harmonious or conflict-prone. A community's boundaries are not limited by geographical space, but by multiple sets of boundaries, such as at household and village levels, as well as by wider networks that may not occupy the same geographical space.[34] As social situations continue to change, such as through dialogues and disagreements involving different groups of people in the society, a community's values and rules can be adjusted to suit changing situations. In other words, 'community' can be seen as a unit, as well as an identity, which is constantly being recreated or reproduced through community members' engagement with wider society.[35]

Community rights discourse can also be seen as a reaction to hegemonic 'mono-right' mentality and legal system which violate the 'complexity of rights' practices in some rural societies.[36] Complexity of rights refer to multiple management principles where different forms of rights can overlap, implying a sense of generosity and self-help in the community to help secure everyone's ability to meet basic needs.[37] For example, one may have an ownership right over a piece of land but others may benefit from byproducts of the land. Leading supporters of CLTD tend to see complexity of rights and community rights as social innovations that challenge the capitalist way of thinking.[38] In a way, CLTD can be seen as ideational extensions of community forest ideas regarding the management of some forest land.[39] It should also be noted that CLTD does not imply giving exclusive rights to local groups, but that other parties, such as the state and civil society, can be involved in the governance of natural resources in a form of checks and balances.[40]

The complexity of rights concept is embedded in CLTD practices as land is owned collectively with democratic rule-setting arrangements, while individual members receive the right to use individual plots of land for agricultural and housing purposes.[41] Main ideas embedded in CLTD are that land is not merely a commodity and that secure land tenure for small-scale farmers is a matter of social justice with implication towards poverty reduction.[42] In CLTD projects, land is decommodified in the sense that members cannot sell their individual land plots through market channels and can only sell their usage rights back to the group at pre-arranged non-market prices. This also helps to prevent land grabs and to secure land tenure for members, as well as future generations.[43]

Preserving land tenure rights for future generations does not mean that the younger generations in these communities are 'locked-in' to the farming profession. As discussed by Ganjanapan, CLTD could be seen as 'cushions' or safety nets for marginalised people, especially in times of economic crisis, given that existing market governance structures are bias in favour of large capital and considering that agriculture is still one of the primary sources of income that requires little capital investment.[44] From this perspective, CLTD ideas and practice are rather like strategic adaptive tools to empower marginalised people, particularly in the short- and medium-run, rather than a static universal solution.[45] As Part 2 discusses in greater depth, the economic necessity of having nil or insufficient land after the 1997 Asian economic crisis prompted some people to occupy land and to join the LRM.[46] During interviews, some LRM members also discuss how their aging physical conditions prevent them from continuing to work as low-skilled labourers in the industrial sector, and that gaining access to land in CLTD projects help them to earn income.[47]

Owing to environmental and food security concerns,[48] as well as a strategic need to gain acceptance from wider society,[49] the LRM and its CLTD discourse also promote sustainable management of natural resource and agricultural production. At least at the leadership level, CLTD is portrayed as a mechanism to safeguard agricultural land for small-scale farmers for food security and for the development of sustainable agricultural food production.[50] Part 3 discusses attempts to promote sustainable agriculture in greater detail.

It is recognised that not everyone in the same areas as that of CLTD projects agree with the LRM's ideas. Even within LRM community groups, there is still a lot of disparity in terms of understanding and acceptance of CLTD ideas,[51] not to mention, some feelings of alienation with academic terms used by some members of the LRM.[52] It has been noted that original CLTD communities in the North tend to have firm beliefs in CLTD principles, whereas latecomer groups only joined the movement because they saw an opening of political space which might allow them to gain access to land.[53] Many people joined the LRM, not necessary because they believe in CLTD ideas, but because they hope to increase their bargaining power and, in the case that they receive CLTD from the state, to stop harassment from the authorities.[54] Some CLTD members prefer to receive individual title deeds but settle for CLTD because they think there is no chance that they will receive the former.[55] It took a while, for example, for a majority of Klongyong co-operative members to join the LRM and promote CLTD because, initially, they were used to complying with the bureaucracy's requests. By 2012, there were still a few people in the minority who disagree with the CLTD approach and prefer to have individual title deeds.[56] Nevertheless, many Klongyong members eventually became convinced of the benefits of CLTD because it guarantees that at least their children will have some access to land.[57] Those in other CLTD projects also reflect similar sentiments. For example, a member of Bantad Mountain group reflects how 'money runs out ... but land is an asset that we have to protect and give to future generations'.[58]

Counter-hegemonic ideas of the LRM resonate with some academic literature and global counter-hegemonic initiatives which similarly question whether the current private property right regime helps to ensure security of tenure.[59] For example, the International Conference on Agrarian Reform and Rural Development (ICARRD), organised by the FAO and Brazil in March 2006 in Porto Alegre, helps to form a new normative basis for future international land governance that also include collective land rights.[60] Contrary to neo-liberal economic thinking, it has been suggested that limiting land sales can protect small-scale farmers from being pressured to cede their land and protect usage rights over communal land.[61] It has also been argued that allowing the emergence of a market for rental rights is a more pro-poor option compared to individual titling schemes which imply the marketability of land rights. Alternatives to individual titling include the adoption of anti-eviction laws in combination with the registration of use rights based on customary forms of tenure.[62] While restrictions on land sales prevent further commodification of land, formal legal recognition of customary rights can provide effective security, promote access to credit, and long-term investment on the land.[63] In addition, distributing land to small-scale farmers can be used to promote productive, equitable, and environmentally sustainable use of land.[64]

The LRM receives help from a few media channels such as ThaiPBS to spread its ideas. It also links up with other groups in society, often under the name P-Move or People's Movement for a Just Society, which is an umbrella organisation consisting of 10 networks including the Four-Region Slum Network, the Assembly of the Poor's Pakmun group, and the Contract Farmer Network. Other allies include Local Act Organisation, Southern Fishermen Network, and the Alternative Agriculture Network.[65] There are also many international collaborations and exchanges of ideas. After land occupations in the North, many leading members visited Brazil's Landless Rural Workers' Movement (MST),[66] the Zapatista in Mexico, and the land movement in Peru.[67] Site visits and exchanges of ideas inspired the LRM in Thailand, but many people also commented on very different social contexts in those countries compared to Thailand.[68] The LRM is also a member of La Vía Campesina (through the Northern Peasants Federation) and participations in international conferences also help to promote interests in the problems of the global agri-food system, as well as the principles of food sovereignty.[69]

Part 2 Counter-hegemonic governance of land

To accomplish their ideas and goals, LRM members campaign for counter-hegemonic land governance which encompasses two dimensions: (1) the development of CLTD as practical examples of democratic local governance of land and; (2) a national campaign to challenge hegemonic legal and policy governance structures. Sections 2.1 and 2.2 discuss these dimensions. Arguably, the CLTD democratic form of local land governance helps to challenge hegemonic hierarchical ideas and informal social relations, which were discussed in Chapter 3. National mobilisation as a social movement also helps to alter members' mentality, from being that of those who tend to wait for help from the bureaucracy, to citizens who feel that they can negotiate with the Thai state, as well as participate in the decision-making process and natural resource management.[70] Section 2.3 takes a step back to explore potential limitations of CLTD and ALRO as counter-hegemonic projects and suggests that it is unlikely for any single form of land governance to be a universally appropriate counter-hegemonic solution that fits all occasions.

2.1 Ground-up land reform and CLTD

After the Asian economic crisis in 1997, many workers in Thailand lost their jobs in the industrial and service sectors and returned home to rural parts of the country. In some places, they found that common land they were once able to used, such as to grow and harvest food, had become private properties often owned by people from outside of the communities. The economic necessity of having nil or insufficient land for subsistence and to produce in exchange for income prompted some groups of people to occupy unutilised land in Lamphun and Chiang Mai from around 1998 onwards.[71] Land occupations in the North have developed into the ideas and practice of CLTD which are then supported by many groups in other parts of the country. In many of these places, land conflicts arise from contestations between citizens and the Thai state over the boundaries of reserved forest.[72]

This section first discusses CLTD projects in the North (Baan Sritia, Baan Pae-tai, Baan Raidong/Mae-aow and Baan Pong) which were the focus of site visits. Then, prominent CLTD examples in other parts of the country are discussed, such as Bantad Mountain group and Suratthani's land reform groups in the South, Samsiew group in the Northeast, and Klongyong co-operative in the Central region. While the nature of land conflicts and practices of CLTD can be quite different, these groups are similar with regards to their acceptance of land reform goals and main CLTD principles.

LRM groups in the North and the origin of CLTD

Sritia was considered the first village that started to occupy and allocate land to members. The land movement in Sritia started around 1989 as a response to the problems with the Nongplasawai land redistribution project.[73] One of its leaders, Mr Thana Yasopa, also joined the Assembly of the Poor's protest in Bangkok in 1997 to pressure the government to solve land problems.[74] Discussions on the lack of land between Sritia and other villages also spurred land occupations in nine nearby villages between 1997 and 2002, including Baan Pae-tai which occupied around 200 rai of land,[75] Baan Raidong/Mae-aow in Lamphun, and Baan Pong in Chiang Mai.

On 9 November 2000, around 300 people from Raidong, Mae-aow and Nong-samanatai villages occupied 426 rai of land which was left unused for three to four decades.[76] In 2001, the land reform network in Lamphun managed to pressure Lamphun's governor to set up a committee to investigate land problems,[77] which found that 290 out of 426 rai have legal deeds that belong to ALRO.[78] After land occupation, participants allocated around one rai per member to approximately 282 members. If members no longer require the land for productive purposes, they can sell their usage rights back to the group and receive some pre-agreed monetary compensation for their work on the land, which is not as high as the market price. This measure aims to prevent the community from losing control over the land and to ensure that land is used productively by small-scale CLTD.[79] Raidong/Mae-aow group also keeps 10 rai of land as common land which have been used to grow crops to earn income for the group's collective fund.[80]

Another strong CLTD group in the North which learned from the experience of Sritia and Raidong/Mae-aow is Baan Pong in Chiang Mai. The group consists of around 79 households or 412 members[81] who occupied over 458 rai of land.[82] Initially, the land was common land that was sold off to people outside of the community for speculation purposes, real estate projects, or as securities to take out loans, but since then they been mostly foreclosed by banks.[83] Baan Pong members occupied the land in 2002 because of economic pressures from having insufficient farm land, which became more acute after the 1997 Asian economic crisis.[84] In Baan Pong CLTD project, around 60 per cent of land is used for agricultural production, 30 per cent for housing, and 10 per cent for common purposes (accommodation for guests, meeting place, collective farm, roads).[85] Each household receives around two rai of land for private usage.[86] Individual usage rights of land can be passed on to their children but members must not sell the land without the approval of the democratically-elected management committee nor leave the land unutilised for more than two years.[87]

Aside from electing five committee officers, Baan Pong members have a meeting every month to vote on issues affecting the community.[88] In addition, members contribute either personal labour or money for agri-food production in collective land to raise money for Baan Pong's community fund.[89] An interesting feature of Baan Pong is the establishment of the community's 'land bank' which serves as a community welfare fund, a source of loans for agricultural purposes, and as a fund for political mobilisation. If the fund becomes significant enough it will also be used to purchase land. The source of funding comes from compulsory monthly saving and exchanges of individual land usage rights; out of 30,000 baht price per plot of land, 10,000 baht is given to the original user of land, 16,000 baht to the land bank, and 4,000 baht to Baan Pong communal fund.[90] The LRM's attempt to pressure the state to establish land banks at the national scale is discussed in section 2.2.

CLTD in the South and Northeast

CLTD land governance ideas and practices in the North spread to other regions of the country through the media and civil society networks. The following paragraphs explore the diversity of CLTD projects using examples from the South and Northeast, namely Bantad Mountain group where members are located across Trang, Krabi and Pattaloong provinces (South), as well as Sai-ngarmpattana groups in Suratthani province (South) and Samsiew group in Chaiphum province (Northeast). The examples suggest that CLTD practices differ depending on local contexts and that one should be cautious not to analyse the LRM as a homogenous movement.

Bantad Mountain group consists of around 80 households or 400 people who occupy over 2,100 rai of land in mountainous areas.[91] Most members claim that their ancestors had lived in the area long before the Thai state declared it a reserve forest area and started to arrest some of the locals in 1989.[92] The Baan Tra community in Trang province was influenced by the Communist movement in the 1970s and 1980s. Since 1991, some members started to mobilise to assert their right to their ancestors' land.[93] They joined the Assembly of the Poor and exchanged ideas with their 'brothers and sisters' from other regions of Thailand, who faced similar problems relating to the control over natural resources.[94]

On 14 October 2000, Bantad Mountain Land Reform Network was established. It consists of 15 member organisations from Trang, Krabi, and Pattaloong provinces.[95] Around 1,200 rai of Bantad Mountain land are used for agricultural and housing purposes while the other 900 rai are designated community forest area.[96] Bantad group adopts a CLTD style of local land governance where the community manifesto and rules, such as regarding natural resource management and saving groups, are established by democratic means.[97] Since Bantad is a remote area bordered with well-preserved forests, the Bantad group tries to establish rules to prevent the destruction of the forest, water resource, and wild life, such as to promote little or no usage of agricultural chemicals[98] and to require additional trees to be planted when members need to cut down some trees.[99]

The experience of Suratthani's land movement in the South is markedly different from the previous groups discussed. Santipattana, Klongsaipattana, and Sai-ngarmpattna communities were accepted as part of the 35 pilot CLTD projects by the Democrat government led by Abhisit Vejchacheewa in 2010, and yet violent oppositions against land reform members in these communities did not cease. As briefly discussed in Chapter 3, there are a lot of large-scale palm oil plantations in Suratthani.[100] Out of around 830,000 rai of palm oil plantations in the province, only 10 per cent belong to around 29,000 farming households.[101] In a 3,000-rai plantation owned by a capital group, only 20 people were hired as labour.[102] Many Thai and foreign companies received license to rent a total of around 200,000 rai of reserve forest areas in Suratthani, and some palm oil plantations continued their operation even though their license over 68,500 rai of land had already expired.[103] Since around 2002, there were large-scale land occupations and some violent retaliations.[104] In 2008, six communities – Santipattana, Klongsaipattana, and Sai-ngarmpattana (1 to 4) – formed the Southern Peasants Federation and joined the LRM, calling for the state to redistribute land and for legal persecutions of private companies whose plantation license already expired.[105] By 2010, ALRO took back some of the land under their jurisdiction, from private companies so that around 400 small-scale farmers could use the land.[106] However, there are still some violent conflicts during the time of research, as section 4.1 discusses.

A relatively new CLTD project includes Samsiew, which adopted the CLTD land governance approach in 2007.[107] Land struggles in Samsiew, however, started since 1932 when the state declared common land over some people's land and tried to evict them.[108] The community which consisted of 24 households in 401 rai of land created its own manifesto which outlines member-agreed rules regarding collective land ownership and management.[109] Unlike the Bantad Mountain group, which encourages all members to participate in the day-to-day decision-making process, Samsiew prefers a more indirect democracy management style where members elect 15 representatives to form a management committee.[110] Samsiew members were also inspired by Baan Pong's experience,[111] but unlike Baan Pong, the division of land between members is based on existing divisions of land among families.[112] However, those who have a lot of land sometimes informally allow others to work on their land.[113] As Part 3 discusses in greater detail, Samsiew is an example of a CLTD project which is rather committed to develop sustainable agricultural production.

Klongyong co-operative

While the Raidong/Mae-aow group received a certificate from the Prime Minister office to support its existence as a CLTD project, the legal status of the certificate is not the same as a land title deed signed by the Department of Land.[114] By 2014, Klongyong co-operative, which covers a total area of around 1,803 rai and consists of 180 households (969 people),[115] is the only LRM group which received a legal title deed in February 2011 that is certified by the Department of Land. This is partly due to its unique status as a rent-to-buy co-operative established in 1980.[116] In 2006, the Co-operative Promotion Department transferred Klongyong land to the treasury department which then increased land rent significantly from between 3,000 to 4,000 baht to around 40,000 to 50,000 baht per 20 rai per year. In addition, the treasury also allowed non-farmers to rent the land.[117] Most of Klongyong co-operative members then protested against the hike in rental price in 2008, and compiled documents to show that Klongyong co-operative was initially set up as a rent-to-buy land co-operative to help small-scale farmers. In 2009, Klongyong joined the LRM[118] and most members also agreed to adopt the CLTD land management approach.[119]

Klongyong leaders received help from Prapart Pintoptang, an academic from Chulalongkorn University, to bring their problems to national attention.[120] Media exposures from ThaiPBS, a national television news station, also encouraged Klongyong members to be less afraid of local village headmen and treasury department officials.[121] Media exposures also helped Klongyong to build alliances with other groups in similar situations, such as in Utraraditr and Utaithani provinces.[122] Klongyong has an advantage over other CLTD projects due to its close proximity to Bangkok and its ability to establish a wide supportive network. As section 4.1 discusses, some CLTD groups in other regions face more obstacles such as violent retaliations from landlords, or are at a more disadvantaged position to build national networks and to receive media coverage.

2.2 Laws and policies regarding land governance

Some studies point to the key role of the state in the maintenance of hegemonic land governance and in facilitating land grabs. The state, for example, has the control over the definition and classification of land and is also able to justify large-scale land investments, as well as appropriations and reallocations of land.[123] In addition, it is suggested that land grabs are not merely contests for control over resources, but also contests for authority over institutions.[124] As this section discusses, the LRM also attempts to change the Thai state's legal and policy structures to promote land redistribution and prevention of land grabs in addition to CLTD projects. Building on the community rights discourse and its own experience, by the early 2010s the LRM started to campaign for four laws to be passed to support: (1) progressive land tax; (2) the establishment of land banks; (3) community rights in the management of land and natural resource; and (4) the establishment of a Justice Fund to help marginalised citizens with their legal fees.

The 1997 Constitution is the first Constitution which favours some decentralisation of power, such as in Articles 284 and 290, as well as recognises community rights.[125] The 2007 Constitution also recognises community rights in Articles 66 and 67,[126] which helps LRM members to legitimise their cause.[127] Many subsidiary laws relating to natural resource management, however, contradict community rights and instead legitimise the centralisation of power in the hands of the government while laws that aimed to decentralise power to local administration are unclear. This results in the lack of checks and a balance system which would allow local citizens to participate in the decision-making process.[128] A lot of land conflicts occur in around 6.4 million rai of forestry areas due to unclear borders[129] and forestry laws also give a lot of power to the Ministry of Forestry, which supports top-down hierarchical control of the state over natural resource.[130]

The LRM initially focused on revoking formal land title deeds which were not obtained legally but found that it is a cumbersome process; the Department of land rarely revokes land deeds because taking individual cases to the administrative court for a ruling is very time consuming.[131] This is problematic because in legal cases involving land conflicts between individual citizens and the state or private companies, the court tends to give higher weight to titling documents even though they had been obtained through illegitimate practices, compared to witnesses and other lines of arguments, such as arguments based on community rights.[132]

Difficulties in revoking formal land deeds led the LRM to advocate other strategies.[133] Since around 2008, the LRM puts forward three main demands for the government: (1) to support CLTD land governance; (2) to establish land banks and; (3) to implement progressive land taxation. The main goal is to redistribute land in the form of CLTD to groups which have established reliable democratic local governance systems. Land banks, partially funded by progressive land tax, will also aid CLTD by helping to facilitate land purchases for redistribution to small-scale farmers and as a fund to facilitate land exchanges within CLTD projects.[134] Progressive land taxation is suggested as a measure to encourage those who have large holdings of land to release these land and to discourage land speculations.[135] Some studies have also noted, for example, that land tax has relatively low enforcement costs and is easy to implement compared to other options.[136] Over the years, the LRM has built alliances with other groups in society, such as academics, lawyers, and even a few politicians, as well as linkages with other civil society groups such as the Fishermen Network and Farmer Debt Network.[137] The Parliamentary Committee to Study Land Problems also supports similar land reform ideas such as the enforcement of maximum land holding limit, the establishment of land banks, the protection of agricultural land, and progressive land taxation.[138]

In 2011, the Democrat Party's Abhisit Vejchachewa government (December 2008 to August 2011) made a few sympathetic moves. By 31 January 2012, 435 communities or 242,798 people in around 2.2 million rai of land across 47 provinces in Thailand had applied for CLTDs from the government.[139] However, only Klongyong and Raidong/Mae-aow were granted CLTDs on 12 February 2011 and 26 March 2011 respectively,[140] but Klongyong was the only group given a legal land title deed signed by the Department of Land. In early 2011, the Abhisit government also agreed to a budget of 167 milion baht to fund community land banks in five pilot communities which include Rai-dong/Mae-aow and Baan Pong.[141] This is not to say, however, that the Abhisit government was actively promoting CLTD, national land bank, and land reforms. It can be argued that they could have done more by, for example, drafting a law on CLTD instead of relying on the Office of the Prime Minister to issue a CLTD certificate to Raidong/Mae-aow because the certificate has lower legal status.

Succeeding the Abhisit government in August 2011 was Phua Thai party's Yingluck Shinnawatra government. The LRM suggested that the party supported CLTD principles during the electoral campaign, and also in its policy statement after coming into power, but the LRM was not satisfied with policy progress by late 2012. The government established a committee to consider land reform proposals suggested by the LRM and promised to speed up the process of passing the law to guarantee community rights in the management of land, forests, water and the sea. However, the LRM felt that in practice there was more or less no following up,[142] and it also tried to pressure the government to act faster by demonstrating in front of the Government House in 2012 and 2013.[143]

Building on the original three proposals, the LRM started to campaign for 'four laws for the poor' in 2014[144] which include laws regarding progressive land taxation, land banks, and community rights in the management of land and natural resource (CLTD law), as well as a law to support the establishment of a Justice Fund for marginalised citizens who need help with their legal fees.[145] After the coup d'état on 22 May 2014, through Order 64/2557 and the Master Plan to End Deforestation, the military-led government clearly adopted a hard-lined position to remove 'encroachers' from the reserved forest which intensified land conflicts between the state and many communities.[146] The LRM's campaign events are also often obstructed by the military government,[147] and at the time of writing (December 2014) it is unclear how the situation will unfold.

It has been suggested that the LRM almost has to 'start from zero' every time there is a change in government.[148] Nevertheless, what seems clear from history is the lack of political will by Thai state managers, civilian or military, to decentralise power and control over the management of natural resource. The autocratic bureaucratic culture entrenched in the Thai state means that issues are often 'frozen' unless the Prime Minister chairs the committees to solve those particular issues,[149] which can be seen as part of the hegemonic structures which obstruct the progress of the LRM. Moreover, as 507 politicians from 11 main political parties held a total of 35,786 rai of land worth 15.7 million baht in 2013, it is perhaps not surprising why land reform is not a priority.[150] Phua Thai politicians, for example, own an average of 85 rai of land per person, while Democrat politicians own an average of 63 rai of land per person.[151]

Limited success in challenging hegemonic laws and national policies constrains the potential of CLTD projects. Raidong/Mae-aow and Baan Pong, for example, need legal legitimacy and financial support to purchase some land that they are currently occupying, as well as to develop public utilities in the areas. However, the lack of clarity in the policy obstructed these developments.[152] Aside from the constraints of national laws and policies, the next section discusses other potential limitations of CLTD and ALRO forms of land governance. Part 4 continues the discussion on obstacles facing the LRM.

2.3 Possible limitations to the potential of CLTD and ALRO land governance

This chapter has focused on CLTD and ground-up land reform initiatives of the LRM. However, CLTD is not necessarily the best form of property ownership that is appropriate in all contexts.[153] There can be other forms of counter-hegemonic governance mechanisms and complementary measures that can help guard against land grabs and promote sustainable agriculture, but it is beyond the scope of this book to explore them in detail. Moreover, although CLTD projects formally subscribe to the democratic decision-making process, further studies on informal norms and social relations within CLTD projects are needed, to evaluate the extent that members do subscribe to democratic principles, and to see whether there are still hegemonic elements that should be contested, such as discrimination based on gender and age. The following paragraphs explore other potential limitations of CLTD and ALRO uncovered in this research, and also suggest the importance of revising CLTD and ALRO to suit changing circumstances.

It has been suggested that CLTD projects may only work in areas with strong family relations and a sense of community which help them to organise and collaborate, such as in Baan Pong.[154] In most places, such as in the Central region and areas near the cities, such a sense of community probably no longer exists (or never existed in the first place). Moreover, by 2014, most land occupations and CLTD projects are on marginal land. There is also a question of whether the second generation of CLTD members will adhere to the principles of CLTD.[155] In addition, although land banks could facilitate a rent-to-buy type of land purchases for co-operatives in CLTD projects,[156] if land prices continue to climb then it is unclear how long it will take to complete each purchase. In the case of Klongyong CLTD co-operative, land prices are very high because the location is close to Bangkok. A few Klongyong members have also questioned whether the group can keep to agricultural production when there is increasing pollution from nearby sources, and when it is a lot more profitable to use the land for other purposes.[157]

Despite these questions and potential problems, one could still argue that the main benefits of CLTD and of the LRM are that they stimulate debates on how to implement equitable distribution and just governance of resources. Practical examples of CLTD can be used as inspirations, and to show that that people can organise to empower themselves so that they have more say in Thai society. This could be a stepping stone towards the building up of larger social movements which, through further discussions and collaborations, push for other (perhaps even better) demands that contest the current centralisation of political-economic power and hegemonic land governance. Moreover, CLTD projects can help provide short-term economic relief for marginalised people, as previously discussed.

To a certain extent, CLTD was created as a reaction to the perceived ineffectiveness of ALRO in preventing redistributed land from being sold off to non-farmers. In the early 2010s, however, it seems that ALRO has rather genuinely been trying to improve its performance. With the help of satellite photographs, ALRO has sued and retaken misused land more efficiently compared to the past where they lacked human resources to inspect over 30 million rai of ALRO land.[158] Although it is still difficult for ALRO to take on some politically and economically powerful landlords, ALRO hopes to send a message that it is taking the issue seriously to encourage other landlords to start releasing ALRO land in their holdings.[159] Moreover, ALRO considers altering its rules to allow for some monetary compensation to encourage farmers to return their land to

ALRO instead of sub-letting to non-farmers, so that ALRO can allocate land to other farmers.[160] One problem facing ALRO is that although it has jurisdiction over 29.3 per cent of agricultural land in Thailand, most of them are marginal land with poor soil quality in rain-fed or dry areas. Only 2.9 per cent of ALRO land are in irrigated areas.[161] The Secretary General of ALRO argues that the state has the legitimacy to safeguard prime agricultural areas for food security purposes because a lot of public investments were spent on irrigation in these areas, such as in the Klong Rangsit area. However, so far there is no national policy to do so.[162]

The discussion on ALRO above suggests that one should not be too quick to rule out ALRO's counter-hegemonic potential. Although ALRO and CLTD land governance seem like polar opposites – top-down bureaucratic management versus ground-up democratic local management – there is still room for collaborations and exchanges of ideas. At least in early 2014, the LRM and ALRO are both receptive of sustainable agriculture. Section 3.3 discusses this issue in further detail.

Part 3 Counter-hegemonic production–distribution practices

The previous part of the chapter has discussed the LRM's attempts to promote land reform and build counter-hegemonic land governance. The LRM, however, is also concerned with sustainable production methods and raising the quality of life for farmers in CLTD projects. Section 3.1 discusses relevant literature and the LRM's recognition that to address land grabs and access to land for small-scale farmers, one has to address structural production–distribution problems of the mainstream agri-food system as well. This section also discusses linkages between the LRM and sustainable agriculture groups in Thailand. Section 3.2 then discusses the development of sustainable agriculture in CLTD projects, while section 3.3 discusses ALRO's promotion of sustainable agriculture as a parallel counter-hegemonic attempt.

3.1 Land and sustainable agriculture

It has been suggested that land grabs should be seen as 'control grabbing' or contests over the future of global agriculture regarding what should be grown, how, by whom, and for what markets.[163] Although studies on land grabs tend to focus on the role of companies and states, it has been pointed out that small-scale farmers can also be seen as potential agents of land grabbing to grow cash crops (boom crops), and the consequences are not that dissimilar from large-scale plantations.[164] Contract eucalyptus farming arrangements in Thailand with an average holding of 30 to 50 rai, for example, were quite common and were encouraged by the Royal Forestry Department (RFD) between 1994 and 1997.[165] As the following paragraphs discuss, the LRM's concerns are not limited to egalitarian land redistribution but also sustainable agricultural production.

At the leadership level (farmer leaders, NGOs, and academics), the goals of the LRM include safeguarding agricultural land and promoting sustainable agriculture to counter problems of the current agri-food system.[166] Realising that production and marketing of agri-food products are related to small-scale farmers' ability to hold on to their land, some of the leading members were initially very idealistic and wanted to develop all CLTD projects as sustainable agricultural areas. For example, Mr Suebsakul Kijnukorn who, along with the Raidong/Mae-aow community, was credited for being one of the originators of the CLTD term, suggests that land reform is a base for food sovereignty and food security.[167] Some people in the movement also wanted to reject mono-crops in favour of diversified farms[168] and looked for alternatives to the capitalist economy, such as from sufficiency principles and sustainable agriculture.[169] Such ideas also resonate with the transnational counter-hegemonic food sovereignty discourse where land is seen as a necessary foundation for creating a just food system.[170]

Many sustainable farmers and NGO activists, who were interviewed, also suggest that farmers' control over land is crucial to the development of sustainable agriculture.[171] Farmers who tend to switch their production methods to sustainable agriculture tend to have their own land,[172] partly because they have the freedom to develop small-scale water sources and to develop farm areas that are suitable for agro-ecological production.[173] Aside from practical matters, some sustainable farmers also see the farmers' right to land as a core of sustainable agriculture, calling it the 'soul of sustainable agriculture' where employment in large-scale (even organic) plantations would reduce farmers to workers in factories[174] rather than allowing them to be their own bosses.[175]

The LRM also works with sustainable agriculture groups, such as with Dr Chomchuan Boonrahong and the Institute for a Sustainable Agriculture Community (ISAC), to develop governance mechanisms to ensure fair contract farming arrangements[176] as well as to promote sustainable agriculture and fair markets in CLTD projects.[177] Nevertheless, people and groups in the LRM are not as equally committed, ideologically, and leaders in the movement have come to recognise that it is not easy to convince other people in the movement to change their production methods to sustainable agriculture.[178] As Chapter 5 discussed, sustainable agriculture requires a lot of knowledge, time and labour, which means it is often not the first choice for CLTD members. Understandably, it is more risky for poorer farmers to enter organic markets because yield tends to drop during the first few years. Instead, poorer farmers who cannot afford the risks usually rely on conventional agricultural methods, which are less labour intensive, to free up their time for low or semi-skilled labour jobs in and outside of the agricultural sector.[179] The problems with the promotion of sustainable agriculture in CLTD projects are discussed in greater detail in the following section.

3.2 Sustainable agricultural production–distribution in CLTD projects

Some members of a few CLTD projects have started to engage with sustainable agriculture. A rather special case is the Mae-ta community (discussed in Chapter 5) which was already a strong sustainable agriculture group when the Sub-district

Administrative Organisation (SAO) supported the management of over 1,200 plots of land in the form of CLTD.[180] Generally, progress in the development of sustainable agricultural production in CLTD projects is rather limited as CLTD projects face many difficulties, such as the lack of labour and time to learn about sustainable agriculture, as the following paragraphs elaborate.

In the North, many CLTD members tend to have debts and were accustomed to being landless labourers. Hence, they prefer to rely on informal jobs and grow whatever they are used to in conventional production methods, which do not yield produce all year round and do not require much of their presence on the farm.[181] However, some people who have reached a certain age tend to rely completely on their CLTD land plots.[182] It has also been suggested that the need to earn quick cash from mono-crops to pay off debts often reduces CLTD members' bargaining power in the market[183] and the monopoly power of middlemen also reduces prices that farmers received.[184] In Baan Pong, for example, members tend to grow Cha-om (climbing wattle), mangoes, longans, and other vegetables. Both male and female members between the age of 18 and 30 tend to work in factories to earn additional income,[185] but some members, such as Mrs Lom Panyathip, rely completely on her farm. Her rationale is that when she was a low-skilled labourer, income was irregular and unstable. Agricultural production on her own farm, on the other hand, makes her feel more independent and also allows her to save up some money.[186]

Most members in Baan Pong CLTD still rely on conventional practices but a few households have tried to switch their production methods to sustainable agriculture.[187] Problems that they experience include the lack of time and labour (especially that they often have to mobilise, politically, to lobby the state on land issues) to fully engage in sustainable agriculture.[188] As a compromising measure, Baan Pong promotes safe usage of agricultural chemicals alongside restrictions on industrial animal farming which produces many environmental externalities.[189] As for Raidong/Mae-Aow, a small group of around 33 people were supported by Ms Sangwal Kantham, one of the community leaders, to receive production trainings from the sustainable agriculture network in the North.[190] Some members also experiment with growing organic potatoes in common land and with producing organic fertilisers, although they still lack equipment and require additional help from the local administration.[191]

A few CLTD groups in other regions also attempt to develop sustainable agriculture in their own ways. Leader of Samsiew's CLTD in the Northeast, Mr Sawai Kamyoi, is a strong supporter of food sovereignty and self-reliance,[192] and clause six in Samsaew's CLTD charter states that the community advocates sustainable agriculture as well as the promotion of integrated farming and diversity of agri-food products.[193] There are also some exchanges of ideas and knowledge with sustainable agriculture groups, but generally members' interests are rather limited.[194] In the South, some households in Bantad Mountain group are interested in sustainable agriculture such as organic farming and/or diversified farming.[195] One famous sustainable farmer includes Mr Kimpong Sangwongkittiwuth from

Tapkhua-plakmoo community who developed a type of diversified farm consisting of rubber trees, food crops and herbal medicinal plants, which is what he calls a practice of 'food sovereignty in a rubber forest' or 'four-level agriculture'.[196] In the case of Klongyong, there is an attempt to encourage households to grow small plots of organic or pesticide-free vegetables because Klongyong leaders felt it is a more effective strategy than asking members to stop using chemicals completely.[197] In 2012, around 50 out of 240 households started to experiment with sustainable production.[198] Taking advantage of its close proximity to Bangkok, Klongyong members sell their pesticide-free products in many green markets in Bangkok.[199]

3.3 ALRO and sustainable agri-food production–distribution

ALRO's mandate could be interpreted to include supporting agricultural production of small-scale farmers in areas under its jurisdiction. In 2013, Dr Weerachai Narkwibulwong, Secretary General of ALRO, expresses clearly his view that 'organic or pesticide-free agriculture is the only way [for small-scale farmers] to survive' and that 'it is not even an alternative'.[200] This view is supported by a qualitative research of 43 ALRO farms in four provinces which found that sustainable agricultural methods have lesser economic risks, yield higher income, and provide more food security compared to conventional cash-crop agricultural production.[201] To promote sustainable agriculture, ALRO focuses on building and supporting model projects such as the Kammad Sustainable Agriculture group (discussed in Chapter 5) and qualitative expansions of such projects.[202] It also promotes Good Agricultural Practice (GAP), safe usage of pesticides to reduce production costs and improve the health of farmers, and tries to act as a connection hub for farmers and agro-processing industries.[203] Another ideological influence that affects ALRO's work is King Bhumipol's sufficiency economy ideas, taken to mean the importance of building immunity and self-reliance to reduce risks from crises without isolation from society.[204] ALRO tries to translate such ideas to policies by encouraging farmers to form supportive networked groups to learn from each other, and also by working with them to spread useful production knowledge.[205]

As discussed in previous chapters, there can be conservative interpretations and top-down implementations of sufficiency ideas by the Thai bureaucracy, which tend to alienate some civil society groups from working with the bureaucracy. Although more empirical research is needed to evaluate ALRO's promotion of sustainable agriculture and its working relations with other groups in society, it seems that top-level management ideas and policy directions of ALRO in the early 2010s are (at least partially) compatible with those of the LRM and many sustainable agriculture groups. This suggests that further collaborations should not be ruled out, as collaborations do not necessarily imply co-optation of oppositions. The next part of the chapter discusses the possibility of co-optation of oppositions in greater detail.

Part 4 Current obstacles and the possibility of co-optation of oppositions

This part of the chapter explores current obstacles facing the LRM and the possibility of co-optation of oppositions. Section 4.1 discusses violence and legal persecutions facing the LRM as well as the possibility of co-optation of CLTD law. Section 4.2 then discusses the red-yellow divide and potentially problematic discourses that may obstruct counter-hegemonic projects of the LRM. Finally, section 4.3 evaluates the LRM's engagement with transnational agrarian movements.

4.1 Violence, the law and co-optation of oppositions

Land occupations sparked violent retaliations in many places. On 13 April 2002, the first Thaksin Shinnawatra administration promised to help LRM protesters which were occupying Chiang Mai city hall. However, a cabinet order on 23 April 2002 urged relevant authorities to strictly enforce the law on land occupiers which led to an increased number of people being arrested.[206] Often, excessive force was used during arrests.[207] In Lamphun, local village headmen were also mobilised to resist land occupiers, by, for example, accusing them of being communists and violators of tradition and Buddhist morality.[208] It is often difficult to locate the sources of violent retaliations. In the North, there was an attempted assassination of Mr Wacharin Ouprajong on 16 June 2002 and an assassination of Mr Kaew Pinpanma on 23 June 2002.[209] In Suratthani in the South, violent retaliations against the land reform movement in December 2003 caused the movement to disperse into smaller groups that acted independently. In 2007, 3,000 people occupied 1,600 rai of palm plantation operated by the Thaksin Palm Company in Ampur Kiriratnikhom but were then violently dispersed by combined police, soldiers, and volunteer forces, which led to two deaths.[210] During the research period of this book, two female members of the Southern Federation of Farmers from the Klongsaipattana community were assassinated by M16 war gun(s) in December 2012.[211]

As Part 2 has discussed, the Abhisit government gave some support to CLTD ideas and practice, but it can be argued that the government could have done more, such as by passing a CLTD or local natural resource management law. Moreover, the government did not seem interested to redistribute private land[212] and legal persecutions of LRM members continued. Between 2007 and 2008, there were 9,336 cases of people trespassing to use land in forest areas[213] and in 2011, there were over 800 legal cases relating to land conflicts known to the LRM where around 300 to 400 of these cases directly involve LRM members.[214] By 2012, around 20 people involved in land conflicts in the LRM network were in prison.[215] Even if the Thai government attempts to introduce a CLTD law, there is still danger of co-optation. As can be seen from the case of the Community Forest law, the Thai state attempted to redefine community forest ideas and practices in ways that differ from what civil society has proposed.[216]

Another potentially problematic issue is how CLTD projects, such as Raidong/Mae-aow, ought to be registered as co-operatives to receive CLTD certified by the Office of the Prime Minister. However, the current co-operative law allows the bureaucracy to inspect financial accounts of co-operatives. This gives the bureaucracy power to pressure Raidong/Mae-aow co-operative to engage in commercial activities, such as to sell chemical fertilizers or to give out loans, so that there are some movements in the account. If not, the co-operative will be forced to close.[217] However, such suggestions create tensions because Raidong/Mae-aow leaders saw such proposed activities as promotions of conventional agricultural production and as encouragements for individual members to accumulate debt. Instead, Raidong/Mae-aow leaders want to help members to reduce their costs of production such as by producing and promoting the use of organic fertilisers.[218] This problem is related to the hegemonic hierarchical mentality and governance structures of the Thai state and Thai society that ought to be challenged, and a starting point could be to re-evaluate the law governing co-operatives in Thailand.

4.2 The red–yellow divide and potentially problematic discourses

Chapter 4 has discussed the red–yellow political polarisation in Thailand and suggested that it weakens social movements. Some academics and activists in the LRM also voice this issue during interviews.[219] After the coup d'état which ousted Prime Minister Thaksin Shinnawatra in 2006, it was suggested that there was 'a blank' in terms of social movement mobilisation because NGOs were divided on strategies, such as whether to establish dialogues with the military-established government.[220] Similarly, after the coup d'état in 2014 which ousted Prime Minister Yingluck Shinnawatra, people's movements were also bitterly divided. Some groups oppose the coup d'état through symbolic actions while some groups want to use government mechanisms, such as the National Reform Assembly, to push through their reform agenda. Others prefer grass-root mobilisation which includes building the people's forum for reform and civil society's campaign for a new Constitution that supports participatory democracy.[221]

Such differences in strategies hinder collaborations and the red–yellow polarised thinking also lead to scepticisms that obstruct the LRM's counter-hegemonic projects. It has been noted, for example, that community rights which inspired the LRM are viewed sceptically by some red shirts as part of conservative discourses and practices advocated by those who like to support military governments.[222] However, as this chapter has discussed, CLTD ideas and practices are recent constructions with grass-roots backgrounds, are based on democratic principles, and are used to help civil society groups negotiate for decentralisation of power in the management of natural resources. As discussed in Chapter 4, the class-based 'phrai versus ammart' approach to the analysis of Thai politics[223] is problematic and needs to be critically examined so as not to constrain strategy options, potential alliances, and overall effectiveness of social movements. The LRM's ideas and practices cannot simply be labelled as either red or yellow, and interviews of LRM members also suggest that there are both red and yellow supporters among members of CLTD projects.[224] Political parties associated with both sides of the political conflicts – Phua Thai and Democrat – supported CLTD during their 2011 electoral campaigns even though policy implementations were arguably weak, while the National Reform Committee led by Prawase Wasi, often portrayed as 'ammart' by red shirt supporters,[225] helped provide forums and support for social movements such as the LRM.[226] Similar to what previous chapters have argued, the case of the LRM demonstrates the simplistic inadequacy of the red–yellow framework, which serves as a form of distracting false dichotomy, at a time when relationships between people's movements and established political authorities deserve critical scrutiny.

Another potentially problematic type of discourse is one that tends to place smallholders' attempts to secure access to land on the same plane as larger and more powerful actors, such as national states and capital groups. It has been pointed out, for example, that smallholders can also be agents of enclosure and dispossession such as through the discourse of common property.[227] However, it is important to point out that the power of agents to enclose land and dispossess others are massively different, not to mention that *why* and *how* different actors want to secure their access to land are qualitatively different, especially from perspectives of ecological sustainability, social justice, and human rights. Whereas corporations may engage in land grabs for speculation purposes or to grow agro-fuel inputs to mostly feed the demands of the world's wealthier population, some less powerful agents may need access to land to meet their basic needs. The opportunity costs of large-scale land grabs should also be considered, as they might have a less poverty-reducing impact than if access to land and water were improved for local farming communities.[228] Omitting to address differences in power relations help to reduce the legitimacy of civil society groups that engage in community-based resource management, which has political implication that favours the maintenance of the hegemonic status quo.

4.3 The global dimension of land governance and the Thai LRM

The LRM usually focuses on the roles of domestic actors, but elements involved in land issues in Thailand are not limited by its nation-state geographical space. Land governance in Thailand can be seen as part of the global hegemonic land governance structures, supported and maintained by global institutions and hegemonic ideas, as Part 1 has discussed. Foreign land purchases through domestic nominees in Thailand, discussed in Chapter 3, are also parts of a global trend where the food–energy scarcity concerns prompted the recent wave of global land grabs. In this sense, the LRM's national campaign to promote a mechanism of local land governance, and more equal distribution of land in the country, has relevance to, and cannot be seen as separate from, global struggles for land reforms. The following paragraphs first discuss contemporary debates on the benefits and difficulties of connecting local, national, and transnational social movements. Relationships between the Thai LRM and La Vía Campesina are then explored. In summary, there is some progress as well as many limitations in linking up with transnational movements, and the LRM generally tends to concentrate on local and national struggles.

Some studies suggest that land contests are becoming globalised and are taking place in multi-scale terrains of multiple actors, institutions, and frameworks.[229] It has been suggested that the informal complex of transnational land governance can be used to protect vulnerable populations subjected to illegal and violent dispossessions of their land.[230] However, it is not a simple task to orchestrate through the transnational governance network. Rural social movements can justify global engagement only if it generates support for local struggles and opens up a national political space,[231] but there can be many problems in trying to link up with transnational social movements such as with regards to representation and accountability.[232] A few national agrarian groups might be able to link up with transnational movements while other groups are left behind.[233] In addition, transnational agrarian movements tend to look for counterparts in their 'image and likeness' so if they found nothing of the sort in other countries and regions, they tend to assume the absence of movements or that there are weak movements.[234] Within a transnational agrarian movement, some groups also have more resources and influence than others.[235]

The biggest transnational agrarian social movement adopting a radical approach is La Vía Campesina which currently represents more than 150 (sub) national rural social movement organisations from 56 countries in Latin America and the Caribbean, North America, (Western) Europe, Asia and Africa.[236] It tries to connect local, national, and international groups and involve their members through the 'externalisation' of national-local issues or the vertical projection of domestic claims onto international institutions or foreign actors.[237] Issues in countries important to La Vía Campesina tend to be swiftly externalised[238] but there is still room for improvement. For example, the 'gate keeper' problem, where one national organisation relegates other movements to the margin, such as with the case of India and Indonesia,[239] can hinder the representation claim of La Vía Campesina. In addition, La Vía Campesina has no presence in some countries such as China even though Chinese peasants and the rural dispossessed have forged collective identities that potentially provide a basis for conceptualising alternatives to neo-liberal capitalism.[240] Overall, it has been suggested that La Vía Campesina needs to address the diversity of land issues beyond the ones that their main members are concerned with.[241]

In the case of Thailand, the Assembly of the Poor and the Northern Peasants Federation (an important member of the LRM) are members of La Vía Campesina. These organisations also help to connect Vía Campsina with other civil society groups in Thailand, such as the Alternative Agriculture Network (AAN) in the Northeast. As Part 1 has discussed, many local leaders in CLTD projects visited movements in other countries, such as Brazil and Philippines, as well as joined La Vía Campesina's international conferences, such as the one in Mali in 2011.[242] The statement of the Global Alliance Against Land Grabbing, convened by La Vía Campesina and allies in Mali in November 2011, extends the understanding of land governance beyond private property ideas to include communal and community property regimes.[243] While their ideas seem compatible and the Thai representatives learned about food sovereignty and that land grab is a global phenomenon, they had language barrier problems and could not fully share their ideas, such as, with regards to CLTD.[244] A leading activist from the Northern Peasants Federation discusses how information is usually disseminated in a rather top-down manner and aside from international conferences and joint declarations every now and then, there is still a gap in co-ordination between the Thai movement and La Vía Campesina.[245] Even though there was a conference organised by La Vía Campesina and the Thai Community Agroecology Foundation in Surin, in November 2012, many Surin sustainable farmers interviewed for this book also suggest that many farmers in their network did not attend the conference.[246] These examples suggest that local members could be encouraged to participate more in international exchanges of ideas in the future.

The discussion on current problems in this section does not mean to demoralise people in the LRM and La Vía Campesina, but to identify room for improvement and to strengthen the movements. Aside from collaborations with La Vía Campesina, the LRM could also engage with other global counter-hegemonic initiatives such as the Voluntary Guidelines on Responsible Governance of Tenure of Land and Other Natural Resources. The Voluntary Guidelines take into account important issues such as the protection of customary tenure, community consultations, and states' obligations to regulate their corporations' operations beyond their borders. They were negotiated with involvement of rural social movements and formally adopted at a special session of the Committee on World Food Security on 11 May 2012.[247] It is unclear how international governance instruments such as the Voluntary Guidelines can translate to national governance structures[248] but if the LRM does not pay sufficient attention to the issue, it might open room for co-optation.

Conclusion

This chapter has focused on the LRM's critique of hegemonic land governance structures, followed by its counter-hegemonic ideas, land governance structures, and agricultural production–distribution practices. Some advances have been made and the LRM managed to stimulate debate in Thai society regarding land redistribution, but the LRM also faces many obstacles including violence and legal persecutions. The last part of the chapter has also discussed some problems arising from political polarisation in Thailand, as well as discussed the LRM's alliance with La Vía Campesina.

The study of the LRM uncovered some interesting issues for future research which are beyond the scope of this book, such as alternatives to market-led land valuation methods. The next and last chapter of this book will also discuss the importance of analysing the interconnections between land management, the agri-food system, and other sectors of the economy to explore counter-hegemonic possibilities more fully.

Notes

1 Sayamon Kraiyoorawong *et al.*, *A Study of Land Conflicts in Thailand Phase 1* (Bangkok: Thailand Research Fund, 2005), 43 (in Thai).
2 Achara Rakyutitham *et al.*, *Land and Freedom* (Bangkok: Black Lead Publishing, 2005), 40 (in Thai).
3 Derek Hall, Philip Hirsch, and Tania Murray Li, *Powers of Exclusion: Land Dilemmas in Southeast Asia* (Singapore: NUS Press, 2011), 37–38.
4 Haroon Akram-Lodhi, 'Land, Markets and Neoliberal Enclosure: An Agrarian Political Economy Perspective', *Third World Quarterly* 28, no. 8 (December 2007), 1437–1438; Olivier De Schutter, 'How Not to Think of Land-Grabbing: Three Critiques of Large-Scale Investments in Farmland', *Journal of Peasant Studies* 38, no. 2 (March 2011), 269.
5 Rakyutitham *et al.* (2005), 40; Methee Singsootham, *Practical Action Research Report on Sustainable Land Reform and Management by the People* (Nonthaburi: Land Reform Network and Local Act, 2010), 12 (in Thai).
6 Singsootham (2010), 40.
7 Kraiyoorawong *et al.* (2005), 43; Singsootham (2010), 14. A study also suggests that land speculation bubbles contributed to the 1997 economic crisis (Warin Wongharnchao *et al.*, *A Study of Ownership and Usage of Land, as Well as Economic and Legal Measures to Maximise Land Usage* (Bangkok: Thailand Research Fund, 2001) (in Thai)).
8 Singsootham (2010), 39; Kraiyoorawong *et al.* (2005), 43; De Schutter (2011a), 270; Walden Bello, Shea Cunningham, and Li Kheng Pho, *A Siamese Tragedy. Development and Disintegration in Modern Thailand* (New York: Zed Books, 1998), 161.
9 Singsootham (2010), 13 and 71; Hall, Hirsch and Li (2011), 38; Kraiyoorawong *et al.* (2005), 88.
10 1 rai is equal to 1,600 square metres.
11 The Land Reform Network and Local Act, *A Report on the Study "Land Management and Social Justice: A Case Study of the Land Reform Network", Part of the Project to Encourage Social Justice, Chulalongkorn University Social Research Institute* (Bangkok: Chulalongkorn University Social Research Institute, 2010), 107 (in Thai).
12 For example, see De Schutter (2011a), 269.
13 Mr Direk Kong-ngern, Baan Pong, Chiang Mai and Mr Wacharin Ouprajong, Baan Huafai, Ampur Chaiprakarn, Chiang Mai, interviewed 30 September 2012, Nonthaburi; Singsootham (2010), 12.
14 Singsootham (2010), 12.
15 Ibid., 13.
16 Mrs Wilaiwan Konka, Vice-president of Baan Pae-tai, interviewed 30 October 2012, Lamphun.
17 Mr Long Pechsood, Bantad Mountain group, Ampur Palian, Trang, 1 October 2012, Bangkok.
18 Direk Kong-ngern, interviewed 30 September 2012, Nonthaburi.
19 A Parliamentary Committee to Consider Land Problems, *A Report on How to Solve the Problems Regarding Land Use, Land Laws, and the Rushed Property Rights Document Process* (Bangkok: A Parliamentary Committee to Consider Land Problems, 2009), 17 (in Thai).
20 Ibid., 67.
21 Dr Weerachai Narkwibulwong, Secretary General of ALRO, interviewed 14 February 2013, Bangkok; Singsootham (2010), 10–11.
22 Bello, Cunningham and Li (1998), 149.
23 Singsootham (2010), 10–11.
24 Bello, Cunningham and Li (1998), 152.

25 Weerachai Narkwibulwong, '37 Years of Land Reform and the Adaptation of Sufficiency Economy', in *37 Years of the Agricultural Land Reform Office* (Bangkok: ALRO, 2012), 15 (in Thai).
26 Dr Duangmanee Laowakul, Faculty of Economics, Thammasart University, research presentation at the Food Security Assembly 2014 in Thailand, quoted in Isra News, 'Macro View of Land in Thailand Reveals Inequality and Highly Concentrated Land: Wealth in Poor People's Tears', *Isra News*, 14 July 2014 (in Thai).
27 Bello, Cunningham and Li (1998), 155–158.
28 A Parliamentary Committee to Consider Land Problems (2009), 18.
29 Wacharin Ouprajong, interviewed 30 September 2012, Nonthaburi; Mr Rangsan Sansongkwae, Baan Raidong, interviewed 30 October 2012, Lamphun; Mr Somkiat Jai-ngarm, Northern Peasants Federation activist, interviewed 30 October 2012, Chiang Mai.
30 Pasuk Phongpaichit and Chris Baker, 1995, *Thailand: Economy and Politics*. New York: Oxford University Press, 307–308.
31 Mr Prayong Doklamyai, advisor to the Northern Peasants Federation, interviewed 1 November 2012, Chiang Mai.
32 Many leading members and general members of the LRM have made these points such as Prapart Pintoptang, lecturer of Political Science, Chulalongkorn University, interviewed 16 October 2012, Nonthaburi; Prayong Doklamyai, interviewed 1 November 2012, Chiang Mai; Sangwal Kantham, LRM local leader from Ban Mae-aow, interviewed 30 October 2012, Lamphun; Nop Mangkornmai, Raidong member in the Raidong/Mae-aow CLTD project, interviewed 30 October 2012, Lamphun.
33 Arun Agrawal and Clark C. Gibson, 'Enchantment and Disenchantment: The Role of Community in Natural Resource Conservation', *World Development* 27, no. 4 (April 1999), 636.
34 Anan Ganjanapan, 'Village in Thai Society: Conceptual Critiques', in *The Community Dimension: Local Way of Thinking Regarding Rights, Power and Natural Resource Management* (Bangkok: Thailand Research Fund, 2001c), 56 (in Thai).
35 Anan Ganjanapan, 'Community Rights in Development', in *The Community Dimension: Local Way of Thinking Regarding Rights, Power and Natural Resource Management* (Bangkok: Thailand Research Fund, 2001a), 246 and 250 (in Thai).
36 Ibid., 236 and 244.
37 Ibid., 241 and 243.
38 For example, see Prayong Doklamyai, 'From Discourse to Practical Innovation: Land Reform by Communities. Transcript of the Presentation at a Conference on Anan Ganjanapan's Complexity of Rights, 8 March 2008', in *'I Don't Have the Answer': 60 Years Professor Dr. Anan Ganjanapan and 20 Years of Social Movement on Community Rights and Natural Resources Management* (Chiang Mai: Sustainable Development Foundation, 2008), 251 (in Thai).
39 Doklamyai (2008), 251.
40 Ibid.
41 Prof. Dr Anan Ganjanapan, lecturer of Sociology and Anthropology, Chiang Mai University, interviewed 29 October 2012, Chiang Mai.
42 Land Reform Network and Local Act (2010), 10 and Singsootham (2010), 23.
43 Rangsan Sansongkwae, interviewed 30 October 2012, Lamphun; Long Pechsood, interviewed 1 October 2012, Bangkok; Wacharin Ouprajong, interviewed 30 September 2012, Nonthaburi.
44 Anan Ganjanapan, interviewed 29 October 2012, Chiang Mai.
45 Ibid.
46 Achara Rakyutitham *et al.* (2005), 118–119.
47 Mr Nop Mangkornmai and Mr Jai Kiti, Raidong/Mae-aow members, interviewed 30 October 2012, Lamphun; Mr Boonlue Jaroenmee, Klongyong Co-operative, interviewed 10 October 2012, Nakhon Patom.

48 Direk Kong-ngern, interviewed 31 October 2012, Chiang Mai; Long Pechsood, interviewed 1 October 2012, Bangkok.
49 Land Reform Network and Local Act (2010), 11.
50 Pongthip Samranjit, 'A Summary of Research on Ground-up Land Reforms by Communitites', 22 July 2011, www.landreformthai.net (in Thai).
51 Ms Sawitta Teeronwattanakul, Northern Peasants Federation activist, interviewed 29 October 2012, Chiang Mai; Mr Pachoen Choosang, Bantad Mountain group, Trang, 1 October 2012, Bangkok; Boonlue Jaroenmee, interviewed 10 October 2012, Nakhon Patom.
52 Mr Sukaew Fungfoo, President of the Baan Pae-tai CLTD project, interviewed 30 October 2012, Lamphun.
53 This point has also been observed by, for example, Ms Chuleerat Jaroenpon, researcher on the LRM and lecturer from Faculty of Social Innovation, Rangsit University, interviewed 4 October 2012, Pathum Thani.
54 For example: Mr Rachata Rangsiri, LRM farmer from Tambol Mae-faeg, Chiang Mai, 1 October 2012, Bangkok; Mr Jai Kiti, Raidong/Mae-aow CLTD project, interviewed 30 October 2012, Lamphun.
55 Boonlue Jaroenmee, interviewed 10 October 2012, Nakhon Patom.
56 Ibid.
57 Mrs Wantana Iamsuwan, one of the nine management committee members, Klongyong Co-operative, interviewed 10 October 2012, Nakhon Patom; Mrs Wilaiwan Konka, Vice-president of Baan Pae-tai CLTD project, interviewed 30 October 2012, Lamphun.
58 Pachoen Choosang, interviewed 1 October 2012, Bangkok.
59 De Schutter (2011a), 268–269; Matias E. Margulis, Nora McKeon, and Saturnino M. Borras, 'Land Grabbing and Global Governance: Critical Perspectives', *Globalizations* 10, no. 1 (2013), 12; Marc Edelman *et al.*, 'Introduction: Critical Perspectives on Food Sovereignty', *The Journal of Peasant Studies* 41, no. 6 (15 October 2014), 923.
60 Margulis, McKeon and Borras (2013), 7.
61 J.W. Bruce *et al.*, *Land Law Reform: Achieving Development Policy Objectives. World Bank Law, Justice, and Development Series* (Washington DC: The World Bank, 2008), quoted in De Schutter (2011a), 271.
62 UN Special Rapporteur on the Right to Food, 'Access to Land and the Right to Food, Interim Report of the Special Rapporteur on the Right to Food, Olivier De Schutter, to the 65th Session of the General Assembly, UN Doc. A/65/281', 2010, quoted in De Schutter (2011a), 271.
63 For an example from India, see: K. Deininger, S. Jin, and H.K. Nagarajan, 'Efficiency and Equity Impacts of Rural Land Market Restrictions: Evidence from India. World Bank Policy Research Working Paper Series 3013' (2006), quoted in De Schutter (2011a), 271.
64 De Schutter (2011a), 258.
65 See a longer list in Rakyutitham *et al.* (2005), 32.
66 Interviews with various people such as Prayong Doklamyai (1 November 2012, Chiang Mai), Direk Kong-ngern (31 October 2012, Chiang Mai), Wacharin Ouprajong (30 September 2012, Bangkok), Sawitta Teeronwattanakul (29 October 2012, Chiang Mai), Rangsan Sansongkwae (30 October 2012, Lamphun), and Montri Bualoi (31 October 2012, Chiang Mai).
67 Land Reform Network and Local Act (2010), 7.
68 Prayong Doklamyai, interviewed 1 November 2012, Chiang Mai; Ransang Sansongkwae, interviewed 30 October 2012, Lamphun.
69 Direk Kong-ngern, interviewed 31 October 2012, Chiang Mai.
70 As reflected by, for example, Boonlue Jaroenmee, Klongyong leader, interviewed 10 October 2012, Nakhon Patom.

71 Rakyutitham *et al.* (2005), 118–119; Rangsan Sansongkwae and other members from Raidong/Mae-aow such as Jai Kitti, Nop Mangkornmai and Oonjai Akaruan, interviewed 30 October 2012, Lamphun.
72 Examples include Bantad Mountain in the South (Pachoen Choosang and Long Pechsood, interviewed 1 October 2012, Bangkok) and other cases such as in Naan (Mr Wichai, a LRM farmer member from Ampur Wiangsa, Naan province, interviewed during the demonstration in front of Government House, 1 October 2012, Bangkok).
73 Kingkarn Samnuanyen, *Dynamics of Social Movement Tactics: The Case of the Land Rights Movement in Lumphun Province. An Unpublished Masters Thesis at the Faculty of Political Science, Chulalongkorn Univeristy* (Bangkok, 2006), 68 (in Thai).
74 Ibid., 81.
75 Ibid., 81 and 83.
76 Ibid., 92.
77 Ibid., 92.
78 Rangsan Sansongkwae, interviewed 30 October 2012, Lamphun.
79 Phu Chiangdao, 'Lamphun Land: Our Heart is the Land', in *Land of Life*, ed. Ngao-sil Kongkaew and Phu Chiangdao (Nonthaburi: Local Act and Community Organisations Development Institute, 2010), 198–199, 203 (in Thai); Rangsan Sansongkwae, interviewed 30 October 2012, Lamphun.
80 Rangsan Sansongkwae, Nop Mangkornmai and Oonjai Akaruan, interviewed 30 October 2012, Lamphun.
81 Singsootham (2010), 36.
82 The Land Reform Network and Local Act (2010), 235.
83 Ibid., 235; Direk Kong-ngern, interviewed 31 October 2012, Chiang Mai.
84 Pongthip Samranjit *et al.*, *A Documental Report on the Research on What Thailand Will Lose without Land Reform: Land Management and Social Justice – A Case Study of the Land Reform Network in Thailand* (Bangkok: Chulalongkorn University Social Research Institute, 2012), 231 (in Thai); The Land Reform Network and Local Act (2010), 224.
85 Land Reform Network and Local Act (2010), 236.
86 Singsootham (2010), 39–40.
87 Land Reform Network and Local Act (2010), 233–234. Also, Direk Kong-ngern and Montri Bualoi, interviewed 31 October 2012, Chiang Mai.
88 Samranjit *et al.* (2012), 233; Direk Kong-ngern, interviewed 31 October 2012, Chiang Mai.
89 Direk Kong-ngern, Baan Pong, interviewed 31 October 2012, Chiang Mai.
90 Land Reform Network and Local Act (2010), 235.
91 Ngao-sin Kongkaew, *The Event Occured at Bantad Mountains* (Bangkok: Bantad Mountain Land Reform Network and the Thai Health Organisation, 2011), 116 (in Thai).
92 Ibid., 130 and 135. Also, Pachoen Choosang, interview 1 October 2012, Bangkok.
93 Kongkaew (2011), 136–147.
94 Pachoen Choosang, interviewed 1 October 2012, Bangkok.
95 Singsootham (2010), 53.
96 Kongkaew (2011), 116.
97 Ibid., 66 and Pachoen Choosang, Bantad Mountain group, interviewed 1 October 2012, Bangkok.
98 Kongkaew (2011), 67.
99 Long Pechsood, Bantad Mountain group, interviewed 1 October 2012, Bangkok.
100 Land Reform Network and Local Act (2010), 106.
101 Ibid., 108.
102 Ibid., 108.

103 Ibid., 107.
104 Ibid., 108–113.
105 Ibid., 113.
106 Ibid., 113.
107 Singsootham (2010), 72.
108 Mr Hemrach Lobnongbua quoted in Prachathai News, 'Report from the Seminar "CLTD and Solutions to Land Conflicts in Thailand"', *Prachathai*, 4 July 2009 (in Thai). Also, Singsootham (2010), 7 and 70–71.
109 Singsootham (2010), 72 and 74.
110 Ibid., 79.
111 Hemrach Lobnongbua quoted in Prachathai (4 July 2009).
112 Singsootham (2010), 74–75.
113 Ibid., 80.
114 Rangsan Sansongkwae, interviewed 30 October 2012, Lamphun.
115 Kom Chad Luek Newspaper, 'Mae-aow villagers smile for the second CLTDs from the Prime Minister', *Kom Chad Luek*, 18 March 2011 (in Thai).
116 Klongyong community leaders, 'A Summary of the Struggles of the Klongyong Community: A Document Prepared by the Locals for Visitors', obtained 10 October 2012, 1–3 (in Thai).
117 Ibid., 2; Land Reform Network and Local Act (2010), 322.
118 Klongyong community leaders (2012), 3.
119 Boonlue Jaroenmee, interviewed 10 October 2012, Nakhon Patom; Shoti Saiyuenyong, one of the nine management committee members, Klongyong Co-operative, interviewed 10 October 2012, Nakhon Patom.
120 Boonlue Jaroenmee, interviewed 10 October 2012, Nakhon Patom.
121 Ibid.
122 Ibid.; Land Reform Network and Local Act (2010), 317.
123 For example, see Saturnino M. Borras, Jennifer C. Franco, and Chunyu Wang, 'The Challenge of Global Governance of Land Grabbing: Changing International Agricultural Context and Competing Political Views and Strategies', *Globalizations* 10, no. 1 (2013), 167.
124 Margulis, McKeon and Borras (2013), 11.
125 Ittipol Srisaowalak *et al.*, *A Project to Study Appropriate Land Rights for Communities* (Bangkok: Thailand Research Fund, 2007), 165 (in Thai).
126 Wich Jeerapat, 'Reflection on Thai Community Right Ideas', *Julniti Journal* 3, no. 38 (2010), 40 (in Thai).
127 A few interviewees refer to the fact that the Thai Constitution recognises community rights, such as Pachoen Choosang, Bantad Mountain group, 1 October 2012, Bangkok.
128 Ittipol Srisaowalak *et al.*, *A Study Project on the Law to Manage Local Areas* (Bangkok: Thailand Research Fund, 2001), Abstract page II and III (in Thai); Kraiyoorawong *et al.* (2005), 88.
129 A Parliamentary Committee to Consider Land Problems (2009), 18.
130 Ibid., 67.
131 Sawitta Teeronwattanakul, Northern Peasants Federation, interviewed 29 October 2012, Chiang Mai.
132 For example, see: Kraiyoorawong *et al.* (2005), 88; A Parliamentary Committee to Consider Land Problems (2009), 18.
133 Sawitta Teeronwattanakul, interviewed 29 October 2012, Chiang Mai.
134 Singsootham (2010), 30.
135 A summary based on interviews with various people in the movement and from Pongthip Samranjit, 'A Summary of Research on Ground-up Land Reforms by Communities', 22 July 2011, www.landreformthai.net (in Thai).

136 V. Songwe and K. Deininger, 'Foreign Investment in Agricultural Production: Opportunities and Challenges. Agriculture and Rural Development Notes, Issue 45, World Bank', 2009, quoted in De Schutter (2011a), 272.
137 See Samnuanyen (2006), 110–113.
138 A Parliamentary Committee to Consider Land Problems (2009), 61–62, 65 and 68.
139 Community Land Title Deeds Office, Prime Minister's Office, 'Document for Distribution Regarding the Latest Progress date 31 January 2012', www.opm.go.th/OpmInter/content/oclt/default.asp (in Thai).
140 Kom Chad Luek Newspaper, 'Mae-aow Villagers Smile for the Second CLTDs from the Prime Minister', *Kom Chad Luek*, 18 March 2011 (in Thai).
141 Isra News, 'P-move Reminds the Government of the Promises on Land Banks and the Protection of CLTDs Areas', *Isra News*, 23 February 2013 (in Thai).
142 Prayong Doklamyai, interviewed 1 November 2012, Chiang Mai. Also, see P-move Declaration number 18, 26 April 2013.
143 P-move Declaration number 18, 26 April 2013.
144 Drafts of the proposed laws can be found at www.landwatchthai.com/index.php/th/4.
145 Acharawadee Buaklee, 'The North Pushes for 4 Land Laws', *ThaiPBS*, 4 April 2014 (in Thai).
146 Paul Sullivan and Wilder Nicholson, 'Is The Master Plan to Solve the Deforestation or Yet Another Strategy to Remove and Evict People?', 12 December 2014, www.esaanlandreformnews.com.
147 Matichon Newspaper, 'Prapart Pintoptaeng – Politics Lecturer from Chulalongkorn was Arrested after Soldiers Cancelled the Walk for Land Reform Event', *Matichon*, 9 November 2014 (in Thai).
148 Prayong Doklamyai, interviewed 30 September 2012, Nonthaburi.
149 Kraiyoorawong *et al.* (2005), 87; Prayong Doklamyai, interviewed 30 September 2012, Nonthaburi.
150 Research based on information from the Office of the National Anti-Corruption Commission, June 2013, by Dr Duangmanee Laowakul, Faculty of Economics, Thammasart University, quoted in 'Landlords from 11 Political Parties Hold 35,000 Rai: Phua Thai, Democrat and Phumjaithai in the Lead', *Prachachat Turakij*, 19 June 2014 (in Thai).
151 Ibid.
152 Interviews from community leaders such as Direk Kong-ngern, Montri Bualoi (31 October 2012, Baan Pong, Chiang Mai), Rangsan Sansonkwae and Sangwal Kantham (30 October 2012, Rai-dong/Mae-aow, Lamphun), as well as Sarawut Wongnikorn, Northern Peasants Federation, interviewed 30 October 2012, Chiang Mai.
153 For a similar view, see Edelman *et al.* (2014), 924.
154 Samranjit *et al.* (2012), 220; Direk Kong-ngern, interviewed 31 October 2012, Chiang Mai; Pacheon Choosang, interviewed 1 October 2012, Bangkok.
155 Dr Weerachai Narkwibulwong, Secretary General of ALRO, interviewed 14 February 2013, Bangkok.
156 Prayong Doklamyai, interviewed 1 November 2012, Chiang Mai.
157 Boonlue Jaroenmee, interviewed 10 October 2012, Nakhon Patom.
158 Weerachai Narkwibulwong, interviewed 14 February 2013, Bangkok; Narkwibulwong (2012), 20; 'Taking Back 5 Million Rai of ALRO Land', *Post Today*, 29 September 2014. Another source suggests ALRO has 34.76 million rai of land under its jurisdiction in 2014 (Dr Duangmanee Laowakul, Faculty of Economics, Thammasat University, quoted in Isra News, 'Macro View of Land' (2014).
159 Weerachai Narkwibulwong, interviewed 14 February 2013, Bangkok.
160 Ibid.
161 Narkwibulwong (2012), 37.
162 Weerachai Narkwibulwong, interviewed 14 February 2013, Bangkok.

163 Margulis, McKeon and Borras (2013), 3 and 14.
164 Derek Hall, 'Land Grabs, Land Control, and Southeast Asian Crop Booms', *Journal of Peasant Studies* 38, no. 4 (October 2011), 838.
165 Keith Barney, 'Re-Encountering Resistance: Plantation Activism and Smallholder Production in Thailand and Sarawak, Malaysia', *Asia Pacific Viewpoint* 45, no. 3 (2004), 331.
166 Samranjit (2011); Prayong Doklamyai, interviewed 1 November 2012, Chiang Mai; Land Reform Network, *CLTDs – We Can: A Handbook* (Bangkok: Land Reform Network, 2012) (in Thai).
167 Rakyutitham *et al.* (2005), 177.
168 Prayong Doklamyai quoted in Rakyutitham (2008), 250–251.
169 Wacharin Ouprajong, interviewed Nonthaburi, 30 September 2012.
170 Edelman *et al.* (2014), 922.
171 Dr Chomchuan Boonrahong, lecturer at Mae-Jo University, interviewed 3 November 2012, Chiang Mai; Mr Witoon Lienchamroon, BioThai, interviewed 5 April 2012, Nonthaburi; Mr Pat Apaimool, Mae-ta sustainable farmer, interviewed 1 November 2012, Chiang Mai.
172 Mr Kiatsak Chatdee, ISAC, interviewed 31 October 2012, Chiang Mai; Mr Aarat Sang-ubol, CAE, interviewed 19 December 2012, Surin.
173 Landlords usually do not allow tenants to dig a pond because land value will drop. Witoon Lienchamroon and Supha Yaimuang, 'Alternative Agriculture: From Individual Farmers to Social Movements', in *Reform the Agricultural Sector for Food Security: Analysis and Practical Policies*, ed. Witoon Lienchamroon (Nonthaburi: BioThai, 2011), 298–299 (in Thai).
174 Ms Nanta Haitook, President of Baan Tanon Organic Herb and Vegetable Processing Group, interviewed 20 December 2012, Surin.
175 Pat Apaimool, interviewed 1 November 2012, Chiang Mai.
176 Prayong Doklamyai, interviewed 1 November 2012, Chiang Mai.
177 Chomchuan Boonrahong, interviewed 3 November 2012, Chiang Mai.
178 Prayong Doklamyai, quoted in Rakyutitham (2008), 250–251.
179 Sajin Prachason *et al.*, *Market Options of Farmers: Structural Effects on Unfairness and Benefit Distribution* (Bangkok: BioThai and the Social Research Foundation, Chulalongkorn University, 2012), 148 (in Thai).
180 Kanoksak Duangkaewruen, Mae-ta, interviewed 1 November 2012, Chiang Mai.
181 Prayong Doklamyai, interviewed 1 November 2012, Chiang Mai; Oonjai Akaruan and Rangsan Sansongkwae, interviewed 30 October 2012, Lamphun.
182 Jai Kiti, interviewed 30 October 2012, Lamphun.
183 Sukaew Fungfoo, interviewed 30 October 2012, Lamphun.
184 Direk Kong-ngern, interviewed 31 October 2012, Chiang Mai.
185 Samranjit *et al.* (2012), 217.
186 Interviewed 20 May 2009, quoted in Singsootham (2010), 46.
187 Singsootham (2010), 49.
188 Direk Kong-ngern, Baan Pong, interviewed 30 September 2012, Nonthaburi.
189 Ibid.
190 Ms Sangwal Kantham, Mr Nop Mangkornmai, and Mr Oonjai Akaruen, Raidong-Mae-Aow, interviewed 30 October 2012, Lamphun.
191 Rangsan Sansongkwae, Nop Mangkornmai, Jai Kiti, and Sarawut Wongnikorn, interviewed 30 October 2012, Lamphun and Chiang Mai.
192 Quoted on 9 February 2010 in Singsootham (2010), 78.
193 Singsootham (2010), 77.
194 Ibid., 79.
195 Singsootham (2010), 64; Pachoen Choosang and Long Pechsood, interviewed 1 October 2012, Bangkok; Mrs Nerm Nooboon, LRM member of Baan Saikling and Baan Tachang group, Patlung, interviewed 1 October 2012, Bangkok.

196 Singsootham (2010), 65; Kongkaew (2011), 115.
197 Boonlue Jaroenmee, interviewed 10 October 2012, Nakhon Patom.
198 Shoti Saiyuenyong, interviewed 10 October 2012, Nakhon Patom.
199 Wantana Iamsuwan, interviewed 10 October 2012, Nakhon Patom.
200 Weerachai Narkwibulwong, interviewed 14 February 2013, Bangkok.
201 Weerachai Narkwibulwong, Arpapan Pattanapan, and Arthita Pongprom, *Efficient Usage of ALRO Land: A Case Study of Maximum of 10 Rai per Household Land Plot* (Bangkok: Thailand Research Fund, 2011), abstract and 147 (in Thai).
202 Narkwibulwong (2012), 20.
203 Weerachai Narkwibulwong, interviewed 14 February 2013, Bangkok.
204 Narkwibulwong (2012), 17 and 20.
205 Ibid., 19 and 21.
206 Samnuanyen (2006), 98–101.
207 For example, 200 policemen and dogs were used to arrest Sukaew Fungfoo and seven other villagers. In another case, 400 policemen destroyed crops and huts in Baan Pongroo and other communities (ibid., 100).
208 Ibid., 100.
209 Ibid., 102 and Wacharin Ouprajong, Baan Huafai, Chiang Mai, interviewed Nonthaburi, 30 September 2012.
210 Samnuanyen (2006), 108–113.
211 Prachathai News, 'P-move Asks Supreme Court to Stop the Delay of the Enforcement of the Ruling on the Palm Oil Land Conflict in Suratthani, as the Delay Has Led to Violence', *Prachathai*, 25 December 2012 (in Thai).
212 Singsootham (2010), 26–27.
213 Dr Duangmanee Laowakul, Faculty of Economics, Thammasart University, research presentation at the Food Security Assembly 2014 in Thailand, quoted in Isra news, 'Macro View of Land' (2014).
214 Dr Permsak Mokarapirom, quoted during the discussion panel on land problems at the second National Reform Assembly, 2012, Bangkok, Thailand.
215 Prayong Doklamyai, interviewed 1 November 2012, Chiang Mai. A table of legal land conflicts in Thailand as relating to different government policies (five regions, 638 cases) can be found in Kraiyoorawong *et al.* (2005), 21.
216 See: Naruemon Thabchumpon, 'NGOs and Grassroots Participation in the Political Reform Process', in *Reforming Thai Politics*, ed. Duncan McCargo (Copenhagen: NIAS Press, 2002), 197–198; iLaw, 'Third Attempt at Drafting Community Forest Law by the National Reform Assembly is Still Not Relevant to Communities', 23 July 2015, https://ilaw.or.th/node/7328 (in Thai); CODI (The Community Organizations Development Institute), 'Community Forest Network Rejects the Community Forest Bill', (n.d.), www.codi.or.th/index.php/news/documentary-communities-news/42-2009-09-22-05-47-57/848-2010-09-06-06-01-33, received 27 November 2014 (in Thai).
217 Sangwal Kantham, interviewed 30 October 2012, Lamphun.
218 Rangsan Sansongkwae and Sangwal Kantham, interviewed 30 October 2012, Lamphun.
219 Anan Ganjanapan, interviewed 29 October 2012, Chiang Mai; Prapart Pintoptang, Chulalongkorn University, interviewed 16 October 2012, Nonthaburi.
220 Sawitta Teeronwattanakul, interviewed 29 October 2012, Chiang Mai.
221 Prayong Doklamyai, interviewed by Pechra Buranin, 'Four Laws for the Poor Campaign', 10 October 2014, http://4laws.info/2014/10/10/603/ (in Thai).
222 Anan Ganjanapan, interviewed 29 October 2012, Chiang Mai.
223 See the discussion of this approach in Yoshinori Nishizaki, 'Peasants and the Redshirt Movement in Thailand: Some Dissenting Voices', *Journal of Peasant Studies* 41, no. 1 (30 January 2014), 2.
224 Direk Kong-ngern and Montri Bualoi, interviewed 31 October 2012, Chiang Mai; Sawitta Teeronwattanakul, interviewed 29 October 2012, Chiang Mai.

225 Prapart Pintoptang, interviewed 16 October 2012, Nonthaburi.
226 See its land reform proposal in: National Reform Committee, *How to Reform Thailand: A Proposal for Political Parties and Voters* (Bangkok: National Reform Committee, 2011) (in Thai).
227 Hall, Hirsch and Li (2011), 13–14.
228 De Schutter (2011b), 249 and 256.
229 Margulis, McKeon and Borras (2013), 13.
230 Matias E. Margulis and Tony Porter, 'Governing the Global Land Grab: Multipolarity, Ideas, and Complexity in Transnational Governance', *Global Restructuring, State, Capital and Labour. Contesting Neo-Gramscian Perspectives* 10, no. 1 (2013), 66 and also 68–69.
231 Nora Mckeon, '"One Does Not Sell the Land Upon Which the People Walk': Land Grabbing, Transnational Rural Social Movements, and Global Governance', *Globalizations* 10, no. 1 (2013), 117.
232 Saturnino M. Borras *et al.*, 'Transnational Agrarian Movements: Origins and Politics, Campaigns and Impact', in *Transnational Agrarian Movements Confronting Globalization* (Chichester: Wiley-Blackwell, 2008), 11.
233 Ibid., 13.
234 Ibid., 18.
235 Saturnino M. Borras, 'La Vía Campesina and its Global Campaign for Agrarian Reform', in *Transnational Agrarian Movements Confronting Globalization* (Chichester: Wiley-Blackwell, 2008), 105–106.
236 Ibid., 92.
237 The definition of 'externalisation' was from S. Tarrow, *The New Transnational Activism* (Cambridge: Cambridge University Press, 2005), 32, quoted in Borras (2008), 97.
238 Borras (2008), 95–97.
239 Ibid., 111–112 and Nancy Lee Peluso, Suraya Afiff, and Noer Fauzi Rachman, 'Claiming the Grounds for Reform: Agrarian and Environmental Movements in Indonesia', in *Transnational Agrarian Movements Confronting Globalization* (Chichester: Wiley-Blackwell, 2008), 224.
240 Kathy Le Mons Walker, 'From Covert to Overt: Everyday Peasant Politics in China and the Implications for Transnational Agrarian Movements', in *Transnational Agrarian Movements Confronting Globalization* (Chichester: Wiley-Blackwell, 2008), 311 and 315–316.
241 Borras (2008), 113–114.
242 Direk Kong-ngern, interviewed 30 September 2012, Nonthaburi and 31 October 2012, Chiang Mai.
243 Borras, Franco and Wang (2013), 171.
244 Arat Sang-ubol, AAN activist, interviewed 19 December 2012, Surin. Also, Direk Kong-ngern and Montri Bualoi from Baan Pong, interviewed 31 October 2012, Chiang Mai.
245 Prayong Doklamyai, interviewed 1 November 2012, Chiang Mai.
246 Specifically farmers from Tamor and Ta-toom groups in Surin, previously discussed in Chapter 5.
247 McKeon (2013), 110–111.
248 Borras, Franco and Wang (2013), 175 and McKeon (2013), 117.

7 Conclusion and reflections

Summary of important points

Overall, this book has argued that the mainstream agri-food system in Thailand has been shaped to aid capital accumulation by domestic and transnational hegemonic forces, although the SAM and the LRM have managed to challenge and offer alternatives to the hegemonic system, to a certain extent. This book has also argued that counter-hegemony should be seen as a non-linear ongoing process over a long period of time, where forces that are predominantly counter-hegemonic may, at times, retain some hegemonic elements. Hegemonic forces also have many measures to co-opt dissert, and the line between hegemony and counter-hegemony is often unclear. The threat of co-optation means that counter-hegemonic forces should continually refine and develop clear ideas and practices to guard against co-optation.

This book has brought new empirical information from Thailand into existing literature on the global agri-food system, alternative agri-food networks, agrarian movements, as well as Thai agrarian development and politics. It also extended neo-Marxist and Gramscian theoretical perspectives in the study of the agri-food system; Chapter 2 has provided an outline of the combined neo-Marxist and Gramscian theoretical framework, while Chapter 3 to 6 have discussed empirical information through this theoretical lens. Rather than focusing mainly on domestic factors, this book has provided new perspectives on Thai agrarian development and social movements by suggesting the interconnected importance of counter-hegemonic ideas, production–distribution practices, as well as governance structures at local, national, and global scales. This book has also explored the relationships between the SAM, the LRM, and the wider state-society complex in which they are enmeshed. It has argued against a polarised conception of development as having only two options – either a traditional backward localist choice or a modern choice – and provided new perspectives on Thai localism as well as polarised Thai politics. To elaborate, this book has argued that polarised political discourses led to narrow framings of structural problems of agriculture and helped to create divisions which weaken social movements. The book's discussions on how cross-class alliances can further or frustrate counter-hegemonic movements also suggest the importance of analysing social movements in relation to established political authority.

Bridging a gap between materialist analysis in the Marxist tradition and more subjectivist analytical perspectives, this book has argued that transformative change in society should be seen as an evolutionary process over a long period of time and that counter-hegemony should take place at both ideational and material levels. Conceptualising counter-hegemony in this manner challenges the Marxist pre-occupation with 'crisis and change'. Moreover, through the Gramscian concept of 'national-popular strategies' and Stephen Gill's 'post-modern Prince' idea about political agency, the book takes into account heterogeneity within and between social movements in different social contexts. Hence, it does not simply dismiss the SAM and the LRM, which were partially inspired by Thai localism, as fundamentally insular and conservative. Instead, this book suggests that these movements bear seeds of counter-hegemonic transformation even though they do not necessarily resemble stereotypical images of politicised, structured, and leftist national movements.

Reflections and future areas of research

As with all research projects, there can always be room for improvements. This book adopts an international political economy approach so it focuses on the study of the agri-food system in Thailand at the macro-level. Inevitably, many issues cannot be explored in great detail. Moreover, the author tried to gather as much relevant information as possible from a variety of reliable sources, but there are few sources and studies on certain topics such as land grabs, the Crown Property Bureau, and the effects of financial speculations on agri-food producers in Thailand. Limitations of time and resources also prevented the author from conducting extensive investigations into these topics. In addition, some issues were still unfolding at the time of writing, such as the paddy pledging scheme, persecutions of land reform movement activists, and the effects of the 2014 coup d'état on the country in general. However, this book could only take into account developments up until early 2014.

Future research projects could explore the consumption side of the agri-food system in greater depth. In addition, more in-depth studies of the heterogeneity (gender, class, age, ethnicity, type of farm labour) within the agricultural sector and agri-food movements would be interesting. Although there is a minimum wage law in Thailand, some types of farm labourers may not benefit from it. The neo-Marxist and Gramscian theoretical framework could also be improved in four main areas in the future. First, the neo-Marxist concept of 'accumulation by dispossession' is rather broad and encompasses a variety of processes ranging from land grabs to financial speculations. Second, although the Gramscian concepts of hegemony and counter-hegemony are useful as general categories of forces that shape the agri-food system, they may give the impression that hegemony and counter-hegemony are exclusive polar opposites. However, as this book has argued, the lines between hegemony and counter-hegemony can be blurred in some instances, especially as predominantly hegemonic and counter-hegemonic forces continue to change and adapt over time. Third, there are other theoretical perspectives that might yield additional insights to the study of the agri-food system. Anarchist perspectives, for example, might shed new light on localist ideas and practices in Thailand, as well as on the conceptualisation of counter-hegemonic movements. Fourth, engagement with other theoretical perspectives might help with a more nuanced conceptualisation of the Thai state; to show its complexity beyond being a major facilitator of capital accumulation.

Comparative studies with countries in Asia and other continents will also be interesting if they could flesh out how specific local, national and regional conditions influence the mainstream agri-food systems and counter-hegemonic agri-food movements in these countries. As Chapter 5 has discussed, the SAM in Thailand received some influence from agri-food movements in India and Japan, such as with regards to seed sovereignty ideas, natural farming principles, and effective micro-organisms technology. However, further study is needed to explore whether regional Asian perspectives on counter-hegemony in the agri-food system can be generalised.

Future research projects could also explore capitalist agriculture's relationships with other sectors of the economy in detail. It has been noted that global land grabs are associated with the rise of 'flex crops' and commodities with multiple uses across food, feed, fuel and other industrial sectors, which blur sectoral boundaries and sectoral governance instruments.[1] This suggests the importance of further analysing the agri-food system in relation to the governance of other natural resources and other sectors of the economy. As Chapter 5 has discussed, many sustainable producer groups in Thailand try to develop add-value agri-food products to earn a higher income and create more jobs. This raises many questions that should be investigated further, particularly regarding the kinds of agro-processing and industrial development that will be compatible with the goals of the sustainable agriculture movement.

Many technical problems facing sustainable agriculture groups in Thailand are also related to wider social and economic structures. For example, the sustainable agricultural movement can expand faster if governance structures that determine which research issues are prioritised, or who gets funding, become more favourable to the promotion of sustainable technologies. Another example is how high costs of organic products in urban centres, such as Bangkok, can partially be explained by high transport costs which are related to the current logistical system, city planning, and fossil fuel capitalist economy. In addition, as discussed in Chapter 6, many members of the land reform movement occupied land because they lost their jobs following the 1997 Asian economic crisis, or because working as labourers in other sectors of the economy was detrimental to their health. Some people in Thailand have also become interested in sustainable agriculture as a way to make a living because they have seen the negative environmental effects of some industrial activities, or because they feel alienated from office jobs.[2] These examples suggest the interconnections of different sectors of the economy which, from a Marxist perspective, relates back to the capitalist system's cyclical boom and bust tendency, creations of reserve armies of labour, as well as the capitalist tendency to exploit and alienate both nature and labour. Seeing the bigger picture will also help alternative agri-food movements to link-up with other social movements and expand their networks.

To conclude, this research on the agri-food system in Thailand has yielded some useful insights which point to many avenues of further studies, such as a comparative study of the agri-food system in Thailand and that of other countries. In the future, the author also hopes to study the possibility that the primary, secondary and tertiary sectors of the economy can be geared towards more socially and ecologically sustainable paths, or to positively and radically transform the capitalist economy as a whole.

Notes

1 Saturnino M. Borras, Jennifer C. Franco, and Chunyu Wang, 'The Challenge of Global Governance of Land Grabbing: Changing International Agricultural Context and Competing Political Views and Strategies', *Globalizations* 10, no. 1 (2013), 162 and 165.
2 Mr Long Pechsood, Bantad Mountain farmer from Trang Province, interviewed 1 October 2012, Bangkok; Mrs Supha Yaimuang, SATHAI, interviewed 3 October 2012, Nonthaburi.

Appendix

Addresses of Sustainable Agriculture and Land Reform Groups

Sustainable Agriculture Groups

Naso Producer Group

Address: 57 Moo 2 Baan Sokkhumpoon, Tambol Naso, Ampur Kudchum, Yasothon province, 35140

Bak-rua Producer Group

Address: 118 Moo 4, Baan Donphueng, Tambol Bakrua, Ampur Mahanachai, Yasothon province, 35130

Nam-oom Sustainable Agriculture Social Enterprise

Address: 27 Moo 10, Baan Siripattana, Tambol Nam-oom, Ampur Korwang, Yasothon province, 35160

Kammad Sustainable Agriculture Group

Address: 61 Moo 3 Baan Noanyang, Tambol Kammad, Ampur Kudchum, Yasothon province, 35140

The Moral Rice (Thamma-ruamjai) Network

Address: 80 Moo 8, Tambol Krajai, Ampur Pa-tiew, Yasothon province, 35150

Rice Fund Surin Organic Agriculture Co-operative

Address: 88 Moo 7, Tambol Kae-yai, Ampur Muang, Surin province, 32000

Tamor Group

Address: 99 Moo 9, Baan Doan-leng Nua, Tambol Tamor, Ampur Prasart, Surin province, 32140

Ta-toom Group

Address: Baan Nongbua, Tambol Nongbua, Ampur Ta-toom, Surin province, 32130

Taptai Group

Address: 24 Moo 10, Baan Tap-tai, Tambol Tamor, Ampur Prasart, Surin province 32140

Community Land Title Deed (CLTD) groups

Baan Raidong/Mae-aow

Address: Baan Raidong/Mae-Aow, Moo 1, Lamphun-Lee road, Tambol Nakhon Jedi, Ampur Pasang, Lamphun Province, 51120

Baan Pong

Address: Baan Pong, Moo 2, Tambol Mae-faeg, Ampur Sansai, Chiang Mai Province, 50290

Baan Pae-tai

Address: Baan Pae-tai, Moo 11, Tonphueng-Jomthong Road, Tambol Nonglong, Ampur Wieng non-long, Lamphun Province, 51120

Klongyong Co-operative

Address: Klongyong co-operative, Moo 8, Tambol Klongyong, Ampur Puttamonton, Nakhonpatom Province 73170

Bibliography

Please contact the author for a Thai version of the bibliography.

A Parliamentary Committee to Consider Land Problems. *A Report on How to Solve the Problems Regarding Land Use, Land Laws, and the Rushed Property Rights Document Process*. Bangkok: A Parliamentary Committee to Consider Land Problems, 2009 (in Thai).

AAN farmer groups. 'Kaen-Nakhon Manifesto: Local Rice, Secure Food and Farmer Livelihoods,' E-Saan Local Rice Expo, 14–15 March 2009 (in Thai).

Aanthong, Akrapong. 'Organic Product Standards: Symbolic Declaration from Civil Society.' In *NGOs for Social Benefits ... and Social Processes Based on Knowledge and Wisdom*, edited by Sombat Hesakul, Supaporn Worapornpan, and Akrapong Aanthong, 53–73. Bangkok: National Health Foundation, 2004 (in Thai).

Abbott, Jason P., and Owen Worth. 'Introduction: The "Many Worlds" of Critical International Political Economy.' In *Critical Perspectives on International Political Economy*, edited by Jason P. Abbott and Owen Worth, 1–13. Basingstoke: Palgrave Macmillan, 2002.

Agarwal, Bina. *A Field of One's Own: Gender and Land Rights in South Asia*. Cambridge: Cambridge University Press, 1994.

Agrawal, Arun, and Clark C. Gibson. 'Enchantment and Disenchantment: The Role of Community in Natural Resource Conservation.' *World Development* 27, no. 4 (April 1999): 629–649.

Akram-Lodhi, Haroon. 'Land, Markets and Neoliberal Enclosure: An Agrarian Political Economy Perspective.' *Third World Quarterly* 28, no. 8 (December 2007): 1437–1456.

Allen, Patricia, and Carolyn Sachs. 'Women and Food Chains: The Gendered Politics of Food.' *International Journal of Sociology of Food and Agriculture* 15, no. 1 (2007): 1–23.

Altieri, Miguel A., and Peter Rosset. 'Ten Reasons Why Biotechnology Will Not Ensure Food Security, Protect the Environment and Reduce Poverty in the Developing World.' *AgBioForum* 2, no. 3–4 (1999): 155–162.

Altieri, Miguel A., and Victor Manuel Toledo. 'The Agroecological Revolution in Latin America: Rescuing Nature, Ensuring Food Sovereignty and Empowering Peasants.' *Journal of Peasant Studies* 38, no. 3 (July 2011): 587–612.

Amanor, Kojo Sebastian. 'Global Food Chains, African Smallholders and World Bank Governance.' *Journal of Agrarian Change* 9, no. 2 (April 2009): 247–262.

Amekawa, Yuichiro. 'Reflections on the Growing Influence of Good Agricultural Practices in the Global South.' *Journal of Agricultural and Environmental Ethics* 22, no. 6 (2009): 531–557.

Appadurai, Arjun. *The Social Life of Things: Commodities in Cultural Perspective*. Cambridge: Cambridge University Press, 1986.

Araghi, A. 'Global Depeasantization, 1945–1990.' *Atlantic* 36, no. 2 (1995): 337–368.

Araghi, Farshad. 'Food Regimes and the Production of Value: Some Methodological Issues.' *Journal of Peasant Studies* 30, no. 2 (2003): 41–70.

Araghi, Farshad. 'The Invisible Hand and the Visible Foot: Peasants, Dispossession and Globalization.' In *Peasants and Globalization: Political Economy, Rural Transformation and the Agrarian Question*, edited by A. Haroon Akram-Lodhi and C. Kay, 111–147. Oxon: Routledge, 2009.

Arce, A., and T.K. Marsden. 'The Social Construction of International Food: A New Research Agenda.' *Economic Geography* 69, no. 3 (1993): 293–311.

Archetti, E., and S. Aass. 'Peasant Studies: An Overview.' In *International Perspectives in Rural Sociology*, edited by Howard Newby, 107–129. New York: John Wiley, 1987.

Aydin, Zulkuf. 'Neo-Liberal Transformation of Turkish Agriculture.' *Journal of Agrarian Change* 10, no. 2 (2010): 149–187.

Baker, Chris. 'Pluto-Populism: Thaksin and Popular Politics.' In *Thailand Beyond the Crisis*, edited by Peter Warr, 107–137. New York: RoutledgeCurzon, 2005.

Bangkok Business Newspaper. 'Naso, Yasothon: An Example of Self Sufficient Agriculture,' *Bangkok Business*, 22 January 2007 (in Thai).

Bangkok Business Newspaper. 'Wilit Techapaibul ... revolutionary Farmer,' *Bangkok Business*, 11 August 2008 (in Thai).

Bangkok Business Newspaper. 'President of Thai Farmers' Association Reports to DSI about Foreign Land Grabs of Rice Fields,' *Bangkok Business*, 6 August 2009 (in Thai).

Bangkok Business Newspaper. 'Natural Rice Production Method to Survive Flood.' *Bangkok Business*. 13 October 2011 (in Thai).

Bangkok Business Newspaper. 'EU Warns Against GM Papaya.' *Bangkok Business*, 3 July 2012 (in Thai).

Bangkok Business Newspaper. 'Yingluck Government Lied about G-to-G Rice Deal – Damages to the Budget and Rice Stock,' *Bangkok Business*, 17 January 2014 (in Thai).

Bangkok Business Newspaper. 'Thida Condemns Doctors for Joining PDRC,' *Bangkok Business*, 21 January 2014 (in Thai).

Bangkok Post. 'Farmers End Protest in Phitsanulok,' *Bangkok Post*, 28 January 2014. www.bangkokpost.com/breakingnews/391947/farmers-end-protest-in-phitsanulok.

Bangkok Post. 'NAAC Decides to Impeach Yingluck,' *Bangkok Post*, 8 May 2014. www.bangkokpost.com/news/politics/408766/nacc-decides-to-impeach-yingluck-in-the-senate.

Bangkok Post. 'Fresh Struggle Kicks off to Halt GM Crops.' *Bangkok Post*, 24 October 2014. www.bangkokpost.com/opinion/opinion/439241/fresh-struggle-kicks-off-to-halt-gm-crops.

Bantuwong, Chalita. 'Local Sage: Creation of Identity through Sustainable Agriculture.' In *Sustainable Agriculture: Cultural Identity, Agricultural Problems and the Identity of Thai Farmers*, edited by Anusorn Unno, 238–270. Nonthaburi: Sustainable Agriculture Assembly Committee and Heinrich Böll Foundation, 2004 (in Thai).

Barney, Keith. 'Re-Encountering Resistance: Plantation Activism and Smallholder Production in Thailand and Sarawak, Malaysia.' *Asia Pacific Viewpoint* 45, no. 3 (2004): 325–339.

Barndt, Deborah. *Women Working the NAFTA Food Chain: Women, Food and Globalization*. Toronto, ON: Sumach Press, 1999.

Barndt, Deborah. *Tangled Routes: Women, Work, and Globalization on the Tomato Trail*. UK: Rowman and Littlefield, 2008.

Bates, Thomas R. 'Gramsci and the Theory of Hegemony.' *Journal of History of Ideas* 36, no. 2 (1975): 351–366.

Bello, Walden, Shea Cunningham, and Li Kheng Pho. *A Siamese Tragedy. Development and Disintegration in Modern Thailand*. New York: Zed Books, 1998.

Belton, Ben, and David Little. 'The Development of Aquaculture in Central Thailand: Domestic Demand Versus Export-Led Production.' *Journal of Agrarian Change* 8, no. 1 (12 December 2007): 123–143.

Berg, Bruce L., and Howard Lune. *Qualitative Research Methods for the Social Sciences*. New Jersey: Pearson, 2012.

Bernstein, Henry. 'Food Sovereignty via the "Peasant Way": A Sceptical View.' *The Journal of Peasant Studies* 41, no. 6 (8 January 2014): 1031–1063.

Bieler, Andreas, and Adam David Morton. 'A Critical Theory Route to Hegemony, World Order and Historical Change Neo-Gramscian. Neo-Gramscian Perspectives in International Relations.' In *Global Restructuring, State, Capital and Labour. Contesting Neo-Gramscian Perspectives*, edited by Andreas Bieler, Werner Bonefeld, Peter Burnham, and Adam David Morton, 9–27. Hampshire and New York: Palgrave Macmillan, 2006.

Bieler, Andreas, and Adam David Morton. 'Class Formation, Resistance and the Transnational Beyond Unthinking Materialism.' In *Global Restructuring, State, Capital and Labour. Contesting Neo-Gramscian Perspectives*, edited by Andreas Bieler, Werner Bonefeld, Peter Burnham, and Adam David Morton, 196–206. Oxon: Routledge, 2006.

Bill and Melinda Gates Foundation. 'Agricultural Development Strategy, 2008–2011.' 11 July 2008.

BioThai. 'Report on the Problems of Hybrid Rice Seeds: Case Study of Hybrid Rice Owned by the Charoen Pokapand Group,' 2009. www.biothai.net/node/150 (in Thai).

BioThai. *People's Handbook about Food (In)security and Thailand's Solutions*. Nonthaburi: BioThai, 2010 (in Thai).

BioThai. 'Effects of Thai-EU FTA on Plant Genes, Biodiversity, and Food Security,' 26 February 2013. www.biothai.net/node/16573 (in Thai).

BioThai. 'Civil Society Is on Guard against the Passing of GMO Law That Will Benefit Transnational Seed Companies,' 21 January 2015. www.biothai.net/node/25705 (in Thai).

Bjarnegård, Elin. 'Who's the Perfect Politician? Clientelism as a Determining Feature of Thai Politics.' In *Party Politics in Southeast Asia: Clientelism and Electoral Competition in Indonesia, Thailand and the Philippines*, edited by Dirk Tomsa and Andreas Ufen, 142–162. London and New York: Routledge, 2013.

Blakeney, M. 'Recent Developments in Intellectual Property and Power in the Private Sector Related to Food and Agriculture.' *Food Policy* 36 (2011): 109–113.

Boonchai, Krisda. 'Introduction.' In *Sustainable Agriculture: Cultural Identity, Agricultural Problems and the Identity of Thai Farmers*, 7–26. Nonthaburi: Sustainable Agriculture Assembly Committee and Heinrich Böll Foundation, 2004 (in Thai).

Boonchai, Krisda, Bantoon Setsirot, Witoon Lienchamroon, and Anuch Arpapirom. *Ideas and Policies Regarding Agri-Food Resource Base*. Nonthaburi: BioThai, 2007 (in Thai).

Boonrahong, Chomchuan, Witaya Jantawongsri, and Tassanee Palee. *Appropriate Alternative Markets for Sustainable Agricultural Products*. Bangkok: Thailand Research Fund, 2000 (in Thai).

Boonthuan, Karnda. 'Technology That Changes Paddy Fields.' *Bangkok Business*. 2 January 2014 (in Thai).

Borras, Saturnino M. 'La Vía Campesina and its Global Campaign for Agrarian Reform.' *Journal of Agrarian Change* 8, no. 2–3 (2008): 258–289.

Borras, Saturnino M. 'La Via Campesina and its Global Campaign for Agrarian Reform.' In *Transnational Agrarian Movements Confronting Globalization*, edited by Saturnino M. Borras, Marc Edelman, and Cristóbal Kay, 91–122. Chichester: Wiley-Blackwell, 2008.
Borras, Saturnino M., and Jennifer C. Franco. 'From Threat to Opportunity? Problems with the Idea of a "Code of Conduct" for Land-Grabbing.' *Yale Human Rights and Development Law Journal* 13, no. 2 (2010): 507–523.
Borras, Saturnino M., Marc Edelman, and Cristóbal Kay. 'Transnational Agrarian Movements: Origins and Politics, Campaigns and Impact.' In *Transnational Agrarian Movements Confronting Globalization*, edited by Saturnino M. Borras, Marc Edelman, and Cristóbal Kay, 1–36. Chichester: Wiley-Blackwell, 2008.
Borras, Saturnino M., Jennifer C. Franco, and Chunyu Wang. 'The Challenge of Global Governance of Land Grabbing: Changing International Agricultural Context and Competing Political Views and Strategies.' *Globalizations* 10, no. 1 (2013): 161–179.
Bridge, G., P. McManus, and T. Marsden. 'The Next New Thing? Biotechnology and its Discontents.' *Geoforum* 34 (2003): 165–174.
Bruce, J.W., R. Giovarelli, L. Rolfes, D. Bledsoe, and R. Mitchell. *Land Law Reform: Achieving Development Policy Objectives. World Bank Law, Justice, and Development Series*. Washington DC: The World Bank, 2008.
Buaklee, Acharawadee. 'The North Pushes for 4 Land Laws.' *ThaiPBS*, 4 April 2014. www.citizenthaipbs.net/node/4015 (in Thai).
Buck, Daniel, Christina Getz, and Julie Guthman. 'From Farm to Table: The Organic Vegetable Commodity Chain of Northern California.' *Sociologia Ruralis* 37, no. 1 (1997): 3–20.
Buranin, Pechra. 'Four Laws for the Poor Campaign.' 10 October 2014. http://4laws.info/2014/10/10/603/ (in Thai).
Burch, David, and Geoffrey Lawrence. 'Towards a Third Food Regime: Behind the Transformation.' *Agriculture and Human Values* 26, no. 4 (31 July 2009): 267–279.
Busch, Lawrence. 'The Private Governance of Food: Equitable Exchange or Bizarre Bazaar?' *Agriculture and Human Values* 36, no. 3 (2009): 1–8.
Busch, Lawrence, and Carmen Bain. 'New! Improved? The Transformation of the Global Agrifood System.' *Rural Sociology* 69, no. 3 (2004): 321–346.
Business Thai. 'Thanin-Jaroen: 2 Rich Men Are Revolutionising Thai Agriculture!,' 8 May 2008. www.businessthai.co.th (in Thai).
Calestous Juma, 'Feeding Africa: Why Biotechnology Sceptics are Wrong to Dismiss GM,' *Guardian*, 27 May 2014, www.theguardian.com/global-development-professionals-network/2014/may/27/gm-crops-food-security-calestous-juma-africa.
Cameron, Angus, and Ronen Palan. 'Empiricism and Objectivity: Reflexive Theory Construct in a Complex World.' In *Routledge Handbook of International Political Economy: International Political Economy as a Global Conversation*, edited by Mark Blyth, 112–125. London: Routledge, 2007.
Cargill. 'Food Security: The Challenge,' 2014. www.cargill.com/wcm/groups/public/@ccom/documents/document/na3059573.pdf.
Chaowakul, Makasiri. *Revision of Thai Rice Market Structure: A Complete Report for Thailand Research Fund (TRF)*. Naresuan University, 2009 (in Thai).
Chen, C., J. Yang, and C. Findlay. 'Measuring the Effect of Food Safety Standards on China's Agricultural Exports.' *Review of World Economics* 144, no. 1 (2008): 83–106.
Chiangdao, Phu. 'Lamphun Land: Our Heart is the Land.' In *Land of Life*, edited by Ngao-sil Kongkaew and Phu Chiangdao, 180–214. Nonthaburi: Local Act and Community Organisations Development Institute, 2010 (in Thai).

Clapp, Jennifer. 'Food Price Volatility and Vulnerability in the Global South: Considering the Global Economic Context.' *Third World Quarterly* 30, no. 6 (September 2009): 1183–1196.

Clunies-Ross, T. 'Organic Food: Swimming against the Tide?' In *Political, Social and Economic Perspectives on the International Food System*, edited by T. Marsden and J. Little, 200–214. Aldershot: Avebury, 1990.

CODI (The Community Organizations Development Institute). 'Community Forest Network Rejects the Community Forest Bill,' n.d. www.codi.or.th/index.php/news/documentary-communities-news/42-2009-09-22-05-47-57/848-2010-09-06-06-01-33.

Collier, P. 'Politics of Hunger: How Illusion and Greed Fan the Food Crisis.' *Foreign Affairs*, November/December 2008.

Community Land Title Deeds Office, Prime Minister's Office, 'Document for Distribution Regarding the Latest Progress date 31 January 2012', www.opm.go.th/OpmInter/content/oclt/default.asp (in Thai).

Cone, C.A., and A. Kakaliouras. 'Community Supported Agriculture: Building Moral Community or an Alternative Consumer Choice.' *Culture and Agriculture* 51/52 (1995): 28–31.

Coombes, Brad, and Hugh Campbell. 'Dependent Reproduction of Alternative Modes of Agriculture: Organic Farming in New Zealand.' *Sociologia Ruralis* 38, no. 2 (1998): 127–145.

CorpWatch-Thailand. 'Connections between CP, Politicians and Thai Bureaucracy.' In *CP and Thai Agriculture*, 27–38. Nonthaburi: BioThai, 2008 (in Thai).

Cox, Robert W. 'Social Forces, States and World Orders: Beyond International Relations Theory.' *Millennium – Journal of International Studies* 10 (1981): 126–155.

Cox, Robert W. *Production, Power and World Order: Social Forces in the Making of History*. New York: Columbia University Press, 1987.

Cox, Robert W. 'Global Perestroika.' In *The Socialist Register: New World Order?*, vol. 28, edited by R. Miliband and L. Panitch, 26–43. London: Merlin Press, 1992.

CP Foods, *Kitchen of the World: Annual Report 2003*.

Curtis, Fred. 'Eco-Localism and Sustainability.' *Ecological Economics* 46, no. 1 (August 2003): 83–102.

Dailynews. 'Foreign Force Swallows Million Rai of Paddy Field. President of Thai Farmers' Association Exposed Dangerous Sign; Foreign Force's Land Grab Goals in Central and Northeastern Regions.' *Dailynews*, 4 August 2009 (in Thai).

Daly, Herman E., and Joshua Farley. *Ecological Economics: Principles and Applications*. Washington DC: Island Press, 2004.

Dawe, David. 'Have Recent Increases in International Cereal Prices Been Transmitted to Domestic Economies? The Experience in Seven Large Asian Countries.' ESA Working Paper. Rome: Agricultural Development Economics Division, FAO, 2008.

De Schutter, Olivier. 'How Not to Think of Land-Grabbing: Three Critiques of Large-Scale Investments in Farmland.' *Journal of Peasant Studies* 38, no. 2 (March 2011a): 249–279.

De Schutter, Olivier. *UN Human Rights Council: Report Submitted by the Special Rapporteur on the Right to Food*, 2011b.

Deininger, K., S. Jin, and H.K. Nagarajan. 'Efficiency and Equity Impacts of Rural Land Market Restrictions: Evidence from India.' World Bank Policy Research Working Paper Series 3013 (2006).

Delforge, Isabelle. *Contract Farming in Thailand: A View from the Farm. A Report for Focus on the Global South*. Bangkok: Focus on the Global South group, 2007.

DeLind, Laura, and Philip Howard. 'Safe at Any Scale? Food Scares, Food Regulation, and Scaled Alternatives.' *Agriculture and Human Values* 25, no. 3 (2008): 301–317.

Department of Industrial Promotion. *A Study of the Feasibility of Ethanol Production from Cassava 2009*. Bangkok: Ministry of Industry, 2009 (in Thai).

Desmarais, Annette. *La Vía Campesina: Globalization and the Power of Peasants*. London: Pluto, 2007.

Dibden, Jacqui, David Gibbs, and Chris Cocklin. 'Framing GM Crops as a Food Security Solution.' *Journal of Rural Studies* 29 (November 2011): 59–70.

Doklamyai, Prayong. 'From Discourse to Practical Innovation: Land Reform by Communities. Transcript of the Presentation at a Conference on Anan Ganjanapan's Complexity of Rights, 8 March 2008.' In *"I Don't Have the Answer": 60 Years Professor Dr. Anan Ganjanapan and 20 Years of Social Movement on Community Rights and Natural Resources Management*, 247–253. Chiang Mai: Sustainable Development Foundation, 2008 (in Thai).

Dolan, Catherine. 'On Farm and Packhouse: Employment at the Bottom of a Global Value Chain.' *Rural Sociology* 69, no. 1 (2004): 99–126.

Edelman, Marc, Tony Weis, Amita Baviskar, Saturnino M. Borras, Eric Holt-Giménez, Deniz Kandiyoti, and Wendy Wolford. 'Introduction: Critical Perspectives on Food Sovereignty.' *The Journal of Peasant Studies* 41, no. 6 (15 October 2014): 911–931.

Eimer, David. 'Burmese Smugglers Get Rich on Yingluck Shinawatra's £13 Billion Thai Rice Subsidies.' *The Telegraph*. 4 February 2014. www.telegraph.co.uk/news/worldnews/asia/thailand/10618134/Burmese-smugglers-get-rich-on-Yingluck-Shinawatras-13-billion-Thai-rice-subsidies.html.

Elias, Marlène, and Magalie Saussey. '"The Gift That Keeps on Giving": Unveiling the Paradoxes of Fair Trade Shea Butter.' *Sociologia Ruralis* 53, no. 2 (1 April 2013): 158–179.

Elinoff, E. 'Smoldering Aspirations: Burning Buildings and the Politics of Belonging in Contemporary Isan.' *South-East Asia Research* 20, no. 3 (2012): 381–397.

ETC group. 'Concentration in Corporate Power.' *Communiqué* 91 (2005a).

ETC group. 'Global Seed Industry Concentration.' *Communiqué* 90 (2005b).

FAO. *Project on Livestock Industrialisation. Trade and Social-Health-Environment Impacts in Developing Countries*, 2003.

FAO, *Food Outlook*, (Rome: FAO, June 2008), 55–57, www.fao.org/docrep/010/ai466e/ai466e00.htm.

FAO. *How to Feed the World in 2050*. Rome: FAO, 2009.

FAO, IFAD, and WFP. *The State of Food Insecurity in the World 2013. The Multiple Dimensions of Food Security*. Rome, 2013.

Feldman, Shelly, and Stephen Biggs. 'The Politics of International Assessments: The IAASTD Process, Reception and Significance.' *Journal of Agrarian Change* 12, no. 1 (2012): 144–169.

Femia, Joseph. 'Hegemony and Consciousness in the Thought of Antonio Gramsci.' *Political Studies* 23, no. 1 (2006).

Fernandez, Rebec A. 'Agricultural Value Chain Financing in Thailand.' In *Financial Access and Inclusion in the Agricultural Value Chain*, edited by Benedicto S. Bayaua, 81–92. Bangkok: APRACA, 2008.

Fine, Ben. *The Political Economy of Diet, Health and Food Policy*. London: Routledge, 1998.

Forsyth, Tim. 'Thailand's Red Shirt Protests: Popular Movement or Dangerous Street Theatre?' *Social Movement Studies* 9, no. 4 (November 2010): 461–467.

Foundation for Labour and Employment Promotion, Four Regions Slum Network, and Committee of Thai Labour Solidarity. *A Survey of 9 Consumer Products Prices and Effects on the People*. Bangkok, 2008 (in Thai).
Fox, Jefferson, and Jean-Christophe Castella. 'Expansion of Rubber (Hevea Brasiliensis) in Mainland Southeast Asia: What Are the Prospects for Smallholders?' *Journal of Peasant Studies* 40, no. 1 (January 2013): 155–170.
Frank, André Gunder. *Capitalism and Underdevelopment in Latin America: Historical Studies of Chile and Brasil*. New York: Monthly Review Press, 1976.
Freidberg, S. *The Contradictions of Clean: Supermarket Ethical Trade and African Horticulture*. London, 2003, www.iied.org/pubs/pdfs/6361IIED.pdf.
Friedmann, Harriet. 'From Colonialism to Green Capitalism: A Social Movements and Emergence of Food Regimes.' In *New Directions in the Sociology of Global Development: Research in Rural Sociology and Development Volume 11*, edited by F. Buttel and P. McMichael, 227–264. Oxford: Elsevier, 2005.
Ganjanapan, Anan. *Dynamics of Communities in Resource Management: Ideological Framework and Policies*. Bangkok: Thailand Research Fund, 2000 (in Thai).
Ganjanapan, Anan. 'Community Rights in Development.' In *The Community Dimension: Local Way of Thinking Regarding Rights, Power and Natural Resource Management*, 231–250. Bangkok: Thailand Research Fund, 2001 (in Thai).
Ganjanapan, Anan. *Economic Culture in an Economy of No Culture*. Bangkok: Kopfai, 2001 (in Thai).
Ganjanapan, Anan. 'Village in Thai Society: Conceptual Critiques.' In *The Community Dimension: Local Way of Thinking Regarding Rights, Power and Natural Resource Management*, 11–60. Bangkok: Thailand Research Fund, 2001 (in Thai).
Getz, Christina, and A. Shreck. 'What Organic and Fair Trade Labels Do Not Tell Us: Towards a Place-Based Understanding of Certification.' *Journal of Consumer Studies* 30, no. 5 (2006): 490–501.
Gill, Stephen. 'Globalisation, Market Civilisation and Disciplinary Neoliberalism.' *Millennium: Journal of International Studies* 24, no. 3 (1995): 399–423.
Gill, Stephen. 'Toward a Postmodern Prince? The Battle in Seattle as a Moment in the New Politics of Globalisation.' *Millennium: Journal of International Studies* 29, no. 1 (1 January 2000): 131–140.
Gill, Stephen, and D. Law. 'Global Hegemony and the Structural Power of Capital.' *International Studies Quarterly* 33, no. 4 (1989): 475–499.
Glassman, Jim. 'Economic Nationalism in a Post-Nationalist Era: The Political Economy of Economic Policy in Post-Crisis Thailand.' *Critical Asian Studies* 36, no. 1 (2004): 37–64.
Gliessman, Steve. 'Agroecology and Sustainable Food Systems Agroecology: Growing the Roots of Resistance.' *Agroecology and Sustainable Food Systems* 37, no. 1 (2013): 19–31.
Global Harvest Initiative. *Accelerating Productivity Growth: The 21st Century Global Agriculture Challenge. A White Paper on Agricultural Policy*, 2009. www.globalharvestinitiative.org/.
Glover, Dominic. 'Is Bt Cotton a Pro-Poor Technology? A Review and Critique of the Empirical Record.' *Journal of Agrarian Change* 10, no. 4 (2010): 482–509.
Glover, Dominic, and L.T. Ghee. *Contract Farming in Southeast Asia: Three Country Studies*, edited by D. Glover, and L.T. Ghee. Kuala Lumpur: Institute Pengajian Tinggi/Institute for Advanced Studies, 2008.
Goodman, David, and Melanie E. DuPuis. 'Knowing Food and Growing Food: Beyond the Production–Consumption Debate in the Sociology of Agriculture.' *Sociologia Ruralis* 42, no. 1 (January 2002): 5–22.

Goodman, David, and Michael Redclift. 'Internationalization and the Third World Food Crisis.' In *Refashioning Nature: Food, Ecology and Culture*, 133–166. London: Routledge, 1991.

Goodman, Michael K. 'Reading Fair Trade: Political Ecological Imaginary and the Moral Economy of Fair Trade Foods.' *Political Geography* 23, no. 7 (September 2004): 891–915.

Goss, Jasper, and David Burch. 'From Agricultural Modernisation to Agri-Food Globalisation: The Waning of National Development in Thailand.' *Third World Quarterly* 22, no. 6 (2001): 969–986.

Goss, Jasper, David Burch, and Roy E. Rickson. 'Agri-Food Restructuring and Third World Transnationals: Thailand, the CP Group and the Global Shrimp Industry.' *World Development* 28, no. 3 (2000): 513–530.

GRAIN. *Making a Killing from Hunger*, 2008. www.grain.org/article/entries/178-making-a-killing-from-hunger.

GRAIN. *Seized! The 2008 Land Grab for Food and Financial Security*. Barcelona: GRAIN, 2008.

Green Net Co-operative. 'About Green Net Cooperative.'. www.greennet.or.th/about/greennet.

Gurian-Sherman, D. *Failure to Yield: Evaluating the Performance of Genetically Engineered Crops*. Cambridge: Unions of Concerned Scientists, 2009.

Guthman, Julie. 'Regulating Meaning, Appropriating Nature: The Codification of California Organic Agriculture,' *Antipode* 30, no. 2 (1998): 135–154

Guthman, Julie. 'Raising Organic: An Agro-Ecological Assessment of Grower Practices in California.' *Agriculture and Human Values* 17 (2000): 257–266.

Guthman, Julie. 'Room for Manoeuvre? (In)organic Agribusiness in California,' in *Agribusiness and Society. Corporate Responses to Environmentalism, Market Opportunities and Public Regulation*, 114–142. London: Zed Books, 2004.

Hall, Derek. 'Land Grabs, Land Control, and Southeast Asian Crop Booms.' *Journal of Peasant Studies* 38, no. 4 (October 2011): 837–857.

Hall, Derek, Philip Hirsch, and Tania Murray Li. *Powers of Exclusion: Land Dilemmas in Southeast Asia*. Singapore: NUS Press, 2011.

Hall, Stuart. 'The Problem of Ideology-Marxism without Guarantees.' *Journal of Communication Inquiry* 10, no. 2 (1986).

Harvey, David. *The New Imperialism*. Oxford: Oxford University Press, 2003.

Harvey, David. *A Brief History of Neoliberalism*. Oxford: Oxford University Press, 2005.

Hewison, Kevin. *Power and Politics in Thailand: Essays in Political Economy*. Manila: Journal of Contemporary Asia Publishers, 1989.

Hewison, Kevin. 'Localism in Thailand: A Study of Globalisation and its Discontents.' A Centre for the Study of Globalisation and Regionalisation (CSGR), University of Warwick, UK, Working Paper No. 39/99, September 1999.

Hewison, Kevin. 'Responding to Economic Crisis: Thailand's Localism.' In *Reforming Thai Politics*, edited by Duncan McCargo, 143–162. Copenhagen: NIAS Press, 2002.

Hewison, Kevin. 'A Book, the King and the 2006 Coup.' *Journal of Contemporary Asia* 38, no. 1 (2008).

Hewison, Kevin. 'Class, Inequality, and Politics.' In *Bangkok May 2010: Perspectives on a Divided Thailand*, edited by M. Montesano, 143–160. Singapore: ISEAS, 2012.

Hines, Colin. *Localization: A Global Manifesto*. London: Earthscan, 2000.

Hinrichs, Clare C. 'Embeddedness and Local Food Systems: Notes on Two Types of Direct Agricultural Market.' *Journal of Rural Studies* 16 (2000): 295–303.

Hinrichs, Clare C. 'The Practice and Politics of Food System Localization.' *Journal of Rural Studies* 19, no. 1 (January 2003): 33–45.
Holt-Giménez, Eric, and Miguel A. Altieri. 'Agroecology, Food Sovereignty and the New Green Revolution.' *Agroecology and Sustainable Food Systems* 37, no. 1 (4 September 2013): 90–102.
Holt-Giménez, Eric, and Annie Shattuck. 'Food Crises, Food Regimes and Food Movements: Rumblings of Reform or Tides of Transformation?' *The Journal of Peasant Studies* 38, no. 1 (January 2011): 109–144.
Hongthong, Yupin. 'The State Pushes to Solve Farmer Crisis: Open Smart Farmers School in 6 Provinces.' *Bangkok Business*, 11 August 2013 (in Thai).
Huguet, J.W., A. Chamratrithirong, and K. Richter. 'Thailand Migration Profile.' In *Thailand Migration Report 2011: Migration for Development in Thailand – Overview and Tools for Policymaker*, edited by J.W. Huguet and A. Chamratrithirong, 7–16. Bangkok: International Organization for Migration, 2012.
Humphrey, John. 'Policy Implications of Trends in Agribusiness Value Chains.' *The European Journal of Development Research* 18, no. 4 (2006): 574–575.
Hutanuwat, Nanthiya. 'A Strategy to Expand Organic Jasmine Rice Production. A Paper for the 5th National Academic Conference on Agricultural System 5: Alternative Energy and Food Security for Humanity, 2–4 July 2009, Ubol International Hotel, Ubolratchathani Province.' Ubolratchathani, 2009. www.mcc.cmu.ac.th/Seminar/showseminar.asp?type_id=18.
Hutanuwat, Nanthiya, and Narong Hutanuwat. *Before a Community Rice Mill Business Can Be Established: A Case Study of Bakrua Farmer Group, Yasothon Province*. Ubolratchathani: Local Development Institute (LDI), 2000 (in Thai).
Iewskul, Natwipa. '18 Years Track Records of GMOs: Threats to Thailand's Food Sovereignty.' *Green Peace Southeast Asia Website*, 2 April 2013. www.greenpeace.org/seasia/th/PageFiles/505377/18-year-of-gmo.pdf (in Thai).
Iewsriwong, Nithi. 'Changing Thailand with the Rice Mortgage Scheme.' *Mathichon*, 5 November 2012 (in Thai).
Iewsriwong, Nithi. 'Changing Thailand with the Rice Mortgage Scheme (One More Time).' *Mathichon*, 3 December 2012 (in Thai).
iLaw. 'Third Attempt At Drafting Community Forest Law by the National Reform Assembly is Still Not Relevant to Communities,' 23 July 2015. https://ilaw.or.th/node/7328 (in Thai).
Imai, Masami. 'Mixing Family Business with Politics in Thailand.' *Asian Economic Journal* 20, no. 3 (September 2006): 241–256.
International Assessment of Agricultural Knowledge, Science and Technology for Development (IAASTD). *Agriculture at a Crossroads. Global Report*, 2009.
International Fund for Agricultural Development (IFAD). *Rural Poverty Report 2011. New Realities, New Challenges: New Opportunities for Tomorrow's Generation*. Rome, 2011.
Isawilanont, Somporn. *Thai Rice: Changes in Production and Distribution Structure*. Bangkok: Thailand Research Fund, 2010 (in Thai).
Isawilanont, Somporn, and Prue Santithamrak. *A Report on Global and Thai Rice Production and Trade Situation 2011 and Future Tendency (KNIT Agricultural Policy No. 2012–1)*. Bangkok: KNIT, 2011 (in Thai).
Isawilanont, Somporn, Sanit Kao-ian, Weersak Kongrit, and Orawan Bootso. *Dynamics of Thailand's Rice Production Economy and The Future Outlook*. Bangkok: Thailand Research Fund, 2009 (in Thai).
Isra news. 'P-move reminds the government of the promises on land banks and the protection of CLTDs areas,' *Isra News*, 23 February 2013. www.isranews.org (in Thai).

Isra news. 'Judiciary Declared the State Was Not Guilty for GM Papaya Contamination, Greenpeace Feared Monsanto Monopoly,' *Isra News*, 2 April 2013. www.isranews.org (in Thai).

Isra news. 'Against Section 190 Modification. NGOs against an Increase in the Power of the Executive – Elites, and a Reduction of Civil Society's Spaces,' *Isra News*, 18 November 2013. www.isranews.org (in Thai).

Isra news. 'Macro View of Land in Thailand Reveals Inequality and Highly Concentrated Land: Wealth in Poor People's Tears,' *Isra News*, 14 July 2014. www.isranews.org (in Thai).

Issarapan, Pibul. 'Farmers' Risks from Using Agricultural Chemicals and Sudden Illness.' In *An Academic Conference to Monitor Agricultural Chemicals 1, 16–17 June 2011*, edited by National committee to plan for food security. Bangkok, 2011 (in Thai).

Jamarik, Saneh. 'Self-Sufficient Economy in the Globalisation Current.' In *Safety and Stability through Self-Sufficiency Economy*, edited by Pitaya Wongkul, 91–140. Bangkok: Withithat Institute, 2008 (in Thai).

Jantarawong, Sombat. *Election Crisis*. Bangkok: Kopfai, 1993 (in Thai).

Jaroenpanich, Sriracha, Roypim Teerawong, Piriya Siripopankul, Jiraporn Janyaoan, and Unrat Siammai. *A Study of the Effects of the Paddy Pledging Scheme on Thai Farmers' Quality of Life*. Bangkok: Office of the Ombudsman Thailand, 2014 (in Thai).

Jeerapat, Wich. 'Reflection on Thai Community Right Ideas.' *Julniti Journal* 3, no. 38 (2010): 35–53 (in Thai).

Jikkham, Patsara. 'Rice Stockpile to Be Audited.' *Bangkok Post*, 13 June 2014.

Jitpleecheep, Pitsinee, and Piyachart Maikaew. 'Delayed Scheme Payments Lead to Higher NPLs.' *Bangkok Post*, 17 February 2014.

Jitsanguan, Thanwa. 'Sustainable Agricultural Systems for Small-Scale Farmers in Thailand: Implications for the Environment.' Paper at Kasetsart University, Bangkok, 12 January 2001.

Johnson, Craig, and Timothy Forsyth. 'In the Eyes of the State: Negotiating a "Rights-Based Approach" to Forest Conservation in Thailand.' *World Development* 30, no. 9 (September 2002): 1591–1605.

Kaewthep, Kanoksak. 'The Struggle of Thai Farmers 1989–1999.' In *The Path of Thai Farmers*. Bangkok, 1999 (in Thai).

Kaewthep, Kanoksak. 'Rakthammachart Rice Mill: Naso Community, Ampur Kudchum, Yasothon Province.' In *Community Organised Welfare (2): Production Groups. Journal of Political Economy (for the Community) 18*, 111–158. Bangkok: Chulalongkorn University, 2001 (in Thai).

Kam Pakha. 'Morality Leads Thailand towards Destruction.' *Matichon (weekly)*, 14–20 January, 2011 (in Thai).

Kam Pakha. '"Life Must Be Easy" Is Just a Propaganda.' *Matichon*, 18 September 2014. www.matichon.co.th/news_detail.php?newsid=1411041439 (in Thai).

Karnchuchat, Weerayuth. 'Thai Retail Business: Two Cities Divide.' In *The Struggles of Thai Capital 2: Politics, Culture and Survival*, edited by Pasuk Phongpaichit, 217–279. Bangkok: Matichon, 2006 (in Thai).

Karriem, Abdurazack. 'The Rise and Transformation of the Brazilian Landless Movement into a Counter-Hegemonic Political Actor: A Gramscian Analysis.' *Geoforum* 40, no. 3 (May 2009): 316–325.

Kata, Prachathip. *Civil Society and the Path of Self-Reliance: Lessons from the Organic Agriculture Network in Yasothon*. Bangkok: Society and Health Institute, 2005 (in Thai).

Kemp, Jeremy. *Community and State in Modern Thailand (Working Paper no. 100)*, Southeast Asia program, University of Bielefeld,1988.

Kerkvliet, Benedict. *The Power of Everyday Politics: How Vietnamese Peasants Transformed National Policy*. Ithaca, NY: Cornell University Press, 2005.

Keyes, Charles F. *Thailand: Buddhist Kingdom as Modern Nation-State*. Bangkok: Westview Press, 1987.

Khaosod Newspaper. 'Grassroot Voices Regarding the Rice Mortgage Scheme,' *Khaosod*, 16 April 2012. www.khaosod.co.th/view_news.php?newsid=TURObFkyOHlOVEUyTURRMU5RPT0= (in Thai).

Kirwan, James, and Damian Maye. 'Food Security Framings within the UK and the Integration of Local Food Systems.' *Journal of Rural Studies* 29 (March 2012): 91–100.

Kittiarsa, P. 'Becoming "Red": The New Brand of Thai Democracy with a Provincial Base.' *Journal of the Siam Society* 3 (2011): 226–230.

Klongyong community leaders. 'A Summary of the Struggles of the Klongyong Community: A Document Prepared by the Locals for Visitors,' obtained 10 October 2012 (in Thai).

Klonsky, K., Laura J. Tourte, Robin Kozloff, and Benjamin Shouse. *Statistical Review of California's Organic Agriculture 1995–1998*. Davis: University of California, Agricultural Issues Center, 2001.

Kom Chad Luek Newspaper. 'Mae-Aow Villagers Smile for the Second CLTDs from the Prime Minister,' *Kom Chad Luek*, 18 March 2011 (in Thai).

Kongkaew, Ngao-sin. *The Event Occured at Bantad Mountains*. Bangkok: Bantad Mountains Land Reform Network and the Thai Health Organisation, 2011 (in Thai).

Kraiyoorawong, Sayamon, Appayut Jantarapa, Nuntachart Noosrikaew, Rakchanok Jindakam, Ruangthong Janda, Pinyo Jantawong, and Komsan Jan-on. *A Study of Land Conflicts in Thailand Phase 1*. Bangkok: Thailand Research Fund, 2005 (in Thai).

Kraiyoorawong, Sayamon, Appayut Jantarapa, Nuntachart Noosrikaew, Rakchanok Jindakam, Ruangthong Janda, Pinyo Jantawong, and Komsan Jan-on. *Traditional Wisdom: Community and Nature's Ways*. Bangkok: Duan-tula printing, 2008 (in Thai).

Land Reform Network. *CLTDs – We Can: A Handbook*. Bangkok: Land Reform Network, 2012 (in Thai).

Land Reform Network and Local Act. *A Report on the Study "Land Management and Social Justice: A Case Study of the Land Reform Network", Part of the Project to Encourage Social Justice, Chulalongkorn University Social Research Institute*. Bangkok: Chulalongkorn University Social Research Institute, 2010 (in Thai).

Lang, Tim, and Colin Hines. *The New Protectionism: Protecting the Future Against Free Trade*. New York: New Press, 1993.

Laothamatat, Anek. *Thai Democracy as a Tale of Two Cities: Paths to Reform Politics and Economy for Democracy*. 5th ed. Bangkok: Wipasa, 2000 (in Thai).

Laothamatat, Anek. *Changing Areas and Foundation: Building Local Administration and a Foundation for Democracy*. Bangkok: Thammasat University, 2009 (in Thai).

Laothamatat, Anek. *Progressive Locality: Political Theories to Build the Local as a Foundation for Democracy*. Bangkok: Thai Health Organisation, 2009 (in Thai).

Lawrence, Geoffrey, and Philip McMichael. 'The Question of Food Security.' *International Journal of Sociology of Agriculture and Food* 19, no. 2 (2012): 135–142.

Le Mons Walker, Kathy. 'From Covert to Overt: Everyday Peasant Politics in China and the Implications for Transnational Agrarian Movements.' In *Transnational Agrarian Movements Confronting Globalization*, 295–322. Chichester: Wiley-Blackwell, 2008.

Lerche, Jens. 'The Agrarian Question in Neoliberal India: Agrarian Transition Bypassed?' *Journal of Agrarian Change* 13, no. 3 (16 July 2013): 382–404.

Lerche, Jens, Alpa Shah, and Barbara Harriss-White. 'Introduction: Agrarian Questions and Left Politics in India.' *Journal of Agrarian Change* 13, no. 3 (16 July 2013): 337–350.

Levi, Margaret, and April Linton. 'Fair Trade: A Cup at a Time?' *Politics and Society* 31, no. 3 (1 September 2003): 407–432.

Lienchamroon, Witoon. 'Alternative Agriculture: A Path of Free, Independent Agriculture. A Document Summarising the Academic Content of the Third Congress of Alternative Agriculture (18–21 November 2004 at Kasetsart University).' In *Reform the Agricultural Sector for Food Security: Analysis and Practical Policies*, edited by Witoon Lienchamroon, 149–184. Nonthaburi: BioThai, 2011 (in Thai).

Lienchamroon, Witoon. 'Behind the Movement to Extend Agricultural Chemicals Registration.' In *Reform the Agricultural Sector for Food Security: Analysis and Practical Policies*, 54–60. Nonthaburi: BioThai, 2011 (in Thai).

Lienchamroon, Witoon. 'Fighting FTA: the Thai Experience.' In *Reform the Agricultural Sector for Food Security: Analysis and Practical Policies*, 301–319. Nonthaburi: BioThai, 2011 (in Thai).

Lienchamroon, Witoon. 'Lessons from the Struggle over Plant Genetics Protection under the WTO's TRIPs.' In *Reform the Agricultural Sector for Food Security: Analysis and Practical Policies*, 63–77. Nonthaburi: BioThai, 2011 (in Thai).

Lienchamroon, Witoon. 'Suggestions to Avoid Food Crisis for Thailand.' In *Reform the Agricultural Sector for Food Security: Analysis and Practical Policies*, 238–250. Nonthaburi: BioThai, 2011 (in Thai).

Lienchamroon, Witoon. 'The Role of Agri-Businesses and the Changes in Rural Thailand and Thai Society,' 25 November 2011. www.biothai.net/node/10889 (in Thai).

Lienchamroon, Witoon, and Suriyon Thankitchanukit. *From the Green Revolution to Bio-Engineering. Lessons for the Future of Thai Agriculture*. Nonthaburi: BioThai, 2008 (in Thai).

Lienchamroon, Witoon, and Supha Yaimuang. 'Alternative Agriculture: From Individual Farmers to Social Movements.' In *Reform the Agricultural Sector for Food Security: Analysis and Practical Policies*, edited by Witoon Lienchamroon, 267–301. Nonthaburi: BioThai, 2011 (in Thai).

Limnirandkul, Bootsara, Cho-paka Muangsuk, Pratanthip Kramol, and Pruek Yipmantasiri. 'Contract Farming and the Opportunity of Development of Small Scale Farmers.' Paper for the Conference at Agricultural Science Faculty, Chiang Mai University, 22–23 September 2006. www.mcc.cmu.ac.th/research/MCCannualSeminar2006/link/sa.html (in Thai).

Lockie, Stewart. 'The Invisible Mouth: Mobilizing "the Consumer" in Food Production–Consumption Networks.' *Sociologia Ruralis* 42, no. 4 (2002): 278–294.

Lockie, Stewart, and L. Collie. '"Feed the Man Meat": Gendered Food and Theories of Consumption.' In *Restructuring Global and Regional Agricultures: Transformations in Australasian Agri-Food Economies and Spaces*, edited by D. Burch, J. Cross, and G. Lawrence, 225–273. Aldershot: Ashgate Publishing, 1999.

Lockie, Stewart, Kristen Lyons, Geoffrey Lawrence, and Kerry Mummery. 'Eating "Green": Motivations Behind Organic Food Consumption in Australia.' *Sociologia Ruralis* 42, no. 1 (2010): 23–40.

Losirikul, Manus, and Prasit Karnchan. *The Possibility of Hom Mali Rice Production in Organic Farming Systems as an Alternative Farming Career with Poverty Alleviation Potential for Lower-Northeastern Farmer: A Case of Surin Province*. Bangkok: Thailand Research Fund, 2006 (in Thai).

Lynas, Mark. 'Mark Lynas Plenary Speech for International Rice Congress 2014, Bangkok, Thailand.' 31 October 2014. www.marklynas.org/2014/10/mark-lynas-plenary-speech-for-international-rice-congress-2014-bangkok-thailand/.

Lyons, Kristen, David Burch, Geoffrey Lawrence, and Stewart Lockie. 'Contrasting Paths of Corporate Greening in Antipodean Agriculture: Organics and Green Production.' In *Agribusiness and Society. Corporate Responses to Environmentalism, Market Opportunities and Public Regulation*, edited by Kees Jansen and Sietze Vellema. London: Zed books, 2004.

Madeley, John. *Hungry for Trade. How the Poor Pay for Free Trade*. London: Zed Books, 2000.

Malseed, Kevin. 'Where There Is No Movement: Local Resistance and the Potential for Solidarity.' *Journal of Agrarian Change* 8, no. 2–3 (2008): 489–514.

Manager Newspaper. 'CP Advances on Biodiesel Business, Contract Farming of Palm Oil in Indochina,' *Manager (weekly)*, 21 March 2008. www.manager.co.th/iBizchannel/ViewNews.aspx?NewsID=9510000034527 (in Thai).

Manager Newspaper. 'Food Crisis Increases Pressure on Landless Farmers. Watch out for CP's Monopoly Control over 100,000 Million Baht Rice Seeds Market,' *Manager*, 1 May 2008. www.manager.co.th/Daily/ViewNews.aspx?NewsID=9510000050851 (in Thai).

Manager Newspaper. 'Foreign Force's Land Grabs in 25 Provinces. Land Sold in Massive Volume by Farmers and Brokers,' *Manager*, 17 September 2009. www.manager.co.th/mgrWeekly/ViewNews.aspx?NewsID=9520000108424 (in Thai).

Manager Newspaper. 'CP Took over Makro, Swallowed Thailand, Advancing on Asian Markets,' *Manager*, 27 April 2013. www.manager.co.th/AstvWeekend/ViewNews.aspx?NewsID=9560000050426 (in Thai).

Manager Newspaper. 'Rak Chiang Mai 51 Shows Support to "Plod" – Threathens NGOs Causing Chaos at the Water Summit – Prepares to Mobilise Thousands to Resist,' *Manager*, 16 May 2013. www.manager.co.th/Local/ViewNews.aspx?NewsID=9560000058929 (in Thai).

Manager Newspaper. 'Farmers Bittered from Discriminatory Payment as the Government Only Paid Their Supporters,' *Manager*, 29 January 2014. www.manager.co.th/Home/ViewNews.aspx?NewsID=9570000011000 (in Thai).

Manarangsan, Sompop. 'Contract Farming and Thailand's Agricultural Development.' In *Our Lands, Our Lives*, edited by Buddhadeb Chaudhuri. Bangkok: ACFOD, 1992.

Mankiw, N. Gregory. *Principles of Macroeconomics*. 5th edn. Mason, OH: South-Western Cengage Learning, 2009.

Manning, Richard. 'The Oil We Eat: Following The Food Chain Back to Iraq.' *Harper's Magazine*, 2004.

Manopimok, Suphajit, Wanna Prayukwong, and Viroj Manopimok. *A Complete Report on the Research Project on the Possibility of Alternative Agriculture in Thailand: An Economics Analysis*. Bangkok: Thailand Research Fund, 2001 (in Thai).

Margulis, Matias E., and Tony Porter. 'Governing the Global Land Grab: Multipolarity, Ideas, and Complexity in Transnational Governance.' *Global Restructuring, State, Capital and Labour. Contesting Neo-Gramscian Perspectives* 10, no. 1 (2013): 65–86.

Margulis, Matias E., Nora McKeon, and Saturnino M. Borras. 'Land Grabbing and Global Governance: Critical Perspectives.' *Globalizations* 10, no. 1 (2013): 1–23.

Marsden, T.K., and A. Arce. 'Constructing Quality: Emerging Food Networks in the Rural Transition.' *Environment and Planning* 27, no. 8 (1995): 1261–1279.

Matichon Newspaper. '3 Sugar Plants Associations Believe in the Long Bright Future of Sugar Cane and Sugar Industries, Pushing the State to Support Ethanol,' *Matichon*, 25 September 2009. www.matichon.co.th/news_detail.php?newsid=1253896039&catid=05 (in Thai).

Matichon Newspaper. 'National Reform Committee Suggests Land Reform to Take Advantage of Food Crisis,' *Matichon*, 16 March 2011. www.matichon.co.th/news_detail.php?newsid=1300277716&grpid=03&catid=00 (in Thai).

Matichon Newspaper. 'Village Leader Tells of Capitalist Land Grabbing of Rice Fields,' *Matichon*, 4 April 2012 (in Thai).

Matichon Newspaper. 'Prapart Pintoptaeng – Politics Lecturer from Chulalongkorn was Arrested after Soldiers Cancelled the Walk for Land Reform Event,' *Matichon*, 9 November 2014. www.matichon.co.th/news_detail.php?newsid=1415522432 (in Thai).

Matsumura, Masaki. 'Coercive Conservation, Defensive Reaction, and the Commons Tragedy in Northeast Thailand.' *Habitat International* 18, no. 3 (January 1994): 105–115.

McCargo, Duncan. 'Thailand's Political Parties: Real, Authentic and Actual.' In *Political Change in Thailand: Democracy and Participation*, edited by Kevin Hewison, 114–131. London and New York: Routledge, 1997.

McCargo, Duncan. *Politics and the Press in Thailand: Media Machinations*. London: Routledge, 2000.

McCargo, Duncan. 'Populism and Reformism in Contemporary Thailand.' *South East Asia Research* 9, no. 1 (2001): 89–107.

McCargo, Duncan, and Ukrist Pathmanand. *The Thaksinization of Thailand*. Copenhagen: Nordic Institute of Asian Studies (NIAS) Press, 2005.

McCluney, Ross. 'Renewable Energy Limits.' In *The Final Energy Crisis*, edited by Andrew McKillop and Sheila Newman, 153–175. London: Pluto Press, 2005.

Mckeon, Nora. 'The FAO, Civil Society and the Global Governance of Food and Agriculture.' In *The United Nations and Civil Society: Legitimating Global Governance – Whose Voice?*, 17–120. New York: Zed Books, 2009.

Mckeon, Nora. '"One Does Not Sell the Land Upon Which the People Walk": Land Grabbing, Transnational Rural Social Movements, and Global Governance.' *Globalizations* 10, no. 1 (2013): 105–122.

McMichael, Philip. 'Incorporating Comparison Within a World-Historical Perspective.' *American Sociological Review* 55, no. 2 (1990): 285–297.

McMichael, Philip. 'Peasant Prospects in the Neoliberal Age.' *Development* 11, no. 3 (2006): 407–418.

McMichael, Philip. 'Peasants Make Their Own History, But Not Just as They Please ...'. *Journal of Agrarian Change* 8, no. July (2008): 205–228.

McMichael, Philip. 'A Food Regime Analysis of the "World Food Crisis."' *Agriculture and Human Values* 26, no. 4 (31 July 2009): 281–295.

McMichael, Philip. 'Banking on Agriculture: A Review of the World Development Report 2008.' *Africa* 9, no. 2 (2009): 235–246.

McMichael, Philip. 'Food Sovereignty, Social Reproduction and the Agrarian Question.' In *Peasants and Globalization: Political Economy, Rural Transformation and the Agrarian Question.*, edited by A. Haroon Akram-Lodhi and C. Kay, 288–312. Oxon: Routledge, 2009.

McMichael, Philip. 'The Land Grab and Corporate Food Regime Restructuring.' *Journal of Peasant Studies* 39, no. 3–4 (July 2012): 681–701.

McMichael, Philip, and Frederick Buttel. 'New Directions in the Political Economy of Agriculture.' *Sociological Perspectives* 33, no. 1 (1990): 89–109.

McNally, Mark. 'Gramsci's Internationalism, the National-Popular and the Alternative Globalisation Movement.' In *Gramsci and Global Politics. Hegemony and Resistance*, edited by Mark McNally, and John Schwarzmantel, 58–76. Oxon: Routledge, 2009.

Mekong Youth Alliance for Organic Agriculture and Agro-Ecology. 'Occupy Your Life Manifesto.' Obtained at an academic forum on agro-ecology, farmer rights, food sovereignty and farmer movements, 12 November 2012, Chulalongkorn University, Bangkok.

Miliband, Ralph. *State in Capitalist Society*. London: Quartet Books, 1969.

Ministry of Agriculture and Co-Operatives (MOAC). 'Ministry of Agriculture and Co-Operatives Tries to Stop Capitalists from Increasing Rent and Exploiting Farmers, Using Legal Means according to the Agricultural Land Rent Act,' 21 April 2008. www.moac.go.th/ewt_news.php?nid=1911&filename=wimol (in Thai).

Ministry of Public Health. *A Survey on Food and Nutrition of Thailand,5th Assessment*. Bangkok, 2003.

Monsanto, 'Why Does Agriculture Need to be Improved? Growing Populations, Growing Challenges,' www.monsanto.com/improvingagriculture/pages/growing-populations-growing-challenges.aspx.

Moore, Jason W. 'Transcending the Metabolic Rift: A Theory of Crises in the Capitalist World- Ecology.' *Journal of Peasant Studies* 28, no. 1 (2011): 1–46.

Morton, Adam David. *Unravelling Gramsci*. London: Pluto Press, 2007.

Morton, Adam David. 'Social Forces in the Struggle over Hegemony Neo-Gramscian Perspectives in International Political Economy.' In *Rethinking Gramsci*, edited by Marcus E. Green, 147–166. 1st edn. Oxon: Routledge, 2011.

Morvaridi, Behrooz. 'Capitalist Philanthropy and Hegemonic Partnerships.' *Third World Quarterly* 33, no. 7 (August 2012): 1191–1210.

Mutebi, Alex M. 'Explaining the Failure of Thailand's Anti-Corruption Regime.' *Development and Change* 39, no. 1 (January 2008): 147–171.

Naew Na Newspaper. 'Warn the State to Revise Measures for Rubber Prices. Three Strategies to Develop the Rubber Industry,' *Naew Na*, 13 December 2012.

Nakthim, Chonlakanda. *The Roles of Leaders in Knowledge Management of the Farmers' Organic Rice Farming: A Case Study of Natural Farming Group in Thamo Sub-District, Prasat District, Surin Provice*. Thesis from the Department of Social Service, Thammasat University (Bangkok, 2008) (in Thai).

Naranong, Viroj. Presentation at a public conference: 'Rice, Fish, Food: Menu of Inequalities Facing Thai Farmers', Thammasat University, Bangkok, Thailand. 14 January 2013.

Narkwibulwong, Weerachai. '37 Years of Land Reform and the Adaptation of Sufficiency Economy.' In *37 Years of the Agricultural Land Reform Office*, 14–25. Bangkok: ALRO, 2012 (in Thai).

Narkwibulwong, Weerachai, Arpapan Pattanapan, and Arthita Pongprom. *Efficient Usage of ALRO Land: A Case Study of Maximum of 10 Rai per Household Land Plot*. Bangkok: Thailand Research Fund, 2011 (in Thai).

Nartsupha, Chatthip. *Modernisation and the "Community" School of Thought*. Bangkok: Sangsan Publishing, 2010 (in Thai).

Nartsupha, Chatthip, and Wanworn Ja-noo. 'Editorial.' In *Community Culture School of Thought in Thai Society*, edited by Chatthip Nartsupha and Wanworn Ja-noo, 8–11. Bangkok: Sangsan Publishing, 2012 (in Thai).

National Committee to Develop Organic Agriculture. *National Strategic Plan to Develop Organic Agriculture 1 2008–2011 and National Practical Plan to Develop Organic Agriculture 2008–2011*. Bangkok: Sahamit Printing, 2008 (in Thai).

National Committee to Develop Organic Agriculture. *National Strategic Plan to Develop Organic Agriculture 2 2013–2016 (draft)*, received from Ms Wibulwan Wannamolee, senior specialist in agri-food standards, National Bureau of Agricultural Commodity and Food Standards Office, 31 January 2013 (in Thai).

National Committee to Develop Strategic Plan to Manage Chemicals. *National Strategic Plan to Manage Chemicals 4 (2012–2021)*. Nonthaburi: Integrated program for chemical safety, food and drug administration, Ministry of Public Health, 2011 (in Thai).

National Health Committee. *Report of the Meeting 1/2008 on the Topic of Policies and Strategies to Reduce Negative Health Effects from Chemical Pesticides on 14 January 2008*. Bangkok, 2008 (in Thai).

National Reform Committee. *How to Reform Thailand: A Proposal for Political Parties and Voters*. Bangkok: National Reform Committee, 2011 (in Thai).

National Statistical Office (NSO), www.nso.go.th/ (in Thai).

Newell, Peter. 'Trade and Biotechnology in Latin America: Democratization, Contestation and the Politics of Mobilization.' *Journal of Agrarian Change* 8, no. 2–3 (April and July 2008): 345–376.

Nicholls, Clara Ines, and Miguel A. Altieri. 'Conventional Agricultural Development Models and the Persistence of the Pesticide Treadmill in Laitn America.' *International Journal of Sustainable Development & World Ecology* 4, no. 2 (1997): 93–111.

Niles, Daniel, and Robin Jane Roff. 'Shifting Agrifood Systems: The Contemporary Geography of Food and Agriculture: An Introduction.' *GeoJournal* 73, no. 1 (26 July 2008): 1–10.

Nishizaki, Yoshinori. 'Peasants and the Redshirt Movement in Thailand: Some Dissenting Voices.' *Journal of Peasant Studies* 41, no. 1 (30 January 2014): 1–28.

Nontaworakarn, Phuttina. 'Summary of the Current Status of the Revised Dangerous Chemical Acts 2008.' In *An Academic Conference to Monitor Agricultural Chemicals 1, 16–17 June 2011*, edited by National Committee to Plan for Food Security. Bangkok, 2011 (in Thai).

Nostitz, N. *Red vs. Yellow, Volume 2: Thailand's Political Awakening*. Bangkok: White Lotus, 2011.

O'Brien, Kevin, and Lianjiang Li. *Rightful Resistance in China*. Cambridge: Cambridge University Press, 2006.

O'Laughlin, Bridget. 'Gender Justice, Land and the Agrarian Question in Southern Africa.' In *Peasants and Globalization: Political Economy, Rural Transformation and the Agrarian Question*, edited by A. Haroon Akram-Lodhi and Cristobal Kay, 190–213. New York: Routledge, 2009.

O'Laughlin, Bridget, Henry Bernstein, Ben Cousins, and Pauline E. Peters. 'Introduction: Agrarian Change, Rural Poverty and Land Reform in South Africa since 1994.' *Journal of Agrarian Change* 13, no. 1 (12 January 2013): 1–15.

Ockey, J. 'Change and Continuity in the Thai Political Party System.' *Asian Survey* 43, no. 4 (2003): 663–680.

Ockey, J. *Making Democracy: Leadership, Class, Gender, and Political Participation in Thailand*. Honolulu: University of Hawaii Press, 2004.

Office of Agricultural Economics (Thailand). *Agricultural Economics Indicators 2010*. Bangkok: Office of Agricultural Economics, 2010 (in Thai).

Office of Agricultural Economics (Thailand). *Basic Information on the Agricultural Sector 2010*. Bangkok: Office of Agricultural Economics, 2010 (in Thai).

Office of Agricultural Economics (Thailand). *Basic Information on Agricultural Economics of Thailand 2012*. Bangkok: Office of Agricultural Economics, 2012 (in Thai).

Office of Natural Resources and Environmental Policy and Planning. 'Situation on State of Environment,' 2006, 12 November 2008 (in Thai).

Oopayokin, Pricha, and Suri Karnchanawong. *Business/tradesmen and Thai Parliamentary System: A Study Funded by the Secretariat of the House of Representatives*. Bangkok, 1999 (in Thai).

Ouyyanont, Porphant. 'The Crown Property Bureau in Thailand and the Crisis of 1997', *Journal of Contemporary Asia*, 38, No. 1 (February 2008): 166–189.

Paarlberg, R. *Starved for Science: How Biotechnology is Being Kept out of Africa*. Cambridge: Harvard University Press, 2008.

Pananont, Pawida, and Weerayuth Karnchuchat. 'Thai Capital Expands Abroad.' In *The Struggles of Thai Capital 1: Adaptation and Dynamics*, edited by Pasuk Phongpaichit, 293–372. Bangkok: Matichon, 2006 (in Thai).

Pannarong, Sukhum, and Pimolna Boonyasena. *A Study of Development Opportunity and Direction of Organic Crop Production System*. Chiang Mai: Research and Development Center for Community Economy, Economics Department, Chiang Mai University and the National Research Council of Thailand (NRCT), 2009 (in Thai).

Panyakul, Witoon, and Pattarawadee Poomsak. *A Report on the Status of Research and Innovation Relating to Organic Agriculture in Thailand*. Bangkok: National Innovation Agency, 2008 (in Thai).

Panyakul, Witoon, and Jade-sanee Sukjirattikarn. *Organic Market: Opportunities and Paths to World Organic Markets*. Bangkok: Earth Net Foundation/Green Net Cooperative, 2003.

Parliament's Committee of Commerce. *Report on the Study of Problems and Effects of Modern Trade*. Bangkok, 2003 (in Thai).

Patel, Raj. *Stuffed and Starved. Power and the Hidden Battle for the World Food System*. London: Portobello Books, 2007.

Paterson, Bill. 'Trasformismo at the World Trade Organization.' In *Gramsci and Global Politics. Hegemony and Resistance*, edited by Mark McNally, and John Schwarzmantel, 42–57. Oxon: Routledge, 2009.

Pathmanand, Ukrist. 'Globalisation and Democratic Development in Thailand: The New Path of the Military, Private Sector, and Civil Society.' *Contemporary Southeast Asia* 23, no. 1 (2001).

Patrawart, Juthatip. 'Branding as the Marketing Strategy for Organic Products: A Case Study on Moral Rice.' *Asian Journal of Food and Agro-Industry* (2009): 256–263.

Pattanapanchai, Nattapong. *Food – Life or Commodity? Marketable Culture Under the Control of Corporations*, edited by Ubol Yoo-wah. Nonthaburi: SATHAI, 2008 (in Thai).

Pattanapanchai, Nattapong, and Arat Saeng-ubon. *A Report on the Tap-Tai Community Way of Life, Surin*. Surin: Alternative Agriculture Network, 2007 (in Thai).

Patzek, Tad W., and David Pimentel. 'Thermodynamics of Energy Production from Biomass.' *Critical Reviews in Plant Sciences* 24, no. 5–6 (2006): 329–364.

Paul Tharp, 'Hedge Funds Find New Sweet Spot in Sugar', *New York Post*, 30 September 2009, http://nypost.com/2009/09/30/hedge-funds-find-new-sweet-spot-in-sugar/.

Pechpa, Nikhom, Montri Baothong, Adul Klonepan, and Prachak Boontos. *A Complete Report of the Research Project on the Moral Rice Network*. Bangkok: Thailand Research Fund, 2009 (in Thai).

Peluso, Nancy Lee, Suraya Afiff, and Noer Fauzi Rachman. 'Claiming the Grounds for Reform: Agrarian and Environmental Movements in Indonesia.' *Journal of Agrarian Change* 8, no. 2–3 (2008): 377–407.

Peluso, Nancy Lee, Suraya Afiff, and Noer Fauzi Rachman. Suraya Afiff, and Noer Fauzi Rachman. 'Claiming the Grounds for Reform: Agrarian and Environmental Movements in Indonesia.' In *Transnational Agrarian Movements Confronting Globalization*,

edited by Saturnino M. Borras, Marc Edelman, and Cristóbal Kay, 209–238. Chichester: Wiley-Blackwell, 2008.
Peterman, A., J. Behrman, and A.R. Quisumbing. *A Review of Empirical Evidence on Gender Differences in Non-Land Agricultural Inputs, Technology and Services in Developing Countries. International Food Policy Research Institute Discussion Paper 001003*. Washington DC, 2010.
Petras, James, and Henry Veltmeyer. *Social Movements in Latin America: Neoliberalism and Popular Resistance*. New York: Palgrave Macmillan, 2011.
Phetprasert, Narong. *Rice Politics under State-Capital Monopoly. Journal of Political Economy (for the Community)* 27. Bangkok: Edison Press, 2005 (in Thai).
Pholnoi, Arunee. *Retail and Wholesale Trade's Strategies*. Bangkok: Pansan, 2003 (in Thai).
Phongpaichit, Pasuk. 'Developing Social Alternatives. Walking Backwards into a Khlong.' In *Thailand Beyond the Crisis*, edited by Peter Warr, 161–184. New York: RoutledgeCurzon, 2005.
Phongpaichit, Pasuk. 'Thai Politics beyond the 2006 Coup,' Excerpt of Supha Sirimanond Memorial Lecture, 2007, *Bangkok Post*, 31 July 2007.
Phongpaichit, Pasuk, and Chris Baker. *Thailand: Economy and Politics*. New York: Oxford University Press, 1995.
Phongpaichit, Pasuk, and Chris Baker. *Thaksin: The Business of Politics in Thailand*. Chiang Mai: Silkworms Books, 2004.
Phongpaichit, Pasuk, and Chris Baker. 'Thailand, Thaksin and The Temple of Doom.' *Far Eastern Economic Review* 171, no. 6 (2008): 338.
Pongsawat, Pitch. 'The Relationship Between the Economic and Political Changes and Farmers Movement in the Present Thai Society: A Critical Observation', *Fah-Diewkan*, Year 1, Vol. 1, (January–April 2005): 67 (in Thai).
Puapongsakorn, Niphon, Ammar Siamwala, Nareethip Rungkawee, Jeerapa Tosomboon, Kritsadarat Wattanasuwan, Methinee Phongprapapan, Sek Methasurarak, Kiratipong Naewmalee, and Pornchai Sapying. *The Retail Business in Thailand: Impact of the Large Scale Multinational Corporation Retailers*. Bangkok: TDRI, 2002 (in Thai).
Phurisamban, Rapijan. 'Basic Information on the Market and Usage of 4 High-Priority Agricultural Chemicals in the Monitoring List.' In *An Academic Conference to Monitor Agricultural Chemicals 1, 16–17 June 2011*, edited by National Committee to Plan for Food Security. Bangkok, 2011 (in Thai).
Pimbert, Michel P., John Thompson, William T. Vorley, Tom Fox, and Cecilia Tacoli. 'Global Restructuring, Agri-Food Systems and Livelihoods.' *Agriculture* no. 100 (2001).
Pimentel, David, and Tad W. Patzek. 'Ethanol Production Using Corn, Switchgrass, and Wood; Biodiesel Production Using Soybean and Sunflower.' *Natural Resources Research* 14, no. 1 (2005): 65–76.
Pintoptang, Prapart, Supha Yaimuang, and Banchorn Kaewsong. *The Possibility of Developing the Welfare System for the Poor and the Disadvantaged: The Case of Farmers*. Bangkok: Political Economy Study Center, Economics Faculty, Chulalongkorn University, 2003 (in Thai).
P-move (People's Movement for a Just Society). *Declaration number 18*. 26 April 2013 (in Thai).
Pollan, Michael. 'Farmer in Chief.' *New York Times Magazine*, 2008.
Pongthong, Yupin. 'Solving Farmers Crisis through Professional Schools in 6 Provinces.' *Bangkok Business*, 11 August 2013 (in Thai).

Post Today Newspaper. 'Foreign and Thai Capital's Purchases of Foundations of Agriculture,' *Post Today*, 20 February 2010 (in Thai).

Post Today Newspaper. 'Farmers Complain to the Government about Exorbitant Land Rents,' *Post Today*, 3 October 2011 (in Thai).

Post Today Newspaper. 'Expensive Lesson: From Paddy Pledging to Rubber Price Speculations,' *Post Today*, 19 July 2012 (in Thai).

Post Today Newspaper. 'Draft of Thai-EU FTA: Thai Loses More than Gain,' *Post Today*, 10 December 2012 (in Thai).

Post Today Newspaper. 'Yanyong Reveals That Low Prices of Rubber Is due to Depressed Economic Conditions,' *Post Today*, 6 September 2013 (in Thai).

Post Today Newspaper. 'Farmers Complained That Late Payment Made Them Turn to Informal Loans,' 8 January 2014 (in Thai).

Post Today Newspaper. 'Taking Back 5 Million Rai of ALRO Land,' *Post Today*, 29 September 2014 (in Thai).

Prachachat Turakij Newspaper. 'Wave of Land Grabs for Speculations and Agro-Fuels Inputs due to Low Interest Rates and Rising Agricultural Commodity Prices,' *Prachachat Turakij*, 14 May 2008 (in Thai).

Prachachat Turakij Newspaper. 'Top Rice Exporter, Asia Golden Rice, Received Right to Purchase Government's Stock at Low Price – Medium/small Size Companies at a Disadvantaged,' *Prachachat Turakij*, 13 January 2011 (in Thai).

Prachachat Turakij Newspaper. 'Speculations Causes Rubber Prices to Plummet and for Rubber Co-Operatives All over the Country to Lose over 10,000s Million,' *Prachachat Turakij*, 16 March 2011 (in Thai).

Prachachat Turakij Newspaper. 'Famous Business Families Stocking up Land All over Thailand, Jareon Riched with 6.3 Hundred Thousand Rai, Land Tax in Consideration,' *Prachachat Turakij*, 18 June 2014 (in Thai).

Prachachat Turakij Newspaper. 'Landlords from 11 Political Parties Hold 35,000 Rai: Phua Thai, Democrat and Phumjaithai in the Lead,' *Prachachat Turakij*, 19 June 2014 (in Thai).

Prachason, Sajin. 'A Draft Document for the Meeting "Agriculture and Food in Time of Crisis", 22 July 2008.' In *Progress Report to the National Health Commission on Developments of Proposals from the National Health Assembly 2008*, 2008 (in Thai).

Prachason, Sajin. *Food Security in Thai Society: A Report Submitted to UNDP Thailand, January 2009*. Bangkok, 2009.

Prachason, Sajin, Thanaporn Srisuksai, Nattaporn Liemjaratkul, Pornchai Wachirachai, Narisra Saisanguensat, and Patcha Duang-klad. *Market Options of Farmers: Structural Effects on Unfairness and Benefit Distribution*. Bangkok: BioThai and the Social Research Foundation, Chulalongkorn University, 2012 (in Thai).

Prachathai. 'Report from the Seminar "CLTD and Solutions to Land Conflicts in Thailand," ' *Prachathai*, 4 July 2009. www.prachatai.com/journal/2009/07/24960 (in Thai).

Prachathai. 'P-move asks Supreme court to stop the delay of the enforcement of the ruling on the palm oil land conflict in Suratthani, as the delay has led to violence,' *Prachathai*, 25 December 2012. http://prachatai.com/journal/2012/12/44383 (in Thai).

Prachathai. 'NESDB Warns the Government the Unconstitutional Risk of Not Listening to Public Opinions Regarding Thai–EU FTA,' *Prachathai*, 16 January 2013. http://prachatai.com/journal/2013/01/44713 (in Thai).

Prachathai. 'Civil Society Disagrees with Changing of the Law to Aid Seed Companies,' *Prachathai*, 1 March 2013. www.prachatai.com/journal/2013/03/45554 (in Thai).

Prachathai. 'Ammar's Speech "The Future of Thai Agriculture under Changing Circumstances," ' *Prachathai*, 29 August 2013. http://prachatai.com/journal/2013/08/48467 (in Thai).

Prasertkul, Seksan. *Citizen Politics in Thai Democracy*. Bangkok: Amarin, 2005 (in Thai).

Prasertsuk, Kitti. 'From Political Reform and Economic Crisis to Coup D'état in Thailand: The Twists and Turns of the Political Economy, 1997–2006.' *Asian Survey* 47, no. 6 (2007).

Prayukvong, Wanna. 'A Buddhist Economic Approach to the Development of Community Enterprises: A Case Study from Southern Thailand.' *Cambridge Journal of Economics* 29 (2005): 1171–1185.

President of the Thai Rubber Association. 'Rubber Market Situation in 2013,' December 2013. www.thainr.com/th/message_detail.php?MID=187 (in Thai).

Pritchard, Bill. 'Trading into Hunger? Trading out of Hunger? International Food Trade and the Debate on Food Security.' In *Food Systems Failure: The Global Food Crisis and the Future of Agriculture*, edited by Christopher Rosin, Paul Stock, and Hugh Campbell, 46–59. London: Earthscan, 2012.

Puapongsakorn, Nipon. *Study of the Supply Chain Management and Logistics of Agricultural Products*. Bangkok: Thailand Development Research Institute, 2009.

Puapongsakorn, Nipon. 'The Political Economy of Thai Rice Price and Export Policies in 2007–2008.' In *The Rice Crisis Markets, Policies and Food Security*, edited by David Dawe, 191–218. London and Washington DC: FAO and Earthscan, 2010.

Puapongsakorn, Nipon. *Thai Rice Strategy: Research and Development on Thai Rice and Looking Forward*. Bangkok: Thailand Research Fund, 2013 (in Thai).

Puapongsakorn, Nipon, and Jittakorn Jarupong. *Rent Seeking Activities and The Political Economy of the Paddy Pledging Market Intervention Measures*. Bangkok: Office of the National Anti-Corruption Commission, 2010 (in Thai).

Puapongsakorn, Nipon, and Ammar Siamwalla. 'Rural Villagers' Economic Group: Success and Survival, 51.' In *A Report for the Annual Seminar 1995 of Thailand Development Research Institute (TDRI), 9–10 December*. Cholburi, 1995.

Puapongsakorn, Nipon, and Ammar Siamwalla. 'Transform Thailand with the Paddy Pledging Scheme: Facts for Ajarn Nithi and the Public,' 24 November 2012. http://tdri.or.th/tdri-insight/responses-to-nidhi/ (in Thai).

Puechphol, Daoruang, Wanna Thongnoi, Boonkong Suwanpechr, Somnuek Panichkul, Manit Kanjampa, Boonsa Hootachai, Boonsong Thongnoi, Thonglor Kwanthong, Kriengsak Wenwanarak, Anon Ngewlai, and Padung Wenwanarak. *A Complete Report of the Research Project to Study Traditional Rice Genetics to Expand Organic Rice Production in Baan Kudhin, Baan Kammad, Baan Nonyang in Tambol Kammad, Ampur Kudchum, Yasothon Province*. Bangkok: Thailand Research Fund, 2010 (in Thai).

Puntasen, Apichai. 'Applying Self-Sufficient Economy to Systematically Solve Poverty.' In *Dhamma Economics: A Collection of Speeches of Distinguished Professors from the Economics Department, Thammasat University*, 92–94. Bangkok: OpenBooks, 2010 (in Thai).

Puntasen, Apichai, and Paradorn Preedasak. 'Agriculture in Thailand at the Cross-Road.' *ASEAN Economic Bulletin* 15, no. 1 (1998): 90–107.

Rakchat, Jirawat. 'From Farming to Contract Eggs Chicken: The Growth of Agri-Business.' In *Thai Countryside: Medium Size Farmers and Landless Agricultural Labourers*, edited by Jamari Chiengthong, Wattana Sukansiel, Jirawat Rakchat, Swang Meesang, and Priyawal Jaipinta, 245–296. Chiang Mai: University of Chiang Mai, 2011 (in Thai).

Rakyutitham, Achara. 'Anan's Dynamic: From Culture, Na-Moo to Complexity.' In *"I Don't Have the Answer": 60 Years Professor Dr. Anan Ganjanapan and 20 Years of Social Movement on Community Rights and Natural Resources Management*, 11–31. Chiang Mai: Sustainable Development Foundation, 2008 (in Thai).

Rakyutitham, Achara, Tuanjai Tiwong, Jetsada Chotikitpiwaj, Pongthip Samranjit, Krisda Boonchai, and Suriyan Thongnooiad. *Land and Freedom*. Bangkok: Black Lead Publishing, 2005 (in Thai).

Ratsongkwae, Muanfan. 'CP Maize: Naan Case Study.' In *CP and Thai Agriculture*, edited by CorpWatch-Thailand and BioThai, 131–144. Nonthaburi: BioThai, 2009 (in Thai).

Rattanawaraha, Chanuan. *Organic Agriculture*. Nonthaburi: Biotech Center, Department of Agriculture, 2007 (in Thai).

Raynolds, Laura T. 'Consumer/Producer Links in Fair Trade Coffee Networks.' *Sociologia Ruralis* 42, no. 4 (October 2002): 404–424.

Research Institute of Organic Agriculture (FiBL) and International Federation of Organic Agriculture Movements (IFOAM). *The World of Organic Agriculture. Statistics and Emerigng Trends 2014*. Edited by Helga Willer and Lernoud Julia Frick and Bonn: FiBL and IFOAM, 2014.

Research unit on agri-businesses at Kasetsart University. *Strategic Commodity: Rice*. Department of Agricultural Economics and Natural Resource, Kasetsart University, 1997 (in Thai).

Rigg, Jonathan, and Sakunee Nattapoolwat. 'Embracing the Global in Thailand: Activism and Pragmatism in an Era of Deagrarianization.' *World Development* 29, no. 6 (June 2001): 945–960.

Rigg, Jonathan, Buapun Promphaking, and Ann Le Mare. 'Personalizing the Middle-Income Trap: An Inter-Generational Migrant View from Rural Thailand.' *World Development* 59 (July 2014): 184–198.

Ritzer, George. *Sociological Theory*. 5th edn. New York: McGraw-Hill, 2005.

Robbins, Paul. *Political Ecology: A Critical Introduction*. 2nd edn. Chicester: Wiley-Blackwell, 2012.

Rodmua, Nattakarn. *An Analysis of Costs and Process of Thai Rice Export. A Dissertation for a Master's Degree in Economics, Thammasat University*. Bangkok: Thammasat University, 2009 (in Thai).

Roff, Robin Jane. 'Shopping for Change? Neoliberalizing Activism and the Limits to Eating Non-GMO.' *Agriculture and Human Values* 24, no. 4 (8 August 2007): 511–522.

Roitner-Schobesberger, Birgit, Ika Darnhofer, Suthichai Somsook, and Christian R. Vogl. 'Consumer Perceptions of Organic Foods in Bangkok, Thailand.' *Food Policy* 33 (2008): 112–121.

Rojanaphraiwong, Sukran. *A Mission in Self-Reliance: Report of the Study on Tap-Tai Community Way of Life, Surin, by Natpong Pattanapanchai and Arat Saeng-Ubol*. Nonthaburi: Alternative Agriculture Network, 2008 (in Thai).

Rojanapraiwong, Sukran, Kaset Sittinew, Noppawan Sirivejakul, Kanokwan Soponwattanawijit, and Sompat Sreemekarat. *Local Genes and Sustainable Agriculture: A Document for the Third Alternative Agriculture Assembly 18–21 November 2004, Kasetsart University*. Nonthaburi: Pim-dee Printing, 2004 (in Thai).

Rosset, Peter M. *Food is Different. Why We Must Get the WTO out of Agriculture*. London: Zed Books, 2006.

Rosset, Peter M. 'Food Sovereignty and the Contemporary Food Crisis.' *Development* 51, no. 4 (2008).

Rosset, Peter M., and Miguel A. Altieri. 'Agroecology Versus Input Substitution: A Fundamental Contradiction of Sustainable Agriculture.' *Society and Natural Resources* 10, no. 3 (1997): 283–295.

Rupert, Mark. *Ideologies of Globalization: Contending Visions of a New World Order*. London: Routledge, 2000.

Sage, Colin. 'The Interconnected Challenges for Food Security from a Food Regimes Perspective: Energy, Climate and Malconsumption.' *Journal of Rural Studies* (2013): 71–80.

Saito, K., H. Mekonnen, and D. Spurling. *Raising the Productivity of Women Farmers in Sub-Saharan Africa. Discussion Paper 230.* Washington DC, 1994.

Salam, Md. Abdus, Toshikuni Noguchi, and Rachanee Pothitan. 'Community Forest Management in Thailand: Current Situation and Dynamics in the Context of Sustainable Development.' *New Forests* 31, no. 2 (March 2006): 273–291.

Samnuanyen, Kingkarn. *Dynamics of Social Movement Tactics: The Case of the Land Rights Movement in Lumphun Province. An Unpublished Masters Thesis at the Faculty of Political Science, Chulalongkorn Univeristy.* Bangkok, 2006 (in Thai).

Samranjit, Pongthip. 'A Summary of Research on Ground-up Land Reforms by Communitites,' 22 July 2011. www.landreformthai.net.

Samranjit, Pongthip, Suthee Prasartset, Krisda Boonchai, and Piyaporn Arunpong. *A Documental Report on the Research on What Thailand Will Lose without Land Reform: Land Management and Social Justice – A Case Study of the Land Reform Network in Thailand.* Bangkok: Chulalongkorn University Social Research Institute, 2012 (in Thai).

San Saeng-arun magazine. 'From Way of Life and Cultural Roots to Machine-like Farmers: Problems and Solutions in the View of Witoon Lienchamroon.' *San Saeng-Arun Magazine.* Bangkok, 2012 (in Thai).

San Saeng-arun magazine. 'In the Water There are Fishes, in the Paddy Field There is Rice: Farmer Livelihoods, Disintegration and Survival.' *San Saeng-Arun Magazine.* Bangkok, 2012 (in Thai).

Sangthongkam, Wirat, Pantop Tangsriwong and Samsak Damrongsoontornchai *70 years Jirathiwat: Central's competition and growth.* (Bangkok: Manager Classic, 2003) (in Thai).

Sapphaitoon, Athiwat. *6 Mega Retail Business Empire: Various Marketing Techniques for Modern Trade, Case Study and Lessons from Thailand.* Bangkok: Phueng-ton, 2002 (in Thai).

Schreinemachers, Pepijn, Iven Schad, Prasnee Tipraqsa, Pakakrong M. WIlliams, Andreas Neef, Suthathip Riwthong, Walaya Sangchan, and Christian Grovermann. 'Can Public GAP Standards Reduce Agricultural Pesticide Use? The Case of Fruit and Vegetable Farming in Northern Thailand.' *Agriculture and Human Values* 29 (2012): 519–529.

Scott, James. *Domination and the Arts of Resistance: Hidden Transcripts.* New Haven, CT: Yale University Press, 1990.

Senakham, Tirawuth, and Witoon Panyakul. 'The State and Agri-Businesses: From "See-Prasan" to Agricultural Council.' In *Analysis and Policy Suggestions to Develop Alternative Agriculture: A Book for the Assembly of Alternative Agriculture 10–15 November 1992, Thammasat University*, 153–177. Bangkok: Alternative Agriculture Network, 1992 (in Thai).

Senate Committee on Agriculture and Co-operatives. *Report on the Investigation on Contract Farming of the Senate Committee on Agriculture and Co-operatives.* Bangkok: 2003.

Shattuck, Annie. 'Will Sustainability Standards Work? A Look at the Roundtable on Sustainable Biofuels.' In *Agrofuels in the Americas*, edited by R. Jonasse, 75–95. Oakland: Food First Books, 2009.

Shaw, Candice. 'Global Agro Food Systems: Gendered and Ethnic Inequalities in Mexico's Agricultural Industry,' *McGill Sociological Review* 2, April (2011): 92–109.

Shiva, Vandana. *The Violence of the Green Revolution. Third World Agriculture, Ecology and Politics.* London: Zed books, 1991.

Shiva, Vandana. 'The Future of Food: Countering Globalisation and Recolonisation of Indian Agriculture.' *Futures* 36 (2004): 715–732.

Siamwalla, Ammar. *Politics and Business Interests under the 1997 Constitution: A Complete Report for Prapokplao Foundation*. Bangkok, 2003 (in Thai).

Siamwalla, Ammar, and Somchai Jitsuchon. *Tackling Poverty: Liberalism, Populism or Welfare State. A Paper Presented at the Annual Thailand Development Research Institute Academic Seminar, 10–11th November 2007*. Cholburi, Thailand, 2007 (in Thai).

Singsootham, Methee. *Practical Action Research Report on Sustainable Land Reform and Management by the People*. Nonthaburi: Land Reform Network and Local Act, 2010 (in Thai).

Siripat, Decha. 'Diversified Farms: Solutions for Farmers (first Published in 1987).' In *The Path of Sustainable Agriculture*, 75–84. 2nd edn. Samut-Sakorn: BioThai, 2011 (in Thai).

Siripat, Decha. 'Present and Future of Alternative Farmers in Thailand (first Published in 1987).' In *The Path of Sustainable Agriculture*, 85–93. 2nd edn. Samut-Sakorn: BioThai, 2011 (in Thai).

Siripat, Decha. 'The Assembly of the Poor and Alternative Agriculture Policies (first Published in 1997).' In *The Path of Sustainable Agriculture*, 94–100. 2nd edn. Samut-Sakorn: BioThai, 2011 (in Thai).

Sittichai, Pattama, Satien Sriboonrueng, Chusak Jantanopsiri, and Ukrit Marang. *A Complete Report on the Project to Compile and Analyse the Problems of Farmers and Sustainable Development*. Bangkok: National Economics and Social Development Board (NESDB), 2002 (in Thai).

Smith, L. C., U. Ramakrishan, A. Ndjaye, L. Haddad, and R. Martorell. *The Importance of Women's Status for Child Nutrition in Developing Countries. Research Report 131*. Washington DC, 2002.

Songwe, V., and K. Deininger. 'Foreign Investment in Agricultural Production: Opportunities and Challenges. Agriculture and Rural Development Notes, Issue 45, World Bank,' 2009.

Sopranzetti, C. 'Burning Red Desires: Isan Migrants and the Politics of Desire in Contemporary Thailand.' *South-East Asia Research* 20, no. 3 (2012): 361–379.

Southern Alternative Farmer Group. 'Manifesto of the Southern Alternative Farmer,' 6 June 2009, Patlung, Thailand (in Thai).

Sriboonchitta, Songsak. *Overview of Contract Farming in Thailand: Lessons Learned. ADBI Discussion Paper 112*. Tokyo: Asian Development Bank, 2008.

Sricharatchanya, Paisal. 'Thailand's Crown Property bureau mixes business with social concern', *Far Eastern Economic Review*, 140 (26) (30 June 1988): 61

Srimanee, Yanee, and Jayant Kumar Routray. 'The Fruit and Vegetable Marketing Chains in Thailand: Policy Impacts and Implications.' *International Journal of Retail and Distribution Management* 40, no. 9 (2012): 656–675.

Srisaowalak, Ittipol, Weerachai Narkwibulwong, and Tachamai Rerksasoot. *A Study Project on the Law to Manage Local Areas*. Bangkok: Thailand Research Fund, 2001 (in Thai).

Srisaowalak, Ittipol, Sarayut Techawuthipan, Sinee Duangphueng, Anongnart Juajanat, and Patareeya Tepkhajorn. *A Project to Study Appropriate Land Rights for Communities*. Bangkok: Thailand Research Fund, 2007 (in Thai).

Sroythong, Kookiet. 'Pesticides Usage and the Spread of Brown Planthoppers Among Rice Crops in the Central and Lower North Regions.' In *An Academic Conference to Monitor Agricultural Chemicals 1, 16–17 June 2011*, edited by National Committee to Plan for Food Security, 2011 (in Thai).

Starr, Amory, and Jason Adams. 'Anti-Globalization: The Global Fight for Local Autonomy.' *New Political Science* 25, no. 1 (March 2003): 19–42.

Stilwell, Frank. 'The Ideology of the Market: Neoclassical Economics.' In *Political Economy: The Contest of Economic Ideas*, 149–210. 3rd edn. Victoria: Oxford University Press, 2012.

Suksut, Paranat, and Wanna Jarusomboon. 'The Identity of Sustainable Agriculture: A Case Study of the Middle Class.' In *Sustainable Agriculture: Cultural Identity, Agricultural Problems and the Identity of Thai Farmers*, edited by Anusorn Unno, 195–236. Nonthaburi: Sustainable Agriculture Assembly Committee and Heinrich Böll Foundation, 2004 (in Thai).

Sullivan, Paul, and Wilder Nicholson. 'Is the Master Plan to Solve the Deforestation or Yet Another Strategy to Remove and Evict People?' 12 December 2014. www.esaanlandreformnews.com.

Sustainable Agriculture Thailand (SATHAI). *Interesting Knowledge about Commercial Garden Plants: Case Studies of Rubber and Palm Oil*. Nonthaburi: SATHAI, 2009 (in Thai).

Tarrow, S. *The New Transnational Activism*. Cambridge: Cambridge University Press, 2005, 32.

Techa-artik, Sompan. *Diversified Farms Save Lives and Dhamma: Self-Reliance and Growing Wealth in the Soil Sustainably*. Bangkok: Research and Development Institute, Khon-Kaen University, 1995 (in Thai).

Tejapira, Kasian. 'Post-Crisis Economic Impasse and Political Recovery in Thailand: The Resurgence of Economic Nationalism.' *Critical Asian Studies* 34, no. 3 (2002): 323–356.

Tejapira, Kasian. 'Toppling Thaksin.' *New Left Review* 39 (2006).

Terd-udomsap, Thammawit. *The Political Economy of Thai FTAs, Research Document 8*. Bangkok, 2008 (in Thai).

Teubal, Miguel. 'Peasant Struggles for Land and Agrarian Reform in Latin America.' In *Peasants and Globalization: Political Economy, Rural Transformation and the Agrarian Question*, edited by A. Haroon Akram-Lodhi and Cristobal Kay, 148–166. New York: Routledge, 2009.

Thabchumpon, Naruemon. 'NGOs and Grassroots Participation in the Political Reform Process.' In *Reforming Thai Politics*, edited by Duncan McCargo, 183–202. Copenhagen: NIAS Press, 2002.

Thadsanakulpan, Thodsapol. *Farmers' Deadly Noose: Problems and Farmer Rights Under Contract Farming*. Bangkok: Working Committee for the Fair Contract Farming Network, 2013 (in Thai).

Thai Post Newspaper. 'Hand over to DSI to Deal with Corruption in Rice Mortgage Scheme. Threaten to Blacklist Boonsong Organised the Team,' *Thai Post*, 24 February 2012. www.thaipost.net/node/53054 (in Thai).

Thai Post Newspaper. 'World Supply of Sugar Pulls down Prices of Sugar Cane. Thai Producers Ask the State for Help,' *Thai Post*, 6 December 2013. www.thaipost.net/news/061213/83030 (in Thai).

Thai Publica. 'An Interview with Niphon Puapongsakorn, Academic Master on Rice, on Things He Did Not Want to See in Paddy Pledging Scheme and Fear of Politics Destroying the Thai Rice Market,' *Thai Publica*, 21 September 2011. http://thaipublica.org/2011/09/nipon-rice/ (in Thai).

Thai Publica. '"Phongthep Wiwattanadech", Medical Doctor at Chiang Mai University Suggests "Contract Farming" to Be the Cause of Haze Pollution in Northern Thailand . Revealed Statistics Suggesting Peaked Dangerous Chemicals – Lung Cancer.' *Thai*

Publica, 1 September 2012. http://thaipublica.org/2012/09/contract-farming-cause-burning/ (in Thai).

Thailand Industry News. 'The Private Sector Pushes for the Birth of Retail Business Act, Concerns over Foreign Monopoly and Destruction of Traditional Thai Shops,' 16 June 2008. http://thailandindustry.com/indust_newweb/news_preview.php?cid=3756 (in Thai).

Thairath Newspaper. 'The Economics Team's Editorial,' *Thairath*, 15 June 2009 (in Thai).

Thairath Newspaper. 'Rice Mills Slowly Sell Their Rice to Speculate on Prices While Exporters Ask the Government to Sell its Rice Stock. Ministry of Commerce Also Threatens to Sell its Own Brand of Rice,' *Thairath*, 14 December 2009 (in Thai).

Thairath Newspaper. 'Tycoon Jaroen Invested 1.2 Hundred Million in Big C Purchasing the Majority of Shares,' *Thairath*, 8 February 2016 (in Thai).

Than Settakit Newspaper. 'Fat Rice Traders! 6,000/ton Profit Export to Malaysia,' *Than Settakit*, 12 June 2008 (in Thai).

Than Settakit Newspaper. 'Close the Deal Carrefour and Big C, Strategic Take over,' *Than Settakit*, 22 November 2010 (in Thai).

Than Settakit Newspaper. 'Rubber Prices Adjust Upwards according to Speculations in Tokyo,' *Than Settakit*, 12 October 2013 (in Thai).

Than Settakit Newspaper. 'Many Factors Cause Sugar Cane Prices to Drop,' *Than Settakit*, 5 January 2014 (in Thai).

Thanapornpan, Rangsan. *Transient Characteristics of Thai Politics*. Bangkok: Manager News Group, 1993 (in Thai).

Thanapornpan, Rangsan. *The Political Economy of the 1997 Constitution (Volume 1 and 2)*. Bangkok: Thailand Research Fund, 2003 (in Thai).

Thaotawil, Pruek. 'Government Policies and Farmers' Debts: The Failure of Small-Scale Farmers' Debt Moratorium.' In *A Study of the Possibility of Developing a Welfare System for the Poor and Disadvantaged in Thailand*. Bangkok: Chulalongkorn University, 2003 (in Thai).

Thaotawil, Pruek. 'Self-Sufficiency Project at the Village Level: Elitist Control Over the Rural Sector.' *Fah-Diewkan Academic Magazine* 6, no. 2 (2008): 70–86 (in Thai).

The Nation. 'Stress Drives Another Farmer to Suicide,' *The Nation*, 16 February 2014. www.nationmultimedia.com/webmobile/national/Stress-drives-another-farmer-to-suicide-30226933.html.

The Pilot Project to Develop Sustainable Agriculture for Small-Scale Farmers. *Lessons and Experiences of Sustainable Agricultural Development by Farmers and Community Organisations*. Nonthaburi: Sustainable Agriculture Foundation Thailand (SATHAI), 2004 (in Thai).

Tomich, Dale. *Slavery in the Circuit of Sugar: Martinique and the World Economy, 1830–1848*. Baltimore, M.D.: Johns Hopkins University Press, 1990.

Trimakka, Triyada, and Ubol Yoo-wah. *A Study on Alternative Markets in Thailand: Market Access of Small-Scale Farmers*. Nonthaburi: SATHAI, 2008 (in Thai).

Turton, Andrew. *Production, Power and Participation in Rural Thailand: Experiences of Poor Farmers' Groups*. Geneva, 1987.

Udomrat, Suthep. 'Self-Sufficiency Philosophy.' In *Safety and Stability through Self-Sufficiency Economy*, edited by Pitaya Wongkul, 71–78. Bangkok: Withithat Institute, 2008 (in Thai).

Unger, Danny. 'Sufficiency Economy and the Bourgeois Virtues.' *Asian Affairs: An American Review* 36, no. 3 (2009): 139–156.

United Nations. *Foreign Land Purchases for Agriculture: What Impact on Sustainable Development?*. United Nations, 2010.

United Nations Development Programme (UNDP). *Thailand Human Development Report 2007: Sufficiency Economy and Human Development*. Bangkok: UNDP, 2007.

United Nations Environment Programme (UNEP). *Towards a Green Economy: Pathways to Sustainable Development and Poverty Eradication*. Geneva: UNEP, 2001.

United Nations Special Rapporteur. 'Access to Land and the Right to Food, Interim Report of the Special Rapporteur on the Right to Food, Olivier De Schutter, to the 65th Session of the General Assembly, UN Doc. A/65/281,' 2010.

Unnno, Anusorn. 'Alternative Agriculture: Indigenous Knowledge Advances and Counter-Attack.' In *Knowledge and Politics of Natural Resources. Academic Series Number 43*, edited by Darin Inmuan, 191–235. Bangkok: Princess Maha Chakri Sirindhorn Anthropology Centre, 2005.

Unno, Anusorn. *Farmer Rights in Thailand: Learning Process and Agricultural System Development. A Research under Thai Human Rights Project*. Bangkok: Thailand Research Fund, 2002 (in Thai).

Unno, Anusorn. *Sustainable Agriculture Movement in Thailand and the Politics of Sustainable Agriculture Narratives*. Nonthaburi: Sustainable Agriculture Foundation Thailand (SATHAI), 2003 (in Thai).

Unno, Anusorn. *Social Movements for Common Resource Rights in the Thai Society: Alternative Agriculture in the Context of Property Rights System*. Nonthaburi: Alternative Agriculture Fair Committee, 2004 (in Thai).

Vanloqueren, Gaetan, and Philippe V. Baret. 'How Agricultural Research Systems Shape a Technological Regime that Develops Genetic Engineering but Locks Out Agroecological Innovations.' *Research Policy* 38 (2010): 971–983.

Walker, Andrew. 'Environmental Issues in Thailand: A Rural Perspective.' In *Thailand's Economic Recovery: Proceedings of the National Thai Studies Centre Annual Thailand Update 2004*, edited by Cavan Hogue. Singapore: ISEAS, 2006.

Walker, Andrew. 'Beyond the Rural Betrayal: Lessons from the Thaksin Era for the Mekong Region.' Paper presented at the International Conference on Critical Transitions in the Mekong Region. Chiang Mai, Thailand, 29–31 January 2007.

Warr, Peter. 'The Economics of Enough: Thailand's "Sufficiency Economy" Debate.' *International Conference on "Happiness and Public Policy", Organized by PPDO, Prime Minister's Office, UNESCAP, UNCC, Bangkok, 18–19 July 2007* (2007): 1–14.

Wasi, Prawase. *Buddhist Agriculture and Peaceful Happiness for Thai Society*. Bangkok: Mo-chaoban, 1987 (in Thai).

Wasi, Prawase. *Ideas and Strategies for Equality between State, Power and Society, and for Wisdom*. Bangkok: Komolkeemthong, 1993 (in Thai).

Weeks, John. *The Irreconcilable Inconsistencies of Neoclassical Macroeconomics*. New York: Routledge, 2012.

Weis, Tony. 'The Accelerating Biophysical Contradictions of Industrial Capitalist Agriculture.' *Journal of Agrarian Change* 10, no. 3 (2010): 315–341.

White, Ben, Saturnino M. Borras, Ruth Hall, Ian Scoones, and Wendy Wolford. 'The New Enclosures: Critical Perspectives on Corporate Land Deals.' *Journal of Peasant Studies* 39, no. 3–4 (July 2012): 619–647.

Wield, David, Joanna Chataway, and Maurice Bolo. 'Issues in the Political Economy of Agricultural Biotechnology.' *Journal of Agrarian Change* 10, no. 3 (2010): 342–366.

Williams, G.A. 'Gramsci's Concept of Egemonia.' *Journal of the History of Ideas* 21, no. 4 (1960).

Winichakul, Thongchai. 'Nationalism and the Radical Intelligentsia in Thailand.' *Third World Quarterly* 29, no. 3 (April 2008): 575–591.

Wongharnchao, Warin, Ittipol Srisaowalak, Ampon Kittipol, Jarin Teswanich, Supalak Pinijpuwadol, Sawas Phongsuwan, Orapan Srisaowalak, Sopon Pornchokchai, Pratak Simapichaiset, Santipap Jindasaeng, Satitpong Soodchookiat, Boonchana Klankamsorn, and Uthid Khaosatien. *A Study of Ownership and Usage of Land, as Well as Economic and Legal Measures to Maximise Land Usage*. Bangkok: Thailand Research Fund, 2001 (in Thai).

World Bank. *World Development Report 2008: Agriculture for Development*. Washington DC: The World Bank, 2007.

World Bank, UNCTAD, FAO, IFAD. *Principles of Responsible Agricultural Investments*. Washington DC: World Bank, 2010.

Worth, Owen. 'Beyond World Order and Transnational Classes. The (Re)application of Gramsci in Global Politics.' In *Gramsci and Global Politics. Hegemony and Resistance*, edited by Mark McNally and John Schwarzmantel, 19–31. Oxon: Routledge, 2009.

Worth, Owen. 'Reclaiming Critical IPE from the "British" School.' In *Critical International Political Economy Dialogue, Debate and Dissensus*, edited by Stuart Shields, Ian Bruff, and Huw Macartney, 117–131. Basingstoke: Palgrave Macmillan, 2011.

Yaimuang, Supha, Pannee Towakulpanich, and Walaipon Oddoampanich. *Alternative Markets: Partnership for a New Society*. Edited by Walaipon Oddoam panich and Supha Yaimuang. Bangkok: Pim-dee Printing, 1996 (in Thai).

Zurcher, Sacha. 'Public Participation in Community Forest Policy in Thailand: The Influence of Academics as Brokers.' *Geografisk Tidsskrift-Danish Journal of Geography* 105, no. 1 (January 2005): 77–88.

List of interviews and email correspondents

Interviews

Aarat Sang-ubol, Community of Agro-Ecology Foundation, 19 December 2012, Surin.
Adisorn Puangchompoo, 1 rai-100,000 baht project, 13 January 2013, Nonthaburi.
Amporn Suyakomol, Baan Romphothong, 31 October 2012, Chiang Mai.
Anan Ganjanapan, Chiang Mai university, 29 October 2012, Chiang Mai.
Arpakorn Krueng-ngern, Tambol Mae-ta, 1 November 2012, Chiang Mai.
Arunsak Ocharos, farmer from Sri-saket, 6 April 2012, Bangkok.
Bood-dee Piengprom, Ta-toom group, 22 December 2012, Surin.
Boonlue Jaroenmee, Klongyong Co-operative, 10 October 2012, Nakhon Pathom.
Boonsong Martkhao, Kammad group, 25 December 2012, Yasothon.
Boonyuen Arj-arsa, Nam-oom Enterprise, 23 December 2012, Yasothon.
Chanuan Rattanawaraha, Agricultural Advisor Office, Department of Agriculture, 17 January 2013, Nonthaburi.
Chomchuan Boonrahong, Mae-Jo University, 3 November 2012, Chiang Mai.
Chuleerat Jaroenpon, Faculty of Social Innovation, Rangsit University, 4 October 2012, Pathum Thani.
Chutima Muangman, Naso producer rice mill, 25 December 2012, Yasothon.
Decha Siripat, Khao Kwan Foundation, 14 October 2012, Nonthaburi.
Direk Kong-Ngern, Baan Pong CLTD, 30 September 2012 and 31 October 2012, Nonthaburi and Chiang Mai.
Jai Kiti, Baan Raidong/Mae-aow CLTD, 30 October 2012, Lamphun.
Janda Inpan, Tanon Organic Herb and Vegetable Processing Group, 20 December 2012, Surin.
Jirapan Meesap, Thamma-ruamjai network, 23 December 2012, Yasothon.
Kamnueng Maneebool, Nam-oom Enterprise, 23 December 2012, Yasothon.
Kampol Kongsathan, Baan Romphothong, 31 October 2012, Chiang Mai.
Kankamkla Pilanoi, Thamma-ruamjai Network, 23 December 2012, Yasothon.
Kanoksak Duangkaewruen, Subdistrict Administrative Organisation, Tambol Mae-ta, 1 November 2012, Chiang Mai.
Kanya Onsri, Baan Taptai, Tambol Tamor, 22 December 2012, Surin.
Kasemsak Sanpoch, former Surin Governor, 21 December 2012, Surin.
Kiatsak Chatdee, Institute for a Sustainable Agriculture Community, 31 October 2012, Chiang Mai.
Kittithanet Rangkaworaset, 1 rai-100,000 baht project, 13 January 2013, Nonthaburi.
Long Pechsood, Bantad Mountain group (Trang), 1 October 2012, Bangkok.

Lun Saneh-ha, Naso organic farmer, 25 December 2012, Yasothon.
Man Samsri, Naso organic farmer, 25 December 2012, Yasothon.
Mitr Boontawee, Tamor group, 20 December 2012, Surin.
Montri Bualoi, Baan Pong CLTD, 31 October 2012, Chiang Mai.
Nanta Haitook, Tanon Organic Herb and Vegetable Processing Group, 20 December 2012, Surin.
Nerm Nooboon, Baan Saikling/Tachang, Patlung, 1 October 2012, Bangkok.
Nichai Taipanich, Agricultural Advisor Office, Department of Agriculture, 17 January 2013, Nonthaburi.
Nikhom Pechpa, Thamma-ruamjai Network, 23 December 2013, Yasothon.
Nop Mangkornmai, Raidong/Mae-aow CLTD, 30 October 2012, Lamphun.
Oonjai Akaruan, Raidong/Mae-aow CLTD, 30 October 2012, Lamphun.
Pachoen Choosang, Bantad mountain group (Trang), 1 October 2012, Bangkok.
Paisit Panichkul, Chiang Mai University, 7 November 2012, Chiang Mai.
Pakphum Inpan, Tamor group, 20 December 2012, Surin.
Pat Apaimool, Mae-ta farmer, 1 November 2012, Chiang Mai.
Pattarawan Jansiri, Kamkhuenkaew hospital, 24 December 2012, Yasothon.
Pimlada Pheekaew, Baan Romphothong, 31 October 2012, Chiang Mai.
Pitak Saengsin, BAAC Chiang Mai branch, 2 November 2012 Chiang Mai.
Pornpilai Lertwicha, researcher on Thai rural communities, skype interview 17 October 2012.
Praderm Damrong-jaroen, former Farmer Network Party, phone interview on 17 October 2012.
Prapart Pintoptang, Chulalongkorn University, 16 October 2012, Nonthaburi.
Prapat Panyachatrak, National Farmer Council, 29 January 2013, Bangkok.
Pratueng Narintarangkul Na Ayuthya, Farmers' Reconstruction and Development Fund (Chiang Mai branch), 2 November 2012, Chiang Mai.
Prayong Doklamyai, Northern Peasants Federation, 30 September 2012, Nonthaburi and 1 November 2012, Chiang Mai.
Phra Promma Suphatto, Thamma-ruamjai forest temple, Ampur Pa-tiew, Yasothon, 23 December 2012, Yasothon.
Rachata Rangsiri, Tambol Mae-faeg, Chiang Mai, 1 October 2012, Bangkok.
Rangsan Sansongkwae, Raidong/Mae-aow CLTD, 30 October 2012, Lamphun.
Rungroj Kajadroka, Tamor group, 20 December 2012, Surin.
Samrach Thong-iam, Tamor group, 20 December 2012, Surin.
Samrit Boonsuk, Community of Agri-Ecology Foundation, 19 December 2012, Surin.
Samrueng Roopsuay, farmer leader from Sri-saket, 6 April 2012, Bangkok.
Sangwal Kantham, Raidong/Mae-aow CLTD, 30 October 2012, Lamphun.
Sarawut Wongnikorn, Northern Peasants Federation, 30 October 2012, Chiang Mai.
Sawitta Teeronwattanakul, Northern Peasants Federation, 29 October 2012, Chiang Mai.
Shoti Saiyuenyong, Klongyong Co-operative, 10 October 2012, Nakhon Pathom.
Sittiporn Bangkaew, Director of the Office of Commercial Affairs in Surin, 21 December 2012, Surin.
Som Sadomsuk, Tamor group, 20 December 2012, Surin.
Somchai Wisartpong, Organic Agriculture and Development Group, Department of Agricultural Extension, phone interview on 21 January 2013.
Somkiat Jai-ngarm, Northern Peasants Federation, 30 October 2012, Chiang Mai.
Sompoi Jansang, Rice Fund Surin Organic Agriculture Co-operative Ltd., 19 December 2012, Surin.

Somwang Chomchuen, Bak-rua producer rice mill, 24 December 2012, Yasothon.
Suchit Nokham, Maeping Organic Limited Partnership Company, 2 November 2012, Chiang Mai.
Sukaew Fungfoo, Baan Pae-tai CLTD, 30 October 2012, Lamphun.
Supha Yaimuang, SATHAI, 3 October 2012, Nonthaburi.
Suwanna Langnamsank, Health Society Company Ltd. (Lemon farm supermarkets), 11 February 2013, Bangkok.
Suwonasart Konbua, Green Net Co-operative officer, 24 December 2012, Yasothon.
Thamma Sangkalee, Ta-toom group, 22 December 2012, Surin.
Thanachote Jaikla, Vice Director of the Local Administration Office in Tambol Tamor, Surin, 20 December 2012, Surin.
Thaspong Tonklang, Director of the Local Administration Office in Tambol Tamor, 20 December 2012, Surin.
Ubol Yoowah, NGO activist, 22 December 2012, Yasothon.
Uthai Juansang, Bak-rua farmer, 24 December 2012, Yasothon.
Witoon Panyakul, Green Net Co-operative, 23 January 2013, Bangkok.
Wacharin Ouprajong, Baan Huafai, Chiang Mai, 30 September 2012, Nonthaburi.
Wantana Iamsuwan, Klongyong Co-operative, 10 October 2012, Nakhon Pathom.
Weerachai Narkwibulwong, Director of ALRO, 14 February 2013, Bangkok.
Wibulwan Wannamolee, Senior Officer at the Office of Agricultural Standards and Accredition, 31 January 2013, Nonthaburi.
Wichai (undisclosed surname), Tambol Aynalai, Naan, 1 October 2012, Bangkok.
Wilaiwan Konka, Baan Pae-tai CLTD, 30 October 2012, Lamphun.
Witoon Lienchamroon, BioThai, 5 April 2012, Nonthaburi.

Email correspondence

Akinee Jiwattanapaiboon, Xondur Thai Organic Food, 21 February 2013.
Archinya Ourapeepattanapong, Chiangmai Organic and Spa, 16 January 2013.
Kriengsak Suwantharadol, Syngenta (Thailand), 14 March 2013.
Paladisai Jinapak, All Be One Thailand, 18 January 2013.
Pisit Werawaitaya, Earth Born Company, 18 January 2013.
Piyanat Na-Nakhon, Southeast Asia Organic Company, 16 January 2013.
Songpun Kuldilokrat, Managing Director of Arysta LifeScience, 21 January 2013.

Index

accumulation by dispossession 18–19, 37, 39–40
Aden company 101
Agreement on Agriculture 12
agri-business 1–3, 6, 12–13, 15, 19, 39, 46–7, 49, 51–2, 56, 92, 116–17, 122
agri-food governance 19, 50, 110
Agricultural Land Reform Office (ALRO) 71, 101, 111–12, 144–5, 148–9, 151, 154–6, 159
agro-ecology 89, 93, 96, 105
agro-fuels 12–13, 20, 39–40, 42, 51; ethanol 51, 56; *see also* energy crop
Alternative Agriculture Network (AAN) 71–2, 74, 95–6, 98–9, 109, 111–17, 163
ammart 75–6, 161–2; *see also* phrai; polarised politics; red-yellow divide
anarchist thoughts 120
Asian Development Bank (ADB) 54
Asian economic crisis of 1997 40, 49, 52, 54, 94, 98, 131n99, 143, 146, 148, 176
assassination 160
Assembly of the Poor, the 71–2, 76, 114–17, 147, 149–50

Baan Pae-tai 148–9
Baan Pong 148–51, 154–5, 158
Baan Tanon 104
Bak-rua 86, 100, 104, 107–8, 123, 134n200
Bangkok 7, 44, 52–3, 86, 98, 100, 125, 142–4, 149, 152, 155, 159, 176–7
Bank for Agriculture and Agricultural Cooperatives (BAAC) 48, 100, 107
Bantad Mountain Land Reform Network 142, 147–8, 150, 158, 177
Big C 48–9, 65n111
biodiversity 11, 15, 38, 42, 44, 87, 89, 92, 96, 116
Biodiversity and Community Rights Action Thailand (BioThai) 6, 41, 92, 95, 116; *see also* Lienchamroon, Witoon
Biodiversity for Sustainable Agriculture Asia 89
biosafety law 117
biotechnology 1, 25, 54; *see also* genetically modified (GM) seeds
Board of Investment (BOI) 51
Boonrahong, Chomchuan 87, 96, 157
bourgeois ideology 26
Bowring Treaty of 1855 37
Buddhist: communes 90; economics 89; values 23, 120; virtues 93
Burapha Television company 102, 111; *see also* moral rice

capitalisation of nature 20
capitalism 5, 25–7, 51–2, 76–7, 88, 90, 122, 163
Cargill 14
Carrefour 14, 49, 65n111
cassava 40–1, 43, 51, 56
Central group 48–9
central market 48, 79, 84n70
certification 14, 25, 27, 100, 105–6, 109–10, 123; *see also* fair trade; Northern Organic Standard; Organic Thailand
Chaipattana Foundation 113
Charoen Pokphand Group (CP) 41, 46, 48–9, 52, 59, 65n111, 69n186, 123
Chiang Mai 7, 47–8, 73, 77, 86–7, 96–8, 102–4, 109–10, 112, 117, 143, 148–9, 160
circulating capital 17
climate change 11, 107
co-operative 44, 52, 57, 59, 73–4, 87, 89, 98, 100, 102, 109, 114–15, 123, 147–8,

151–2, 155, 161; *see also* community enterprise
Committee on World Food Security 164
commodification 18, 37–9, 57, 92, 96, 143–4, 147
Common Agricultural Policy 14
common knowledge 16
common sense 22–3
community culture school of thought 90, 122; *see also* localism; Nartsupha, Chatthip; sufficiency
community enterprise 79, 99–101, 119; *see also* co-operative
Community Forest law 160; *see also* community rights; complexity of rights
Community Intellectual Right law 116; *see also* community rights; intellectual property rights
community land title deed (CLTD) 7, 71, 73, 77, 143, 145–58, 160–4; *see also* community rights; complexity of rights; land bank; land grabs; land occupation; land reform movement (LRM), the; Northern Peasants Federation
Community of Agro-Ecology Foundation (CAE) 96
community rights 16, 71–3, 76–7, 116, 144–5, 152–4, 161
Community Supported Agriculture (CSA) 26, 90, 98, 103, 110, 122, 124
complexity of rights 8, 72–3, 143, 145–6; *see also* Ganjanapan, Anan
concentration and centralisation of capital 19; *see also* monopoly
Constitution, the 52, 67n142, 77, 144, 152, 161
consumerism 90, 94, 111
contract farming 18–19, 25, 40–2, 45–7, 50–1, 59, 72, 106, 110, 123, 157; Contract Farmer Network 147; contract farmers 46–7, 106
control grabbing 156; *see also* land grabs
Convention on Biological Diversity (CBD) 116; *see also* biodiversity
conventionalisation in organic market 25
corporate social responsibility (CSR) 101, 123
coups d'état 58, 75, 77–8, 113, 154, 161, 175
critical IPE in the Coxian tradition 5
crony capitalism 51
Crown Property Act of 1948 53
Crown Property Bureau (CPB) 41, 53–4, 58–9, 120; *see also* monarchy
cultural identity 92–4; *see also* local sage

debt 11, 20, 38, 52, 75, 88, 145, 153, 158, 161
decentralisation 71, 115, 161; decentralise power 112, 120, 152
Democrat Party 68n160, 82n27, 153–4
Department of Agricultural Extensions 51
Department of Land 153
depeasantisation 18
deregulations 14–15; *see also* neo-liberal policies
developmental monk 88
diversified farming 96, 104, 158
Duangkaewruan, Kanoksak 112; *see also* Mae-ta

Earth Net Foundation 98; *see also* Green Net Co-operative
eco-localism 91
economic efficiency 1, 15, 37
effective micro-organism (EM) 90, 97
energy crop 41–2, 51, 56; *see also* agro-fuels; flex crops
eucalyptus 41, 144, 156
European Union, the 11–12, 14, 44, 54–5
exploitation 5, 17–18, 37, 87
extra-human nature 18

fair trade 25–6, 72, 89, 99–100, 103–4, 107–9, 122–4; fair prices 46, 103, 109; fair trade premiums 103; Fairtrade 98, 100; Fairtrade Labeling Organization International (FLO) 98; minimum fair trade prices 107
Farmer Debt Network 153
farmer rights 89, 92, 116
feminist perspective 5, 10, 26–8; *see also* women
financialisation 14, 28
flex crops 176; *see also* agro-fuels; energy crop
Food and Agriculture Organization (FAO), the 14, 25, 37, 44, 46, 147
food dependence 12
food miles 91
food safety 125
food security 1, 12, 15, 20, 27, 39, 41–2, 72–3, 87, 89, 91–4, 104, 112, 115, 126, 146, 156–7, 159, 164
food sovereignty 72–3, 87–9, 91–2, 122, 142, 157–9, 164
food-energy 13, 20, 28, 51, 56, 144, 162; food-fuel 13, 39, 41

forced under-consumption 43
Ford Foundation 11, 38
Foreign Business Act of 1999 40, 55
formal land titling 143
four laws for the poor 73, 154; *see also* Justice Fund; land reform movement (LRM), the
Four-Region Slum Network 117, 147
Frank, Andre Gunder 19
free market 11, 56; *see also* neo-classical economics; neo-liberal policies
free trade 12, 15, 18–19, 53–4, 112, 116; free trade agreement 12, 19, 53–5, 112, 116–17; *see also* international trade; neo-classical economics; neo-liberal policies
Friedmann, Harriet 25
Fukuoka, Masanobu 89–90, 99; *see also* natural farming

Ganjanapan, Anan 73, 91, 119, 145–6; *see also* complexity of rights
Genetic Resources Action International 89
genetically modified (GM) seeds 11, 15–16, 19, 24, 38–9, 116–17
Ghandi 89
Gill, Stephen 24, 175; *see also* postmodern Prince
Global Alliance Against Land Grabbing 163; *see also* land grabs
global commons 16
global warming 15
Good Agricultural Practice (GAP) 23, 125, 159, 164, 175
Gramscian perspective 3–5, 7, 10, 17, 20–3, 26–8, 49, 55, 70, 73, 121, 174–5
grassroots democracy 71; *see also* decentralisation
green capitalism 25
green market 26, 72, 86, 92, 98, 103–4, 109, 115, 124, 159
Green Net Co-operative 89, 98–100, 103, 109, 123; *see also* Earth Net Foundation; Panyakul, Witoon
Green Revolution, the 11, 37–9, 50, 57, 59, 69n188, 99
Greenpeace 116

Harvey, David 18; *see also* accumulation by dispossession
High Yielding Variety 11, 38–9, 50; *see also* Green Revolution, the
human rights to food 89
humans and extra-human nature 18

individualism 15–16, 88
informal norms 50, 58, 94
informal rules of the market 48
Institute for a Sustainable Agriculture Community (ISAC) 96, 109, 157
integrated farming 72, 96, 158
intellectual property rights 11, 16, 18–19, 39, 50, 54, 72, 89, 116
International Conference on Agrarian Reform and Rural Development (ICARRD), the 147
International Fund for Agricultural Development (IFAD), the 25
International Monetary Fund (IMF), the 12, 14, 21, 54–5
International trade 12, 15, 38
International Union for the Protection of New Varieties of Plants (UPOV) 54, 116–7

Jamarik, Saneh 89, 99
Japanese Tekei system 90
Jasmati 116
JJ Organic Market 98
Justice Fund 73, 152, 154; *see also* four laws for the poor; land reform movement (LRM), the

Kammad 71, 86, 97, 99, 101, 103, 106, 108, 111–12, 159
Khao Kwan Foundation 96–7, 110
King Bhumipol Adulyadej 113, 121, 123–4, 159; *see also* Crown Property Bureau (CPB); monarchy; New Theory of agriculture; royalism; sufficiency
Klong Rangsit 156
Klongsaipattana 150–1, 160
Klongyong co-operative 147–8, 151–2

La Vía Campesina 72–3, 89, 117, 121, 144, 148, 162–4; *see also* Assembly of the Poor, the; food sovereignty; Movimento dos Trabalhadores Rurais Sem Terra (Landless Rural Workers Movement) (MST)
labour reproduction 94
Lamphun 7, 71, 143, 148–9, 160
land bank 73, 149–50, 153–5; *see also* community land title deed (CLTD); four laws for the poor
land grabs 4, 7, 11, 13, 18, 25, 28, 40–2, 50–1, 59, 73, 144, 152, 155–6, 162, 175;

see also control grabbing; Global Alliance Against Land Grabbing
land occupation 73, 147–9, 155, 160; land reform movement (LRM), the
Land Reform Act of 1975 144; *see also* Agricultural Land Reform Office (ALRO)
land reform movement (LRM), the 3, 6–7, 70–4, 77–8, 80, 142–57, 159–64, 174–5; *see also* four laws for the poor; Northern Peasants Federation; People's Movement for a Just Society (P-Move)
Laothamatat, Anek 120
Leekpai, Chuan 72, 82n27, 144; *see also* Democrat party
Lemon Farm 89, 98, 106, 110
lèse majesté law 53–4, 58–9; *see also* monarchy
liberalisation 12–13, 15, 19, 50; *see also* free trade; neo-liberal policies
Lienchamroon, Witoon 95; *see also* Biodiversity and Community Rights Action Thailand (BioThai)
Local Act Organisation 147
local canvassers 53
local sage 93, 96, 113, 122; *see also* cultural identity
localism 2–4, 71, 87, 90–1, 118–21, 174–5; *see also* community culture school of thought; community rights; Nartsupha, Chatthip; sufficiency
longan 47, 102, 158

Mae-ta 97–8, 110, 112, 157
Maeping Organic Company 103, 110
maize 12, 38, 43, 50
Maleenont family 41
Maptaputh, Rayong 90
Mekong Youth Alliance for Organic Agriculture and Agro-ecology 89
middlemen 45, 48–9, 74, 79, 99–100, 158
Ministry of Commerce 51, 116, 124
Ministry of Forestry 152
modern trade 48; convenience store 48; hypermarket 48–9; supermarket 48, 55, 98, 123
modernisation 19, 22, 27, 51, 55–6, 88, 90, 118
monarchy 53, 58, 75, 113, 120; *see also* Crown Property Act; Crown Property Bureau (CPB); King Bhumipol Adulyadej; lèse majesté law; privy council; royalism
mono-cropping 10, 38
monopoly 7, 11–12, 14–16, 18–19, 28, 37–9, 45–50, 54–6, 59, 78–9, 87, 96, 158
Monsanto 6, 14, 39
moral rice 93, 95, 99, 101–2, 108, 110–11; *see also* Thamma-ruamjai
Movimento dos Trabalhadores Rurais Sem Terra (Landless Rural Workers Movement) (MST) 121, 147; *see also* food sovereignty; La Vía Campesina
multi-level market channels 97

Nakhon Luang (Capital Rice) 47, 65n104, 123
Nakhon Patom 142
Nam-oom social enterprise 86, 100, 104, 107
Narkwibulwong, Weerachai 159; *see also* Agricultural Land Reform Office (ALRO)
Nartsupha, Chatthip 71, 90; *see also* community culture school of thought; localism
Naso 49, 86, 90, 99–101, 103–4, 108, 123
National Economic and Social Development (NESD) plan 51, 112, 114–15
National Reform Assembly 161
National Strategic Plan to Develop Organic Agriculture 113
national-popular 23, 118
nationalism 58–9, 69n198, 120
natural farming 87, 89–90, 99, 176; *see also* Fukuoka, Masanobu
neo-classical economics 10, 14–15, 28, 31n36, 31n38, 84n70
neo-liberal policies 12, 14, 16, 19, 21–2, 36, 53, 55, 147, 163
neo-Marxist perspective 2, 4–5, 7, 10, 17, 27, 37, 39–40, 57, 175
Network of the Right of Thai Local Wisdom 116
New Theory of agriculture 91, 96; *see also* diversified farming; integrated farming; King Bhumipol Adulyadej; sufficiency
Nokham, Suchit 97
nominees 4, 40, 59, 162
non-commodified work 5, 27–8; *see also* feminist perspective
Nonthaburi 95–6, 102, 142, 177
North American Free Trade Agreement (NAFTA) 12; *see also* free trade; international trade

Northern Organic Standard 109
Northern Peasants Federation 118, 142, 148, 164; *see also* land reform movement (LRM), the

Occupy movement, the 89
Office of Agricultural Economics (OAE) 45, 51
Office of the Ombudsman 79
Office of the Prime Minister 153, 161
one rai-100, 000 baht training group 96; *see also* Rangkaworaset, Kittithanet
opportunity costs 13, 42, 80, 162
Order 64/2557 154
organic agriculture 71–2, 87, 89, 98–100, 104, 106, 110, 113–14, 122–3
organic intellectual 23
Organic Thailand 108–9; *see also certification*
Organisation for Economic Co-operation and Development (OECD) 11, 38
over-production 17

paddy pledging scheme 14, 45, 47, 74–80, 88, 108, 125–6, 175
Pakmun group 147; *see also* Assembly of the Poor, the
palm oil 40–1, 43, 51, 144, 151
Panyakul, Witoon 98; *see also* fair trade; Green Net Co-operative
Parliamentary Committee to Study Land Problems 153
patron-client mentality and relations 3, 22–3, 36, 48, 50, 52–3, 55, 58, 67n152, 68n161, 74, 76, 88, 93, 111, 120, 124
peak oil 13
Peasants' Federation of Thailand (PFT) 70–1, 145
People's Movement for a Just Society (P-Move) 147; *see also* land reform movement (LRM)
People's Alliance for Democracy (PAD) 75; *see also* polarised politics; yellow shirts
People's Democratic Reform Committee (PDRC) 75; *see also* polarised politics; yellow shirts
philanthropy capital 14
Phongpit, Seri 100
Phra Promma Suphatto 111; *see also* moral rice; Thamma-ruamjai
phrai 58, 75, 77, 161; *see also* ammart; polarised politics; red-yellow divide; Sakdina
Phua Thai 153–4, 162; *see also* Thai Rak Thai (TRT)
Pilanoi, Kankamkla 111
pilot programme for sustainable agriculture, the 71, 100–1, 111, 113–15
Pintoptang, Prapart 152
polarised politics 4, 52, 80; *see also* ammart; phrai; red shirts; red-yellow divide; yellow shirts
populist policies 3, 7, 68n161, 74, 76, 82n31
postmodern Prince 24; *see also* Gill, Stephen
poststructuralist perspective 5, 26, 28
Prasertkul, Seksan 120
price competition 15, 84n70, 107, 109
primitive accumulation 18
privy council 75; *see also* monarchy
processed organic agri-food products 106
producer rice mill 49, 79, 86, 99–100, 102, 104, 107–8, 123, 125; *see also* Bak-rua; co-operative; community enterprise; Kammad; Nam-oom social enterprise; Naso; Rice Fund Surin Organic Agriculture Co-operative
progressive land tax 152

Raidong 71, 148–9, 151, 153–4, 157–8, 161
Rangkaworaset, Kittithanet 97
red shirts 75–7, 161; *see also* polarised politics; red-yellow divide
red-yellow divide 160; *see also* polarised politics
relocalization 91
research on organic agriculture 114
reserve army of labour 18, 20, 42, 57, 94
rice 12, 37–8, 40–1, 43–5, 47, 49–50, 52, 56, 76, 78–80, 86–8, 93, 95–105, 107–12, 114–16, 123, 125; *see also* paddy pledging scheme
Rice Fund Surin Organic Agriculture Co-operative 87
Rockefeller Foundation 38
royalism 58; *see also* monarchy
rubber 37, 41–4, 78, 159

Sai-ngarmpattana 150
Sakdina 3, 23, 52, 54–5, 58–9, 75, 93, 120, 124; *see also* monarchy; patron-client mentality and social relations
Samsiew 148, 150
Sangkalee, Thamma 103

Santi Asoke 90, 96, 110; *see also* Buddhist communes
Santipattana 150–1
Sayamol, Tool 96
Schumacher, E.F. 89; *see also* Buddhist economics
seasonal migrants 94
Sekai Kyusei Kyo group 90; *see also* effective micro-organism (EM)
semi-dispossessed 19
Shinnawatra, Thaksin 53, 74–5, 82n36, 160–1; *see also* red shirts; Thai Rak Thai (TRT); Shinnawatra, Yingluck
Shinnawatra, Yingluck 75, 78, 153, 161; *see also* paddy pledging scheme; Phua Thai; Shinnawatra, Thaksin; Thai Rak Thai (TRT)
Siam Makro 48, 65n111, 66n112
Siripat, Decha 93, 96; *see also* Khao Kwan Foundation
Small-scale Farmers of the Northeast (So Ko Yo Oo) 71; *see also* Assembly of the Poor, the
social distance between consumers and producers 25
social relations 15, 21–2, 58, 72, 86, 88, 92, 94, 106, 109–11, 120, 145, 148, 155
social safety nets 28, 94
Sor Por Kor 4–01 scandal 144; *see also* Democrat Party
Southern Fishermen Network 147; *see also* Assembly of the Poor, the
Southern Peasants Federation 142; *see also* land reform movement (LRM), the
speculations 1, 7, 11–12, 14, 20, 37, 43–4, 50, 56, 59, 117, 153, 175; *see also* financialisation
Sritia 148–9
Suan-ngern Meema 89
sufficiency 2, 71, 76, 90–1, 96, 113, 118–24, 157, 159; *see also* localism
sugar cane 37, 40–1, 43, 51, 56
Sunthornchai, Mahayoo 96
super-exploitation 18
Suphanburi 96, 110
Supreme Court, the 75
Surin 7, 86–7, 95–100, 102–5, 107–10, 112, 115, 125, 164
surplus appropriation 5, 19, 45
surplus value 17, 31n44
sustainability premiums 107; *see also* certification
sustainable agriculture movement (SAM), the 3, 6–7, 70–2, 74, 80, 86–125, 174–6; *see also* Alternative Agriculture Network (AAN)
Sustainable Agriculture Thailand Foundation (SATHAI) 92, 96–7, 177

Ta-toom 87, 103
Tamor 87, 96, 100, 103, 112
Taptai 87, 97–8, 100, 103–4
tenure 146–7, 164; customary forms of tenure 147; security of tenure 147
Tesco 14, 48–9
Thai Beverage 41, 48, 65n111
Thai Health Promotion Foundation 97
Thai Rak Thai (TRT) 52–3, 68n160, 68n161, 74–6, 82n33, 82n34; *see also* paddy pledging scheme; Phua Thai; populist policies; red shirts; Shinnawatra, Thaksin; Shinnawatra, Yingluck
Thailand Research Fund 112
ThaiPBS 147, 152
Thamma-ruamjai 86–7, 93, 95; *see also* moral rice
Thonburi hospital group 41
Tosritrakul, Rosana 89
Trade-Related Aspects of Intellectual Property Rights (TRIPS) 18, 89, 116–17; *see also* intellectual property rights
trasformismo 24

United Front for Democracy Against Dictatorship (UDD) 75; *see also* polarised politics; red shirts
United Nations Development Programme (UNDP) 113
United Palm Oil Industry Plc. 41
United States, the 11–12, 14, 21, 38–9, 44, 51, 53–4, 100, 107, 117
Usage rights 73, 146–7, 149–50

Vejchacheewa, Abhisit 150, 153, 160; *see also* Democrat party
Voluntary Guidelines on Responsible Governance of Tenure of Land and Other Natural Resources, thev25, 164
vote buying 52–3, 76

Wal-Mart 14; *see also* modern trade
war of manoeuvre 22
war of position 22, 27
Wasi, Prawase 71, 89, 112, 119, 162
women 26–8, 104; *see also* feminist perspective

World Bank, the 11–12, 14, 16, 21, 25, 37, 57, 117, 143
World Trade Organization (WTO) 12, 14, 19, 89, 116

Yaimuang, Supha 95, 177; *see also* Sustainable Agriculture Thailand Foundation (SATHAI)
Yasothon 49, 71, 86, 90, 95, 97–103, 107–8, 110–12, 125
yellow shirts 75; *see also* People's Alliance for Democracy (PAD); polarised politics; red-yellow divide
Yongchaiyut, Chavalit 114

Zapatista 147